My Dear Kristen, … you lemons. I know you will mak… fabulous lemonade. Remember you are much bigger than your problem.
Much Love and Light

365 Ways to Connect with Your Soul

[illegible] May 21st, 2016

Jodi Chapman, Dan Teck

& Over 200 Soulful Contributors

DandiLove Unlimited

This book comes from our hearts and is here to support you in connecting with your soul. Please know, though, that it is not a replacement for therapy or medical advice. If you are feeling like you could use some extra support, please seek out a professional in your area.

The authors who contributed to this book are from all corners of the world, and we have kept their native English spelling for each of their pieces. For this reason, you will see words like "color" and "colour" or "realized" and "realised" throughout the book – just depending on what part of the world the author is from. We also wanted to find a balance of maintaining consistency throughout the book while still honoring each author's belief system. For this reason, you will see that some words are capitalized in some pieces and not in others. For the most part, we capitalize words relating to God, Source, the Universe, and a Higher Power.

Ordering information available at:
www.365waystoconnectwithyoursoul.com.
For wholesale inquires, please write to: info@365bookseries.com.

Printed in the United States of America
ISBN: 13-978-0-9893137-7-3
Library of Congress Control Number: 2015917110

www.365bookseries.com

DEDICATION

We would like to dedicate this book to each of the contributing authors who shared such heartfelt and soul-filled pieces.

We would also like to dedicate this book to each of the readers. We are so grateful for your love and support. This book comes straight from our soul, and we are honored to share it with you.

And lastly, we would like to dedicate this book to everyone in the world who is brave enough to connect with their soul and to stay in that open, vulnerable, loving space. It takes true courage to do this, and we honor you. Our world becomes that much brighter the moment someone aligns with their soul. Let's keep shining!

Table of Contents

Introduction

We would like to begin this book by welcoming you home. We're so glad that you listened to that soft whisper inside – asking you to slow down, go deeper, and connect with something more. By being here in this moment, you've taken the crucial first step toward creating a truly magical life – one where you are engaged, present, and filled with joy. One where colors seem brighter and people seem sweeter. One where the world seems like a loving place to live in. One where you feel grounded and completely plugged into the Universe. One where you have given yourself permission to come home.

Oftentimes, it can feel like we live in a world that is moving faster and faster; that our to-do lists are getting longer and longer; and that there is less and less time to get in touch with who we are, what we want, and why we're here. We feel pulled to work more and stay busy and keep up; and yet, at the same time, we hear a soft whisper inside of us asking us to do the exact opposite: rest, pull back, be still.

It's certainly not uncommon for us to ignore this whisper – to shove it down and do our best to continue our life as usual. But the whisper usually gets louder and louder and louder until we eventually listen and remember and feel on a deep level that this wise part of us – our soul – is speaking the truth. We realize that we yearn for a deeper existence, we yearn to walk through each day connected to something bigger, we yearn to find meaning in it all. We yearn to come home.

We've both felt these urges – these callings. And we've both ignored them, stuffed them down, thought we were too busy to listen. What we've found, however, was that disconnecting from our soul and from the Universe didn't make us feel good. It actually made us feel exhausted and worn down and disheartened and apathetic and just blah – definitely not how we wanted to feel. So we decided – over a period of time – to give our soul a chance. We decided to hear it out, trust its wisdom, and treat it like the loving friend it is. In doing so, our entire world opened up. It felt like we had been living in black and white before then, and we now are surrounded by the most beautiful colors. Everything is brighter, lighter, and filled with love.

Does that mean that everything always goes smoothly and we never experience heartache or frustration? Of course not. It simply means that we now have an ally who is always on our side. Our soul comes with some pretty powerful friends, too: the Universe, angels, spirit guides, our loved ones on the other side, and the most loving energy we've ever felt. All of this is available to each of us at any moment. We had just forgotten that. And then we remembered.

Since reconnecting with our soul, our hearts have completely opened and our lives have transformed. Because of this, we're passionate about supporting others with their connection as well.

If this is the first time you've connected with your soul in a very long while, we're so happy for you! We can feel your soul rejoicing – jumping up and down with excitement. Reading this book is sure to be a heart-opening journey for you!

If you're already plugged into your beautiful soul and already feel the light and love that this connection brings, then we hope that this book will help you find fun, new ways to deepen this connection.

One of the things that we love most about our soul is that we can connect with it at any moment – no matter what we're doing or where we are, it's always available to us. Our intention for this book is to show that the ways we connect with our soul are truly endless. There is no one right or wrong way to do it – each way is equally important and equally magical. Our soul doesn't care if we connect through meditation, through cooking a great meal, or through smiling at a stranger. This wise part of us simply wants us to be happy and filled with joy – it wants us to remember how completely tapped in we always are to infinite love. Whatever we do to raise our vibration and connect with this love is completely up to us.

Your soul is always with you. When you're busy, it's there. When you're meditating, it's there. When you're filled with joy, it's there. And when you're filled with anger, it's there. It's always with you and is always loving and supporting you. It's up to you to welcome its presence into your life and to allow yourself to slow down enough to hear its wisdom. Reading this book is such beautiful confirmation that you value your soul and also yourself – that you are excited to see what kinds of magic the two of you can experience together.

Defining the Soul

Because this book is all about connecting with our soul, we want to do our best to define and describe the soul itself. We realize, though, that trying to define the soul is next to impossible, since it's bigger and brighter than any words in any human language. It's a feeling, an experience, an embodiment, a knowing, and a connection all wrapped up into one amazingly loving being.

Here is how we can best define it:

> Our soul is our connection between the spirit world and the physical world. It's our best self. It's our loving confidant; our inner cheerleader; our all-knowing, peace-loving, completely present self. It's our inner voice, our infinite wisdom, our Godliness. It's eternal. It's our truest essence. It's who we've always been and who we have yet to become. It's the embodiment of all of our desires and all of our experiences. It's our blueprint and our possibility. It's energy – pure, loving, infinite energy. It simply is and will always be. It's that inner whisper that asks you to dream bigger and trust yourself more and live on purpose. It's that soft nudge that lovingly pushes you to show up as your true self in the world. It's the gut feeling that you can't quite explain but know is real. It's you. All of you. And all of everything. All wrapped up into one. It's light. Pure light. It's love. Pure love.

How This Book Came to Be

Very few people like doing their taxes, and we're certainly no exception. Last year, we were going through the endless stacks of paper and methodically entering in each item when we came across a receipt from several years back. We pulled it out of the pile – wondering how it ended up there. We were about to toss it aside and get back to the taxes when we noticed something written on the back. It turned out that it was a seedling for this book idea. Before going to sleep that night, we asked for more clarity regarding our next step, and this fully formed book idea popped in immediately upon waking. We were so excited about it but weren't sure if anyone else would be. When over 200 heart-centered souls quickly signed up to be part of it, we were absolutely elated. This book has been surrounded by loving energy right from the start, which is such a beautiful example of what happens when we open our hearts and let our soul lead the way.

How to Read This Book

This book is divided into 10 sections and contains one way to connect with your soul for each day of the year. There are many ways to enjoy this book: you can read each entry in order on the day it appears, or you can flip through at random and let your soul guide you. You can read each piece and leave it at that, or you can read it and then take action by giving the tip a try.

You can also build a spiritual practice around this book. For example, in the morning, you might want to make a cup of tea, go to your sacred space (either inside or in nature), take a few deep breaths to center yourself, read one passage, and then spend a few minutes journaling about it or simply close your eyes and allow yourself to be with it for a moment or two. If you would like to create a nightly spiritual practice, you can take a relaxing bath, curl up in bed, and read a passage before falling asleep. It's a loving way to begin or end the day.

We suggest that you keep a journal nearby when reading this book. Journaling is a great way to start an ongoing conversation with your soul – getting into the habit of connecting with it on a regular basis. You can write down any emotions and experiences you feel after reading a passage or simply use the passages as a starting point to go even deeper. Your journal can also be a wonderful place to jot down any inspiration that comes to you while reading this book. We've found that once we begin this conversation with our soul, the words and ideas begin to flow freely and effortlessly. So it's a good idea to be prepared in case some really wonderful wisdom starts flowing from you! (But please know that it will all flow in the right time – it may feel like a small drip at first, which is completely okay! Everyone's experience with connecting with their soul is unique, and trusting that everything is happening at exactly the right time is so important.)

You can also read this book with your friends and deepen your relationships! You can meet (either in person or online) and go through the days together, or you can pick and choose them at random and share what you learned about yourself after reading them and taking them into your heart.

Please remember that however you go through this book is perfectly right – just by having it around, you will be opening your heart and letting your soul know that you're ready to connect. You'll be setting the intention that you're ready and open, which is a beautiful first step.

Giving Back

Because nature and animals are two ways that help us connect with our own soul, we'll be donating 5% of all profits from sales of this book to the Jane Goodall Institute. (You can learn more about this charity by going to www.janegoodall.org.)

Thank You

Thank you so much for giving yourself this gift of soul connection. We hope that it feels as good going into your heart as it did pouring out of ours. We feel so blessed that we live in a world where deepening our connection with this wise part of ourselves is valued and seen as important. And we're so grateful that you're here on the journey with us – that makes it extra special.

We hope this book serves as a daily reminder to you that your soul is always with you – cheering you on and loving you. Our lives have already been changed during the process of compiling the pieces. We found new ways to connect with our own soul – either ways that we hadn't ever heard of or ways that we had forgotten but now remember. It's our hope that through reading this book, your life will be changed as well.

Hugs, love, and gratitude,
Jodi and Dan

Chapter 1
Soulful Practices

There are many different ways to connect with your soul. Some have you go into a deeper state of consciousness (such as meditation), and others simply are silly and playful (such as swinging or spinning around and around). There is no wrong way to connect with your soul, which is a huge relief!

One of our favorite soulful practices is to go on a mini retreat each afternoon. We lie down together, and usually one or two of our cats will come join us. We just close our eyes, listen to their purring, pull away from the world for a little while, and plug back into our connection with each other and with our soul. Sometimes (depending on how stressed and frazzled we are) it just takes a few minutes to feel better, and other times it can take up to an hour. But we always leave feeling refreshed and ready for the world again. We're so grateful for this practice and for all of the new ones that we've learned while compiling this chapter.

On the following pages, you'll be introduced to concrete things you can do to slow down and align with your higher self. You'll most likely have heard of (and even done) many of the practices. If so, the pieces can serve as a loving reminder to try them again – to welcome them into your daily experience. Some may be new for you, which is exciting and heart expanding! Please view them all with an open mind and an open heart – try each one out at least once to see how it feels. You never know which ones might resonate with you and also with your soul.

Give yourself permission to have fun with this! And remember to smile along the journey. While connecting with your soul is super important and meaningful, it's also a joyful experience that we hope you'll embrace and let flow through your body, heart, and spirit.

Bookending: Routines with Soul

by Vanessa Codorniu

"You don't seem yourself; are you okay?" my mom asked me one night during a visit. I scanned my day quickly and realized that, in the midst of traveling, I had skipped my daily morning and evening "bookending" rituals!

As an empath and professional intuitive, I have based my life on leveraging my sensitivity to serve others. That means that walking my talk and managing my own energetic self-care are key. For the last decade and a half, bookending has been at the heart of my inner balance and joyful success. I start and end each day with a solid and peaceful foundation. This way, whatever may happen in between, I know where I am coming from and where I am going to: my peaceful center.

My morning routine begins in bed. Here are some of my favorite morning "bookend" rituals: Reiki hands-on-healing self-treatment; gratitude list; creative visualization; yoga child's pose; speaking affirmations out loud; and an intuitive-guidance meditation where I ask my higher self, angels, and guides, "What do I need to know right now?"

My evening routine must include some form of clearing and releasing – consciously clearing away a day's worth of thoughts, beliefs, emotions, cells, feelings, energetic hooks, expectations, and anything that no longer serves me. Technology off. Candles on. Bath running. I enter the water and release the day. I emerge fully myself and ready for slumber.

Bookending your day with positive rituals can shift your energy immensely. Here are a couple of quick tips for creating your own rituals:

- *Sacred rituals should be personal.* Do you like to wake up quietly? Or is a reggae tune and a booty-shaking start to your day what gets you centered and feeling connected?
- *Intention is everything.* It doesn't matter if you are doing one yoga pose or five, or if you begin your day breathing and sipping peppermint tea as you look out into your garden. What matters is that you do it and it feels good!

Bookending rituals invite our sacred presence in. Starting one is a great way to honor yourself and support your soul!

Dark Showers

by Jodi Chapman

As a highly sensitive person, it's easy for me to feel overwhelmed by life. It's easy to feel that the incoming stimulus is sometimes just too much to handle. Today was one of those days. It was filled with worry, emotional ups and downs, external and internal noise, and taking others' energy into my body. I felt completely frazzled and wasn't sure how to find my center again. And then I heard my soul softly whisper, "Take a dark shower."

At first, this sounded silly to me. I couldn't see how this would fix anything. But I figured I would try it simply because I didn't have any other suggestions and really did want to feel better. So I closed the bathroom door, turned on the water, turned off the light, felt my way around, and stepped into the shower in complete darkness. I stood under the stream and allowed the purifying water to cleanse my spirit and wash away each part of the day that either I had taken in from someone else or that belonged to me but wasn't coming from a high vibration.

In my mind's eye, I visualized all of the unwanted energy flowing down the drain – seeing it as impermanent and no longer a part of my present moment. And I gave it permission to flow away from me. I closed my eyes and took several deep breaths. Almost immediately, I began to feel my body loosen and my heart open. I began to sense my inner light growing brighter. After a few minutes, I turned the water off, stepped out of the shower, turned on the light, and reemerged into my life – feeling much more at peace and much more connected with my soul than I had just moments before.

I'm so thankful to my soul for suggesting this practice. It's definitely something that I plan on continuing.

The Most Powerful Question to Ask Each Morning

by Jaden Sterling

I clearly remember the first morning I received guidance from my soul.

The previous night, as my head hit the pillow, I'd been haunted by thoughts of a pressing business situation that desperately needed resolution. My mind swirled with various outcomes, yet no clear strategy emerged. I was doing what I was taught: "Think carefully and give situations thorough consideration." These tactics weren't working, though, which unsettled me to the point of feeling panic. Finally, exhaustion prevailed and I drifted off to sleep.

The following morning, before my eyes opened and my conscious mind kicked into gear, a new thought "dropped in." I had never before considered this thought as an option, but it completely resolved my business situation in a way that was simple and elegant. At that moment, I realized that I had tapped into my soul's guidance through a process that is available to everyone.

Here are the simple steps to help you hear your soul speak on any topic you desire:

- Before sleep, think of a situation that needs clarification.
- Ask the Universe to bring you clarity early in the morning so that you'll remember it.
- Upon waking and while still lying in bed, connect with your soul (before your conscious mind awakens) and ask, "What do I need to know right now?"
- Be aware of thoughts, feelings, ideas, and visions that come to you, and notice how they answer your question.

Give it a try tomorrow morning. Before your conscious mind wakes up, ask your soul the most powerful question that will change your life: "What do I need to know right now?" Then listen for the answer.

A New Twist on Affirmations

by Cindy Jones Lantier

I've been working with affirmations for years, and I've had a love/hate relationship with them this whole time. The love part comes from the fact that they can feel so hopeful. Until they don't. I often feel as though I'm lying to myself. I am not thin and wealthy. I do not do housework with ease. I don't always trust divine guidance. I try to be positive and treat myself with compassion, but most positive affirmations are just too much of a stretch for me to believe in.

Now I do things a little differently. Rather than affirming that I'm wealthy when I'm not, I start with a statement that is true: "I want enough money to pay off that pesky student loan with ease and take an Alaskan cruise next fall."

Then I start to play with words until I feel an energy shift. I might say, "I want to experience financial abundance." Again true, but it doesn't always feel possible.

So I affirm what I already have: work I love, a comfortable home, two cars in the driveway. I let myself appreciate the abundance that is already mine. Acknowledging the wealth I have makes it easier for me to slide into my desires. I am among the richest 1% of the world's population, after all! Now I can say, "I am a healthy kind of wealthy; I have more than enough…" and believe it!

When I move on to, "I easily make my student-loan payments" or "I enjoy cruising Alaska with my husband," they don't feel like distant dreams. They feel true.

Abraham-Hicks teaches that when we feel bad about ourselves, it's because we're thinking a thought that Source Energy – or the larger, non-physical part of ourselves – wouldn't think. Conversely, when we feel good, it's because our thoughts are in alignment with Source.

That's why traditional positive affirmations don't work for me. They stir up thoughts that my ego believes, even though they aren't the truth about who I am. Taking it more slowly allows me to find that alignment with the expanded version of myself – and connect with my soul.

The Power of Presence

by Julie Jones

There are days as a nurse when my soul sings! Strangely, these powerful and often transcendent times are not usually attached to the "heroic" moments you might expect – such as saving someone's life. They are not triggered by medical treatments, "fixing" someone, or *doing* anything at all. Rather, they are based in quiet, intense, and sacred moments of simply *being* with another person.

One such time was spent with a patient whose first words to me were, "Today is most likely my last day on Earth." I had my plans for the night: medications to pass out and assessments to perform. In this moment, however, my tasks seemed small. Instead of racing through my to-do list, I chose to get present and just be.

I pulled up a chair, and the man continued: "My surgery is scheduled for the morning. I have absolutely no chance of survival without it and only slightly better odds if I go ahead with it." He went on to tell me about his life and shared that he was alone – widowed with no children. All day, he had been angry with the nurses and complained about his meals. His physical presence on Earth was most likely nearing its end, and he had spent the day upset and angry. He wished for a do-over.

Being fully present with this man, I was reminded of the sacredness of soul-to-soul connection. I couldn't do anything to save him, and I wondered if simply being present with him was enough. But in that moment, it felt like the most important gift I could offer.

The next day, the room was empty. I paused in the doorway and reflected on how precious and fleeting life is. And I was reminded that being present allows me to have a choice in how I respond to even the most heartrending situation.

This experience and other moments of quiet, soulful connection have shown me that the greatest gift to offer is a willingness to simply *be* – to notice another's journey of joy or suffering, to share the power of presence.

Clear Your Clutter, Free Your Soul

by Bree Orata

Your outer state of affairs is a perfect reflection of your inner situation.

There is a lot to be said about chaotic spaces that are full of papers, dust, disorder, and *stuff*. I know, because I lived this way for many years! I was surrounded by what I like to call "too-muchness." I clearly remember feeling overwhelmed and bombarded by all manner of things. I even had a heavy tomato crate repurposed as a shelving unit right above my head that was filled to the brim with books, magazines, and all sorts of other things. My life was overcrowded, and there was no space for anything else to come in.

I finally became serious about decluttering when I was challenged to come up with a project for which I would be 100% accountable. After much self-reflection, I realized that my greatest need was to create space. (After all, you need to have space in order to create and manifest!)

Any clutter in your life is trying to tell you something, and you must be willing to hear that story. My clutter told me that I was holding on too much to a past that neither served me nor brought me joy. It revealed to me that I was still stuck on getting things done the hard way. Most of all, it showed me that I was not honoring my soul. Through all that confusion, I was threatening to shut down under the burden of *too much*.

As I began to release the clutter (such as arithmetic books that I'd held onto since elementary school!), I came to appreciate the importance of letting go of unnecessary things that burden me and make me heavy. My soul now feels lighter and freer than it ever has before.

Clearing your clutter will leave you with what you truly need in order to get clear on your next step. I hope that you, too, will get to experience the joy and the lightness that comes when you clear your clutter and free your soul.

Make a Sacred Space Indoors

by Heather Boon

Nature has always been the place for me to find connection; it wraps me safely in peace and tranquility. So when the ability to retreat into nature was taken from me, I became filled with frustration.

It was just over two years ago when I found myself confined to a wheelchair for three months with a broken leg. This was to be followed by many months of physiotherapy before I could navigate the outdoors again.

I felt so resentful of what had been taken from me; I couldn't see the opportunity I'd been given to create a new way to connect with spirit. Eventually, I looked around my home for what I could use to capture the same peace and calmness that I felt in nature.

I needed to open my heart to other possibilities; and in doing so, my eyes sought out things that held great meaning for me: crystals, scarves, Tibetan bowls, and statues. Each of these items held part of my essence in them. They had come from various places, times, and people, each piece holding a soul connection in some way.

With difficulty, I brought everything together, feeling inspired to create something really special. What was I going to do with these personal treasures?

Looking around for the perfect place, I saw the sideboard in my dining room. Painstakingly, I managed to clear this off and laid a beautiful, colourful scarf over it, then gently placed each piece of my precious collection on the scarf. When I looked at my completed sacred space, I could feel the power of what I had started.

The process of creating this was, without a doubt, guided by my soul. Throughout the following months, this sacred space helped me keep my focus positive. Since that time, I've continued to add new pieces, and I still revel in the space today.

I'm so grateful for this experience, as I learned that we always have the ability to connect with our soul – outside in nature or inside our home. We simply need to listen.

Going Nowhere

by Nicole Levac

On days when I find myself feeling stuck, hitting a personal roadblock, or stagnating in my business or any other area of life, I know I have to go out for a walk. Not just one of my normal daily walks but a "nowhere walk."

When I take a nowhere walk, I set out with time on my hands and no specific destination in mind, other than to deepen my connection with myself and to feed my soul.

These walks are about being present, in the moment. I tap into my intuition and get out of my own mind – and out of my own way! I make sure to feel my core, pay attention to the small nudges I notice there, and not only listen but also *act* on them. Allowing myself to trust and act on my feelings/instincts always energizes me and strengthens my connection to self during times when it would be easy to stop trusting myself.

The beauty of this activity is that it can be done in many ways. If you are in a city, go for a nowhere walk through the city. You could even do this while driving. It works well either way. The key is to trust yourself and pay attention to your feelings.

I generally prefer walking outside, where I use my senses to enjoy the moment – looking at birds, the sky, and the landscape, and listening to different sounds that create the music of nature. On particularly cold winter days, however, I'll often go for a "nowhere drive" while listening to my feelings.

However I take my nowhere walk (or drive), I always come back rejuvenated, recharged, and re-energized. These times always reveal something beautiful, magical, and inspirational. They help me to reconnect with my own inner voice – with my experience of being me.

I hope you'll try "going nowhere" on your own – and let me know where it leads you!

How Three Coins Became a Lifeline

by Jane Duncan Rogers

After my husband, Philip, died in 2011, all I wanted was to be able to bring him back. My worst fear (no children, no man) had come true. I found myself in a place that felt unbearable, but I had to bear it. I didn't want to kill myself, but I didn't want to live either.

One of the things I turned to was a stalwart that had helped me often before. I had used it many years previously when I woke at 4:00 each morning for several months, worrying about a legal situation we were going through. I used it in my 20s to help me get clear on whether to embark on a relationship or not. And I used it to help discover any ulterior motives that might be going on whenever we were having marital challenges. Each time I used this tool, it calmed me down, spoke the truth, and brought me back to my soul.

I was first introduced to the I Ching by my Mum in my early 20s, and it's been a constant and loving companion ever since. I throw three coins onto a table six times, noting the order of heads and tails. These correspond to a pattern of lines laid out in my copy of *An Introduction to the I Ching* by Carol Anthony, the six lines making up a pattern known as a hexagram.

Then I look up the reading for that hexagram in the book. Invariably, there will be at least one phrase that reaches my soul, and I feel immediately reconnected and soothed. When the truth is spoken or read like this, something inside me just relaxes. With that relaxation comes a clarity of insight and a wonder and awe that I could ever have gotten disconnected in the first place.

In the face of Philip's death, the I Ching returned me to a connection with him, with love, and with the essence of life. A return to being here, right now. In stillness. In beauty. In love.

Sitting Down

by Lori Thiessen

Our souls can get so lost in the noise and busyness of daily life. Often, we need stillness and silence to connect with them. One of my favorite ways of settling down and connecting with my soul is sitting down. Now, I don't mean just sitting on a chair or slouching on the couch, I mean sitting *down*. On the floor. On the ground. It is one of my most comforting ways to be with my soul and converse with my Higher Power.

In the quiet pre-dawn, I sink down to the floor in my bedroom and stretch my legs out. Resting my back against the bed, my small electric fireplace fills the room with a soft glow and a gentle warmth. I relax into a deep state of stillness and connection where I find the courage I need to get up and begin my day.

With the evening dusk, it's the front step I choose to go to. I sit on the hard concrete, which has been warmed by the heat of the day, with my knees tucked up tight to my chest. Folded up on the outside, I pull together the parts of me that have become loose from the chaos of the busy day. The outdoor sounds of wind and birds remind me of a bigger world than the one that consumed my thoughts and energy during the day. As darkness falls and the tea in my oversized mug cools, my swirling thoughts and emotions settle down, and my soul reminds me that above all else, hope still exists. And I find the courage I need to let go of the day that has ended.

This practice of sitting down has given me a deeper understanding for the religious ritual of praying kneeling or prostrate. I find there is such a different connection achieved and perspective gained when I drop below my normal eye level, below the face-to-face interaction zone. Down to the level of my soul where clarity of thought is achieved, where I interact with my soul and my God.

Color Your World

by Sherry VanAntwerp

Most of the time we take color for granted. We only think about it when we encounter a majestic pink and purple sky, turquoise blue waters, the lush green of a meadow, or when a social-media poll asks, "Which dress color do you like better: white and gold, or blue and black?" But what would happen if we started to pay more attention to color and recognize the patterns and repetitions that arise?

Color is one way that our soul, or higher self, communicates with us. Think of color as a roadmap that your soul is sharing to direct you to areas of life that need attention.

Within our human bodies lies an energy system, our chakra system. Each of the chakras is linked to a color that reflects the vibrational energy of that chakra. Our soul communicates which chakra may need attention by bringing the corresponding color into our awareness. For example, I was recently on a two-hour drive and happened to notice a bright orange car that zipped by me. I think it is safe to say that orange is not a common car color, but soon after that I noticed yet another orange car, and then another. In total, I saw 12 orange cars on that drive. (I should mention that my two hours of driving were on a rural interstate in Iowa, not rush hour in Chicago!)

Orange is the color associated with the sacral chakra, which is home to our feelings, emotions, intimacy, and connectedness. When I reflected on what was happening in my life, it became clear that my soul was definitely sending me a message that I needed to spend some time working on the matters of this chakra.

What might your soul be trying to tell you? What colors have you been drawn to recently or keep repeating in your day? Spend some time reading your "color map," and remember that your soul is the most accurate GPS you will ever have!

Embrace Your Senses, Embody with Soul

by Nishaan Sandhu

I hear that life on Earth takes the cake for the longest waiting list…and with good reason! It's a wonderful stage on which to learn, evolve, and reconnect. And it's a place to experience the miracle of physical life.

I see the body as a vessel – a physical manifestation of our soul in this present time and place. We embody life most fully not by rejecting our physical reality but by embracing the wisdom of our *whole being,* including our senses.

Our senses teach us how to navigate survival, intuition, and pleasure on Earth. They warn when something is unsafe. They share what we love and what we don't. They flavor decisions; inspire comfort; and keep us creative, alive, and thriving. They're a navigation system, embodying the voice of our soul.

We all come into this world honoring our sensory wisdom and our soul's voice. But at some point, many of us develop doubt toward our inner compass in order to keep the peace. If this has happened to you, don't worry – that wisdom isn't lost; it's just waiting to be honored again. When we honor our sensory wisdom, gut instincts, intuitive insight, and yes, even earthly pleasures, we heighten our soul's experience of embodiment and clear the lines to our soul's navigation.

To help facilitate this process, start to notice and honor your preferences: What sensory experiences do you love? What do you dislike? What are your favorite creature comforts?

Remember, this process isn't about judgment or criticism but about enjoyment of life in alignment with Soul, one detail at a time. It's about honoring and nurturing (rather than denying or discounting) your senses.

You can start simple. Visit a garden or greenhouse and notice what colors, scents, and textures of nature make you feel most aware or present. What lights your heart and brings vitality? Or start wherever you are right now, asking yourself: *Where can I pour pleasure into my unique experiences? What sights, sounds, tastes, scents, and textures do I love?*

Honor your body's wisdom. Embrace your senses. Embody with soul.

Walking the Route to Yourself

by Nadean Ollech

I took the bus from Galway into a little village, deciding that I would walk and find beds as I went. It just seemed like what I was supposed to do. Before I got off the bus, the driver asked me what I was looking for. "I don't know," I said, "but I'll know it when I find it."

This was in June 2014, in the midst of a year-long journey of self-discovery in Europe. The experience brought me more gifts than I ever expected, but it wasn't until the seven-day solo ramble across the Irish countryside that I felt my inner self receiving what I had been asking for throughout the year: a deeper connection to self, a new way of listening, and personal peace. Somewhere between Galway and Doolin, I walked through a door to my inner self. The door was the pathway to my soul, and now I live whole.

Since returning home, I've continued to walk 1-3 hours a day. My body sometimes complains, but my inner self could not cope without this walking meditation. I know that my inner self wants the best for me; and if I listen, it will take care of me. I also know that when my inner self, my body, and my conscious mind work together, I am comfortable and free to be me and live happily. So I continue to walk. And when I do, I get to connect with a part of myself that goes beyond aching legs or conscious thought, a part of me that is connected to the Universe.

During my walks in Ireland and the walks I've taken since then, I learned that a great way to connect with your soul is to find the pathway between the conscious and unconscious and then keep revisiting it so that the path stays clear and open. For me, long solo walks opened this pathway. Now all I have to do is to keep the pathway open…and keep on walking the route to myself.

Give Your Soul a Gift

by Christine Tomasello

Sometimes your soul just needs a little TLC. After all, it's so easy to get disconnected from it when you put all of your focus and energy toward something (or someone) else – such as a project at work, your kids' activities, starting school, helping a partner, or taking care of an aging parent. Anything that drains your energy can cause this disconnection.

Any time we're feeling depleted, we can take special care to reconnect with our soul. One way to do this is to give your soul a gift. Try taking yourself on a date, making a special meal, re-reading a favorite book, playing dress-up in your best clothes, or people-watching at your favorite coffee shop. The point is to take time to do something that you know will nourish your soul.

You can inquire about what your soul might want at that moment. Does your soul want something stimulating, like a fun movie? Or would it rather have some quiet time on a bench? You can even ask your soul, "What is it that you need right now? What would be nurturing to you? What will make you feel loved?"

If you ask these questions, be sure to sit in silence for a few moments. Give your soul some time and space to respond. Don't worry about doing it "right." Believe that your soul will provide you with the clarity you're looking for. Trust yourself and trust the process. You'll know what the right gift is.

It is easy to get caught up in life and neglect our soulful beings. Giving your soul a gift will help you slow down, get centered, and stay grounded through the chaos. Just being intentional with your time and directing your energy toward something that you enjoy, even if it's only for an hour, is powerful. And your soul will thank you for it.

Reflect on Your Child's Soul

by Kathy White

I became a parent under the most difficult of circumstances: my first child was stillborn.

After a very normal pregnancy, in the last stages of a natural labour, my baby started to show signs of distress. We were rushed to have an emergency C-section, and tragically he never breathed outside of the womb.

My subsequent journey was to love my son, even in his death, by connecting with his soul. In my grief and shock, I was catapulted into a deeply spiritual place of connection beyond the body. That soul connection was profoundly sad and incredibly beautiful at the same time, as I strove toward healing and accepting our souls' journey as mother and son and seeing his death as perfect.

When my other two children were born, I was compelled to be a perfect parent. And yet, I found myself getting bogged down with worry, stress, the whirlwind of day-to-day activities, and trying to get everything done. In this busy-parent mode, I lost the wonder and wisdom of what it truly means to be a parent. I longed to connect with my two children on the same level of soul that I had connected with their older brother.

I created *Child Soul Cards* and used them to help me go beyond any disturbing or irritating behaviour in my children and to view that behaviour as a message from their soul trying to say something to me. *Child Soul Cards* gave me a pointer into the souls of my children; so rather than reacting to them with anger or frustration, I became able to see their soul force at play and therefore develop more compassion, love, and understanding for them.

So, parents, this is your invitation. Reflect on your child's soul. See their potential, their vulnerability, their wisdom, and their journey from a soul perspective. Rekindle the amazing gratitude, honour, and wonder of being a parent. In doing so, you'll connect with your soul as well.

Connecting with Crystals

by Pam McKinney

I've always loved sparkly things! As a child, I collected beautiful stones that I found or bought on our family travels. As an adult, I've always been drawn to jewelry made with beautiful crystals. Now, as a Certified Crystal Healer, I've learned that not only are crystals beautiful, they're also a way to connect with your soul. I use crystals for many purposes, such as balancing my chakras, assisting in meditations, manifesting intentions, and facilitating healing for myself and others.

Crystals each have their own unique energy frequency that you can tune into. Because their energy frequency is very stable, you can align your body's energy to theirs. This helps your body get into a balanced state, which allows it to heal.

When using crystals to balance my chakras, I allow my guides to assist me in choosing the stones that are aligned with what I most need at the time. When my chakras are aligned, my energy flows freely and I feel my connection with Source.

During meditation, crystals help me expand my energy and open up even more to receive messages from my guides. My favorite crystal for this is my Lemurian seed. I also use other stones as I'm guided, such as labradorite. There's lots of magic in that stone!

Another way to connect with your soul is through crystal grids – groups of crystals arranged to help you manifest your intentions. One way to use crystal grids is to write out your intention, place it at the center of a sacred geometrical pattern, and surround it with crystals that resonate with you and support your intention. You can also make a ritual around the creation of your grid – such as burning sage, lighting candles, or placing the grid in a sacred area of your home.

However you use crystals, you will be led to the ones that most resonate with your soul. You will definitely feel more connected to certain crystals, just like you feel more connected to certain people. Most important, you will feel a closer connection with All That Is.

Finding Daily Hearts

by Tanya Levy

It began purely by accident. I snapped a picture with my new phone through the bathroom window with the flash on by mistake. In the light, I saw what looked to me like a heart. Then I started seeing heart clouds in the sky. Then I graduated to photo apps where I would mirror photos and augment colour, and hearts started showing up in my mirrored photos. Eventually, I came to realize that this was no accident after all. Clearly, all that is Divine wanted me to see hearts.

It had been a difficult couple of years. My Mom was in and out of the hospital and died in March 2015. She would get out of the hospital, and my Dad would go in. It seemed that each time my faith would waver, a heart would appear in the sky. It became like a secret sign: when I saw a heart, I knew that God was watching over my folks and me.

Seeing hearts helped me connect more deeply with my soul. I learned to become more present when I was outside or walking in nature. I learned to breathe the air more deeply and search the sky, the ground, trees, and the flowers with more presence. On a day when I was feeling out of sync, I would stumble across tiny hearts made out of snow. If I took a break at work and walked over to my office window and snapped a photo, I would later see a heart amongst the clouds.

Everyone's signs are different. For me, the Divine chose to speak through hearts. For you, it may be feathers, animals, or numbers. If what you see or find helps you connect more with your soul, then the journey becomes easier and life is brighter. I know that my heart still leaps with gratitude and joy whenever I stumble upon a new heart.

Ask Yourself Penetrating Questions

by Thea Westra

Just as it's said that eyes are the window to our soul, I believe that questions are the key to our soul.

Could you imagine a world in which everything is taken at face value and the question mark is never used? Surely that world would quickly dissolve inside its limits. We would never dream, watching the night sky and wondering what lies far, far away.

I am not talking about mundane subjects of concern like what to eat for lunch or what color to wear. Beyond the shell of daily existence there are more poignant matters that also want our attention. In fact, we crave purposefulness and mindful intention for our life.

When we ask ourselves those prickly kind of questions, we are making contact with the heart. Powerful questions can sometimes need a lifetime, and there is no guarantee they will even receive closure.

The purpose of asking meaningful questions for self reflection is to expose yearnings and perspectives that might not always be in clear view. We become quite expert at keeping secrets from our conscious mind, yet your feelings when hearing a pointed question will quickly let you know the truth of your soul.

I know you have felt it. For example, ask yourself this gorgeous question from Debbie Ford's book *The Right Questions*: "Will this choice propel me toward an inspiring future or will it keep me stuck in the past?" Never mind your well thought-out answer. How did your heart respond? Did you notice? What was your first thought?

That first response, before you spend a lot of time analyzing or internally debating, THAT is the voice of your soul.

Spend regular time with powerful questions, even ones that you find a little uncomfortable or might make you squirm a little. Then, check in with the soul part of you.

Are you listening to your thoughts (or worse, someone else's voice answering for you, like a parent or close friend), or will you listen instead when your soul replies?

Become a Pro at Psychic Self-Defense

by Puja Madan

Have you ever left a room full of people and felt completely depleted? Or had an unpleasant exchange with a store clerk that left you feeling exhausted and irate?

Our energetic body field can be affected both positively and negatively by the thoughts and actions of people around us. When it is protected we can raise our vibration and connect more easily with our souls.

Here are some tools to help you become a pro at psychic self-defense:

- *Bubbles, force fields, and armors* – With visualization techniques, we can create a protective bubble or armor around us. Sit comfortably and relax your body and mind. Imagine yourself inside a bubble of yellow or white light, totally safe and protected. This bubble will protect both your physical and energetic body from psychic harm. You can also build armor or a shield of mirrors to protect you.
- *Crystals and essential oils* – The live energy of plants and crystals can be used to protect energy fields very effectively. Crystals that are great energy protectors include smoky and rose quartz, onyx, labradorite, amethyst, and amber. Keep a few around your home or office. Essential oils that protect the aura include juniper, eucalyptus, vetiver, cedarwood, and sage. These oils can be inhaled, mixed with a carrier oil to rub on the skin, or added to water to make sprays that can cleanse your home or office.
- *Cord cutting and protection from psychic attacks* – A psychic cord or hook can develop when someone gets hooked onto us energetically or psychically. Archangel Michael is known for his work in helping people with cord cutting. Invite him to help and ask other deities, spirit guides, or guardian angels you work with to help you.

In addition to these techniques, water is always a good way to flush out negative energy from the energy field. And nothing beats good sleep for keeping your aura strong and healthy. Whatever method you use, you can keep your energetic field safe and protected at all times!

Rush Hour or Happy Hour?

by Anissa Centers

When we ask ourselves what is best for us, our mind's answers are often what we think we *should* feel, based on what our family, friends, or peers have told us we should want. But there's a part of us that knows our core truth without being told by others. This is the part that just *knows* when someone or something is or isn't good or doesn't feel right.

I've come up with a fun, easy way to access your inner wisdom at any moment, just by asking one simple question.

Before we get to the question, though, let's take a short inner vacation. Imagine the most relaxing vacation spot ever. For me, it's a Jamaican beach with white sand and blue-green water. The wait staff "magically" appears with what I want, without me having to say a word, then quietly disappears. (Sometimes, the guy bringing my drink looks just like Idris Elba, but don't tell anyone I said that.) Once you're in your perfect place, how do you feel? Did you just exhale? Did your shoulders drop into a relaxed posture?

Now let's visit a very different location. Imagine being on a six-lane highway at 6:45 on a Monday morning, with traffic backed up for miles. How do you feel now? Did your shoulders creep back up? Chest tighten? Breathing become shallow?

Think about any aspect of your life, and then ask yourself this question: *Does it feel more like rush hour or happy hour?*

Your physical response to this question is your body's way of talking to you. Your body is always giving you feedback or, better yet, a heads-up about what needs attention in your life. You can always get the truth about whether a person, place, or thing is good for you – simply by asking…and then allowing your deeper wisdom to emerge through your body's responses.

Use this method often. It's like duct tape. It can work on anything!

Four-Bodies Check-In Ritual

by Stacey Hall

I am blessed that I experienced a physically debilitating illness that kept me in bed 90% of the time for more than two years.

For years leading up to the day I collapsed, I had lived each day as if I were playing "beat the clock" – packing in as many activities as I possibly could before dropping exhausted into bed late each night, having missed meals and other ways to nourish myself physically, emotionally, mentally, and spiritually.

When my energy finally ran out, lying in bed day after day gave me plenty of time to breathe, meditate, and pray. All day long, I would pray for answers as to how to restore my energy, my hopefulness, and my enthusiasm.

I began noticing other activities that made my soul feel refreshed and uplifted and started crafting my days with specific daily "chi-generating" rituals. I woke up visualizing my chakras while saying "I AM" affirmations followed by prayers. I took baths with Epsom salts and essential oils. I nourished my body. I focused on my breathing, played with my dogs, or watched shows like *Ellen* to laugh.

Now that my wellness is restored, whenever I feel my energy sinking and want to connect with my soul, I immediately practice my "Four-Bodies Check-In Ritual." I check in with my physical body, my emotional body, my mental body, and my spirit body. I ask each one to let me know the score it gives itself (on a scale of 1-10, with 10 being fully energized). Then I ask each one to let me know what it requires to come up to a 10. I make an agreement with each body as to when I will give it what it needs, and I thank it for letting me know.

The entire process takes less than two minutes, after which I always feel "chi-lifted" again!

Writing with Your Non-Dominant Hand

by Catherine Walters

For years, I've used two-way writing to connect regularly with my Divine Friends. Until recently, however, I felt like a piece was missing: I didn't have a real relationship with my true self, my own soul. Because of this, I felt disconnected and empty, and I longed for something more.

Looking for guidance, I turned to one of my inner-child books. As I flipped through the pages, I noticed a page that alternated typed text with the childish writing of the non-dominant hand. At that moment, something clicked. I had already used non-dominant handwriting to give my inner child a voice, and I suspected I could use the same tool to communicate and develop a deeper connection with my soul.

Excited, I grabbed a journal, markers, colored pens, and fat crayons; and I began to write – alternating using my left and right hands:

> Dear Precious Soul, I love you and thank you for always being there.
>
> Precious, I like that. I love you, for all you are is love.
>
> Is it really this easy to communicate with you?
>
> Yes, I am always here for you. Can you feel my love?

I took a deep breath and felt myself held in the most loving embrace. Tears of love and gratitude flowed down my cheeks. This gift of love was right inside of me, yet until using the tool of non-dominant handwriting, it had eluded me.

Once I read those wise words that came from deep inside me, I made a promise to myself to include non-dominant handwriting as part of my daily spiritual practice. Now, instead of feeling empty or disconnected, I start my day feeling full of love, joy, and wholeness.

I invite you to try this practice, too! Remember to have fun and enjoy connecting with your inner child…and with your soul!

The Gift of Sensitivity

by Nancy Ferrari

When you are identified as a sensitive soul, this means that you are sensitive to energy within you and around you and that you have an elevated intuition. These are special gifts; however, they can easily be misunderstood by others and can bring possible challenges, such as:

- feeling overwhelmed by elevated noise and energy
- feeling exhausted at the end of the day
- skin sensitivity to clothing and/or touch
- feeling others' emotions within an environment
- being labeled and misunderstood by others

These experiences can feel overwhelming and disempowering; however, there are techniques you can use to help you along your journey.

An effective way to tune in with your sensitivity is to connect with yourself at the soul level (which is love and truth) through simple practices, such as stillness and/or meditation. While focusing on your breath (or practicing another type of simple meditation), your sensitive nature will calm down, clearing your mind as you shut off the "noise switch." This can be done at any time of day – whenever you want to manage the amount of energy that comes your way.

Another simple technique is grounding, which is achieved by just standing in the grass with bare feet. As you are innately sensitive, you will draw in the positive energy from the earth, which helps you feel more centered and harmonious.

It is also especially important, as a sensitive soul, to utilize your intuition to invite positive people into your life – people who will support you and enhance your life. Anyone of a negative nature will have the capacity to cause interference within your energy field and drain you.

The more you make time to connect with yourself at the soul level, the more easily you'll see that your sensitivity is a true gift.

Tapping into Your True Essence

by Julie Jones

I've noticed an interesting pattern in my life: When everything is running smoothly, I often forget to take time to connect with my soul or even to be grateful. But when life presents challenges (such as a frightening report from the doctor, problems with the kids, or a relationship that's not living up to expectations), that's when I do the most inner work. That's also when I tend to reach for holistic tools, such as essential oils.

Essential oils are a wonderful pathway to help us connect our body-mind-spirit, especially during stressful times. Two of my favorite essential oils for these moments are frankincense and sandalwood. One or two drops diluted in a teaspoon of carrier oil and applied to my temples, forehead, and the back of my neck help me to slow my breath and release fear. In this moment of release, a gap opens, allowing me to connect with the Divine, tap into my inner wisdom, and reconnect with my true self – my essence.

In a sense, this experience mirrors the process that the oils themselves go through. When an essential oil is still in the plant, it is called the "essence." But when a skilled distiller applies just the right amount of heat and pressure, the plant releases the essence and the essential oil slowly emerges.

I love this example from nature, and I relate to it in my own life. In moments of "heat and pressure," I try to remember that my circumstance is temporary and that it is helping to release my true essence. And I know that I will emerge stronger.

Passing Through Two Gates

by Susan Mullen

Growing up clairsentient with a strong, clear inner knowing created some of my earliest and harshest lessons. As a young woman, I was often conflicted between what I was feeling and what was being presented. I often chose to ignore my inner guidance in order to keep the peace or go with the flow.

Ignoring my intuition was like holding a candle but choosing to navigate in the dark. It set me up for disappointment every time. My decisions were typically based on outside opinion rather than on what my inner voice was trying to convey. As I began respecting and using my intuitive gifts, however, my entire life changed.

Some of us are more wide open and connected to the field of consciousness than others, but we all have the same potential to tune into and further develop our natural gifts in this area. We can tap into our inner knowing at any time to discern what is right for us or what is not.

The next time you want to access your inner wisdom, try passing whatever you're trying to discern through these two "gates":

- *Does it allow you to live peacefully in your body?*
- *Does it sit right in your soul?*

After asking these two questions, *feel* where the answers land in your body. Feel the energetic weight. Does it feel as if you are pulling it, or as if *it* is pulling *you*? If it feels like it's pulling you forward, it is a *YES*…and to be explored further. If you feel a heaviness in your body, as if you are pulling it along, that is your consciousness saying, *NO, it is not to be explored at this time.*

This is an internal look with no judgment of self. It is about honoring where you truly stand in your life. Only you can discern what truly sits right in your soul.

For me, this process never fails to deliver my next right step!

Baking with Intention and Love

by Nancy Merrill Justice

Christmas in my home has always been a time of celebration, creativity, giving, and enjoying family traditions. Through the tradition of baking Christmas treats each year with my grandmother, Namo, for our family and friends, I learned the joy and peace that came through making something from the heart – and then giving it away with love. My spirit was always in harmony with Namo's, and our souls connected in celebration through baking.

As I review my life's journey toward self-actualization, I realize that my Christmas baking experiences have accurately reflected the level of my soul awareness at those times. In my youth and early adulthood, although I loved my grandmother and baking with her, I was often impatient with the entire baking/packaging process, and our conversations were on a more superficial level.

As the years passed and I grew more in touch with myself and with spiritual awakenings, my baking experience with Namo changed significantly. The "strategic planning" of our 150 dozen baked creations became a much more sophisticated and thoughtful process – from the selection of the ingredients to the complementary gourmet varieties we chose to make. We were much more intent in our desire to create the most exquisitely delicious experience for our family, friends, and associates than we had been in years past.

But more significant was the highly soulful experience Namo and I created as we spent time baking together. I was fully present – cherishing every moment – asking her questions about her childhood, her memorable life experiences, and her thoughts on a wide variety of subjects. I got to know and experience her loving, kind, and generous spirit as she shared her creativity and wisdom with me. The expressed joy, peace, and happiness we felt listening to our favorite Christmas music and singing together while we baked all translated into the most important ingredient being added to our baked creations: LOVE.

Now, at Christmas and around the year, I still bake with intention, from my heart and soul – always adding ingredients of love and joy from memories of connected souls.

Tuning Up Your Inner Antenna

by Gabriele Engstrom

A dear friend of mine once told me that I was constantly retuning my antenna. At first this confused me; but as I pondered her words, I realised she was correct.

An antenna is a finely tuned instrument that can read different frequencies or vibrations. I have been using (and tuning and retuning) my own "inner antenna" since early childhood.

I was a very shy little girl who was bullied in kindergarten because I spoke a different language. To protect myself, my antenna constantly scanned my surroundings. As soon as I felt a frequency that made me uncomfortable, I would make myself invisible. I'd hide under tables, in corners, or any place where my teachers and parents would have a hard time finding me.

Each of us has an inner antenna, which constantly picks up signals from the world around us. This remarkable tool does more than just protect us; it can lead us step by step to our goals and dreams.

When my antenna finds an object, person, or situation I want, I get goose bumps. And bingo – I know it's the right thing. The opposite is true, too. When my life isn't working the way I would like, I know my frequency is low. I don't make myself invisible anymore, but I still retreat when I'm feeling off or "out of tune." Fortunately, I've discovered several ways to center myself, raise my vibration, and "retune" my antenna.

One way I do this is by listening to the sounds of nature, such as the wind, birds, fire, water, or the humming of insects. When I'm not able to get outside, I re-energise myself through breath. I imagine that with each breath my body becomes lighter and lighter, and that every cell is being healed and rejuvenated.

My suggestion to you is to use your breath, nature sounds, or any other technique that helps you connect back to your inner antenna. As you do so, you will feel more at peace with yourself and your environment, and you'll be able to attract the love and abundance you desire.

Express Lane to the Higher Self

by Linda Voogd

Our bodies and minds can take us only so far on our journey. Our hearts take us further. And our soul takes us to the deepest regions of our core. I try to connect to this higher part of myself as often as possible; but sometimes, when I get caught up in day-to-day distractions, I need a quick reminder of who I really am in this lifetime.

On mornings when life is hectic, I look for ways to jumpstart the connection to my higher self. When I can't do my ideal exercise routine (a 45-minute walk or a 25-minute workout on my elliptical machine), I find five minutes for intense movement to energize my body and get my blood flowing. I do the same for my soul. When I don't have time for longer spiritual rituals, I head for the fast track. I use a shortcut, or as I think of it, "the express lane to my higher self."

I find that short poems or quotes send me a direct message, bypassing my rational mind. Short phrases by Rumi, Hafiz, Tagore, or other great writers are VIP passes straight to the soul. They're like going on a ride at Disneyworld without having to wait in line.

What phrases work for me? This short poem by Rabindranath Tagore offers a great example:

"I CANNOT keep your waves," says the bank to the river.
"Let me keep your footprints in my heart."

Reading these words, I hear my soul whisper, "Accept change; it will point you in right direction." Poetic lines like this put in perspective what is truly important and remind me that I am nurtured.

The following quote by Albert Camus acts as a tool helping me visualize my soul holding the lamp that guides me through life's darkest storms:

In the depth of winter, I finally learned that within me there lay an invincible summer.

When I read this quote, I imagine my soul saying to me, "I will provide warmth and shine light to illuminate your path."

With just a few words, I am energized and connected to my eternal self – in almost no time at all!

Singing Bowls: A Note for the Soul

by Stella Tassone

"Music washes away from the soul the dust of everyday life."
- Berthold Auerbach

When I first heard the sound of a singing bowl, it struck a chord and vibrated my heartstrings. The feeling throughout my whole body was divine.

The harmonic vibration in singing bowls slows down your heart rate, relaxes the brain, and creates a feeling of peace and tranquility. This form of sound healing naturally restores the vibratory frequencies of the body, mind, and soul that are out of tune.

When I decided to purchase a singing bowl (which I got from a beautiful Tibetan monk who blessed it and taught me to play), I knew this little instrument was going to assist me in finding peace within and connecting my body, mind, and soul.

I now have five of these bowls, and when it all seems too much or when I'm feeling out of alignment, I know my bowls are waiting for me to strike them so they can sing to my soul.

I place them in a row, inhale and exhale deeply, and allow my brain to move into the theta brainwave frequencies that place me into a deep, meditative state. This assists in bringing clarity of mind, heightening intuition, and allowing me to listen not only through my ears but through my soul.

My children also love these bowls and our ritual of sitting in a circle and playing them. I hope that through this ritual, they are able to learn from an early age how important it is to stop, breathe, and connect with who they are and listen to their soul.

Tapping Your Way to Self-Connection

by Cindy Jones Lantier

"Even though I am acting and feeling defensive with my friend, I deeply and completely love, honor, and accept myself."

Thus began a recent tapping session.

Tapping (whether in the form of Thought Field Therapy or Emotional Freedom Technique) is a great way to discover, process, and clear the blocks that keep us from fully connecting to our greater self, our soul. These blocks can be caused by pain (either physical or emotional), anger, resentment, and unhelpful self-beliefs. All these things – and a whole host of others – can foster a sense of disconnection.

Tapping works with the energy systems in our bodies. It is non-medicinal and non-invasive. It's easy, and anyone can learn it. The only drawback that I know of is that it looks and feels a little silly to do, especially when you're just learning it.

Through tapping, I have seen some amazing results – both personally and in my clients. I have made connections between issues that I didn't know were related, allowing me to finally find some healing.

When I was dealing with a stressful friendship issue, I tapped on my feelings of uncalled-for defensiveness. Following the trail of whatever came up next, I realized that those feelings were related to my feelings of not being seen and heard for who I was as a child. Realizing this connection helped me to feel less defensive with my friend; I could see that those emotions weren't always authentic responses to her words and actions.

But most importantly, the tapping that began on this stressful friendship issue actually helped me clear and process those painful feelings from my childhood.

We don't have to be perfect to feel connected with our soul – if that were the case, nobody would ever feel that connection, much less be able to live out of it! But the more toxic memories and long-held pain we can work through, the stronger that connection will become. Doing the work of self-development only increases the connection with our higher self. Tapping can help.

Fingerprints of the Soul

by Christine King

Trying to figure out our life's purpose can sometimes prove very frustrating. It is often difficult to distinguish the signs and messages coming directly from our soul from all the other thoughts and ideas going on in our head. We can end up feeling confused and unsure, resulting in a sense of disconnection from our higher wisdom.

After many years on the spiritual path, with all its challenges and triumphs, I was finally led to my life's work as a Soul Guidance Practitioner and Workshop Facilitator.

I can remember joking with a friend that the journey would have been a whole lot easier if the Universe had just provided me with a map, clearly marked, "Soul's Purpose – This Way!" Little did I know at the time that it already had! In fact, I came to discover that before we are born, each one of us is already in possession of our own individual "Soul Map." We come into this world with it and have been carrying it around with us ever since, but most of us are unaware of it because it is hidden in a place where we might never think of looking: *in our own hands!*

Around 16 weeks, while still in the womb, a set of fingerprints appeared on your hands, and those fingerprints have never changed. Not only do these fingerprints serve as a unique mark of your physical body, they also can hold the key to your soul's purpose – which can be decoded by the process of hand analysis.

Open your hands, palm side up and rest them in your lap. Take a little time to study your hands. Everything there is a map of your soul. Gently close your eyes and say silently to yourself, "My soul has a plan for me and is guiding me to it." If it feels right, explore this more. By searching online, in books, or wherever else you feel drawn to, you'll find that a whole world of information on this topic will open up to you. And it all begins, quite literally, at the tips of your fingers!

Messages from the Light

by Elizabeth Harper

Your spirit is filled with a magnificent light. It is a reflection of the Divine that keeps you in communication with your true self. When you journeyed to Earth as a soul, your light split into a multitude of rays. You emerged as a beautiful rainbow. Your personal soul rainbow is your unique color thumbprint. No other light-being on the planet contains the same colors in the exact proportions as you.

If you are the rainbow, then do you know where to find your pot of gold? All the riches the universe has to offer are hiding in plain sight, right there within your heart. This is the doorway to the wisdom and guidance of your soul. When you find and *become* that pot of gold, then all the knowledge, abundance, and love you have sought will be yours.

One of the easiest ways to connect with your soul is through color. The colors you choose every day mirror the soul's light. If you want to know why you have been guided to a particular color, simply close your eyes, relax, and ask yourself, "What does this color mean for me?" If the answer is elusive, ask this question instead: "If I knew, what would this color mean for me?"

Expand on this technique to receive a daily message from your soul. Close your eyes. Make an intention to connect. Place one hand over your heart. Imagine that it is overflowing with vibrant golden light. Step into and *become* the light. Look above you and notice if one color within your rainbow is pulsing with more energy than the others. Let this color flood your heart and allow its message to flow through your consciousness. As before, ask what the color means for you.

Whenever you want to communicate with your soul, go into the pot of gold that is your heart. Invite it to speak to you through the vibration of your personal rainbow, and allow it to guide you to the colors your individual soul needs for your own enlightenment.

Discovering "Peaceful Dragon Energy"

by Hue Anh Nguyen

On March 25, 2005, I was in a near-fatal car crash. My SUV was totaled, I was knocked unconscious, and I had an out-of-body experience that seemed to go on forever. Miraculously, when I regained consciousness I learned that I had only been out for a few moments and that nothing was broken (other than my SUV).

Despite emerging relatively unscathed, I did experience excruciating pain all over my body that no medication could relieve. After months of trying different methods to alleviate my pain, the doctors gave up their efforts to heal me and settled on a diagnosis of Fibromyalgia.

After several years of suffering from chronic pain, I traveled to Australia to meet Lynn – a woman who could certainly relate to coming back from the brink of death. Several years earlier, she had been on her death bed, saying goodbye to her family. As a final attempt to save her, she was taken to Vuon La (which translates into "strange garden"), a special place in Vietnam known for the healing properties of the magnetic field that surrounds it.

While in Vuon La, Lynn meditated within the healing field and also practiced "Peaceful Dragon Energy" – a spiritual movement technique that combines elements of qigong, t'ai chi, meditation, and intuitive energy. Not only was she healed, but she ended up healthier than ever!

During my visit with Lynn, she demonstrated Peaceful Dragon Energy for me. As I watched her body's graceful movements, flexible and full of wonderful energy, I felt a powerful energy flowing through me, and my body started to move intuitively. Although I kept moving for 1½ hours, I didn't experience any pain or fatigue – for the first time in years!

After Lynn attuned me to this energy, I learned how to attune it to others – in person and even remotely! Over the past few years, I've experienced (both firsthand and through working with others) just how powerful this practice is.

While I never would have chosen to be in that car crash, I'm so grateful that it initiated the journey that led me to the profound healing of Peaceful Dragon Energy.

Surrender to Your Soul – Morning Intention

by Helen Jane Rose

The "Surrender to Your Soul" Morning Intention is one of my favourite ways to wake up – especially when I'm not feeling centred and present or have slipped into worrying about something.

This intention came about in response to a question I was asked at a seminar. A woman wanted to know how she could begin her day feeling connected to her soul. I suggested that she start each morning by asking what her higher purpose for the day was and then writing the first thing that came into her head. But the woman said that she'd already tried this many times, and it didn't work for her.

At this point, another woman asked if, instead of the question about higher purpose, I could suggest a morning *intention* to start the day. While I didn't have an immediate answer, one came to me the next day during a meditative writing session. This intention has since helped me – and many other people – to start our day feeling connected and really tuned into our souls, with the peace of knowing that all is okay and just as it's meant to be.

The intention works best if you say it just after you wake up, silently or out loud:

"Today I intend to surrender to the agenda of my soul. My soul knows exactly what is planned for me, and I surrender to what unfolds, fully accepting all that I will experience today. As I surrender to my soul's agenda, I understand that I will feel more and more peace, knowing that everything is as it should be. My soul has been in charge all along, and I am so grateful for finally realising that it's true that everything is unfolding exactly as it is meant to."

Remember, remember – the great power in surrender!

Embrace the Mystery, Enjoy the Journey

by Sue Kearney

Your human self wants to know what's going to happen. You want to know that your efforts and plans will have the results you crave. But you never really do know, do you? You like to *think* you know, to have the certainty that you're on a clear path from here to there. But what can you really know besides this moment?

When the steps you take and the outcomes that will result from these steps are unclear, how do you stay grounded, wrap yourself in ease, and claim the joy in the journey? These suggestions will help you, even when you can't see very far in front of your feet.

- *Develop a consistent spiritual practice.* Regularly pray, meditate, or engage in any other spiritual activities that strengthen your connection with your soul.
- *Cultivate a support system.* Connect regularly with friends, a coach, a mastermind group, or anyone else who can support you in your life's journey.
- *Trust that the right and perfect outcome is already written.* It's already in the book! Your job is simply to keep putting one foot in front of the other with your eyes up and your heart open.
- *Stand sovereign in the mystery.* You are exactly where you are meant to be. There is big magic in accepting what is still unknown and unclear.
- *Call in compassion and remember that you are not doing this alone.* Wrap yourself in the love and safety of the Divine.
- *Set aside sacred time in your calendar to lovingly and joyfully do the tasks that move you in the direction of your goals.* When things feel hard or challenging, take a look at breaking your tasks into more manageable chunks. And get support as you go. Give the powerful gift of asking for help.
- *Implement your sacred self-care so that all your actions nourish you instead of depleting you.* Stay balanced; take exquisite care of yourself.

Add these practices to your self-love toolkit to stay connected with your soul, embrace life's mysteries, and enjoy the journey.

Ask Your Soul Questions

by Katja Rusanen

When I was a teenager, I started to connect with my intuition by asking questions. Even though the most burning ones back then were along the lines of whether the hottest boy in my class liked me or not, this inner questioning opened a door to the wisdom of my soul. I started to hear my soul's voice, which became my decision-making tool.

As an adult, whenever I need to make a big decision, I tune in for inner guidance. Time after time, I'm surprised how I just receive an answer. Oftentimes, however, I've done the opposite of what my inner guidance suggested…and later realized that this wasn't the smartest choice! But I'm still learning to trust and take full responsibility for all the choices I make.

Asking questions can be a simple way to connect with our soul. Here's one way to do this: Take five deep breaths and shower yourself with love. Allow your mind to become peaceful and calm, and then ask a "yes or no" question. Always request an answer that will be for your highest good. Answers come in different forms – you might simply know it or it might come through your senses, as it's possible to hear, feel, taste, smell, or see the answer. Sometimes you might not get a clear answer, as there may be certain useful learning experiences with both choices.

Muscle testing is another approach. When using this technique, first ensure that you are well hydrated. Stand in a relaxed and comfortable position and calibrate your body by asking a question that you already know the answer to. Pay attention to how your body reacts; it might lean forward for "yes" and backwards for "no," or the other way around. Once you know which way is which, ask your question and use your body to connect with your soul's wisdom as it gives you an answer.

When we ask questions, we find answers. When our mind is quiet, we can hear the voice of our soul. We have infinite wisdom within us.

Using Human Design to Improve Your Life

by Yvonne Peraza

Last year, I was introduced to a fascinating tool called Human Design. It's a personality-assessment tool that shows you your unique decision-making strategy, your special gifts and talents, where you carry your pain, and your potential for healing and wisdom. It's a synthesis of eastern and western astrology, the I Ching, the Kabbalah, the chakra system, and modern science.

Through Human Design, I learned that conditioning tends to interrupt our natural tendencies. Many of us are raised to "just go out and do it." So we try and try and try, but we just end up failing. Yes, I've been there...many times.

For most of my life, I was living according to society's "rules" – all the expectations about how we should act, how we should dress, what we should do for a living, who our friends should be, and who we should marry. But much of what I was told I "should" do just didn't match up with what I was feeling and seeing.

When I learned about Human Design, however, everything finally made sense. This system helped me look beyond external rules and connect with who I am at the soul level. My life *really* began to change when I started to understand and practice the strategy for my specific Human Design type.

I found this so helpful that I decided to discover my husband's and children's types as well. Their characteristics totally matched the system, and I felt that I understood their personalities and behaviors better than I ever had before!

Thanks to Human Design, I'm finding myself more confident as an individual and able to interact more effectively with my family. Perhaps best of all, I no longer have to depend on society's "rules" to tell me who I should be, because I have found out who I am at the soul level.

Spiritual Hypnosis

by Vanessa Codorniu

"I cannot shake this feeling I've had since I can remember that something is wrong with me," my client shared.

Bright, beautiful, and successful, this woman in her 40s lit up a room like the Fourth of July, yet she could neither feel it nor believe it.

I began to guide her into a session of spiritual hypnosis created to take her directly to the point where she first received or believed this story/belief that something was wrong with her…

"I am just born! They are saying, 'Too bad something is wrong with her – she has an infection.'" She began to cry as she witnessed her birth and heard the negative diagnosis she received in the hospital. "You see! Something *has* been wrong with me all along! I was born weak – just not good enough for this life!"

I continued the hypnosis session by guiding her up the steps of a rainbow-colored staircase, where her Higher Self met us. I asked, "Higher Self, can you explain why she was born with an infection and why this has impacted her life this way?"

Her Higher Self replied: "You believe you were punished in some form or that you are somehow not whole because you were born with an ailment. In truth, you have never been broken, lacking, or less than. You are a courageous and expansive soul who chose to enter this lifetime in this way to teach your family the meaning of unconditional love and compassion. Embrace the truth of who you are."

Once awakened from hypnosis, the woman gasped and began to cry tears of joy. She was overcome with love, feeling lighter and at peace. There was a palpable shift in her voice and heart. "There was never anything wrong with me," she said. "I am whole. I have *always* been whole! *All* of us are truly whole!"

Connecting with the soul through spiritual hypnosis requires a willingness to explore the possibility that each of us has a Higher Self, an inner wisdom that can shepherd us through our life experiences and an expanded earthly perspective. As we connect with this higher awareness, we transform and are inspired to live the life we desire.

Divine Drumming

by Maura Smith

The magical sound of the drum speaks directly to our soul in a language shared by all. With its simplicity and power, drumming offers an instinctual way of connecting with your innermost being. This power is multiplied in drum circles.

Whenever I participate in a drum circle, I feel its magic working from the first moment. As it begins, all is quiet and still. In the deep silence, I hear the first drumbeat. It echoes down to the depths of my being, resonating fully as I soak up this experience. In the drum circle, I sense the flow of life running through me as it tunes any discordant parts into harmony.

Other beats join in, one by one, enriching the vibration and captivating me. With every beat, I allow myself to become more fully present and go deeper into the experience. When it is my turn, I feel the motion of my hands responding to the inner flow and allow my beat to emerge naturally.

A light breeze in the night air rides the wave of the drumbeat. I look up to the starry sky and feel grateful for being part of this circle where I connect with the sound, the light of the fire, and the shadowy faces. As the beat ebbs and flows, so do my emotions. The fire in the center of our circle crackles, as if to add exclamation marks to the repetitive *Boom! Boom! Boom!* The vibrations echo through me and lift my spirits to soar and dance freely. The rhythm is intoxicating; I sense it running through every fiber and transforming heavy energy to light, stagnation into flow.

As this pure form of sound subsides, tranquility emerges and welcomes the coming stillness. The last beats eventually fade out, leaving nothing but peace.

While the drum circle offers a powerful path to peace and connection, you don't have to wait for a drum circle to feel its magic. You can invite this experience at any moment – even in *this* very moment – by tuning into the sounds around you and connecting with the divine vibrations…and with your own soul.

Create a Signature Soul Space™

by Jimena DeLima

Growing up as a clairsentient little girl, I learned early on that the moment I stepped into a room, my vibrational state was altered. It became routine for me to play with my surroundings to temper my mood and define a space that was "mine" – free of external influence.

This practice made a significant difference to my energetic health and state of mind since feeling my soul and coming back to "me" both comforted me and kept me grounded. Eventually, I realized that what I was doing was anchoring my soul's vibration through its reflection. Since the soul uses its personality to navigate its human experience, the personality is the soul's instrument and thus a gateway that can lead us back to it.

The spaces we inhabit can be soulful, as they hold their own consciousness, energetic field, and vibration – just like you and me. This energy is translated and absorbed through our energetic bodies and subconscious. Colors, photos, artwork, books, furniture, shapes, and smells all communicate. Collectively, they tell the story of who someone is or who they want to be. By adjusting the vibration of our surroundings to reflect our soul's expression (personality), we rewrite the narrative and create a signature vibration that keeps us in constant communion with our soul.

Here's how you can create what I call a Signature Soul Space™:

- Examine each space and every single item in them – from the large right down to the small.
- Declutter and remove what no longer resonates, clean all surfaces, and perform a space-clearing ritual (e.g., smudging).
- To create the highest vibration and most accurate reflection of your soul, add items that represent aspects of your life (e.g., relationships, career) and personality (e.g., colors, music, hobbies, quotes) that evoke feelings of love and joy.

Seeing and feeling my soul around me became a sacred way to connect with my divinity. I hope you, too, will experience the joys of creating a Signature Soul Space™ and immersing yourself in your true essence.

An Ode to Reading

by Shannon Brokaw

Thank you, Beatrix Potter, for my foray into the written word and illustrious drawings via *Peter Rabbit.* I learned what true love was when my father would get off of work from his graveyard shift and take his daughter, who was eagerly awaiting his arrival, from her bed, to care for and read to, while he let my mother sleep.

Thank you, Dr. Seuss, for teaching me that I indeed liked *Green Eggs and Ham*, and that my penchant for storytelling was just beginning to surface. How enthralled I was reading to my friends, family, or anyone who would listen as I recited each and every word.

Thank you, Beverly Cleary, for introducing me to such a compelling and lovable character as Ramona Quimby. I learned that there were good and bad behaviors in everybody, but that in the end, goodness would prevail.

Thank you, Anne Frank, for showing me that no matter what evil lurked outside your tiny attic window, that what can never be taken from any individual is their mind. You taught me that, regardless of circumstance, it is right to set forth dreams in life: to think about the future, to create, to inspire.

Thank you, Jane Austen, for proving that a woman could choose her own path in life, regardless of what societal norms dictated in a time when your station in life was set from birth. You graced my world with six of the greatest novels.

Thank you, J.K. Rowling, for inspiring me to step into that imaginative world that had escaped my very essence. Once again, I was reminded of how reading enabled my overactive imagination and creativity to stir by having the courage to step outside of my comfort zone and write.

To every author, past and present, I thank you for giving me the gift of reading. Reading has not only created a thirst for the expressive word in me, but ignited my soul into taking the leap to put words onto paper, with a hope to inspire all who read them.

What authors have inspired you, expanded your world, and helped you connect with *your* soul?

A Crown of Many Colors

by Mariët Hammann

I've been receiving a lot of messages from my soul recently. It turns out she likes to have fun, is adventurous and creatively colorful, and...*wears a crown?* I have to admit, this last message left me baffled but also curious. I stayed open and found myself receiving clear soul invitations onto a colorful path of health and healing. Before long, my soul's invitations were being echoed by messages from Facebook, YouTube, email, books, music, gatherings...pretty much everywhere I looked!

I gradually pieced together a "crown" of questions corresponding to the colors of the spectrum:

- *Red:* Who *am* I?
- *Orange:* How do I want to *feel*?
- *Yellow:* What do I want to *do*?
- *Green:* How do I want to *love*?
- *Turquoise:* What do I want to *speak*?
- *Blue:* What do I want to *see*?
- *Purple:* What do I want to *understand*?

I delved deeply, reflected truthfully, made adjustments, and aligned with the answers I received inwardly and outwardly. I always felt my soul connect with me in those breathless moments just before I got my answers, acknowledging that these truly were "crowning moments."

Here are some of the answers that I received to the colorful questions: *I am a SoulStory Connector. I feel like a Joyful Jumper. I love being a Colorful Soul. I understand that I am an Eternal Optimist.*

Wearing my soul's crown reminds me to ask these important questions:

- What am I sending from within myself out into the world, and what impact is it having "out there"?
- What is the world sending back to me, and what impact is it having "in here"?

My wish for you is that your soul connects your adventurous life journey into crowning moments, illuminating you "in here" as well as "out there."

Needing Less, Having More

by Deena Gray-Henry

For many years, I was one of those people who felt more alive and creative in controlled chaos. I would often say, regarding my messy home, "I want people to know that someone actually *lives* here!" As the years passed, however, my chaos became less controlled and more overwhelming because I kept bringing more and more things into my life.

The solution? Get organized! I read numerous books and articles, tried many organizational techniques, purchased boxes and bins, put up shelves, and paid for storage lockers…but the changes did not last!

I kept trying. This time, I increased the intensity not only of my efforts and actions, but also of my prayers, my energy, and my affirmations. That's when real changes began. I was inspired to make a vision board of the home I wanted. I created a collage of beautiful, clutter-free rooms, and an immediate miracle happened: our kids surprised us by painting four rooms in our home, and a friend who had a business doing one-day makeovers helped us. Within three weeks, four rooms were totally transformed! Our home was amazing, beautiful, and exactly what I wanted. But once again, the transformation didn't last, and feelings of disappointment set in.

Fortunately, I never gave up! Day after day, year after year, I continued to focus on what I wanted: a clutter-free, organized life.

Eventually, I came to understand that the problem wasn't the *things* themselves, it was my *attachment* to them. I realized that I viewed my things like cherished pets that I would never give away. As I began to release this attachment, I saw clearly that I needed LESS to have MORE! I finally understood the statement, "You cannot organize clutter"! Immediately, another miracle happened: two "Earth angels" called within hours of each other and said, "I have the feeling that I need to help you declutter." They did help me; and my life, home, environment, and relationships have been transformed forever.

I've finally learned that having less truly creates more – more creativity, inspiration, intuition, contentment, freedom, happiness, peace, joy, and love – and it creates a clear path to connect with my soul.

Activating Your Divine Navigation System®

by Ronda Renee

You were born with your very own Divine Navigation System®, which helps guide you to the experiences (and lessons) your soul intended to have in this lifetime.

Your Divine Navigation System® is made up of the four centers of being: your heart, mind, body, and spirit. The heart represents your feelings and emotions. The mind, your thoughts and consciousness. The body, your physical existence and action. The spirit, your connection with Source. Each of the centers plays an integral role in allowing your soul to make itself known. One is not more important than another. They all have a special role to play. You can't just use your head or your heart. You can't just take action or focus on your connection with Source.

The centers also each hold a specific energy in each person on the planet. I call these your Divine Coordinates®. In order to fulfill your soul's intention, all four centers of being must be activated and aligned with your specific energies and must be functioning together as they were meant to. When they are, your soul is fully able to express itself in your life and do the navigating for you.

Until you know what your specific energies are and understand how to get your Divine Coordinates® to work together, it is not uncommon to have a "go-to" center of being that acts much like an overused muscle. This quick check can reveal which one(s) of the centers is your "go to."

- *Heart:* Do you tend to react emotionally to circumstances?
- *Mind:* Do you over-analyze or over-think? Are you emotionally reserved?
- *Body:* Do you regularly over-do or over-commit? Are you a massive action-taker?
- *Spirit:* Do you see the big picture but have a hard time getting things accomplished?

As you move through your day, practice bringing all four centers into your decision making. When you bump up against challenges, practice balancing the centers to allow your Divine Navigation System® to chart your course to your soul.

Spiritual PhytoEssencing

by Cathie Bliss

Over the course of our lives, we layer up. We add t-shirts of co-dependency, sweaters of fear, and jackets of anger. It's natural to do this, no shame involved. It's the human way of staying safe and fitting into a family, a school, a world where we want to be loved and accepted. We inhale this stuff as kids, and then, somewhere along the way, realize that what we breathed in became "who we are." The light turns on: that's not our truth; that's not our Real Self!

As we become conscious of our co-creative role in life, we long to remember our soul, our Real Self. Spiritual PhytoEssencing (SPE), developed by Dr. Bruce Berkowsky, is a beautiful, potent, soul-level healing art that utilizes essential oils to encourage our return to Self. SPE synthesizes aspects of aromatherapy, Kabbalah, homeopathy, depth psychology, and other modalities into a system focused on psycho-spiritual harmonization.

For countless reasons, a soul can become overwhelmed by daily life, and feel separated from the Divine. When one feels psychically disconnected from their soul, with a sensation of being stuck or incomplete, a custom SPE blend can be used as a mirror for the Real Self. The blend shows the Self a glimpse of pure soul energy around which it can reorganize, and a spiritually sensitive individual will be inspired to reorient to their unique soul-nature.

Like all living beings, plants are ensouled, animated with life-force. The essential oil is a plant's most fragrant and spiritual part and expresses specific archetypal qualities. In turn, each person's soul-nature is a unique combination of many distinct archetypes. In creating a custom blend, these soul-level archetypes are carefully matched with essential oils that have corresponding qualities. It is this resonance between human and plant souls that allows and encourages the Self to embrace an SPE blend.

SPE is not a quick fix back to the soul. However, if you are ready to remove layers of false identity and revitalize your Real Self, you may be very interested in the deep, life-changing art of SPE.

Lose Your Mind and Drop into Your Heart

by Jaden Sterling

How often have you known that something was going to happen in your life…and it did? Perhaps the moment you laid eyes on someone, you knew beyond a shadow of a doubt that this person was meant for you…and they were. Or maybe you knew while walking down the aisle that it wasn't such a great idea after all…yet you were too afraid to say anything. How did that work out for you?

True knowing has nothing to do with the brain but everything to do with the heart.

To tap into your inner knowing, you simply must lose your mind and drop into your heart. Your heart holds the key to anything you want to know. Why is this? Simple: ego has no access to the heart. Your soul's "border patrol" stops ego from crossing into this sacred territory.

The heart houses your feelings, which always ring true. The heart knows your truth – well before your brain does – and will guide you well, as long as you allow and trust. Feelings of joy, love, and inspiration remind you that you are on the right track and that your soul is on board!

The heart is the seat of the soul, and together they create a juicy elixir for you to gain nourishment from. When you listen to your soul's whispers, they will resonate, and your heart will corroborate the message. The only question is: Are you over-thinking with your brain or listening to your heart?

The next time you're looking for clarity, take the most impactful 16-inch journey of your life – from your head to your heart – and discover the truth that's waiting there for you.

Shattered-Glass Ritual

by Vicki Talvi-Cole

"Pain of the past is only held in place by your own judgments, how you define yourself. You are your own worst enemy. To put it more accurately: you are your *only* enemy," whispered one of my horses.

I frequently communicate with my horses in this way and have learned so much from them. This particular piece of wisdom stung, though. I could feel the discomfort rise within my body – chest tightening, breath becoming shallow. At the same time, I felt the love and truth of these words gliding through my heart, landing deep within my soul.

I saw the glass wall that I had built around myself to keep imagined enemies out. I realized that it was me who had locked myself behind this wall of judgment and my own projections. Tears fell gently as I recognized that I was my own hostage.

Opening my willingness to dive deeper, into the stillness I sank, asking, "What can I do to free myself?"

I gazed at the beauty and wonder of my horses standing within the stillness of morning light, reflecting to me my own beauty and wonder. I felt a gentle breeze that came with an answer from my soul: "Change your mental habits! Any ritual will do. Throw a rock. Shatter the glass each morning against the painted backdrop of your terrors. Muster up more self-love and fully embrace self-acceptance. Ask yourself: *What did I paint with my emotions, thoughts, and actions on that blank canvas?*"

With a deep breath, I decided to take my soul's advice and threw a rock. In doing so, I could hear and feel glass shattering within me. Exhaling, a new painted backdrop began forming. One with new, brighter colors, laced and aligned with emotional energies that uplifted me. It felt amazing!

I continue this ritual, allowing it to shift and change. Some days I find that more than one rock is needed; other days a little pebble is enough to bring about the breakthrough I need – enough to shatter the glass within me.

The Healing Power of Crystal Singing Bowls

by Michelle Anne Gould

Mary had come here out of a commitment to take better care of her health; but when her eyes caught sight of the glistening crystal singing bowls, she wondered what she'd gotten herself into. What were these things? And how could they help her heal?

Hesitantly, she settled into a comfortable place in the room and undid her sky-blue scarf. Taking a few deep breaths, she gently closed her eyes and opened herself up to the unknown.

The Zen master began with expert patience, tapping the sides of each bowl, as though connected to a rhythmic dance.

The rich, full vibrations took Mary by surprise. Effortlessly and almost immediately, she slipped into a state of deep relaxation. Her whole body not only absorbed the sounds, it took on the vibrations and soared higher. The magical music seeped into her cells, into her bones.

She began to feel dizzy. The sweet, echoing sounds danced within her ears and stirred her heart. Her mind drifted to an unseen paradise. With each chime, she felt closer to the angelic realms, closer to Heaven.

Unbeknownst to her, at that moment all of Mary's chakras had become balanced, aligning her body and soul. The sounds from the bowls allowed her to move into a theta brainwave frequency that induced a deeply meditative and peaceful state.

The voice of an angel joined the singing bowls. Wonderful emotions caught in Mary's throat as she realised the angelic voice was her own. The vibration had led to her inner true self.

The music stopped. In the deep silence, Mary could still feel the energy. She opened her eyes, feeling brand new, fresh, and alive. The magic had captivated her, cleansed her energy, and purified her soul.

With her scarf lightly grasped in one hand, her other hand caressed the lump on her neck. Somehow it seemed smaller. Smiling, Mary stood up and walked to the blessing table, where she placed her scarf among the offerings. Feeling at one with her universe, she opened the door.

S.E.L.F. Check©

by Destrie Sweet Larrabee

If at first you don't succeed, think again! If it seems as though your life is not where it should be, take some time for reflection – it just might set you free! You may have just gone through a life-changing moment!

Every experience is a learning opportunity and, therefore, an opportunity for soul connection. But how does one know for sure? That very question makes all the difference, for it is the first step in actively taking part in your life experience!

Certainly, you can go through life experiencing many things; but in order to truly grow and evolve, the experience alone is not enough. We don't learn by experience; we learn from thinking about and *processing* the experience.

S.E.L.F. Check© is a quick guide to keep you actively engaged in your evolutionary growth and wellbeing. After experiencing an event, just thinking about this process actually engages your brain in higher-level thinking. After some practice, you will find yourself automatically asking yourself the S.E.L.F. Check© questions:

*S*ee:	What do I see happening with me and/or the people around me?
*E*xperience:	What am I experiencing and feeling?
*L*earning:	What am I learning? Do I need more information?
*F*ocus:	As I focus on my next steps/action plan, what will I do with this knowledge? (Once you know, you can grow!)

As a teacher and a lifelong learner, I developed this acrostic and process to help my students realize their learning so they would know what they know – and it worked! But I also learned that this was a wonderful tool for many other uses, and I went on to share it with all of my students, as I taught grades pre-K through graduate school.

This has proven to be an amazing tool for me in my never-ending journey of self-discovery and soul connection, and I have never felt more alive and excited about all of life's amazing gifts, for which I am infinitely grateful! Trust this process – it will work for you, too!

30 Days of Positivity

by Natasha Botkin

Many times during the past few years, I could barely manage to make it through the day. I felt like a shell of a human being, a sleepwalker. I could feel myself vibrationally sending out S.O.S. signals: *Oh, dear God, what am I going to do? I think my soul wants to leave my human form!*

Knowing that something had to change, I began to look for what had gone missing in my life. My search led me to a 30-day positive-affirmation challenge. I accepted the challenge…and even expanded on the idea, deciding to dedicate the next 30 days to positivity in many forms.

I began my month-long journey by focusing on a couple of my favorite positivity tools: a dream board and a "Just Be Present" meditation. These provided some glimmers of hope and moments of peace, but soon enough I found myself once again lying on the floor in a jumbled mess, praying for divine help. I knew I needed to end this cycle, so I didn't give up. I vowed to stick with the positivity program for at least 30 days.

The turning point of my journey came in an unexpected way: when my higher self urged me to start taking photos. I turned my regular hikes into "beauty walks" during which I'd look for – and *find* and *photograph* – anything beautiful. These walks revitalized my soul and helped train my eye to find the positive. As I continued this practice, I also found that wise words began to flow from within me – and I ended up writing my own daily affirmations for 30 days.

The positive energy gained momentum, spiraling upwards and leading me to seek even more ways to express my love and illuminate my positivity. By the end of the month, I felt like I had returned to the true me – a peaceful, joyful, and wise source of light!

Whether you are feeling lost and empty (as I was before I began this positivity journey) or are already feeling good and would like to be lifted even higher, I invite you to try your own 30-day journey of positivity. You can use photography, affirmations, or any other tools that lift you up and return you to your source of inner beauty and light.

The Empty Chair

by Linda Voogd

I grew up believing that my soul was an entity positioned somewhere in my chest, existing solely to collect sin. I tried not to think about it too much, though, lest I be bombarded by my imperfections. Yet the more I grew and the more I experienced, the more I was drawn to stories by others seeking a spiritual path. I began to see the soul as the higher self – an energy within that is connected to everything else.

One day, I had a spiritual reading by someone who could interpret messages of the soul. Although the wisdom she offered rang true, the experience made me realize that if my soul had messages, I wanted to find them myself. So began the journey within.

As a therapist, I use many techniques to help my clients increase communication, locate buried memories, and recognize their gut reactions. When it's difficult to express emotions related to someone in particular, I use the Gestalt technique of "the empty chair." In this powerful technique, you talk to an empty chair and pretend it is the person with whom you most need to communicate. This method works so well that I decided to try it with my soul. I began to share my feelings, thoughts, and fears on a regular basis with this empty chair. I waited in silence for direction.

Then one day, in a workshop designed to cut through the ego and bring you closer to your eternal nature, I was able to hear my soul's message more clearly than ever. When the workshop leader asked me to write a letter allowing my soul to communicate through me, my body shook and words spilled out onto the page.

I know that what came that day was from my soul, because the letter was filled with incredible love, kindness, and forgiveness. It was a message to move forward and let go of past mistakes, words I could not otherwise have written at that time. Although in my handwriting, the letter transcended my ego and rose above my mind's day-to-day chatter. It spoke its own beautiful language – the language of my soul.

Although I no longer believe that my soul resides in my chest (or in an empty chair), addressing it directly has led me to deep healing and a two-way connection with my higher self.

Step out of Separation, Step into Being

by Jane Duncan Rogers

Feeling agitated at what the lecturer was saying, I adopted my usual way of calming myself down: Imagining a column of white light above my head, I pictured it coming down over, around, and through my body. The light moved down through my head, my torso, my hips, and my legs, right down to the floor. I imagined it flowing out of my body and connecting with the white light that was now surrounding me.

Quickly, I began to feel calmer, as I murmured to myself, "All is well. You are a peaceful soul. All is very, very well."

Then suddenly there was a flip. It was as if there had been a "me" observing this delicious column of peaceful white light, and now there was only the light. "Me" had disappeared, and there was a revelation: "Oh! I AM the light itself!"

The lecture continued. All the participants continued looking attentively towards the front of the room. Despite this momentous happening, it appeared that no one else had noticed.

When we recognize that we ARE the light (or the peace, the love, or whatever you want to call it), it is a different thing entirely from the light soothing the mind. This is being, simply being.

And when you are *being*, there is nothing to be done. For whatever is happening (in this case, listening to a lecturer), that is the being-ness happening right now.

Accepting *what is*, right now, IS being. Being in the moment. It's actually always happening, but usually we are not accepting what is, and herein lies the struggle. With simply being, the mind no longer needs soothing. When you are *being* like this, there is nothing to be soothed.

It's the resisting of *what is* that causes the suffering. One way to interrupt the suffering, though, is to ask, in any situation, "What would light do now?" This immediately enables the apparent separate "you" to recognize that it has believed it is separate, and to simply "be the light" and act from that.

Using Mudras for Emotional Release

by Laura P. Clark

Emotions. We all have the full spectrum of them. They are our natural response mechanism to life. They serve us well when we understand that they are one part of our natural being but do not define who we are. They *don't* serve us well when we react based on negative emotions (such as fear or anger), allowing them to dictate our decisions. Negative emotions can disconnect us from our soul and play havoc on our vibrational self – and on our lives!

One way to release emotions that do not serve us is through the movement of mudras.

Mudras are a series of arm-and-hand positions that express an action or attitude of spirit. Commonly used during yoga sessions, these gestures serve many purposes by supporting the flow of positive energy through the body and returning you to a place of centeredness and peace. They clear your mind of thoughts that do not serve you, engage your spiritual self, realign your emotional energy for your highest good, and allow for the expansion of your consciousness.

You most likely have your own movements and mudras already. It may be the yawn-and-stretch pattern that energizes you in the morning. It may be a shoulder roll that refreshes you at your desk during the day. Or it might be a fist pump that motivates you when you face a challenge. Discovering, refining, and using your gestures with intention is the practice of personal mudra movement.

Today, pay attention to your motions and *emotions*. See if you have a movement pattern that helps you with certain feelings or situations. If so, fine-tune it, practice it deliberately, and expand upon it. If not, consider what movement might release negative emotions, and try it out! Create a pattern, slow it down, and use it with the intention to release emotions that do not serve you. Before long, you'll discover your own powerful mudra movements to refuel you with joy and love!

Open to Direct Connection with Divine Source

by Melissa Sarazin

In my 20s, I decided to become a chef because I imagined myself living a dream life, travelling and working in exotic locations. In this dream, I was happy, smiling, content, and living high on the hog! When this became my reality, however, I felt lost. No matter where I was or who I was with, this feeling persisted – a constant sense of something missing, like there was some cosmic joke that I had missed out on.

Even living on an Australian island paradise, it wasn't long before depression kicked in. I went numb inside. I couldn't get myself into life, and I remained on the periphery looking in from the outside.

Little did I know it then, but this was to become the greatest blessing of my life. In my state of depression, I received so much support, love, and guidance. I finally realized that I was never lost, just disconnected!

During this journey of healing, reconnecting, and revitalization, I began a simple daily practice that cultivated connection, support, and love. My life transformed, and I lived each day with renewed purpose.

I continue this practice to this day. Every morning, whether I am on my meditation mat or in the shower, I ask for a direct connection with Divine Source. I take deep breaths and feel into this connection. I imagine I am being held by the Universe, like a mother cradling her child. I open to the support and love and draw it into my heart centre, breathing in all that is available to me. Once I feel this energy expanding in my heart, I create an intention to feel this connection throughout my day. I ask that it feeds my activities, helps me to solve any problems, and inspires me to live from my true, radiant essence.

This simple ritual feeds anything that feels empty, stuck, or impossible. Now every location becomes exotic (no matter where I am), and the beauty of life flows through me. I am living in my dream!

Grounding

by Karrol Rikka S. Altarejos

As part of my morning ritual, one of the first things I do upon opening my eyes is to set the intention of being grounded. During these few precious moments, I meditate, taking slow, deep breaths. I allow my awareness to settle within my body, noting any tension while easing into a quiet reverie. My mind focuses and my muscles relax, and in this state I connect with my energy.

Tuning in, I identify needless worries and stress. Accepting that these thoughts carry energies that do not serve me, I willingly release them down through my body and into the earth. I visualize myself as a strong and powerful tree with roots that extend not only past the soil and rock layers, but also deeply into the core of Mother Earth. Through this link, an exchange of energy occurs. What was once perceived as negative is transmuted and transformed. Silently giving my thanks, I accept the loving and nurturing energy that is provided in return. When the meditation is complete, I'm ready to start my day feeling more aware, centered, and refreshed.

For me, this has become an essential practice. As an empath – an individual who is highly sensitive to the energetic vibrations of emotions and feelings – grounding acts as a foundation that anchors my energies, strengthens my boundaries, and brings my attention to my soul and the precious body that it occupies. I become even more mindful and present within my body, knowing that my spirit is at its essence. Acknowledging this connection between the spiritual and physical reminds me that the same pulse I feel within is a rhythm that can be found in the very heart of nature. The balance and harmony that is then created from my being spreads beyond myself and encompasses all that I encounter.

Imagine what it could do for the world if we all invited our soul energy to ground into our physical beings and awakened to the peace, clarity, and self-awareness that it brings.

Create a Personalized Process

by Sallie Keys

Just as everyone has their own specific talents and style of learning (such as visual, auditory, or kinesthetic), we each have a way that works best for us to connect with our soul.

For example, you might be more adept at receiving soulful messages visually, in the form of images popping into your mind, rather than receiving communication through feelings or sensations. If this is the case, using your mind's eye to imagine that you are having a meeting with your soul would be a wonderful way to communicate with your soul. This method would create a strong connection that you could reference over and over again – just return to your visualization any time you need guidance. Your soul will be there waiting for you!

Or perhaps your soul tends to communicate through inner urges or physical sensations. If this is the case, you might frequently feel a strong impulse to take action on something without logically knowing why. You might even feel a physical sensation in your body, making you feel excited (or cautious) about something. Take note of repetitive communication like this so that you recognize it in the future and make it a permanent part of your process of connecting with your soul.

Receiving messages will look and feel different for each of us. We each have unique abilities, which we can utilize in the way that suits us best. Discover what your strengths are when it comes to receiving spiritual guidance. Create a personalized process for soulful connection – one that feels right for *you* – and develop your gifts to the fullest extent possible. A great way to do this is to find some time alone, then quiet your mind, close your eyes, and pretend you are actually having a meeting with your soul. What does your soul look like? What does he or she have to tell you? Ask your soul some questions and see what responses you get.

And remember: your soul *wants* to communicate with you and *wants* to be heard. It's just waiting for you to open yourself up to receive its guidance and wisdom.

A Mystic's Cloak: Ritual of Release and Renewal

by Vicki Talvi-Cole

Sun rising, I was acutely aware of the horses' rhythmic munching sounds. Letting my mind wander, I began to feel that I was floating on a breeze.

On a post above me sat a vulture with its wings extended, catching the morning rays. Intuitively, I raised my arms and sensed something being draped across my shoulders and flowing down my body. I felt a grounded sensation, yet I felt so light.

A giggle of delightful joy burst from deep within. "A Mystic's Cloak," I heard ever so gently. It felt wonderfully light, airy, and flowing – appearing to be woven together with millions of stars. Fully embracing this gift from Soul, I could feel its weight, how it moved as I moved, the texture, what it smelled and tasted like. As I enjoyed the experience, an inner wisdom began to bubble up, bringing me a sense of renewal.

Later that night, I stood with my horse, the Goddess Mare, in complete stillness – only her breath being heard.

"Drop your cloak," I heard her gently whisper.

What? I felt that I was just getting used to it, and it felt pretty darned good having it on!

"Just as the shadows cast by the sun are absorbed into the earth," she continued, "you, too, can drop your cloak and release this day."

I trusted her wisdom and let the cloak go. I felt the energies from it dropping off my shoulders and sliding down my back.

Then one of my other horses whispered, "Now physically shake your body; and as you do, imagine a dog shaking, as if repelling water. Step forward, up and out of the disappearing energies. Create a release-and-renewal ritual – intentionally putting on a new cloak each morning and removing it each night."

I realized then that I could welcome this magical cloak, a gift that connects me to my soul, and you can, too! Every day when you awaken, imagine your soul essence around you, feel your magical cloak and the energies of it around you, and release it every single night as the sun sinks beyond the horizon.

Living Life in Full Color

by Mariët Hammann

Living is not for the faint-hearted…or the "grey-hearted"!

I realized this when my soul started steering me in colorful directions that I would have passed by while sleepwalking with a grey outlook on life. In my mind, I was pretty much living a decent life. I was easygoing, accommodating, going with whatever landed on my life path. Yes, perhaps it could be called a "grey" life, but I just thought this meant that it was neither black nor white.

But then I had a soul-awakening that this grey-heart/life was one-dimensional. I needed more. I needed clarity, meaning, and direction. I needed *color*!

Luckily, my soul knew I was meant to live on purpose and soon began speaking to me in color – reflecting a whole spectrum back into my life. Here's what I experienced:

- Engaging with colorful people nourished my heart.
- Expressing colorful creations nourished my voice.
- Eating a variety of colorful foods nourished my body.
- Experiencing a full spectrum of colorful emotions (positive *and* negative) nourished my feelings.
- Exploring colorful dualities nourished my mind.
- Having colorful dreams nourished my inner wisdom.
- Acknowledging the impact of different colors nourished my soul.

Who would have thought that nurturing color would nourish my body, mind, and soul?

These days, I'm allowing my soul to freely show up in true color, gently reminding my "grey-heart" to reflect my colorful soul story. I am living in full color!

How about you?

Your Last Day on Earth

by Heather Bestel

My client is in a downward spiral of negativity and self-doubt. Everything is collapsing around her, and she is desperately holding onto the last fibres of her faith, her trust, her knowing, and her belief in life. Nothing is helping. She is falling into the pit of hopelessness.

She has lost her way.

And so I gently invite her to come with me into the future. We take five slow, deep, beautiful breaths...the kind that break open our resistance and take us down into the very core of our being. We feel the air in our lungs. We allow the promise of relaxation to flow over us. And then we let go and sink into the darkness behind our closed eyelids.

I ask her to imagine that this is her last day on Earth, that her journey here is over and she's about to embark on the next stage of her adventure. Then I ask her the question: *What does your soul need to tell you?*

The answer comes: *Be still. Make peace. Accept. Be grateful. Let go. Believe. Trust yourself. Be love.*

In that moment of stillness, she is able to reconnect with her inner wisdom and hear her soul's message. She is able to find her purpose, her joy, her gift. Once again, she knows who she is. She knows her role, her place, and her mission. She has let go of the worry, anxiety, stress, and anger. She feels whole once more. She has given herself the gift of perspective, and she knows that she can visit this last day again whenever she needs to.

And so can you.

Chapter 2
Gratitude, Love, & Prayer

At the heart of a soulful life is gratitude – feeling appreciation and giving thanks for life's blessings. And at the heart of this appreciation is love – love for the world, for self, for others, for the Divine, and for life itself. This love and gratitude can be expressed in many ways: through prayer, through formal rituals of thanksgiving, or simply by offering a quick smile of appreciation.

Gratitude, love, and prayer are central components of our daily lives. We like to start and end our day by focusing on what we appreciate – big things (such as life itself), little things (such as a perfectly ripe avocado), and joyful moments (such as watching the cats play with a new toy). We frequently offer prayers of gratitude, as well as prayers wishing for the best for friends, loved ones, and the entire world.

All of these prayers and expressions of gratitude come back to love: they are expressions of love, helping us focus on and expand this love within ourselves and throughout the world. And while we always hope that love continues to expand over time, it always feels good right away, in the very moment we feel appreciation, give thanks, and pray.

The pieces in this chapter provide many ways to deepen your own gratitude, love, and prayers – including saying prayers and mantras, finding fun ways to express gratitude, appreciating the power of soulful friendships, connecting with spiritual communities, finding comfort in life's little pleasures, and deepening your love for the Divine. We hope that these pieces help you feel greater appreciation and love for yourself, for others, and for life itself. And we hope that they help you deepen your loving connection with your soul.

The Gratitude Game

by Dan Teck

The past 20 minutes haven't been so hot: The dog we're fostering destroyed her bedding. Our cat puked on our comforter. And the Yankees lost to their rivals. Oh yeah, and it's also tax day.

My generally sunny disposition took a nosedive. I started worrying about the animals, worrying about taxes, and worrying that I was forgetting to worry about something that I should be worrying about.

Fortunately, before I slid too far into this downward spiral, my wife reminded me of one of my favorite ways to reconnect with my soul: "The Gratitude Game."

The Gratitude Game is exactly what it sounds like: One person says something that they're grateful for, then the other person says something that *they're* grateful for…and so on, until you're both feeling better.

(If you're playing alone, you can write down your gratitude list, which has the added benefit of letting you return to it again and again.)

So Jodi and I went back and forth: I said that I'm grateful that the animals are (generally) healthy and well behaved. She said that she's grateful for her friends. I said that I'm grateful that I get to spend so much time doing what I love. She said that she's grateful to live in such a beautiful area. And we both said how grateful we are for each other. (Yes, we're really that sappy.)

And even though nothing external changed, I'm already starting to feel better. I've stopped the downward spiral of negativity, I'm feeling good about my life right now, and I'm looking forward to a future filled with even more to be grateful for.

Above all, I've reconnected with my soul: that part of me that knows that everything's going to be all right – or, more accurately, that everything already *is* all right. (Even when the Yankees don't win.)

A New Way to Pray

by Cindy Jones Lantier

Like many people who follow an independent, eclectic, spiritual path, I've struggled with what place prayer would have in my life. I wholeheartedly believe in the power of prayer, but I'm uncomfortable praying for a specific outcome – after all, I don't know the big picture, and I can't possibly know which outcome is best.

But when my friends and family are in crisis or transition and ask for prayers, I want to support them. I want to add my energy to the energy of others in lifting them up.

After months of struggle, I finally came up with the idea of using my prayer beads to help me with these intercessory prayers. Instead of praying for a specific outcome, I pray for a series of what I call "Divine Blessings." If I were praying for my husband, for example, I would say, "May John know Divine Love," as I touched the first bead. Then, I'd move to the second bead and say, "May John know Divine Grace." I'd cycle through the nine beads on the strand as I prayed these nine Divine Blessings: Love, Grace, Compassion, Wisdom, Healing, Comfort, Peace, Presence, and Clarity.

Praying for the people I love in this way allows me to participate in the ritual of intercessory prayer and offer them my support, yet still be in integrity with my beliefs. I get to connect to that higher part of myself – my soul – as I express my love and compassion for others.

Ripples of Love Flow Outwards

by Fiona Louise

When we want to connect with our soul, our first thought is often to look inwards. Today, how about we focus outwards? When we choose to focus outwards, we do so to give, not to receive. I therefore encourage you to act in order to create meaning in someone else's life, brighten their day, or lessen their burden.

In doing so, we experience a connection with our soul through loving, selfless acts, which others can see, feel, and be touched by. Without expectation of return, our service to others inspires other loving, selfless acts. Focusing outwards is like dropping a tiny pebble in a pond: it causes ripples of positive love for all beings.

There are so many ways to focus outwards, such as: holding a door open for a stranger, smiling at everyone whilst walking down the street, thanking a server by name. You could give way to let a car enter your lane or pay for the coffee for the person next-in-line at a café. How about volunteering your time to teach someone literacy, rehabilitate abused animals, read to kids in the hospital, or mentor through apprenticeship? Perhaps you could cook a meal for a struggling family or pay for their groceries, or visit with an elderly neighbor so that they feel valued and remembered. You could offer to mow lawns, prune a tree, or clear someone's guttering. When a friend needs cheering up, you could send flowers or write a letter telling them how much they mean to you. You could write positive-message cards and leave them inside books at a bookstore, donate goods/clothes to a second-hand store, or drop money on the ground for someone to pick up.

The possibilities are limited only by our imagination. We can outwardly focus in any way that resonates with us. Connecting with our soul by focusing outwards creates a sense of peace and a warm feeling that radiates in our heart. We can think of this as a hug from our soul.

What outward action can you do today to create a ripple of positive love?

A Simple Blessing

by Ashley Pierson

"If the only prayer you ever say in your entire life is thank you, it will be enough."
- Meister Eckhart

During my days in Catholic school, the nuns always led us in prayer before lunch. I would throw a look my best friend's way, and we would laugh with bowed heads, hoping that Sister Theresa wouldn't see our folly. To say the reverence of the moment was lost on me would be an understatement, but the ritual did develop a habit.

Saying a blessing before a meal doesn't have to be specific to religion. A thank you to God, the Universe, or just in general has a direct connection to soul that is undeniable.

My practice starts in the quiet of the morning with a hot cup of coffee. I take in the smell of fresh-roasted bliss, wrap my hands around the steaming cup, and take a moment to give thanks. With my days often overbooked, I say a silent thank you and feel a transformative energy take root, filling me with energy and gratitude. My reflection from early morning continues as my family prays over dinner in our small but powerful nightly ceremony. Prayer seems to convert the food so that it feeds not only our bodies but our souls as well. The linking of food and prayer forms a circle that brings unity and connection to God.

It's true that my prayer of appreciation has changed from my early days; however, I am glad that the ritual was set in motion. Many years passed before I anchored a ceremony of acknowledgement that feeds my soul every day. It is not elaborate or as formal as taught by the nuns at my childhood school, but it's just as powerful. I find that in the hustle and bustle of life, the moments when I stop and say thank you before a meal are more than enough to reconnect with my soul.

From Gratitude to Mindfulness

by Cindie Chavez

I'm not sure exactly when my mindfulness practice began, but I know that it grew organically from a desire to expand my gratitude.

I decided that each night before falling asleep I would spend a couple of minutes connecting my five senses to things I was grateful for that day. It would be a short, quiet, meditative act.

The first night was easy. I still remember a few of the things I felt grateful for: the taste of chocolate, the smell of coffee beans grinding that morning, and the softness of my little puppy's fur.

The second night I reviewed my day and began my practice realizing that once again I was feeling grateful for chocolate, coffee, and my puppy. Soft puppy snuggles are the best, right?

On the third night, I began to realize I was choosing more or less the same list each night, and although puppies, coffee, and chocolate are wonderful, I knew I could find many more things to be grateful for.

One afternoon shortly after that, I found myself enjoying a beautiful bouquet of roses. I remember feeling overjoyed when I realized that "the smell of roses" could be on my list that night. Yay!

That's how it started. Each day, my senses were even more aware of everything I was experiencing, enjoying, and discovering, because I knew those things might "make the list."

My two-minute gratitude practice was now asserting itself into every waking hour, and it was sensational!

Each day became a sensory treasure hunt. Each evening became a gratitude fest of new and epic proportions. The whole world was opening up to me because I had opened up to the world around me. What started as a small, sleepy gratitude process had become a full-out mindfulness practice.

Since then, I've learned that bringing my awareness to my five senses is the quickest way to come into the present moment, where I can find relief, peace, empowerment, and maybe even some puppy snuggles, chocolate, and a café au lait.

What's on *your* gratitude list for tonight?

"Use Your Faith" Mantra

by Lori Thiessen

Only recently have I been introduced to mantras, after avoiding the whole topic for most of my life. Somehow, I had the mistaken belief that they were repetitive chanting, not unlike sorcery or fairy-tale spells, and the entire concept seemed to offend my Christian roots.

Lately though, I have come to understand them along the lines of a team's cheer that is repeated throughout an edge-of-your-seat playoff game – or similar to the famous line from *The Little Engine That Could*, in which the engine keeps repeating, "I think I can, I think I can, I think I can…"

Mantras have lost their scary mysticism for me and gained in practical application. I can be my own cheerleader and support group with a well worded and appropriately timed phrase.

I've developed a few that I keep in my back pocket. One of my favorites is "Use your faith." It's not so much that I *choose* to use that one, but more that I *hear* it in the back of my head as a reminder from my Higher Power that this is just the right time and place to stop trying to manipulate the circumstances, stop whining and fretting about the situation, and instead determine to use faith to navigate the challenge. "Use your faith" echoes in the back of my mind in a voice not unlike that of Obi-Wan Kenobi as he reminds Luke Skywalker to "Use the Force."

Immediately upon hearing the words of my mantra, I am bumped into a new frame of mind and a new emotional space of faith and trust. "Use your faith," repeated as a mantra, reminds me to take a step back and connect with my soul and my Higher Power, and allow things beyond my control to work themselves out.

Feel free to use this mantra for yourself – or create one that speaks directly to you and connects you with your soul.

Find Deep Joy in Simple Things

by Steve Tallamy

All of us lose the joy in our lives at one time or another. We get sucked into the relentless pressure created in our outer world, whether that is simply a bad day at work or some bigger problem that comes from out of the blue and smacks us full in the face. Reconnecting with the simple things in life will always bring us back to that place where deep joy resides: our soul.

I remember a time when I had just completed a hectic 12-hour shift at a local care home for dementia sufferers. It had been "one of those days." The whole world seemed determined to get the better of me. Residents, staff, and managers had all joined in the game of "Let's Get Steve"! Slamming the front door of the home behind me, I felt as washed out as the damp evening air. I let out a huge sigh before starting the short walk home, mumbling complaints as I shuffled into the night.

All I could think of was getting home and shutting myself away for a few hours before the next long shift would start. I looked to the heavens to scream a silent prayer, but before the breath could leave my body a blackbird started his song of thanks for having been gifted with another day of aliveness. His melodic calling carried his inner joy out to me and immediately began to lift my spirits; my dark mood slowly melted into a smile.

This fleeting moment had the effect of changing my whole outlook on how I perceived the day. I was now excited to get back to my family; take a refreshing, hot shower; eat a sustaining meal; read an inspirational book; and sleep in a warm, comforting bed. It had put everything into perspective. Those disruptive and challenging residents, the annoying staff, and pedantic managers dissolved into their true selves. They, too, had experienced as hectic a day as I had, but here I was standing in deep joy – the joy that can be found in the simple things of life.

I Trust in You

by Lisa Hutchison

How many times have I held on and obsessed about someone else's life in the name of caring? More often than I can count, I thought I was being helpful and acting out of love when I worried about others, but I couldn't have been more wrong.

I lost myself and my direction in life because this anxiety disconnected me from my soul. The more time I spent attending to others, the less time I had to listen to my divine guidance. How did I get out of this habit? I practiced the Serenity Prayer (by Reinhold Niebuhr):

God, grant me the serenity to accept the things I cannot change
[this means other people]
the courage to change the things I can
[this means me]
and the wisdom to know the difference.

I wore this prayer out many times over. Luckily, it stands the test of time.

Letting go and detaching did not come naturally and was a struggle at first. With practice, however, I noticed a sense of peace that came from discovering that I could only see my soul's light clearly when I released judgment, control, and fear.

The secret to detachment is one breath at a time. I learned to mindfully shift my focus from my thoughts into my body and soul. I practiced being in the present moment, not focusing on what was said or how I felt in the past or how I imagine it may be in the future.

I used to think that detachment meant not caring, but I learned that detachment is one of the highest forms of unconditional love. It says: "I care about you so much that I trust in your ability to navigate your life's journey without my interference. I am going to be a loving, faithful observer of your life. If you ask for help or assistance, I will provide it to the best of my ability. Otherwise, I am going to mind my own business, thereby setting you and myself free."

Lovingly detaching from others allowed me to connect with my true self.

The Periphery of Belonging

by Shelley Lundquist

For years, I existed on the periphery of belonging, feeling isolated and disconnected from my soul and also from others. I tried becoming what I thought others wanted me to be in an effort to fit in, but it never felt right.

Then one day I realised that what was really missing in my life was *me*. It dawned on me that I had wanted people to accept me when I had not yet accepted myself. In letting go of judgment and embracing all aspects of myself, the healing that comes with self-acceptance rippled through my life.

Guided by my inner voice, I began to see life with a new clarity. I stopped taking myself so seriously, embraced my carefree nature, let go of the struggle to fit in, and began living from my truth. I watched as the pure expression of who I am and the love I bring to the world illuminated my life. I no longer needed to seek outside myself for recognition.

I marvelled at the change and delighted in the understanding that every moment presents us with exactly what we need to tune our awareness. The people and places I had moved toward in the past were there to teach me to make different choices – ones that would honour who I am. With that gentle reframe and a heart full of gratitude, I opened to old friends and new, with ease and grace. Notably, in learning to accept myself I also became more accepting of others, and past conflicts simply melted away because I was no longer willing to play a part in them.

Those who see the light in me and appreciate me for who I am naturally gravitate toward me, as I do to them. Now, I flourish in relationships that nourish me and respect differences, where communication is open, and where there is unconditional freedom to be and to share without fear of judgment.

It is in having the courage to give the gift of our authentic selves to the world that we finally find our tribe.

Finding Soul-Deep Love

by Jenni Ryan

Have you ever met someone and love shows up the instant your eyes connect? When you feel like you already know each other, and you wonder why you haven't met before? It feels like home – as if nothing in your life had made sense until that very moment.

Love can show up in unexpected ways, often without any apparent rhyme or reason, and fill us with passion and emotional intoxication. But love can also bring up negative emotions – many of them stemming from childhood – such as feelings of unworthiness or the fear of abandonment. These reactions are often our ego's way of protecting us, but they can also block us from experiencing true love.

So how do you move beyond fear and open yourself up to soul-deep love? How do you approach a relationship with a pure heart and no expectations? While there's no formula that guarantees this experience, here are some approaches that I've found helpful.

- *Silence the mind and listen to your heart.* Go to a quiet place – externally and internally – and really listen to your heart instead of the voices in your heard. When I did this, I found a pure heart that was detached from my ego. In this place, there was no fear and no expectations – just love.
- *Allow yourself to be vulnerable.* To experience unconditional love, we must be open to being completely vulnerable without any fear of the outcome. We must accept ourselves, trust that love is enough, and trust that *we* are enough.
- *Love yourself.* Unconditional love for someone else can only happen when you first love yourself unconditionally. Let go of all the self-judgments and self-critical beliefs that weigh heavy on your heart. The more you love yourself, the more you release anything that is not love. And the more you see the light in yourself, the more you see the light in others.

When you open yourself up to soul-deep love, you open yourself to loving connections with others, with yourself, and with your own soul – for at the heart of the soul is pure, unconditional love.

Safe, Protected, and Very Blessed

by Bonnie S. Hirst

I watch as my one-year-old granddaughter plays with two oversized magnets on the fridge. She pulls them off and then delights in the magnetic click as they reattach to the metal surface. With her pudgy fingers, she tries joining the magnets together, but their opposite polarization resists her efforts.

The push-pull of the magnetic forces resembles our lives. Our souls yearn for the heartfelt joy of positive thinking, but worry pushes into our lives and negative thoughts envelop us: *Will my family be safe in their daily activities? Will the loss of a loved one fracture the family unit? Will I be financially able to provide for them? Will devastating health issues determine our fate?*

Hardships sometimes overflow in our lives, and our negative thoughts can outweigh our positive ones. When this happens, I struggle fiercely. I question if my soul is strong enough to wade into the pain and surface on the other side.

In my attempts to connect with the positivity of my soul, I created a mantra: *My family and I are safe, protected, and very blessed.*

As I say *safe,* I imagine my mom's arms from Heaven wrapping warmly around me. On the word *protected,* I feel my guardian angel's love envelop me; and on *very blessed,* I envision God's light and love surrounding me and my loved ones.

As I mindfully repeat these words, my soul opens and unites with the warm-heartedness of my mantra. My fears and worries begin to fade.

Just like the positive pull of the magnets that my granddaughter is so fascinated with, my soul (when I listen to it) pulls me back into a positive mindset.

My family and I are safe, protected, and very blessed.

A Jar Full of Gratitude

by Janice Lawrenz

Most of us are so busy that we don't often take time to appreciate the wonderful details in our lives. We forget so many good things that happen over the days and years. A gratitude jar can help us remember and appreciate those wonderful moments…again and again.

There are many ways to use gratitude jars, and I would love to share my own process, which has given me uplifting and profound results.

Each morning, I write down three things I'm grateful for. It can be an uplifting quote, a special moment I experienced, or something as simple as the fresh air I breathe. At the end of each week, I look over what I've written and choose three that really speak to me on a deep, energetic level. To make these three look extra special, I trim the edges of the paper using patterned scissors and outline the border with a gel pen. I then put the paper in a special jar (which I've decorated with paints and ribbons). I place the jar where I can see it every day. Each day and week I repeat this process.

I use the gratitude jar in a number of ways: When I feel down, I pull out one piece of paper from the jar. Reading it and closing my eyes gives me a feeling of goodness and uplifts my spirits. On special occasions and holidays, I use the jar as the basis of a gratitude ritual. In the stillness of the early morning, I light incense and candles, put on meditative background music, and empty the jar's contents onto the floor. I pick up one piece of paper at a time, reading each one aloud, allowing its energy to infuse my heart, body, and soul with a warm, comforting feeling.

My gratitude jar helps me turn vagueness into clarity, sadness into happiness, procrastination into action, and feeling stuck into recognising that I have choices – and I can always choose gratitude! However I use my gratitude jar, I always end up feeling more appreciative, energised, and ready to embrace whatever life has to offer!

Anam Cara

by Kylie Mansfield

We all have a soul. It is the very essence of who we are, and it is made up from all the experiences we harvest from this garden we call life. Most of all, I think our soul is fashioned through the people who dwell alongside us in our gardens – particularly those we label as friends.

I have always believed that it is friendship that will get you through life. Friends are one of God's greatest blessings. Like a vase full of beautiful flowers, friends can make your heart sing, encouraging you to bloom at your best.

Just as there are many types of flowers in a garden, there are many different types of friends in life. For me, the most important to our being are those who the Irish call *Anam Cara.*

In Gaelic, *Anam* is "Soul" and *Cara* is "friend" – so *Anam Cara* is a *Soul Friend.*

Anam Cara is eternal. It is the type of connection that ties hearts together. It breaks through all barriers, all restraint, and all emotion. It is supportive, encouraging, vibrant, loving, and trusting. It is a connection that surpasses all other. It is unconditional.

Oftentimes, we go through life shackled to a façade in order to feel accepted. Without realising it, we become stunted. With a Soul Friend, we are liberated. For Anam Cara frees us and helps us to grow.

However, Anam Cara doesn't always just *arrive.* This sort of relationship has to be cultivated from within. In order to appreciate it, you must first sow the seeds of your own inner light and beauty – for everything stems from you and radiates out.

Be always on the lookout for Soul Friends; and when you find them, invite them into the garden of your life. These connections will produce the sweetest and most exquisite of blooms.

But above all, when you have them in your garden, remember to nourish them – for they will expand your own heart's song and make the garden you dwell in such a wonderful and fulfilling place.

Prayer: Putting Faith into Practice

by Katie Power

For as long as I can remember, my soul and faith have been closely intertwined. I've always been keenly aware of a greater life-force that weaves intricately through us all. Starting from a young age, I have tremendously enjoyed exploring this connection at a deeper level.

As a little girl, I started my spiritual path through the formal route. I went to church, read my Bible, and attended religious classes. With time, however, I started hearing about people who'd had near-death experiences. What they claimed happened when their souls left their body was miraculous, and it expanded my faith even more.

Then one day I came across a well-known psychic on TV who spoke of things like reincarnation and communicating with the spirit realm. I was deeply enthralled and yearned to do this myself. This was when my soul's true calling to be a spiritual messenger came to the forefront. I wanted to put my faith into practice and help others receive messages from spirit, too. So I began learning about the Akashic Records and other healing tools and intuitive modalities.

Over the years, I have learned a lot (and continue to do so). Out of everything I have learned, though, there is one ultimate, tried-and-true way to connect with spirit that I've done almost every day of my life. This practice spans across most religions and cultures worldwide. It is extremely powerful yet so gloriously simple that even a child could do it with their eyes closed.

I am talking about prayer.

Prayer is the single most powerful way that I know to connect with my soul and my faith. It has lifted me up, changed my life, and seen me through my most difficult times. If you, too, are seeking to connect more with your faith – and to put your faith into practice – then I highly recommend starting with prayer.

Letting Go

by Josh Medici

"Life is a balance of holding on and letting go."
- Rumi

My marriage ended a few years ago. It was a painful and confusing time, but we thought it was the best decision for both of us. We did manage to stay close, though; and as time passed, I started wondering: *We don't need to be together to be a family, but could we try to rekindle our relationship?*

After all this time, I still wanted to control what the relationship should look like. By constantly judging the situation, I was trying to control it, and that meant suffering when the results were not what I hoped for or expected. My attachment to my idea of what I thought the relationship "should" be was so great that I could not see that we had managed to solve most of our problems by merely talking and listening; I was too busy worrying about whether or not she wanted to be together again.

In the end, I let it go, realizing that it was not my decision to make. I could not tell her who to love and when to love. By letting go, I realized that she was exactly where she wanted to be, and I was exactly where I needed to be. There was no need to get anywhere else.

Now, a few years since our last goodbye as a couple, I can say that I don't know what the future holds for us. And that's okay. We still manage to spend time together. And even if we're not together, love is what makes us be there for each other and for our son. Love is what unites us.

Through this experience, I learned to let go, and I got my life back in the process. Letting go made me look beyond the illusion of separateness, look within my own soul, and realize that whatever I thought I had lost was actually inside me the whole time.

Daily Appreciation

by Bree Orata

I loved *The Oprah Winfrey Show*, and during its heyday I wouldn't miss an episode for the world. One day when I was going through a particularly low moment, I tuned into the show and heard Oprah describe a very interesting practice: *Find at least three things to be grateful for at the end of each day.*

Right then and there, I took out a notebook and paper and immediately began writing. Even in the midst of my turmoil, I was pleasantly surprised to find that I did in fact have a lot to be thankful for.

That marked the start of my gratitude journal.

On some days, I am thankful for the most basic of things, such as life itself. At other times, I am moved and inspired to give thanks for the littlest of things, including having a full head of tightly-curled coils. Most times, I give thanks for the same things over and over again, such as friends, family, and health. But I give thanks all the same.

I can't quite explain the power behind being grateful. But what I have learned is that whenever I look for something to appreciate, I am immediately flooded by thoughts of wellbeing, positivity, and love. It is as sure as the sun rises.

My experiences with this gratitude practice reminds me of a song that I used to sing over and over again as a young girl:

Count your blessings, name them one by one.
Count your blessings, see what God has done.
Count your blessings, name them one by one.
And it will surprise you what the Lord has done.

To this day, each time I sing these beautiful words, I am reminded to always give thanks and allow myself to become filled with love. I am also reminded of this truth: *Our souls appreciate appreciation.*

Be Your Own Soulmate

by Autumne Stirling

Popular media repeatedly tells us that one day we will find our true soulmate…and the "fairy tale" will begin. Usually, this "soulmate" refers to another person. We fall in love, our lives become one, and we live happily ever after. They "complete" us. As appealing as this may sound, what if this idea has led us astray, taking our focus away from what the ideal conceivably could be?

Would it be possible for you to be your *own* soulmate?

Marinating in this for a moment, how would this shift in perspective impact your daily life? What would you need to do, change, or practice on a daily basis to make this a reality? Would you practice greater self-kindness? Would you ensure that your needs were consistently met? Would you love yourself regardless of how others perceived you? Would you finally forgive yourself? Would you release resentments toward others (knowing that this gesture would provide you with emotional freedom)? Would you invest more time, energy, and soul into ventures that make you feel peaceful? Would you be less invested in outcomes and more connected to the process (knowing that joyful action is its own reward)? Would you commit to consistent soul-searching and self-discovery for a luminous relationship with yourself? Would you favour love, even when loving appears to be impossible?

If we would like all of these blessings in our lives, self-love is paramount. Change occurs when we are willing to be brave, vulnerable, and strong. When we are willing to practice self-expansion, compassion, and commitment, we can unquestionably achieve self-completion.

We can choose to be our own soulmate.

Finding an Oasis of Gratitude

by Murray James

Positive psychology and many spiritual practices have a strong focus on gratitude – yet, for me, the busyness of modern-day life often crowds this out. I therefore decided to create an "Oasis of Gratitude" – to set aside an allotted time to focus on gratitude, which moved me from a negative space to seeing my life with newfound appreciation.

If you would like to experience your own "oasis," set aside two hours, half a day, or a whole day if you are able. Depending on the time of the year, you could spend a period outside in a quiet park, garden, or beach. Or you may prefer to stay home. (Being warm and cosy – and having access to your favourite food and drinks – could assist the process. If you do stay home, though, make certain you will not be disturbed.)

I suggest starting your Oasis of Gratitude experience with a statement of intent or a prayer of praise. Next, turn your focus to people and things you appreciate in your daily life or immediate surroundings, such as family, friends, or your local community. You may then find that your gratitude spills over to charities and people of integrity in public life. You might then focus on work, business, or a certain project that you appreciate. You could also direct your awareness to your inner life, health, wellbeing, and all of your gifts.

If you are outside (or even if you stay indoors) you might find yourself concentrating on your gratitude for the natural environment, such as gardens, forests, and animal life. Mindfully observe, listen to, and if possible, touch nature. You could even create a little altar of flowers, or perhaps you could make a collage.

When you are nearing the end of your Oasis of Gratitude experience, sum up the day with a prayer or statement of blessing. I think you will find that your oasis experience expands your world and leads you to ever greater abundance, joy, and appreciation.

Five Special Ways Friends Tap into Our Soul

by Christine Tomasello

Friends play a special role in our lives. They are the trusted ones who bear witness to our vulnerability and show their love in supportive and nurturing ways. They connect with us on a deep level and can tap into our soul – even when we don't feel able to tap into it ourselves.

Here are five ways that your friends can help you tap into your soul:

1. *They see the best parts of you.* When we're feeling lost, frustrated, inadequate, or broken, friends look into our eyes and remind us of our deeper purpose. They see past the pain or doubt we feel, and find the essence within our soul – even when we can't.
2. *They help you laugh.* Laughter connects us to our soul by getting us out of our heads, keeping us in the moment, and highlighting the good in our life. Friends put a smile on our face and a twinkle in our eye when we need it, and they stand with us until the laughter comes.
3. *They hear you, even when you're not talking.* We want to know that we matter, that our needs are important, and that someone is listening. Friends can tell when we need this validation, even if we don't know to ask for it. They tune into our soul, hear what our heart is whispering, and help us see what we need when we can't figure it out ourselves.
4. *They challenge you and push you to grow.* Friends have an uncanny ability to push our buttons; and while this can be frustrating, it can also serve an important purpose. Friends want us be the best versions of ourselves. They know what we're capable of in our heart and soul, and will gently (or not so gently!) nudge us outside our comfort zones to achieve it.
5. *They love all of you and help you love yourself.* Whether we're at our best or at our worst, friends love us. They remind us of our value when we make mistakes and act as a magical mirror, showing us the goodness in our soul when we've forgotten it.

Friends are those special people who share your soul's journey, celebrate the person you are, and help you tap into your highest self – just as you do for them!

Quiet Wisdom from the Elders

by Marva Collins-Bush

Until I started first grade, all my friends were over 50 years old. I was raised by my grandmother, and I accompanied her everywhere she went. I sat in on her club meetings, I listened to her telephone calls, and I sat at her feet as she and my aunts had those interesting conversations about life. While my peers were playing, I was listening.

I walked with Poppa to the bayou to sit and fish for hours. He pointed out snake skins and poison ivy to me. He showed me edible berries. He made a wonderful drink – using nothing but hot water, evaporated milk, and sugar – which became my favorite treat. We made ketchup sandwiches when Momma wasn't around.

I learned the wisdom of simplicity. I learned about the uncomplicated life. I learned peace. I learned to see life though the eyes of the elders.

I never heard them complain, so I learned not to complain. They were accepting. I once asked, "Momma, how do you stand Mrs. Ida?" I went on to tell her all the things I didn't like about Mrs. Ida. Momma shook her head and said, "Marva, that's just the way Ida is." So I, too, learned to be accepting.

I think the most important lesson I noticed and learned from the elders is that they didn't talk very much. They didn't talk just for the sake of talking. When the elders spoke, we listened, because wisdom poured out from the time in the quiet. The elders spent much of their time in the quiet, so I also learned to sit in the quiet. The long walks to the bayou were quiet walks. I watched Momma sit in her rocking chair in the quiet. I learned as I watched.

The elders called this time in the quiet "collecting" their thoughts. I call it my time of allowing Spirit to talk to me while I listen.

Turning Heartbreak into Self-Love

by Linda Wheeler Williams

Many of us have gone through the pain of rejection, mistreatment, and heartbreak. These experiences can be devastating. They can make you doubt your self-worth. They can shake your confidence in love and make it hard to trust that *anyone* really loves and cares for you.

Perhaps hardest of all, once you have experienced this kind of pain, odds are that you will continue to experience it…over and over again. Your beliefs about your unworthiness cause you to be attracted to people who aren't capable of healthy love at this time. And they will also be attracted to you because you don't expect to be loved. The Law of Attraction will bring you together because you're sending out vibrations and thoughts that say, "Hey, don't love me; I'm unlovable, even by myself." And their vibrations and thoughts are saying, "Then I'm your perfect match, because I'm incapable of loving anyone – including myself and *especially you*!" Then you throw yourselves at each other, both fearing (and, on some level, *expecting*) that it won't work.

While this situation may seem pretty bleak, there is a higher purpose here! To see it, begin by asking yourself these questions: *What if these experiences aren't happening in order to make me miserable, but in order to help me realize my self-worth, find true love, and connect with my soul? What if my soul has brought me these experiences to help me learn to love myself?*

If you want to find true love and connect with your soul, loving yourself is an absolute priority. If you're open to starting this process, begin with baby steps by observing and listening to your self-talk. Your job is to be nicer to yourself than to anyone else. Nurture yourself. Do caring things for yourself. Treat yourself with love! If you want to have a better life, it has to begin with *you.*

The next step is to forgive everyone who has ever hurt you. You're not doing it for them – you're doing it for yourself. And finally, forgive yourself for allowing others (including yourself) to mistreat you.

When you do these things, you will be on your way to loving yourself, and you will no longer attract or *accept* anyone who does not share this healthy, soulful love – for themselves and for you!

Community Worship

by Kristen A. Hemming

As a Wiccan who practiced my faith alone, I didn't think there could be anything more beautiful than the soulful solitude of worshiping the Divine on my own.

As time went on, though, I began to miss the connection and sense of community that I felt as a child going to church. I longed to experience once again that soul-comforting sense of belonging to a community where I could practice my beliefs.

So I began reaching out to the Wiccan community and soon found myself running a temple. Through running this temple, I've learned the following:

- When you take time to worship or meditate in a community, you open yourself to connection with others on the soul level. In recognizing their souls, you honour and recognize your own.
- In community, we create bridges to each other. Worshiping in a community allows us to open our hearts not only to each other, but to ourselves. Through this opening, we step more into our soul and become more of our authentic selves.

As I experienced these openings and connections for me and my community, I realized that there are ways to connect with my soul other than on my own. I now believe that there is nothing more beautiful than when people come together as a community and share in the celebration of their beliefs. The connection to the Divine and to others during worship, contemplation, or meditation can reignite your faith and deepen your connection with your soul.

Someone to Believe in You

by Hue Anh Nguyen

Thirty-five years ago, when I was a little girl, my family and I fled Vietnam to find freedom. After two years of surviving in refugee camps, we finally made our way to Australia.

Because English was my second language, I struggled with school. I also struggled to believe in myself. On the outside, I looked bright and happy, but inside I felt insecure and unworthy.

Then one day I met a girl named Cheung Ye. Although she was shy and barely spoke a word, we quickly became best friends. She believed in my nickname, "Power House," which I got because of my power and energy. Every day, Cheung Ye would cheer me on: "YOU CAN DO THIS! YOU CAN DO THIS!" With this encouragement from my friend, I started to believe in myself, too.

Before long, I finished high school and went on to university, where I would eventually graduate with a Bachelor's Degree in Science. While at university, I met a special friend named Tresha who was working on two bachelor's degrees at once. Her example inspired me – giving me the strength and belief I needed to finish my own nursing degree.

Once I completed my degree, I was very full of life – excited to become a healer, to reach my goals, and to provide others with the tools to transform their lives. Above all, I encouraged others to see in themselves the beauty and potential that they couldn't yet see – just as my two childhood friends had done for me.

Sometimes with a cloud always over your head, you cannot see the beauty of the rainbow. But it only takes one person to believe in you to ignite your inner fire, connect you with your soul, and give you the encouragement to believe you can succeed.

Gratitude as an Antidote to Deprivation

by Sue Kearney

Here's what I've learned in my long journey of putting on my big-girl panties with finances – owning, borrowing, having, and wanting. These lessons extend well beyond the realm of money.

First, the problem: Dysfunction around money and things is, in most cases, built on two really ugly pillars: deprivation and entitlement. Deprivation tells you there's never enough and convinces you that you aren't safe and your needs won't be met. Combined with entitlement, which wants to be given everything without ever having to ask, you've got quite a double whammy going on.

Here's the solution: When gratitude is "in da house," deprivation is healed and quieted, and you can make miraculous changes.

Here are my top five ways to connect to gratitude in a way that will change you from the inside out.

1. Write a daily gratitude list. "I am grateful for…" Go for 10 things. Write the full statement (no cut and paste). Get a gratitude buddy and share your lists with each other.
2. Appreciate others. Out loud. So they hear you.
3. Say "thank you" a lot. More often than is comfortable. Stretch that muscle!
4. Give thanks for your body – the vehicle of your consciousness. Even (especially!) if there are health issues going on.
5. When challenged, find the good. Credit card declined? Less money in your account than you thought? Be grateful you had money in savings to cover. Or be grateful you don't really need this purchase at this moment. (Why yes, this just did happen to me!)

To strengthen the good effect of your gratitude, add a generosity practice. Generosity heals entitlement. Give of your time, your talent, and your treasure.

1. Do you drive and pay tolls with cash? Pay for the car behind you.
2. Carry a bunch of dollar bills with you and hand them out to street people.
3. Smile at strangers. (Yup, that's generosity!)

Soon you won't even recognize yourself – you'll feel so light and free!

Praying from the Heart – Anytime, Anywhere

by Deena Gray-Henry

My favorite and most powerful tool for connecting with my soul is prayer. Prayer is amazing. It is available 24/7; it changes lives, creates miracles, and connects us to higher energy!

My prayers have changed and improved over the years. When I was little, I regularly recited a prayer that my parents taught me, but I focused more on getting the words "right" rather than on the feeling and intention behind the prayer. When I was 24, though, I was introduced to a totally different way of praying: from my heart.

From that point on, there was a definite transformation that took place when I daily communicated with my Heavenly Father from my heart. I had always believed that He was really there, and I had some evidence that He was really there – but when I started "talking" with Him and He answered, I *knew* He was really there and that He knew me personally.

Answers to prayers come in different ways: some are a "burning in our heart," some are a "sure knowledge," and some are things that "REALLY happen"! Here is an example of one of my "really happened" prayers:

One day I realized that I had not been praying frequently for a person I care about. I immediately said a prayer from my heart: "Dear Father in Heaven, please bless ____ and let them know they are loved." I continued to say prayers for them throughout the day: "Please help them have a great day at work. Please keep them safe." That night, my phone rang, and it was the very person I had been praying for! I thought they were calling for someone else in our home and instinctively asked, "Do you want to talk with ____?" They said, "I didn't call for them; I want to talk with you." I instantly recognized that this was an answer to my prayers. After we had a great conversation, I said another prayer – a prayer of gratitude!

I am continually awed by the power of prayer – that it creates *real* miracles and that it easily and quickly connects me with my soul… anytime, anywhere.

Counting Our Blessings

by Kathy Perry

I was exhausted after being up all night in the Lima airport waiting for my flight to Cusco. Finally, we were coming in for a landing when the pilot suddenly pulled the plane straight up to get over the mountains in front of us. My thoughts immediately jumped to a series of questions: *Did we get hijacked by terrorists? Is the pilot going to crash us into the mountains? Is this an omen of things to come with my dental work?*

When my friend in Peru told me she got her teeth done at a bargain price, it sounded like such a good idea. I thought that everything would flow with ease and grace – boy was I wrong! Instead, it was pain and trauma. What was I thinking when I scheduled dental work in Peru? And who goes to Peru and doesn't see Machu Picchu? (I bought the postcard.)

Instead of seeing the sites, my time was spent in the dentist chair – 23 hours in two and a half weeks, plus a three-hour bus ride from the Sacred Valley to Cusco and back each day.

What got me through this experience – and helped me feel connected with my soul – was counting my blessings and repeating the following mantra: *I am blessed. I am thankful for all the blessings in my life: my family, my friends, and the many people I meet and greet throughout the day; my health, my clients, my work, the beauty surrounding me, the majestic mountains; and the beauty in nature, in people, in each breath I take. I am blessed.*

Thankfully, I made it to Cusco safely. And despite the (sometimes literal) ups and downs of this experience, it reinforced my appreciation for the power of counting my blessings – and provided me with two new ones: I am truly blessed to be back home, and I am truly blessed for my new teeth!

Shining God's Light on Earth

by Barbara Royal

Even though we are in individual bodies, we are one at the level of our soul. In our humanness, we see ourselves as separate and, in our confusion, oftentimes have hurt not only ourselves but the rest of our human family. By acknowledging and forgiving these injuries, we can change the course of our lives, connect with our soul, and help the world. We are each needed to shine God's light on Earth. Let us be as one soul expressing love and forgiveness through this prayer and meditation for individual and world peace. (Please pause and experience the Presence between each paragraph.)

> Beloved Presence of God I AM, and the entire Company of Heaven, enfold me and all humankind in your radiation of Divine Wisdom, Light, and Love.
>
> The Divine Wisdom, Light and Love in which I AM now eternally embraced tells me and all humankind that anger, fear, hatred, violence, and war are illusions of power.
>
> The Divine Wisdom, Light and Love in which I AM now eternally embraced tells me and all humankind that You are Love and Love is the only true Power that will bring about permanent inner and world peace.
>
> Knowing this and knowing that I must be the peace I desire in my world, I allow myself to experience Your Flame of Divine Love cleansing me of any fear, anger, hatred or disharmony brought about by my own confusion.
>
> I then imagine public officials and world leaders. I experience Your Flame of Divine Love cleansing them of any fear, anger, hatred or disharmony brought about by their own confusion.
>
> In my imagination, I see terrorists, dictators and anyone creating discord in my world. I experience Your Flame of Divine Love cleansing these people of any fear, anger, hatred or disharmony brought about by their own confusion.
>
> Knowing that your Divine Wisdom, Light and Love is now permeated and active within me and all humankind, I say thank you, God, and the entire Company of Heaven for the peace in my heart and my world. And so it is.

A Person to Be Loved

by Shelley Lundquist

I listened as he talked, surprised by the call and sensing his silent plea to be heard and loved no matter what he was to reveal.

In the past, our conversations swiftly turned to eruptions, followed by the inevitable presenting of his back as he walked out the door. That our relationship has been tumultuous for more than half my son's life is an understatement.

Looking back, I can see the harshness with which I had judged him, blindly justifying that my words and actions came from a place of love and caring. I always believed he was capable of so much more than his choices reflected, and I railed in resistance as he embarked upon a path that no parent would choose for their child.

As parents, we often do not see that our reactions to our children's choices are distorted by our attachments to the dreams we have for them. Such was the folly of my ways. I had pushed him to live up to the vision for his life that I had created in my mind. What I reaped was his withdrawal from my life.

With a gaping hole in my life, I came to understand that focusing on being right would not mend the relationship. In stillness, where I could hear my soul's whispers, I realised that all I ultimately wanted for my son was his happiness. Because I wanted a relationship with him, I had to accept that his path was his, whether I approved of it or not.

In taking responsibility for my emotions, I opened to the awareness that whatever I decided to bring to the relationship would either heal or hinder – the choice was mine.

Today, I listened without expectation. When he suggested that perhaps we fought so much because we are more alike than not, I smiled at the truth of it.

Moving forward, I will lead with an open heart and an open mind, all the while reminding myself to never let a problem to be solved be more important than a person to be loved.

Share the Love

by Gia Reed

What if there were a way to connect with your soul *and* increase your happiness, joy, and energy? There is! The key is…*giving*!

When I am stressed, going through a difficult time, or just feeling low…I give. When I need inspiration or want to share excitement or happiness…I give.

Giving is a powerful force that kicks ego to the backseat and sends its buddies – fear, lack, and limitation – along for the ride. When we give, our attention shifts solely to the present. It allows us to connect with our soul and harmonize with the flow of life and the power of the Divine.

Sometimes we give back to those who have given to us; other times we "pay it forward" to someone we don't even know. Paying it forward doesn't have to involve large sums of money or grand gestures. I compliment the cashier at the grocery store. I leave an encouraging sticky note on a restroom mirror. I call a friend and tell them how much I appreciate them. I pay for the person behind me at the drive-thru. Wherever and however you pay it forward, one thing is certain: it infuses love and kindness into the air.

The cherry on top is the ripple effect. When we pay it forward, the positive energy expands. When we reach out and share the love, it not only affects the recipients of our kindness but it inspires them to pay it forward, too. For instance, I routinely pay for the car behind me at my favorite bagel shop. They started a running count of how many other people did this, and on a recent visit they were excited to tell me that we had reached 20 cars!

Ultimately, giving is not about the giver. It's not about acknowledgment or expecting anything in return. I love that I do receive something in return, though. That amazing feeling of gratitude inside my heart, that connection with my soul, is a gift without measure!

A Daily Gratitude Practice

by Tandy R. Elisala

As a four-time cancer survivor, I've integrated a lot of healing strategies into my life. Without question, my #1 go-to practice is gratitude. From personal experience, I've learned that gratitude is key to living your life with passion, peace, and joy. It is the foundation for developing your greatness. It is also a profound way to connect with your soul.

When things aren't going right in life, it's easy to complain or focus on what we don't have. But when we give thanks for all the blessings we *do* have, we allow even more to be grateful for into our lives.

There are a number of great ways to integrate gratitude into your daily life. One way is to start every morning – before you even get out of bed – by affirming (silently or aloud) three things you are grateful for. This can be as simple as saying: "I am grateful for each breath that I take. I am thankful for my health, my eyes to see, my ears to hear, my family…" or anything else you appreciate. This really sets a positive tone for your day, which can lead to even more to be grateful for!

Another great way to integrate gratitude into your daily life is to start a success jar. Every night, I take a few minutes and write down one thing that went well that day. It can be something you are thankful for or something new you learned. At the end of the month, you can have a "gratitude fest" and read them. Even better, involve your family with this practice and have everyone participate. It's a great way to focus on the positive and connect with your family in a meaningful way.

The key ingredients to miracles and connecting with your soul are: courage, love, the knowing that we are all connected, and gratitude. When your heart is open and full of gratitude for all that is good, you can change the world…starting with yourself!

Mantra Magic for Jumpstarting Your Day

by Karen Marie Palmer

One beautiful way to connect with your soul and manifest a wonderful life is through the use of mantras. For thousands of years, people have used mantras – sacred words, phrases, or even a single syllable (such as *Om*) – to help them connect with the Divine and live more fulfilling lives on Earth.

I have witnessed incredible manifestations thanks to the use of mantras. They have taught me to believe in infinite possibilities and have helped me and many of my students to live happier, healthier, and more peaceful lives. Now, I'd like to teach you the simple steps to begin using three very powerful mantras:

- *Ong Namo Guru Dev Namo* – The English meaning is: "I call on my inner wisdom to help me do my best." This is a wonderful way to connect with your soul. I say this mantra three times slowly, bringing my hands in a prayer position over my heart. This helps quiet and neutralize the mind.
- *Loka Samasta Sukhino Bhavantu* – The English meaning is: "May all beings be in peace. May my actions contribute to the peace of all beings." I sing this with the children at the after-school programs I teach. It is such a beautiful message, and the children sound like angels. We discuss ways we can contribute to a more peaceful world, and what the children share is truly inspiring.
- *Aham Prema* – The English meaning is: "I am Love." This mantra is such a powerful vibration. I have witnessed many lives transformed by singing this mantra daily. Our world needs more love; and the more love we share, the more our love expands.

These mantras have changed my life and have helped me see and feel the oneness and unity that is possible for our world. This is your invitation.

Love Notes from the Divine

by Cindy Jones Lantier

One evening, when I needed to know that I was worthy and deserving – when I needed to be reminded that the Divine has my back, I decided to take control of my needs and find a way to tell myself what I needed to hear. I pulled out a set of pretty notecards and my favorite pen. Then, I spent the next few hours writing out the messages that I needed to hear at the time. I felt as though I was channeling from my Inner Being or the Universe – so I signed them that way!

I finally decided to seal the envelopes, address them to myself, put a love stamp in the corner, and give them to my husband to mail at random times. I asked him to wait a few weeks to mail the first one, so the project would have time to slip my mind.

Sure enough, when the first card arrived, I almost didn't recognize it for what it was. When it clicked, I practically tore the envelope open! The message was fresh. It didn't even feel as though I'd written it; it still had that inspired feeling. It was exactly the message I needed to hear at that moment.

For the next several months, these cards – these gifts from the Divine – found their way back to me with uncanny timing, always saying exactly what I needed to be reminded of in that moment.

The last one from that first batch came on Valentine's Day. I had already received flowers and a lovely card from the greatest guy ever. And then, totally unexpectedly, a love note from the Divine showed up to brighten my day!

I really believe that these positive, supportive messages came from that higher self (my soul), which is always connected to the Divine. I jokingly call them "love notes from the Divine," but I'm only half joking. Even though the handwriting is mine, the messages are not.

My husband loves being the messenger. And I love being the receiver of these divine messages.

Walking Each Other Home

by Clarissa Coyoca

My friend sat on the floor with me, yoga mat to yoga mat, ready to guide me through the upsetting emotions swirling within me – and back into the light of healing and expansion.

For days, my inner critic had been relentlessly harassing me: "Why haven't you gotten over this yet? What's wrong with you?" In these all-too-familiar moments of inner judgment, I'm not connected with my soul. And, as I've learned from painful experience, when I try to face my upset alone, accessing my soul can be quite challenging. But when I share my feelings with an awakening friend, my soul more naturally feels a pull to the light. In these moments of tender heart-longings, I'm especially grateful for my loving community of conscious friends, particularly my spiritual-warrior sister who is here with me now.

In this session, my friend holds the space for my healing – just as I hold space for her when she is in need. She feels my jumbled emotions and invites me into meditation. She encourages my breath to slow down and my tears to flow. My body relaxes with each slower breath. The tears soften their urgency each time I gently acknowledge their presence. I remember that I am *having* a feeling, but I am not the feeling.

I am love.

As I feel the love returning, I send it to the places inside that are sad and longing. Before too long, I feel a shift from the grip on my head to an expansion in my chest – my heart! I'm connected back to my soul through the loving of my heart.

I open my eyes and see my friend wipe her tears. She felt my sadness through our soul-connected friendship. She reminds me how to connect back into that quiet place inside, the place where my soul rests sweetly, always connected to Spirit.

I have such deep gratitude for the community of soul sisters and brothers sharing this journey of conscious living and loving. Each a beacon for the other. Each walking the other home – back into the love that is abundantly available. Back into our magnificent and beautiful souls.

A Soul-Connection Prayer

by Sharon Rothstein

I would like to share a prayer that helps me connect with my soul. It's my hope that it will help you, too.

Thank you, dear spirit, my soul, my inner knowing, for our divine connection.

I intentionally align with you, and my insight is magnified. Your vibration leads the way to right decisions, allowing my own magnificence.

Oh wise and divine partner, you always pay attention to my requests. You sense my needs and expertly manage my affairs, exceeding my highest expectations. You answer my questions and enfold me with protection, strength, safety, and courage. You commend my right decisions through deliberate relief.

I tune into my soul radio dial, which provides peaceful, easy listening. You clear the static in my mind and soften the chatter. The music of my soul is filled with resonant sound and self-assuredness. I can hear your voice whispering sweet guidance through a song on the radio, a sign on a bus, from words of another, or my own creative ideas.

Happiness is mine, and most anything can be when I call out to you. You easily show up with improved outcomes. With practice, our connection remains a constant in my world. My insecure moments lessen. No longer am I a lost child. I am never alone. You are everywhere that I am.

I provide your enjoyment through my actions. I am here for your benefit and pleasure. I see others with love through your eyes. Your steadfast assistance allows me the freedom to reach my personal best. I appreciate all that we conspire to become together. Thank you for all that you have given me and for all that I am about to receive.

I am beyond grateful to walk this path beside your grace. What can I do to create a better tomorrow? How can I assist others?

Dearest soul, I sense your presence, and all is right in my world.

Amen.

Chapter 3
Nature & Animals

One of the ways we like to connect with our soul is to spend time in nature. We feel grateful to live on such a beautiful planet. Being in nature (whether it's going to the beach, walking through a forest, or spending time in our backyard) grounds us. Whenever we're feeling disconnected and need to plug in, just taking a moment to go outside always brings us back to our soul and to the present moment. We especially love the beach, and every time we go there and sit by the shore – taking in the ocean's energy – we instantly feel more alive and vibrant.

There are so many ways to connect with your soul through nature – many of which are shared throughout this chapter. You may like more vigorous activities – such as hiking or running, or you may prefer to take in nature at a more relaxed pace – such as sitting on your back patio and watching the trees sway in the wind. Either way is soulful and beneficial – you really can't get it wrong. Simply making time to step outside and breathe nature in is often enough to instantly connect you.

One of our favorite things to do is to sit on our back patio and watch the birds. There are so many different types that fly by, and hearing their chirps helps us feel at peace. We love animals, and being around them is a great way to connect with our soul. There are many wonderful ways to tap into the love that animals bring. We've certainly found that to be true in our own life. We can be in the worst mood where nothing seems to be going right, and then we'll see our cats playing or will hear them purring, and we immediately feel connected to the present moment and aligned with our soul again.

We hope that you'll find new ways to connect with your soul in nature and through animals on the following pages.

Long Nature Walks

by Holly Worton

Long walks in nature are a deeply spiritual activity for me. I have always felt a strong connection to nature, and in connecting with nature, I connect with my higher self or soul.

The key word for me is "long," as it usually takes me at least two or three hours to disconnect from my train of thoughts and slip into a peaceful, meditative state. It might take a while, but eventually my thoughts settle and my soul pops up to greet me. Then the messages really begin to flow, and new ideas materialize in my mind, seemingly from out of nowhere. When I get these types of downloads, I know that I've reconnected with my soul, and I make note of the wisdom it shares with me.

My favorite walks range from four to five hours and usually follow a roughly circular route. Usually, I'll go on a long walk just once or twice a week, but recently I walked the South Downs Way in southeast England, which was a 100-mile walk split into eight consecutive days. I find that the longer I walk, the deeper the connection with my soul.

If this appeals to you as a way to connect with your soul, I invite you to explore what works best for you. Try different lengths of walks or different locations. You might find that it's easy for you to reconnect with your soul after just one hour of walking in nature, or you may find that you prefer extended walks of four to five hours or even multi-day hikes. Go for a walk in the woods, by the sea, or near a lake or river. You might discover that walking near water is the best way for you to connect with your soul, or you may prefer forest walking, as I do.

Above all, enjoy the process. Long walks are not meant to be a hardship. They can be relaxing, enjoyable, and a great way to connect with your soul!

Cloud Messages Bring Peace

by Carolyn McGee

God speaks to my soul through the clouds and the images that they shape. When I feel troubled or am looking for confirmation, I ask for guidance and then look to the clouds for the answer.

Some of my earliest childhood memories are of lying on my back in the warm grass and looking at the clouds to pick out images. My cousins and I would spend hours watching the clouds shift from one image to another. I felt so happy playing the "name that cloud" game. At the time, it was great entertainment for us!

As I grew older, I realized that clouds provide divine messages for me and are a way for me to connect more deeply with what my soul wants me to know.

When I was starting my angel-communication journey, I questioned the reality of what I was feeling, seeing, and hearing. I wondered if I really was communicating with the Divine. I asked for a sign that the messages were truly guidance for my soul from the angels and God. Later that day I was walking a dog, and as I walked around a corner, I looked up and saw a magnificent angel in the clouds. It was clear confirmation that what I had already felt in my soul was true: Spirit does communicate to me through the clouds.

When my dad was dying in another state, I was driving to be with my mom and sister before he passed. I saw his face as clear as a picture in the clouds. I knew in my soul that he had already started his transition, that he was at peace, and that I would be there in time. My worry ceased, and my love for him filled my soul as I calmly completed my journey.

The joy, serenity, and clarity that I feel when I see cloud images and know that they are direct messages from God to my soul makes my heart expand with the wonder of such a beautiful gift.

Love Letter from a Pet

by Andrea Bryant

The gremlin voices had started again. Just when I was feeling more confident, they returned. The voices told me I was useless. Lazy. Insignificant. The voices were trying to keep me small and safe. To not grow or learn or evolve. Their purpose was to prevent me from living up to my greatness.

So I got frustrated. I got annoyed. Not at the voices, but at myself. For listening to them. For giving them power.

It was then that I decided – no more. It was time to take action.

I needed to find a way to remind myself of my greatness. A way to empower myself again. To ensure that I DID live up to my potential.

And at that moment, I looked at my beautiful pet rabbit, Apple.

What was one thing I knew for sure? That Apple loved me. Unconditionally. He only saw the good in me. He thought I was the most amazing human who ever lived!

Ahhh. I started to feel better. I started to feel connected. Inspiration hit me. I would write a love letter to myself from my darling boy, Apple. What a beautiful gift that would be. To receive a letter filled with love and appreciation for all my wonderful qualities. And so I began to write.

I saw myself through the eyes of my pet. I saw myself from his perspective. I saw what an amazing Mama I am to him. I saw that I am filled with love for animals. And those quirks I have – they make me special. They make me unique. I saw my compassion, my strength, my sense of humour. I saw the "curse" of sensitivity as a beautiful gift. I saw ALL the potential deep within me. Trying to break free. Trying to birth itself.

It was time. Time to step up. Time to be ME. No more hiding.

I sighed with relief. I felt enormous gratitude and love for my pet. I felt centred. I felt whole. I felt connected. I felt loved.

Walking on Rainshine

by Dedra Murchison

I stepped off the curb and into the rain. My umbrella was in the car. I left behind the huddled masses who feared they would melt. A sudden rainstorm had caught Houston off guard after a long period of drought. I felt the first drop hit my skin. It was unexpectedly warm and soothing. This was not the chill cool mist of a Seattle rain on a dark spring night after a movie. It was something else entirely.

I walked slowly. Instead of avoiding puddles, I reveled in them – splashing with childlike abandon. When I finally made it to my car, I wished that I had parked farther away. I felt the soaking wetness of my clothes as they molded to my skin while I sat waiting for the car to warm up. Tina Turner crooned about how she can't stand the rain. I found myself heartily disagreeing with that sentiment this afternoon.

I was delighted to find that the rain had not stopped when I got home – yet another opportunity to walk "umbrellaless" in the rain. I reached my apartment and stood dripping in the entryway. My faithful cat was not amused by my wetness and scampered for the safety of her special hiding space. I caught a glimpse of my reflection in the mirror. My hair was wet and frizzy. My eyes were clear, bright, and shining – the windows of my soul blown wide open. I made a mental note to do this more often.

Planting Soul Seeds

by Debbie Perret

Since becoming disabled, I have learned to embrace the gift of more time to myself. This has led me to quieter, gentler avenues of connection with my soul.

One principle that has become central to me is to tread as lightly as I can on dear Mother Earth. I buy from local farmers; choose organic if I can; and, now that I have more time, I am growing my own food.

Gardening is a magical, multi-sensory vehicle for me to connect with my soul. It begins with tentatively placed tiny seeds, then patient waiting and watching for the first hopeful sprouts of green. The past weeks have seen the careful nurturing of the tiny plants: watering, feeding, replanting, and relocating them strategically for the best mix of sun and rain.

I have been generously rewarded with a jungle of lush plants – some bushy, some wandering vines – but all laden with beautiful flowers and the promise of fruit.

The soul connection happens on different levels. I feel honoured to be an agent in the process of helping to birth and nurture new life. Then there's the deep satisfaction from knowing that I am growing food that is truly nourishing.

For me, though, the biggest piece is the immediate physical experience – the colours, the scents, and the feel of the soil in my hands. It is often warmed by the sun but always cool and moist beneath the surface. I love the feeling of gently cradling the roots and earth around the baby plants as I transplant them to larger pots.

For me, this is the most precious treasure – feeling the earth in my hands. Therein lies a soul connection that is almost a form of prayer or meditation. It instantly transports me from the most distressing mind-chatter and worst spells of fear or pain. It brings me back to the present moment and gives me a sense of peace, comfort, and gratitude. I know that all is well.

Now you know, too. All you need are a few seeds and a little bit of dirt.

Soul of the Ocean

by Jody Rentner Doty

The ocean is an amazing presence – embodying the feminine, symbolizing our feelings and emotions, and reminding us of the vastness of our world with its constancy and changeability. Its fluidity and movement activates and stirs our soul, inviting our attention.

We can choose to surf the waves of life, going with the flow of change, or we can fight the tides and find ourselves caught in the undertow, the riptides, and the whirlpools of resistance. We may bravely dive in, engaging and embracing the adventure of life, or we can gently test the waters, dipping in our toes and calmly wading into the surf, slowly feeling the movement of its wake. We may decide to sit on the shore and watch the comings and goings of life as an observer, taking a time out. But sooner or later, the tide will come in and the ocean will rise and envelop us. It happens whether we actively engage or not.

The ocean whispers truth daily; the constant is change. How we respond to the ups and downs, the corresponding events and emotions, is up to us. We decide whether to dive in, belly flop, wade, or swim. We intuitively answer the call because we are comprised of both body and water.

If the soul is feeling waterlogged, it is good to ask for clarity from our divine compass and allow our emotions to flow in and out like the tides, releasing and purging as they renew our body and quench our soul.

Our soul, like the ocean, evolves each moment. The best we can do is grab our fins, our scuba gear, a raft, a surfboard, or water wings…and hang on, rejoicing in the thrill of the ride! Bring along a buddy for companionship, a life vest for safety, and whatever else helps you brave the changing tides.

Calm or choppy, it's always surf's up!

Birds' Song: Divine Doorway to Spirit

by Lumi Vasile

This morning I was sitting on my couch trying to make an important decision. I contemplated all the possibilities, which just made me more confused. So I stopped for a moment and looked out the window. Gazing without any focus, my mind just drifted away, lost in the symphony of the birds' song outside. They were chirping happily, communicating with each other and with Spirit.

I got lost in their conversation and allowed myself to become one of them – feeling the breeze moving the leaves and branches of the trees, paying attention to the sudden silence and the rolling thunder in the distance, feeling the air changing and the rain coming.

I became aware of the presence of Spirit everywhere around me and within me. And I knew that any decision would be fine and that Spirit would always have my back. What was important, I realized, wasn't the choice from among the many possibilities but my attitude toward the imagined results.

Delving even deeper into the birds' song, I felt again the unspeakable peace, harmony, beauty, and rightness of everything; and I accepted that any outcome of my decision would be the right one. In that moment, Spirit whispered into my ear: "Everything that comes on your path is perfect for you. Allow it to be what it is and allow yourself to receive it."

I came back to the reality of my living room, and the decision was easily made. I became aware of what had just happened: I had stopped doing anything and simply allowed myself to be present. The song of the birds became the doorway to Spirit, and I passed through it. I let their song take me away, and I allowed myself to connect with Spirit, my inner wisdom and guidance.

An immense gratitude filled my whole being as I realized that I had just found another way to connect with Spirit, and I gracefully thanked the birds for their service.

Listen to the Storm

by Lori Thiessen

It had been almost a year since I had told my husband that after 21 years of marriage, I no longer wanted to live with him. The pain, anger, freedom, fears, and opportunities had scrimmaged daily in my mind and heart. I knew I had made the right decision, but the challenges of "Where do I go from here?" and "How will I manage to finish raising our five kids?" and "Am I strong enough for this?" kept me on edge.

One evening was particularly difficult for me, and I was feeling particularly overwhelmed, lost, and alone. It had been a hot summer day, but the sky was rapidly closing over. The thunderstorm that ensued was loud and violent. I stood in the doorway to my backyard, watching the strobe-like lightning and feeling the sound of the thunder rattle in my chest.

I let myself breathe in the energy of the wind as it blew through my soul – bringing me a deep inner calm and filling me with a strong grounding energy. The powerful noise from the wind pummeling the massive trees that surround my house and the crashing booms of the thunder infused my soul with energy and extinguished the burning pain in my heart. I found the courage and strength to move into the unknown.

Since that evening, I have often stood as close as I can to a storm and have drawn that same energy deep into my soul, where it strengthens and restores me. When I feel those same kinds of questions racing through my mind, I go out to the wind and let it speak to my spirit and soothe my heart.

Recently, engineers have come up with a device that uses sound waves to extinguish fires. It was fascinating to watch their demonstration of how it works. The first time I saw it, a light bulb went off in my head, because I knew and understood how the sound of the wind and thunder can do exactly that with the fires of fear inside me.

Sacred Spaces in Nature

by Heather Boon

As a young child from a troubled home, fear was my constant companion. In order to cope, I spent a lot of time in solitude (despite coming from a large family).

When I was seven, my parents divorced and we moved to the country. It was here that I found a sense of belonging. I spent much of the next six years finding sanctuary in nature.

Life at home rarely felt safe to me, so I spent my time creating secret hiding places in the lantana (dense Australian scrub), where I felt completely safe. These became my first sacred spaces in nature. Sometimes my brother or sisters would find me there and share my space for a short while. More often, they had their own sacred spaces they had created for themselves.

As the years passed, these sanctuaries allowed me to connect with the love and support I so desperately needed to feel. When I was the only child left at home, it was decided we would move to Brisbane. I was 13 and found myself in a large city with no nature to retreat to. For the next three years, I lost that feeling of connection and safety.

On turning 16, I left home, and a close friend took me to Mt. Tamborine in the Gold Coast hinterland. In this beautiful and very spiritual place, I immediately knew I had once again found my sacred space. The connection was instantaneous, and peace enveloped me. This mountain became my retreat and sanctuary when life became overwhelming. My sacred places on the mountain have changed over the years; however, it is still my favourite place, and it still fills me with peace and connection whenever I go there.

The connection I instantly feel in nature has sustained me through some tough times, and I know it can do the same for you. Where do you feel most connected? Is it the mountains, the beach, or the country? Create a sacred space in nature where you can connect to your soul, and it will always sustain you.

Turn Your Face to the Sun

by Allanah Hunt

I was busy with my chores: cleaning up the house after the children had left for school, washing their uniforms for the next day, preparing vegetables in advance so that dinner would be easy to complete when I got home from after-school activities…all the usual daily tasks that keep the house running and my family comfortable. It seemed like any other day, and it was…except for one moment that changed my entire day. And all the days since.

On this particular day, as I took the clean washing outside to dry in the fresh air, the singing of a beautiful bird broke through the busyness of my mind. It was just a little sound, but for some reason it lifted me from my task into the beauty around me. As I looked up to try to locate the source of this lovely sound, the warmth of the sun on my face caused me to catch my breath. I closed my eyes against the light and tilted my head backward. I breathed deeply, watched the sunlight play behind my eyelids, and felt my soul fill with bliss.

I would have expected that something so life-changing would be enormous and was surprised that it was just a tiny moment – a shift that allowed me to connect with myself in a new way. This new awareness quickly became something that keeps me in tune with my soul on a daily basis – something that always brings a smile to my face and allows me to stop and simply *be.*

Such a tiny moment…and yet a life-changing one. Because of this experience, I now take time each day to stop, look up, breathe, and appreciate the moment – which always brings me back to my soul and the beauty that surrounds me.

Receiving from Nature

by Nicole Levac

I believe that nature is our physical connection to the Universal Soul. My daily walks reinforce this connection and allow me to receive nature's gifts.

At the start of each walk, I open myself to receiving and to the unknown. I don't ask for anything specific. I simply allow myself to receive what I came to receive on this particular day. No expectations.

As I take my first steps, I allow my senses to receive the beauty of nature through my eyes, ears, nose, breath, feet, and skin. I allow myself to connect more deeply to the experience and to my feelings.

I also disconnect my tongue from the roof of my mouth. This small action allows me to disconnect from the mental chatter that could take place during this sacred time. Whenever I become aware that my attention is not in the present and that my mind is off thinking about something other than the moment I am in, I bring my attention back to the experience that I am living in nature. This is a conscious choice that I make over and over again during the course of my walk.

During my walks, everything I receive is kept inside to feed my soul, to help me nourish my connection to the Universal Soul. I go on these walks to fill up so that I can bring what I have received into my daily life. I always come back rejuvenated, recharged, and liberated because nature knows what I need and what to give me. I just need to show up to receive it.

The Unconditional Love of Animal Wisdom

by Jennifer "Elemental" Larkin

My heart is racing, my inbox is full, I'm late for a conference call, I've entirely missed at least five deadlines…and it's only 9:30 a.m.! I'm in the midst of launching several big ventures at once, and life is exhilarating in the flow of conscious creation. In this moment, however, I have reached my capacity for plate-spinning. I leave my home office and go to the bedroom. Sitting on the bed with my eyes closed, I begin a breathing technique that I hope will help me become calm and present.

Before I complete the breathing exercise, though, something pulls my energy. I open my eyes – then, POP! I am back. Fully embodied. Fully engaged. Fully aware. Staring deeply into my eyes from the foot of the bed is a furry friend who entered my life five years earlier. She is an adorable white Bichon Frisé with the sweetest teddy-bear face and the cuddliest cotton-ball body.

This dog has the capacity to bring me back to center like a Jedi. She is not just a dog. I have often wondered, "Who ARE you?" as I gaze into her deep brown eyes. She is a service animal – trained in the art of energy healing. For her 10-year life, she has known nothing but lying on massage tables in mind-body-spirit fairs and healing centers throughout North America – gifting bodies, hearts, and minds with what they require to come home. She will always lie on the place that requires her attention as she sends yummy vibrations directly to the core of whomever is lucky enough to be receiving a treatment.

In my moment of overwhelm, it was her presence and infinite, unconditional love that brought me back to the present moment – and back to my center. As she had done so many times before, she saw me and reminded me of what was real and true and unshakable.

Animals *know*. They have the ability to *be* with us in ways we do not allow ourselves to truly see or be with ourselves. In this moment, how might *you* connect with the animal kingdom and flow love and light through your core?

Finding Harmony with the Elements

by Yvonne Peraza

My days used to start in a rush. My morning routine consisted of getting ready for work, walking my son to school, walking my dogs, packing breakfast, and catching the train. My checklist had to get done before I left for the day. It felt like a frenzy that I could not get out of. Something had to give.

Then my soul noticed a simple triangle. I kept noticing it everywhere. I did a little research, which led me to the four elements (each of which is represented by a different configuration of a triangle): Air (inspiration), Fire (creativity), Water (emotions), and Earth (stability). On a deep level, I somehow knew that in order to ease my frenzy, I needed to align with the energy of these elements.

One night before going to bed, I invited the elements to become part of my life. I asked for their energy to be infused with mine and to assist me before I started my day. The next morning, I intuitively began to ask questions such as: *How can I benefit from inspiration? How can I tap into my creativity? Why am I having a hard time with my emotions? How can I be more stable?*

It took some time for me to receive answers and notice a change, but my soul persevered.

This practice of simply asking questions relating to the elements helped my soul understand the lessons that I happened upon throughout my day. These questions evolved into asking how I could use this wisdom with others. I started to notice subtle changes. I'd often stop during the day to think back to my morning questions, which always resulted in an "aha moment" for me.

Now, whenever I feel flustered, I always go back to Air, Fire, Water, and Earth. There's always a reminder to stay calm and enjoy the ride. Thanks to the elemental energies, my morning routine now has a new perspective, and I find harmony throughout my days.

Soulful Connection with Animals

by Sarah Dennison Berkett

Animal lovers are a diverse bunch. We come in many different shapes and styles, but one thing unites almost every one of us: we want and need to be around animals.

The deep spiritual bond between humans and animals has been felt for thousands of years. In ancient times, animals were held in high esteem and worshiped by the mystics. Today, animals are just as powerful in the lives of humans. My own life and work has been marked and blessed with animals I call *spirit animals*. Spirit animals mark the passages of our lives. They are magical helpers that guide us on our own hero journeys. They come when they are needed, and they go when their work is finished.

Living with animals is also a spiritual experience. In all the world, there is nothing more natural than for people and animals to live, work, and love together. Yet, the relationships are sometimes difficult, painful, and uncertain, as all relationships are. They are mirrors of humans – reflecting the good and the bad within us.

Animals are a gift to humans. They shape every part of our life in one way or another. They heal and comfort us. They guard and protect us, ease our loneliness, and open our hearts to love. They connect us with Mother Earth and remind us of our obligations to her. They are our partners in this world and are essential to our spiritual lives – to connecting with our soul. We need them as much as they need us. We belong together.

Releasing Through New-Moon Shadow Work

by Cindy Harpe Hively

When I was a little girl, I loved to play with my shadow. I delighted in seeing how tall I became when the sun was low, or how I could make my shadow walk beside me. At night, I made shadow animals on my bedroom wall with a flashlight…until I'd get in trouble for giggling too loud!

As an adult, I'm still captivated by my shadow; but now the shadows that intrigue me are the ones that live deep within my soul. Everyone has these shadows: repressed emotions that can be shameful, traumatic, depressing, or even hateful. These are the parts of ourselves that we generally hide so that we don't have to deal with them, but bringing these shadows to light can bring about profound healing.

Over the past year, I've experienced the benefits of looking at my shadows through the ritual of new-moon shadow work. Each new moon, when the night is at its darkest, I set the intention to explore my shadow, cleanse my soul, and renew my spirit. I go outside, light a candle, look up into the darkness, and call upon Spirit to guide my thoughts, words, and actions for the good of my soul.

And then I allow the shadows to emerge.

A few months ago, I came head to head with one of my biggest shadows: the blame I'd been carrying around for years over a failed marriage. When I allowed these feelings to surface, I saw that the deepest shadow wasn't my pain over the marriage, it was the feeling of "not being enough." Feeling the depth of this pain – this *lie* – wasn't easy. But I stayed with the experience, and soon I felt a deep, soul healing wash over me. Mother Earth soaked up my tears and cradled me as I released these shadows from my soul.

We all have wounds, scars, and blemishes. If we hold onto them we never heal. If we can look at them, especially in the new moon, we can cleanse our soul and live in the truest essence of who we are meant to be.

Messengers of Serenity

by Susan Huntz-Ramos

Our dogs are not really geniuses, although one of them pretends to be – especially when it comes to chasing lizards.

I enjoy sitting outside in our woodsy backyard and have realized that many of the times when I head out there to be by myself are the times when my soul is screaming for peace and reconnection.

As soon as I open the back door, our dogs are right there ready to run outside. They're barely out the door when their bodies do almost a 360, running beside the wall, knocking over random plant pots, hoping to be fast enough to catch that one unsuspecting lizard (which they rarely do). While sitting there watching the dogs, I am totally immersed in the moment – just like them! All that concerns them at this time is that lizard. I don't imagine they're stewing over the little tussle they had before they came outside, wondering if their "boss dog" will let them have the weekend off, or thinking, "Ugh, why am I out here chasing lizards when I have so much work to do?"

Our genius dogs, being clueless about my overworked brain, have no idea how much they have taught me about life, serenity, learning to slow down, and living in the moment.

We all have so much going on in our lives. So much noise in our heads. It is vital to our health to find ways to slow down and simply enjoy the moment. I'm the master of excuses, but I also know that we can carve out 10-15 minutes of time to ourselves. There is nothing selfish about taking quality time for yourself. In fact, doing so will not only work to keep you healthy, your "me" time can also improve every other area of your life.

So go ahead and take 10-15 minutes for yourself. Kick off your shoes and let your bare feet feel the earth. Find shapes in the clouds. Stargaze. Count flowers. Chase lizards. Whatever you choose to do, be patient with yourself, and be all in!

Human Tree

by Jody Rentner Doty

While walking in the woods close to my home, it occurred to me that one of my favorite teachers inspires me by its mere presence on the planet. It does not speak in words but has a universal language that resonates with each soul it encounters. Blessed are our trees, nature's enduring gift.

Trees teach us to be rooted, to be present, grounded in our being and fully connected with our soul. They are a green, living timeline, a reminder that we are always growing, spreading our limbs, and reaching upward toward to the sky.

Trees illustrate the gift of generosity, of unconditional sharing and giving. They provide us with shelter, comfort, shade, warmth, and food. They encourage our resilience during trying times, inspiring us to hold strong and weather life's storms. Trees remind us that we, too, are beautiful beings, self-sufficient in our individuality and quite powerful when we unite as a group, a human forest.

Trees are accepting of other creatures in our world. Unprejudiced, they happily share themselves with birds, squirrels, chipmunks, owls, and raccoons. Trees provide us with a tranquil place for reflection and meditation, a sturdy wooden foundation for reading a book or painting a picture on a sunny afternoon.

On days when I am feeling stressed, overwhelmed, or out of sync with life, I love to stand in the woods, feel the earth beneath my feet, and the wind in my hair, and imagine that I am a human tree – grounded, strong, beautiful, resilient, comforting, accepting, and receptive – living my life fully, growing my soul.

Walking is More Than Just Exercise

by Carolyn McGee

My ego had tricked me into believing that the only way to meditate was to sit quietly in a chair with my back straight and be in stillness. My ego was so wrong!

I have a very active and logical brain, so getting my ego to cooperate and allow the peace that my soul yearns for has not always been easy. To achieve the connection with the Divine that my soul desired, I tried many techniques to meditate…but with little consistent success. I asked God to help me find a simple and enjoyable way to connect with Spirit, which I discovered in a simple activity I was already doing each day!

At the time, I was walking dogs on a regular basis. I noticed that my mind cleared when I was walking. The familiar routine, with the distraction of keeping track of the dogs, provided just the perfect amount of energy for my mind to let go, be free, and reconnect with God. I had many revelations and deep connections with Spirit during my dog walks.

Once I realized that this technique opened a spiritual path, I practiced walking meditation with and without dogs. I love walking around the local reservoir, letting the soothing sounds of nature be background noises to distract my mind as I connect my soul with the Divine.

My neighborhood is another place where I can walk – allowing my thoughts to be free and letting the Divine speak to me. The background sounds and familiar space provide comfort and just enough activity for my ego to let go and for God to speak to me.

My soul craves this connection with God, and it easily comes to me when I am walking.

The Ocean's Symphony

by Stella Tassone

"Listen to the sound of the waves within you."
- Rumi

There's something about the ocean that whispers gently to my soul. Whenever I feel I need time for myself – time to reflect, time for clarity – I hear the calling. It's a signal from the Universe, as clear as a phone call. As soon as I hear it, I get my car keys and go to the place that grounds me and reconnects me with my higher self.

As I walk by the ocean, I feel the waves wash over my soul. I take a deep breath and truly connect. The rhythm, the movement, the symphony of the ocean takes me to a beautiful place within myself. It's instant. I listen to what it tells me.

The sound of the crashing waves, the flowing of the water, the peace is music that fills my heart and soul with pure joy. My soul – my inner vibration – orchestrates with the frequency of the waves, and I'm reminded of how powerful I really am.

I take my shoes off and am always guided to where I sit. Each and every time, magically, after finding my place, I always see a black and white feather. I know my angels are with me.

I take a notebook and pen, and I write freely. I receive answers to questions I've been asking and sometimes I receive information for others that assist them.

By the shore, my soul always allows me to be sure. By the sea, I clearly see.

The Gift of Support from a Power Animal

by Andrea Bryant

I am a worrier. I always have been. It started in childhood. I was always worrying about something. This has carried through into adulthood. When I get stuck in my worrying cycle, I feel anxious, off balance, and ungrounded. I feel like a helium balloon loose in a wind storm! I get so caught up in the worry that I lose sight of what is happening around me. I fail to see the beauty in the world. I become oblivious to life's wonders.

Fortunately, when this happens I now know exactly what to do: I reach for my *Power Animal Oracle Cards* by Steven Farmer. The deck is filled with a variety of different animals. Each of these animals has a particular quality that the species embodies.

When my most recent worry cycle started, I reached for support from the animal realm. I grounded myself and took a deep breath. I shuffled the deck and asked the Universe to give me the power animal I most needed at that time. (I always trust that I will receive the perfect card for the situation.) I continued to shuffle until a card jumped out – as one ALWAYS does. This was the card:

BEAR – Have Courage, Stand Your Ground.

This was the perfect card and message for the situation I was worrying about. I imagined myself as a bear – tall and strong, standing on my hind legs. I allowed that power to fill my whole body. I asked Bear to stand beside me, offering courage as I navigated through this worry. I then thanked Bear for infusing his beautiful qualities into me.

Using this deck always makes me feel connected to nature and the animal kingdom. It helps me feel an amazing sense of calm and peace. And most of all, it helps me feel an enormous amount of trust.

Harmony with the Earth

by Michelle Anne Gould

I had felt so unlike myself for weeks. One incident after another had piled on top of me until I felt like I couldn't breathe. Emotionally and physically, I felt like I was drowning, like I couldn't swim.

Certain that I'd never find my way out of this downward spiral on my own, I turned to nature. Looking up into the sky, I asked, "What do you want me to do?"

In the stillness, I heard the whisper: "Renew your heart." I knew what was needed. I headed into nature.

I felt the excitement coursing through my body. There was a spring in my step and a burst of exhilarated energy. "Renew your heart…gently," the whisper repeated.

Intentionally, I slowed my pace. With each step, I became more aware of my surroundings. My breathing grew naturally deeper. My eyes took in the exquisite views while the sunshine kissed my skin. I abandoned my shoes.

As I climbed the hill, the trees lining the dirt track seemed to embrace me. My senses became heightened. With each step I took, layer upon layer of built-up stress peeled away from my body. A sob escaped from deep within me. I let myself feel it and release it.

By the time I reached the hilltop, I felt cleansed, renewed, rejuvenated. Respectfully, I announced my arrival: "I'm here; may I come in?" The rustling of leaves and the chirping of birds welcomed me. My heart and soul felt overwhelmed by the beauty surrounding me. As if by magic, a whole new world opened up – a doorway into paradise.

Bursting with wonder, I explored further. I jumped down, mesmerised by a flowing stream. Without fear or hesitation, I dipped my toes into the cool and silky water. I playfully grasped it with my hand and watched each droplet return to the stream. A rock caught my eye. I settled down on it and lightly caressed a nearby shrub. It sent a wonderful pulsing vibration through the tips of my fingers.

I closed my eyes, feeling completely, effortlessly at one with the Earth. I was in tune with nature, in perfect harmony.

The Robins' Tale

by Destrie Sweet Larrabee

I was blessed to watch a pair of robins build a nest under the eaves of the house next door – right outside my window. Observing the devoted pair of beautiful birds, I marveled at how they worked together so harmoniously through the building of the nest, the constant feeding, and then that day when... *Oh no! The nest is empty!* Alarmed, I ran outside, joyfully finding all of the babies safe, following Mom, learning how to be robins. Everything was right with the world. I realized then that I felt such happiness, gratefulness, and honor for this gift of soul connection through these beautiful birds. Little did I know that this was just the beginning!

One day, it was time to water the garden, and I was comfortably sitting in a chair watering away. After a bit, I heard the ever-uplifting "Cheerio-Cheerio" of a robin, joyfully sung when it's going to rain. I began drifting off into contemplation, becoming one with "Mom Nature," when I was startled into awareness by a great deal of wing-flapping sounds. Opening my eyes, I thought I was dreaming – I was totally surrounded by a yard completely full of robins! They lined the yard on the fences and garage! Some were waiting patiently for their turn to go under the mister to get a shower; others were at the edges of the spray, looking for worms; still more were happily splashing in the birdbaths, flapping their wings as they exited, making way for the next bird. And I? I was thoroughly transfixed. And transformed. In that moment, I was entirely embraced by this beautiful robin clan. I had consciously and soulfully become one with Mother Earth/Father Sky/Creator of All That Is.

While sharing the robins' genesis, I was also experiencing my own, empowering me to fit yet another piece of my complete connection with my soul. I have never felt more alive, more at peace, more clear in my path.

Messages are everywhere. And robins don't always sing "Cheerio" just when it's going to rain! Sometimes they're announcing a Big Message, and it's up to us to be open to hearing it. I'm so glad I did!

Lessons from a Lobster

by Christine King

Many years ago, I saw a wonderful movie entitled *Into the Deep* – a documentary about marine life and the diverse species that inhabit our oceans.

At one point, the camera focused on a lobster rubbing its back against a very sharp rock. It was explained that this was helping it to shed its old shell. Although this looked very uncomfortable, unless it took place, the lobster would be unable to grow.

Lobsters grow by molting. Before shedding their old shells, they instinctively develop a new thin shell underneath. After secreting various enzymes that soften the old shell, they begin struggling out of it.

Depending on the size of the lobster, it takes anything from 15-30 minutes for this process to take place. In a young lobster, this ritual is repeated about five times a year for the first five years of its life, as it goes through many stages of growth. For adult lobsters, this happens roughly once a year.

For a time after shedding an old shell, the lobster is very vulnerable because the new shell is not yet fully formed. Consequently, in order to protect itself, it usually retreats into a cave or rock crevice until the new shell is hard enough to enable it to return to its larger oceanic world – stronger and more resilient.

This whole process could be applied to our own spiritual growth. During our soul journey, we sometimes rub up against some hard rocks, which although uncomfortable, often act as catalysts for change, assisting us in shedding the "old skins" that have kept us stuck.

While we wait for our new skin to grow stronger, like the lobster, we may feel a little vulnerable and need to retreat into our cave of soothing self-care and allow our soul to support us.

During any period of transition, I find it helpful to repeat this prayer morning and evening for a period of 14 days: "Only greater good can come from this change. I give thanks and am ready to accept the wonderful new blessings my soul has prepared for me."

Like the lobster, at the end of our own periods of growth, we can emerge into a bigger world – feeling stronger than ever.

Let Your Heart Beat with the Ocean

by Allanah Hunt

I remember so clearly a time in my life when I was overwhelmed by my emotions: grief over a recent loss, apprehension about what the future might bring, and anxiety about which direction to turn. I was paralyzed and afraid, and I doubted my abilities to make any kind of decision. I was in a cycle of dread, afraid to be awake yet terrified to sleep. Round and round the thoughts would tumble, night and day, telling me the horror story of my life.

One day, in a state of desperation, I went to the beach, hoping that some time out might quiet the distraught voice in my head. I spread my towel onto the warm, white sand; laid down; and propped up a book in front of me. But I couldn't read; the words all seemed to blur, to rise up off the page and fade away before my eyes.

Setting my book aside, I closed my eyes, rested my head on my arms, and gave myself up to the world around me: the shrill cry of a bird as it celebrated the freedom of flight, the soft whoosh of the gentle breeze, the warmth of the sun on my back, and the splashing of the waves as they broke gracefully onto the sand.

Slowly but surely, my body began to relax and my mind began to quiet. Soon there was nothing but the rhythmical beating of my heart, which kept pace with the breaking waves. In this moment, I became one with the ocean and part of something so much bigger than myself. In this moment, my soul began to heal.

Aligning my heartbeat with the ocean's waves was just the spiritual recharge that my soul needed.

Pets as a Mirror for the Soul

by Carolyn McGee

Being aware of my pets and how they act around me helps me focus on being present and open to my soul. I am highly connected to my pets and find them to be a beautiful mirror for how in touch I am with my energy.

Animals, especially cats, are extremely present creatures. They truly live in the moment and are highly intuitive and open. When I feel upset about something, my cat will jump up on a high shelf and move objects around to get my attention. As I step toward him, I realize that I am disconnected from my soul, that my mind is taking over. The movement toward my cat breaks me out of my disembodied energy. As I realize what is happening, my cat gives me an "I told you so" look and hops down off the shelf. He reminds me to get back in touch with my desire to be peaceful and present.

Another example of an animal being a mirror for my soul connection was when my dog left his toys all over the floor for me to trip over. This wasn't typical behavior for him. As soon as I realized what in my life kept tripping me up, he stopped leaving the toys everywhere – and I was reconnected with my soul!

My new puppy is also a wonderful indicator of how connected I am with my soul and body. He has lots of energy and is a mirror for my own vitality. When he begins to frantically run around the house or yard, it is an invitation for me to slow down and look at how I am expending my energy. As I breathe in, center myself, and connect with my soul, my puppy also settles down.

My pets' open and loving energies provide a clear view into my own connection with spirit. They remind me to breathe, slow my heart rate, and connect deeply with my soul and with the Divine.

Modern Goddess Full-Moon Ritual

by Cat Williford

The moon represents the Divine Feminine, emotional intelligence, creativity, and reflection. The focus of a full-moon ritual is self-healing, self-love, and self-advocacy. The goal is to balance your "can-do" masculine energy by honoring your Divine Feminine. The lasting result is deep connection with your soul and the rhythms of life and nature.

Whether you set up an elaborate altar with representations of the elements, light candles, and invite friends to join you, or decide to keep it simple and sit quietly under the full moon in contemplation, you will experience the power of Divine Feminine connection when you perform this ritual:

1. Close your eyes, sit quietly for a few minutes, and clear your mind of undone to-dos by focusing on your breath. Become aware of your body's comfort or tension levels, breathing gently into any tension you feel. Invite your Divine Feminine Spirit to emerge. Invite any combination of the four directions, four elements, spirit guides, angels, and loving beings to join your circle. Say aloud: "This is a safe space of love, healing, and creation."
2. Speak three gratitudes. Your gratitude may be for people, achievements, personal growth, or even for setbacks and delays.
3. Speak three intentions you will hold for the next 28 days (e.g., physical goals, states of being, or feelings you choose to experience). Make sure you speak with positive-creation language, beginning intentions with "I am" or "I have" or "I experience."
4. Howl at the moon! Stand up, sway your hips in a figure eight, reach up toward the moon, and let sound organically emerge from you.
5. Place your palms on your heart center for an out-loud self-blessing: "I am a love- and light-filled being, contributing positivity and possibility to the world, offering and receiving love equally. I am connected to my Divine Feminine, Source, and the light of others. And so it is."
6. Enjoy a potluck feast with your circle! If celebrating solo, sit under the moon, journal your insights, and then eat a snack to ground your ritual.

Your Personal Four Elements

by Barbara Schiffman

As my day rushes by, my big orange cat, Lucky, demands that I pet him whenever I pass him peacefully lounging on a table or cool tile counter. He's just being a cat, but I hear his "ME-ows" as reminders for me to pause and tune in.

Recent studies report that petting our cats (or dogs) is healing for humans. This simple action reconnects us with nature, which most of us ignore while we're plugged into our screens. I slow down when I pet Lucky, who purrs as I brush circles around his forehead. This stimulates his third eye – and mine too!

My "feline guru" demonstrates the Earth element within us all – human, animal or otherwise. In fact, each of us embodies all four of nature's building blocks, a.k.a. the Four Elements. Our skin, bones, and internal organs vibrate with slow, dense Earth energy. Our blood and bodily fluids surge with Water energy, constantly moving and cleansing. Our breath – flowing in and out from our first to our last – is as light as Air. And our 98.6 degree "Divine Life Spark" – our temperature – proves we're alive, until it cools when our soul departs the body to "go home."

I'm glad our souls have chosen truly creative vehicles for our life journeys. Each has its own shape, size, color, gender, age, talents, and skills. For me, the four elements also reflect the way our souls absorb life energy through our experiences, thoughts, feelings, actions, relationships, and creations. Nature is always in a state of change: birth, growth, death, renewal. This is also true of our human lives and souls.

As you move through your life, become more aware of your personal four elements – your feelings, thoughts, actions, and environment – and how these connect with nature's four elements. This can help you stay joyful and soul-centered. If you find this challenging, start by communing with your nearest animal or human companion. Connect with them first through your eyes – the "Windows to the Soul." Then give them a pet or a hug, heart to heart and soul to soul!

Horses as a Reflection of Your Soul

by Susan Viljoen

What if, whenever you felt overwhelmed, you could reach the touchstone of your innermost self, the part that remains stable no matter what is happening?

During some really painful times in my own life, when I was swept about by emotion, I wished fervently that this could be true. Then I met a remarkable person who showed me how to interact with horses in a way that helped me connect not only with the horses but also with my soul.

I learned that the key was *awareness* – noticing everything about the horse and about myself, noticing what my body was doing, noticing what my mind and my emotions were doing, and noticing how any changes in me affected the horse.

Often people assume they have to be in a really peaceful frame of mind in order to get a horse (or the world) to respond to them with positive energy. I did. As a result, I covered my emotions so I would seem open and relaxed. The horses instantly saw right through me.

When you get real and stay in touch with what is actually going on in your mind and body, your soul speaks directly to the horse, and you get an authentic reaction back, often a very empathetic one. In an inauthentic state, you see your own confusion reflected in the horse's behaviour.

There is no way to get lost here. You receive feedback in every moment: just look at what happens with the horse, and you'll see exactly what energy you are conveying!

While working with horses, I have come to learn that the way the horse experiences you is the way the *world* experiences you. When you exude authentic energy, even when it's not particularly peaceful, people feel inexplicably drawn to you. Aligned in body, mind, and soul, you find that the horse, and the world, moves to follow you.

When you approach a horse from a place of soulful alignment, and you know what that feels like, you can start experimenting with your own methods to get there…with or without a horse!

Communing with Trees

by Milada Sakic

The last year of my 16-year corporate career became almost unbearable. Suddenly, I could no longer stand noise, fluorescent lighting, or even people's voices. I started urgently craving a palpable closeness to nature on a daily basis.

Prior to this year, I had regularly sacrificed my lunch breaks in the name of "getting all the work done." Now, however, every minute of my one-hour break became precious – a sacred me-time, spent on nature walks, walking meditation, and communing with trees.

One day, after a very stressful morning at the office and finishing my meal at one of the park benches, I suddenly noticed the trees in the nearby park in a way that I had never noticed before. They appeared to be filled with so much love, light, consciousness, and energetic support. It was as if the more I noticed them, the more energy was sent back to me – a very calming, loving, and gentle breezy energy.

I decided to send them my love and gratitude, and their love and gratitude came back to me amplified! At first, I sent them a gratitude prayer. Then, I began voicing an "OM" sound while walking. Then, when I sent a question, I was amazed to receive back an incredibly soul-affirming answer. I experienced the most beautiful energetic support, full of so much grace and love. It was a vibrational conversation with an energetic exchange. My body and heart rejoiced!

I gradually started breathing and walking more consciously, and returned to the office with so much calm, clarity, confidence, and joy!

The next time you take a walk, send a gaze of acknowledgment and love to each tree that calls your attention. You will be amazed at the joyous, serene consciousness tuned into you in that moment of grace-filled presence. Simply acknowledging and appreciating the trees helps us open our hearts and stay open to cosmic energetic support and infinite joy!

Trust the Flow of Life

by Kat Ellis McIntyre

"To have faith is to trust yourself to the water. When you swim, you don't grab hold of the water because if you do you will sink and drown. Instead, you relax and float."
- Alan Watts

Water is a gift from the Divine. It is the giver of life – the way one enters the world and the element needed to sustain it. It is the ultimate healer and the ultimate teacher.

Spend time by any river, ocean, or other body of water, and you will surely absorb some of its essence. (If you don't have access to an actual body of water, watch a video of a flowing river – or even just contemplate one in your mind's eye – and immerse yourself in water's soulful wisdom.)

Water teaches us to give abundantly, to have faith and know that we are supported, and to trust the flow of life. Trusting the flow of life means that we do not cling to the past or resist the future. Holding onto that which no longer serves us keeps us stuck and stagnant. Resistance can stifle passion and creativity. But allowing life to flow through us releases our natural creative essence.

When we trust the flow of life, we remember that there is no need to hurry, that everything will be accomplished in the right time. We remember that – just as the moon causes the tides' ebb and flow – we, too, can attune to the natural rhythms of our lives and align with the cycle of the moon's phases, the rhythm of Mother Nature's seasons, and our own heartbeat.

And when we feel disconnected from the flow of life, we can always dive into the depths of our own soul – exploring the layers of our subconscious, returning to the source of creativity: the womb space, where all creation resides. And when we re-emerge from this deep space, we will be refreshed, rejuvenated, and reborn.

As you contemplate water – in person or in your imagination – soak in its wisdom and allow it to reconnect you with the depths of your own soul…and with the flow of all life.

Mindfully Connecting with Your Dog

by Karen Marie Palmer

I believe my connection with my soul began during my difficult childhood, when I found peace and serenity with animals and nature. I soon noticed I was hearing, seeing, and feeling experiences with animals differently than other people. Now, as a conscious dog trainer and Kundalini Yoga instructor, I help people connect with their pets on a deeper and more spiritual level.

Many pet parents have struggled with walking their dog, and I offer them a practice of mindful dog-walking, which will work with any dog. I'm happy to share this simple process with you now.

Be mindful as you approach your dog with the leash. Walk your dog slowly over to the door and have him sit and stay as you calmly open the door. Please make sure your dog stays calm as you open the door; this is setting the tone. Claim the space of the open door and do not let the dog walk through until you lead. Offer treats for good listening. Slowly walk out the door with your dog by your side and a loose leash in your hand.

The walk will begin with you setting the pace. You can walk as slowly or quickly as you would like – just make sure your dog is by your side or behind you. Your body language is very important. Keep your shoulders back and your spine straight. If the dog tries to pull, correct by slightly pulling up on the leash and making a sound that your dog responds to. I use the word "slow" and walk slowly and mindfully.

When your dog is walking perfectly, you can reward him by inviting him to an area where he can sniff. It is important that you keep a bonded connection on the walk and calmly enjoy each other. Mindful walking is very therapeutic to both you and your furry friend. This experience will open your soul to even more ways to connect.

The Elemental Walk

by Nicole Levac

During my daily walks in nature, I invite the four elements and integrate them into my body. This practice connects me deeply with nature and with my own higher self.

To begin, I invite each of the four elements – Earth, Air, Fire, and Water – through a different direction in my body. The Earth element comes in through my feet. The Water element comes in through the crown of my head. The Air element is invited in through my right hand. The Fire element comes in through my left hand. It's as if I become a human compass where the four elements come together.

Each element plays an important role in our lives:

- The Earth element, the most concrete, creates the foundation and the grounding to the physical earth and to our body, making sure to support us.
- The Water element helps to cleanse and clear away the murky and foggy parts, helping us to gain clarity.
- The Air element elevates us into higher parts of ourselves, allowing us to see the bigger picture.
- The Fire element is the transformative element, the igniter and the changemaker.

Although I invite the elements in one at a time, they build upon one another. Once I feel my connection to the Earth element through my feet, I invite the Water element, connecting them together. Once I feel that both are well connected, I invite the Air element and connect it to the other two. The Fire element is the last one I invite in to join with the other three.

Once I feel all four elements inside my body, I unite them together in my heart area. I also recite these words: *I invite the Earth element to join with the Water element, to elevate me with the Air element and transform me through the Fire element so that they unite and support me to be all that I AM.*

Chapter 4
Playing & Having Fun

Some people think that connecting with your soul has to be a solemn and serious endeavor. But just because it's important doesn't mean that it can't be fun! This chapter is filled with fun ways for you to connect with your soul – such as singing, dancing, spinning, and laughing.

We believe that while the soul may be the older, wiser part of you, it also possesses the childlike qualities of innocence, wonder, and playfulness. By allowing your joyous spirit to come out and play, you experience the lighter side of the soulful path. You allow yourself to lighten up and enjoy the game of life. You enjoy *yourself*!

Although we both tend to take life fairly seriously, we also like to sing, dance, play Wii and other games (backgammon is an essential component of our nightly routine), and watch silly movies and YouTube videos (especially if they involve talking cats). We believe in the Abraham-Hicks motto that *Life is supposed to be fun!* We believe that laughter truly is the best medicine. And we believe that our lighthearted activities are great ways to connect with each other…*and* with our soul!

We hope you enjoy reading and experiencing the fun ways of connecting with your soul shared in this chapter. And we hope they help to infuse your soulful journey with a spirit of play, lighthearted joy, and fun!

Take More Vacations

by Arielle Ford

Last April, my soulmate Brian sat me down and said, "We have to talk." I felt a sinking feeling in the pit of my stomach, followed by the thought, "Oh no, what have I done?"

With the passing of my sister, Debbie, just months before, we were both trying our best to survive – not getting much sleep, deep in grief, and yet still keeping up with work's endless demands.

In the sweetest, most gentle voice, Brian shared his concern for my health and wellbeing. With tears in his eyes, he told me he felt that if I didn't stop working and stressing so much, he was afraid I would get very sick and possibly even "work myself to death."

As someone who has always been able to accomplish major things, juggle several simultaneous projects, and withstand huge amounts of pressure, I normally would have just assured him that I could power through.

But there was something in his open-hearted approach that made me stop and listen. I realized that I was no longer the person who could do it all. My nervous system was shredded. I was out of reserves and running on fumes. As I sat there, trying to take it all in and figure out what to do, I remembered something Debbie whispered to me in the middle of the night: "Take more vacations."

I spent the next several days looking at the calendar, trying to see when I could take a vacation. And then it dawned on me: I didn't just need a week or two on a tropical island. I needed a long, extended break. I needed to rest, rejuvenate, and reboot. So on August 1st, I stopped working. Completely! I turned off my cell phone and turned on my email's auto-responder. And, for 90 days, I slept in, took naps, cooked, read, played tennis, walked on the beach, and traveled to beautiful places. But mostly, I rested.

I experienced a new kind of aliveness that isn't fueled by adrenaline. I took Debbie's loving advice to heart, and I feel more connected to my soul because of it – something I definitely can get used to!

If You Want to Feel Free, Just Play

by Peggy Nolan

I watched my six-year-old granddaughter pump her legs so she could swing higher and higher. A smile lit up her whole face. The back-and-forth pendulum motion infused her with carefree joy. Pure bliss radiated from her entire being.

I remember being six and swinging as high as I possibly could. Once I had the speed and the arc of the swing just right, it felt like I was flying. I felt lighter than air…weightless. As I got older, I learned how to leap from the swing at just the right moment and, for a split second, I floated freely through the air until gravity pushed me back to Earth. My friends and I would swing and jump until the sun went down and the street lights came on.

I wondered when I stopped swinging and playing – maybe when I was 11 or 12 – when the playground became uncool and the teenaged pressure to conform took center stage. For years, my soul's deepest longing – to feel free and unencumbered by the weight of the world – remained buried under layers of half-truths, false beliefs, and the expectations of others. All because I stopped playing.

A few months before I turned 40, I became reacquainted with play in a yoga class. I kept going back because the same sensation – of feeling lighter than air, releasing all my worries and anxiety, and being free – cut through the lies I built around my soul.

I came to realize that play is still important, even as an adult – *especially* as an adult! My soul is ageless; it wants to feel free, light, weightless, and giddy with joy. And playing – whether it's riding to the beach with the top of my Jeep down, doing yoga, or watching my granddaughter swing as high as she can – is one of the fastest ways I can center myself, feel intensely joyful, and connect with my soul.

Discover Your Soul Song

by Carol Tuttle

We each have songs that rank among our favorites. But your "soul song" is more than just a song you really, really like – it's a song that moves you and resonates deeply on a soul level. Your soul song is about more than just the music and lyrics – it's about the emotion, vibration, and energy.

All sound is vibration. As a human being, you have an energetic vibration, too. So, because emotion is energy in motion, all music has an effect on our emotions. This means that the music we listen to has an energetic vibration that can either lift our energy up or bring it down.

Without consciously thinking about it, people tend to choose music that matches their mood: sad songs when they're feeling down, upbeat songs when they're happy. Your soul song, on the other hand, is a song that makes your spirit soar no matter what mood you're in. It energizes you, inspires you, and can even bring healing to your soul. The song that does this for me – my soul song – is "Ain't No Mountain High Enough" by Marvin Gaye and Tammi Terrell.

Would you like to discover your own soul song? There's no precise formula for this process. It's an intuitive choice, so let your heart guide you. Here are a few pointers to get you started:

- Come up with a list of a few songs that always seem to move you, energize you, or speak to you on a soul level every time you hear them.
- Notice which songs you go to when you need a boost of encouragement.
- Which songs do you turn up when you hear them on the radio?
- Which songs are on your "Most Played" list in your music collection?
- What do these songs do to your energy? Which ones truly resonate with your soul?

I'm excited for you to discover your soul song – and for you to feel its high-vibration energy resonating with your soul...every time you hear it!

Let Your Joyful Soul Laugh

by Annie Price

I love to have a good laugh. It feels wonderful to express the bubbling joy that rises up from deep within. It's even more fun when you can share lighthearted experiences with friends or family. Laughter is also a great stress release when you're overwhelmed, yet you begin to see a bit of humor in a troublesome situation. Life is just plain easier when you can gently laugh with your silly self.

As we grow up, we learn how to control our emotions and pick up on socially appropriate behavior. There's a "right" and a "wrong" time for boisterous laughter; you know when you shouldn't do it. Unfortunately, being told *not* to laugh can be like throwing gas on the fire – especially when you're a kid. For example, when we were kids at a church service, one of my siblings would certainly start tee-heeing, and before long the contagious giggling overtook the four of us. (My poor mother!)

I remember, years ago, being thrilled to attend a live ballet production. I was quietly absorbed in the show – until they began performing an overly creative piece. The only sound was their bare feet slapping the floor. I stayed with it until, to my complete horror, the mirthfulness would not be denied. I was trapped in the middle of a long row of seats, my shoulders shaking as I tried to suppress giggling that became louder, tears running down my face. People around me began to chuckle along. Very soon, several of us were roaring with laughter – practically rolling in the aisle. Maybe not the intended response, but we enjoyed the show in our own way.

Laughter can help take away the discomfort when you're hurting. There's nothing like letting go with a good belly laugh to help you pass through the pain. A sense of humor can turn your gray sky blue, allowing your sunny soul to shine through.

Don't hold back. At every opportunity, let your soul express itself with plenty of joyful laughter. It will serve you well!

When Movies Make Your Soul Sing

by Christine Tomasello

One of the first times I remember being moved by a film was when I watched *Julie & Julia*. It was a rainy afternoon, and though it was a while ago, I still remember how I felt when it ended – like my soul was singing!

As the credits rolled, I was acutely aware that my entire energy had changed. My mood lightened, my heart lifted, and my mindset opened. What had started as a casual way to pass the time had become a catalyst for me to see all the wondrous possibilities in the world. Suddenly, I was filled with hope, joy, and inspiration *all the way to my core*. Something about this movie had nudged my soul awake.

I don't know why that movie touched my soul so deeply; but I do know that whenever I feel disconnected and discombobulated, I can re-watch it and feel flooded with love and light all over again. And I carry those feelings with me for days.

If a movie ever leaves you feeling this way, take notice. Within that movie are messages you are meant to hear – messages of hope, encouragement, validation, and inspiration. You may not understand the messages on a conscious level, but your soul hears them and brightens with joy. And your soul holds onto these messages long after the movie is over.

We live in a busy world – a crazy, chaotic world composed of never-ending to-do lists, errands, and chores. It's easy to lose our connection with our soul when life takes over. Blessedly, if we can find a spare hour or two, movies that touch and inspire us are a simple way to reawaken that soulful connection.

Whenever you feel disconnected from your soul, take some time to nourish it by watching a movie that moves you. Revel in it, and take notice as your soul starts to stir. You'll know that happens when you suddenly find yourself smiling as you look around the room, contemplating the wondrous possibilities that exist in the world. Cherish that feeling. That's your soul singing.

REACH Your Soul Through Travel

by Debbie Lamb Turner

One of my favorite ways to connect with my soul is through travel. While I'd be hard-pressed to summarize in a single word just how greatly travel affects me, I can come pretty close with a single acronym – REACH – and a bit of explanation for each letter:

*R*elaxation – I regain balance. Traveling provides a meaningful break in my busy life. I feel nurtured when I suspend my daily responsibilities, step back, and reconnect with myself. I receive a new perspective and revived energy.

*E*xcitement – I come alive! When I have a pending adventure planned, I research the place, talk to people who've visited, check the weather, and plan what clothes to pack. The anticipation of going is exhilarating and lasts even longer than the actual trip!

*A*ppreciation – My heart opens. When I'm in a place for the first time, the sky appears bluer, the food smells more delicious, and I feel exhilarated. I become more in tune with my surroundings, and my appreciation is heightened. This renewed state of awareness doesn't dissipate when I return home. I find myself continuing to delight in my world again.

*C*onnection – I connect on a new level. When I travel with others, a different relationship is formed, regardless of whether it's with a spouse, partner, friend, or sister. I step out of my daily life to create a unique moment in time. When I share that special moment with someone I care about, a precious bond unites us.

*H*ealing – My wholeness is restored. A mini respite that nourishes my spirit and delights my senses is exactly what my soul craves.

In everyday life, unexpected (and often unwelcomed) challenges can drain, discourage, and sometimes even devastate us. It's important not to let these situations own us, and to remember we are much more than these experiences.

Regardless of our outer destination, travel can help all of us "REACH" beyond the daily trials of life and reconnect with our soul.

Add a Little Twist to Your Routine

by Thea Westra

Ever wake up tired, in the knowledge you're about to reenact the same play? Perhaps it's time to shake things up a little!

Routine can become very comfortable, avoiding any need to define and challenge your comfort zone. Although it may feel safe, however, allowing yourself to remain stuck in a dull routine of existence can bring you to a very low energy point and will strip the joy from your experience of life. It's a certain path to the death of soul and life spirit, leaving you to swirl inside a circle of limiting beliefs and disappointments in life.

If you want personal growth and soul evolution (and if you're reading this, I am sure you do), sometimes you'll need to leave some of the old behind and stretch yourself into something new.

Soul was never designed to support a life of monotony and routine. Connection with soul is your access to your sense of aliveness. It needs to be set free; allow it to jump out of your skin sometimes! That twinge of aliveness that comes from even minor adjustments in routine, THAT is your soul's response to being released from its cage, even if only for a few moments. The more often you release it, the more often you begin to recognize the path that your soul would want you to travel.

We can develop quirky ways of hiding the things that our soul wants and needs, only a couple of yards from the track that our routine takes us on each day.

You don't have to make dramatic changes in lifestyle, like changing your profession or ending a relationship. Don't buy into the myth that instant change is a magic pill that you can take in the evening, to have you wake up a different person next day.

Steer your life outside the often-walked road and gradually teach yourself to see things from a different vantage point. In those moments of a twist in your routine, you may experience an "Aha!", and THAT is your soul speaking.

Waking Up with Soul

by Anne Aleckson

"Good morning, Soul. What adventures shall we get up to today?" These are the first thoughts that come to mind as I teeter on the edge of wakefulness before my alarm shocks my sleeping body into action.

It wasn't always this way. The first thing that used to jump into my mind on waking was a feeling of regret that I had to pull myself out of a sleep time that was never enough in order to get ready to spend most of the day doing a job I disliked with people who I could not relate to in order to make the money I needed to maintain the unhappy life I had created.

I didn't recognize it as an unhappy life until I first heard my soul urging me into a new way of being. Up until that point, I was simply living life like everyone else – doing what was expected.

It was a subtle awakening, beginning with a statement that I had heard often enough: *Happiness is a choice.* For some reason, this time I felt something deep inside me asking me to find out if this was in fact true.

I know now that this was my soul connecting with me. It felt as though something was sitting behind my heart and knocking, as if to ask for an invitation to enter and be part of my life.

You might have even felt this yourself, a knowing that there must be more to life than this and that there is some part of you hidden away, just waiting to be found.

I found that part of myself, and every day now I nurture this connection by greeting my soul with an invitation to come and play with me, to adventure with me through the day.

Since beginning this practice, every day has been filled with happiness, unexpected connections, incredible synchronicities, and grand adventures.

Invite your soul into your day (*every* day!), and you'll gain a new best friend, a confidant, and a connection with something bigger than life itself.

The Beauty of Childlike Wonder

by Christine Callahan-Oke

I'm a big kid at heart. I love to be silly. What I especially love, though, is seeing the amazingness of the world through my young boys' eyes.

Until I had kids, I didn't think about how beautiful it is to experience life through eyes that aren't clouded by experience.

When we're kids, we do things with such passion and enthusiasm. We don't see limitations; we see opportunities for adventure. And we're not held back by funds or practicality. If we can't have or experience something firsthand, no problem! We can still experience it – by imagining it.

One of my favorite pastimes as a child was leafing through my parents' *National Geographic* magazines, imagining the amazing places I'd travel to and the incredible things I'd do.

Want to go to the Taj Mahal? Sure, let's go this afternoon!

The Amazon Rainforest? Yep – but let's have a snack first.

Want to be a princess in a castle? Yeah, of COURSE!

As we grow up, though, we become burdened with responsibilities and self-imposed limits. We rush around on autopilot, then search for the meaning in it all. And in our flurry, it's easy to lose touch with our innate childlike gift – the ability to find beauty in the moment, to see wonder and possibility in everything around us.

So now, when I find myself spiraling into stress or overwhelm, I'm reminded that I can drop everything for a bit and call out my inner kid. I play, dance, giggle, explore with my kids, or just do something spontaneous. I allow myself to strip away the adult layers and find joy in whatever calls to me, without judgment. In those moments, I'm more easily able to see the beauty in the smallest thing.

Rekindling my childlike wonder brings me back to center and makes my soul come alive. In those moments I feel lighter, freer, and like anything truly is possible.

And what a gift that is to my adult heart.

Non-Song Songs

by Amy Gage

Sound has such a powerful way of taking us to a new vibration, which can then make it easier to connect with our soul's vibration and receive messages from our higher self. One way I experience this is by creating what I call "non-song songs."

To do this, I sit down at my piano and play around with whatever notes feel good to me in that moment. I follow my inner rhythm. Although I'm not a particularly good piano player, this isn't about being a virtuoso – it's just about the *experience.*

After playing for a while, I start to sing whatever comes to my mind. It's like free-writing, but with singing. I don't censor my words, even if they don't make sense. When I'm in a flow of sound and not censoring what comes up, I'm allowing my soul to be heard and felt. I feel that the words are symbols – messages that my soul has for me.

When I feel complete, I usually like to write down whatever I sang, even if it doesn't flow quite yet. I just write the most important parts that stand out to me. After I write it down, I may clean it up, and I usually create a poem from it.

You don't need a musical instrument for this process, but I find that it helps me to have my piano. If you are a seasoned musician or songwriter, you could even use this as a way to create songs. For me, though, I think of these creations as "non-song songs" because I feel that when we get too caught up in something being a "real song" or sounding "good," our brains tend to edit too much, which can inhibit us from hearing our soul clearly. And the main point here is to use this process as a meditation to connect with the soul.

"Non-song songs" have been a beautiful sound meditation for me over the years. I hope that if this idea resonates with you, you'll give it a try. I truly believe that it will help you connect more deeply with your soul.

Shake It Out

by Isla Selupucin

"Oh come on, shake it out," is a theme in our household – the catalytic catchphrase for when tensions are rising and empathy is declining.

We all have times when even our most zen selves get lost in the noise and the stress. There is nothing graceful about the moment when you feel as though the world is exploding around you.

And although we might *know* that we can take control of our actions and change our patterns, just *knowing* isn't always enough to stop the surge of stress and energy pulsing through us.

For these times, my seven-year-old daughter and I have a special way of clearing and rebalancing. It requires embracing our inner silliness by simply taking time out in the moment to physically and mentally shake it out.

Here's how you, too, can take the reins and control rising anxiety by shaking it out:

Take a few deep breaths, find some privacy if you need to, and let loose. Let your whole body go. Dance around the living room, on the corner of a street, or in the aisle of a store. Let yourself be a crazy person for a while, but let the act be meaningful. Take another deep breath, smile, have fun, and embrace it.

The next time someone steals your parking space, jumps the line, or makes you want to cry…*shake!* Let the energy that has built up in your body explode out of you, and give it a clear signal that it's time to leave. Then, let the stillness that comes afterwards comfort you and ground you.

Shaking it out helps me and my daughter to release negativity and replace it with humour, love, and joy.

Give it a try yourself. Go on – shake it out!

Forget About Prim and Proper...and Get Messy!

by Keyra Conlinn

Whether we came from Adam and Eve, naked in the Garden of Eden, or from apes in the jungle, we came from a place where prim and proper didn't exist.

There's something primal about making a mess, about letting what you do show all over you. Kids know this, but adults forget. There is tremendous joy in allowing your expression to flow without restriction, and that openness and freedom can connect you to your divinity.

Opportunities to make a joyful mess abound in everyday life: that green hill in your neighbourhood that begs you to roll down it despite the possibility of grass stains, the puddle in the road that says "you know you want to," and that rich mud of the bay nearby that longs to be used as a canvas.

When nothing presents itself naturally, or it's too cold to be outside, get creative: finger paint (you don't need kids to do it!), bake something messy (anything with flour usually works well), or eat greasy food without cutlery...and without worrying about where the sauce ends up or how silly you might look!

Join in on messy local festivities or events. There's a reason why the Tomato Festival in Spain and the internationally known Color Run (billed as "The Happiest 5K on the Planet!") are so popular: socially approved abandonment of all protocol about being prim and proper! If these events, or others like them, aren't available where you live, get a group of friends and make some messy memories together!

Holidays are also a great excuse to get messy. At Halloween, dig out the pumpkin seeds and flesh by hand. At Christmas, put a gingerbread house together. (Whenever I do, I end up getting icing all over me – unavoidably, of course!)

If you're used to worrying about how you look, let go once in a while. Go within and connect with your soul, who truly doesn't care if you're prim and proper. Regardless of the season or your circumstances, there is always a way to get joyfully, soulfully, and thoroughly messy!

Awaken Your Inner Senses with Soulful Imagination

by Colleen E. Millett

Did you know that your imagination is a great way for you to connect with your soul? This process requires using not just one or two senses but all of them combined. This might sound like a lot of effort, but it actually comes very naturally to us. Whether you know it or not, you use your imagination every day. For example, when a friend is telling you a story and they are describing a person or a place, you probably find yourself imagining the person or scene in your head, right?

Let's play with this right now, shall we?

Picture a narrow path with sea grape trees on either side, leading you down a trail to a white sandy beach. Once on the beach, you remove your shoes and sink your feet into the warm sand, which flows between your toes. You feel the warm sea breeze dance gently across your skin and blow through your hair. You smell the saltiness in the air with a hint of coconut from the tanning lotions of the sunbathers who you see speckled along the beachfront. You watch and listen as one wave after another rises, crests, and then crashes at the shoreline. The rhythm soothes you like a lullaby. The seagulls caw as they glide overhead and fade into the brilliant red and orange sunset. You sit at the shoreline to enjoy a fragrant and juicy peach; the first bite causes you to salivate wildly as you remember picking peaches with your grandparents as a child. You feel the joy of your soul spring forth as all of your senses awaken you and remind you of who you really are.

Uniting your imagination and your senses is the perfect way to reconnect with your soul – and the possibilities for soulful imagination are endless! It only takes a few minutes to feel, smell, taste, see, and hear the things that you love most and reconnect with your soul in this very special way.

Soul Singing: Reconnecting to Joy

by Cynthia L. Ryals

Music has always held a special place in my life. As a baby, I loved cooing at the radio hidden inside of the pink, stuffed bunny placed in my crib. Music was a soothing companion – a constant friend that always brought me joy.

Throughout my youth, I experienced the power of music as a performer. I loved singing as much as I loved breathing. It was an honor to create and witness the emotion and magic of just the right song before an audience. Music has a way of reaching inside of us, touching places in our hearts that we dare not share with the world.

Over the years, I have come to understand that music is not just entertaining, it is spiritual – a soulful connection to our subconscious. Have you ever found yourself suddenly experiencing an emotion and then realized that a song was playing in the background that reminded you of a particular time in your life? That is music connecting with your soul.

In my spiritual journey, singing has become a powerful part of my meditation practice. It brings me into a place of joy and peace, where I can more easily connect with my soul. More importantly, I have discovered that my soul is longing to sing me love songs. These are the songs that have yet to be written; spontaneous songs of Spirit that celebrate my authentic self. When I allow those words and melodies to come forth, I find great healing. To me, this is true soul music.

Soul singing is simply allowing my inner voice of truth and wisdom to rise above the limiting beliefs and stories in my mind. I create a space for this connection by singing a simple verse or chorus that resonates with my spirit – something soothing and uplifting. As I relax, I allow other words and melodies to come forth, creating a new song. Connecting with my soul in this way brings me joy and strength for whatever life brings my way.

Today, allow your soul to sing you a love song, and reconnect to joy on your journey.

Leap into Soul Connection Through Adventure

by Diana Onuma

On a lazy afternoon of my relaxing holiday, I noticed the paragliding stand at the resort. The idea of gliding high in the sky both excited and scared me. I pondered…and went away. I returned and asked questions. I went away again. I pondered some more. And eventually, I booked my scary, exciting adventure.

At this point in my life, I had been procrastinating in making some important decisions. There was a very clear conflict between what I wanted to do and what others expected of me. I felt nervous and conflicted about making a change; but I felt a gentle, persistent prompt from my inner wisdom, urging me to take bold steps towards what I wanted. I instinctively felt that this paragliding adventure – jumping from a mountaintop into the "unknown" – would provide the inspiration I needed to follow my heart, push through my all-too-familiar comfort zone, and take a (literal) leap of faith!

When the big day finally arrived, however, my resolve began to waver. Moments before the jump, my internal gremlins started working overtime – telling me all the reasons why I should back out, reminding me of the risk involved, begging me to keep my feet on solid ground…until my inner wisdom shut down the gremlins with a single word: "SILENCE!!!"

And with that, I leapt.

During the flight, I felt a shift in the core of my being. I reconnected with a part of me that had been lost. I was no longer concerned about expectations. All of my earlier reservations and misgivings simply fell away, leaving me with a powerful sense of peace and freedom.

Thanks to this adventure, my old "friends" – procrastination and fear – have been replaced with what I call "the art of allowing and living in my light." I've learned to honour the whispers of wisdom that persistently call to me, offering soulful guidance, filling me with courage, and helping me blossom.

I invite you, too, to connect with your spirit of adventure, to walk the path to your deeper truth, and to break through your comfort zone and leap into the fullness of who you truly are.

Finding Joy Inside a Hula Hoop

by Arwen Lynch-Poe

Before I became a professional joy-seeker, I was a bitter woman – happiest when I was shredding someone for something I deemed foolish. I didn't care if I hurt them; my own pain needed release. Talk about the wrong kind of projection!

I lost friends because of my toxicity – friends who have never allowed me back in their lives. I lost more than that, though; I lost my connection to my own self. I lost the thread that had always led me back to my soul. Like Theseus entering the labyrinth, I seemed doomed to be lost with no one to hear me cry.

Mythological drama aside, I needed help. That came in the form of my younger sister and a hula hoop. She told me that the smartest thing she'd learned was how to hold a hula hoop. As I questioned her sanity, she demonstrated by putting her hands out to either side of her waist, saying, "That's my hula hoop. I can only control what's inside my hula hoop."

That brought my tower down. In tarot, my favorite introspection tool, the Tower tends to be built on lies we tell ourselves. When it falls, it is a significant energy shift. In that moment with my sister, I experienced an immediate shift. I realized that my anger, pain, and bitterness were all self-inflicted. My life was toxic because I was focused on what I couldn't change or control. I was focused on everything outside my hula hoop, and all the anger and bitterness that I had been carrying were useless time-wasters.

The healing shift didn't happen right away. I had to continually remind myself that I could only control what was inside my own hula hoop. Repetition and dedication to the concept of seeking joy as a way of life pulled me out of that ugly, soul-crushing life I'd been living. I gave up trying to manage anything other than myself. I've re-emerged as a more compassionate woman. I reconnected to my own soul's purpose and even adopted a new motto: *Seek joy, y'all. Pass it on.*

What's in *your* hula hoop?

Honoring Your Quirkiness

by April Williams

For so many years I tried to hide my light, my truth, my soul. I toned down my spunkiness, rounded my jagged edges, and really focused on replicating my surroundings so as not to stand out. I forced back into the margins anything that didn't fall neatly into place:

- My made-up words
- My lack of grace
- My "distinguished" dance moves
- My daydreamy, somewhat spacey demeanor
- The way I ate french fries (always leaving the "butts")

What I didn't realize in these times of suppression was that I was actually disconnecting myself from my soul – my true self. As time passed, however, I gained wisdom within, which pointed me to many truths – a major one being that my quirks were the very points that distinguished me from everyone else on this planet.

Quirks arise from rarity. They undeniably stand out amongst the crowd. Whether they are acceptable or not seems to depend on the audience. So with this information we can conclude that, in all reality, we are all quirks – unique, exquisite, one-of-a-kind gems that cannot be reproduced. This is why it would make sense to own, embrace, and honor the quirkiness that emanates from within in order to connect more closely with our soul. So today, ask yourself:

- What are my peculiar patterns?
- My tragically textured – yet treasured trademarks?
- My wonky, weathered, scrumptiously silly, or favorably fruity traits (the ones that stand out like a sore thumb – the ones I couldn't hide if I tried)?

Then *own* these quirks of yours! Get down and dirty, funky and flirty with as many quirks as you feel comfortable with today. I think you'll find, besides being one of a kind, that to your soul you'll be a lot less blind. I'm confident that the more you honor the unique quirkiness that is you, the more you'll start to see and more closely connect with your one and only soul.

Allow Your Soul to Sing

by Monica Wilcox

I close my eyes, take a deep breath, feel the beat, and visualize the notes.

In my mind, the piano strokes metamorphosize as blue slits sparkling between my ribs. I imagine the steady melody of the cello winding in and out of my skull like a cascading aurora borealis. The hum of a female voice blooms as a purple spiral from my gut to my breastbone. I feel yearning – my own or another's, I do not know. I accept whatever the music stimulates within me. In this moment, my soul sings.

Music fell out of my life the day I moved to Germany in 1996. The wide spectrum of American radio shriveled down into a single channel of NPR's talk radio. My stereo, useless without a large electric converter, stayed in its moving box. The day I returned to America, I turned on my car radio and rediscovered the power of music. Its sway returned to my hips, its vibration burned in my bones, its rhythm tugged at my toes, while the lyrics dusted my lips. Oh, how I had missed it!

Now, I will not let a day pass without a melody to carry me through. I wake to pop music, dress to Irish folk, drive to country, write to New Age, and sleep to chirping crickets and running streams. My playlists are titled by the mood I wish to invoke inside myself.

Music is a magic carpet that rides upon sound waves. A few notes of a specific song and suddenly we are revisiting our first homecoming dance, our favorite movie, or our grandfather's funeral. One song can take us out of a bad mood while the next one plunges us into heartbreak. Music encompasses the vast totality of our human experience: past, present, and future.

Start with a tune that feels like the song of your soul. Find another and another until you have a playlist. Now close your eyes, take a breath, feel the beat, visualize the notes, and allow your soul to sing.

Spinning with Joy

by Pam McKinney

Remember as a child when you looked outside and saw the season's first snow begin to fall? Can you feel how excited you were to rush outside and be in it, even though nothing had yet accumulated on the ground? You looked up into the sky and watched those unique little snowflakes floating down toward you. You reached out your arms and started to spin around, feeling the snowflakes lightly fall on your cheeks and your tongue. The anticipation of a "snow day" spent sledding or building a fort or a snowman made this the most perfect day in the world. You were spinning with joy!

As adults, we tend to get so absorbed and overwhelmed with our to-do lists that we forget to connect with our soul through simple, joy-filled moments. I was reminded of just how important and precious these moments are when I had the opportunity to care for a friend's beautiful little girl for the first two years of her life. Through her, I learned how connecting to my soul in moments of joy could transform my life. I began to see the innate beauty of my own soul. She brought back those feelings of ultimate joy and freedom as we spun around, danced, and laughed. Her pure and complete connection helped me feel my own, and I allowed myself that inner knowing that nothing is impossible for me to be or do.

During that time, I also began taking an NIA (Non-Impact Aerobics) class. One of our routines involved us spinning around, eyes closed, arms outstretched. As I was spinning, engrossed and enthralled with the music, tears began to flow as I found myself releasing all my cares and worries and once again feeling connected with my soul. In that moment, I was a beautiful, innocent child, anticipating all kinds of wonderful adventures and knowing that I could do anything and everything I want to because I am always connected and free to choose. I was literally spinning with joy, which felt amazing!

I welcome you to give it a try. I hope it reconnects you with your childlike wonder as well!

Embracing New Experiences

by Donna S. Priesmeyer

My weekend in the country cottage was absolutely idyllic. I savored the beautiful simplicity in those quiet moments of the morning when I was awakened by a ray of sunlight and felt inspired to sit on the porch, listen to the birds sing, watch the sun rise over the meadow, and become one with the beauty and solace of nature. I felt such gratitude that I had responded to the calling of my soul, urging me to come away, breathe in the cool air, rest in the countryside, and be healed by the pristine palette of nature. It was Grace magnified on so many levels.

For years, I had longed to stand on holy ground where pilgrims once stood. The sacred sites spoke to my heart, calling me to experience life apart from the normal, day-to-day routine. Then a spiritual teacher invited me to travel to a number of sacred locations. I embraced these new experiences with the openhearted anticipation of a child. In my travels, I connected with the ancient Anasazi in the American Southwest, was amazed by the metaphysical symbolism of the Rosslyn Chapel, visualized a more loving and expansive world in the stone circles of Scotland, watched the sun rise from the center of Stonehenge, reflected on my life in the Oracle's Cave at Delphi, prayed in the Basilica of St. Francis, and had profound visions while meditating in the Great Pyramid of Giza. Filled with gratitude for each new experience, I connected with past memories that prepared me for insights yet to be revealed. It was amazing to get out of my comfort zone and embrace these opportunities.

Reflecting on these experiences, I realized that this simple weekend in a quaint country cottage was also amazing. It seemed centuries away from the fast-paced lifestyle to which I am accustomed. It offered the quiet and solitude that led to the adventure of going within, feeling one with nature, opening my heart to the Creator of All That Is, and truly connecting with my soul. I had traveled all over the world to feel the deep-soul connection I was experiencing in that moment.

The Peekaboo Process

by Mimi Quick

Connecting with your soul can be fun!

Let's bring up those energy levels today. Did you know that adding play to your day can reduce stress levels and help you perform better in business and all areas of your life? Did you know that many people are living on automatic pilot, doing the same thing day in and day out, living lives with little hope and not ever really connecting with their souls?

If you don't want to be stuck in a rut and are ready for deeper connection with yourself, I have created a really fun way to do it. I created this process years ago for a client who seemed to allow her mind to get in the way of her deeply connecting with her soul. She loved it, and I think you will, too.

Let's raise your energy vibes to a higher level and move into fun while connecting with your soul. Here's what you'll need:

1. Yourself
2. A quiet place
3. The openness and willingness to have fun
4. A mirror

All you have to do is allow your inner child to play along with you in this process.

Are you ready?

Standing or sitting in front of a mirror, place your hands over your closed eyes. You'll see darkness and maybe a few swirls of light. Notice the quiet, notice the light, and watch as the light gets brighter. As you do, also notice the inner part of you – your soul.

Connect deeply with that sacred part of you – that magical, powerful, and all-knowing place within you.

Now, get ready to share that amazingness with the world. Take your hands off your eyes and shout "Peekaboo!" and open your eyes. Do you see your amazingness looking back at you? Do this three times to shift to a more playful energy, give yourself a deep connection with your soul, and bring up the fun!

The Art of Inner Celebration

by Laurie Seymour

When was the last time you celebrated something? Did you celebrate a birthday or an anniversary? A promotion or some other big achievement?

Frequently, celebration means acknowledging something outside of ourselves, giving it special attention, significance, and value. But you can also do this with your inner life – you can practice the art of inner celebration!

If you look within, you'll find so much that's worthy of celebration. Consider something as fundamental as your own breath. Spend a quiet moment appreciating its life-giving quality, and you'll realize the miracle it entails. There's no need for you to control the breath, nothing to orchestrate as it does the job of nourishing you. No chemistry degree is required to conduct the complex oxygen/carbon interchange. You release your breath naturally, effortlessly; and as you receive, you are energized and nourished. Take a moment to celebrate this all-too-often overlooked process.

Continue your celebration by considering how a similar process – the exchange of circulating energy, giving and receiving – plays out in your daily life. You receive and can then offer out. If you turn your back on receiving – with thoughts of insufficiency or denial – you stop the flow. Something inside of you begins to shrivel. Likewise, if you hold back from giving, you deny yourself the fullness of who you are and the joy that you can experience.

Celebrate and appreciate the natural flow of energy in all areas of your life. Through your gratitude, you extend thanks for the creative partnership that exists between you and the Universe. And as you do so, your connection with yourself, your soul, and the entire world is enriched.

When you practice the art of inner celebration, you acknowledge yourself – and life itself – with a feeling of reverence. A door opens within you to worlds of new possibility. You remember that you are a miracle in this very moment. You celebrate being alive.

Soul Playing

by Carol Owens

It started like any other day. I attended to my morning routine of exercise, a shower, getting dressed, and eating breakfast. I picked up clutter and put away the endless things that had been left where they were dropped.

Then I headed to my office to begin my workday. (I work from home as a writer, so my office is close by!) I had deadlines to meet and clients to talk to. Within minutes, however, I knew it wasn't going to be a typical day.

My son needed someone to take care of his two kids for the day. I said I would – thinking that they could play while I worked. My grandkids had other ideas, however. Each time I sat down to work, one of the girls needed me to help them play. I began worrying that I wouldn't get my work done on time. I was getting stressed and cranky.

Finally, the older of the two (who is five), asked me to play pretend with them. She knows this is something we can do together and have fun. On this particular day, she decided we were going to pretend to be butterflies. Being a butterfly meant we had to fly freely, leaving our worries and responsibilities behind.

We pretended to fly, fluttering from one flower to the next in the yard. Each time we landed, we had to say, "Thank you for this beautiful flower." Both girls were laughing and carefree. At first I felt silly. Then I heard my soul saying, "Let go. Be yourself."

I felt myself being free and innocent. I felt my soul expand, and I let my worries go – placing all my love and attention on pretending to be a butterfly. In the end, I felt more connected to who I am than I had in a long time.

Just watching the innocence of children as they put their heart and soul into everything they do brings joy to my soul. Their little spirit shines a bright light that connects to my soul – especially when I join in the playful, soulful fun!

Experience the Infinite Through Travel

by Keyra Conlinn

Travel ignites our senses and helps us connect with our soul in ways we might never know if we remain static our whole lives; it opens our eyes to new possibilities.

I've never lost the curiosity of a child, so whenever I encounter people from other cultures, I observe intently – sometimes staring in awe, sometimes giddy. I marvel at the sounds they make that are so natural to them but which I would need training to produce. It amazes me that we're all given the same vocal organs but we use them in such different ways!

Experiencing the multitude of vibrations from unimaginable instruments also lifts me to another place. I feel a deep connection in such moments – not usually because of the music itself but because of the joy of discovery. Sure, there are some sounds that my ears decide they'd rather not hear again, but even that brings a chuckle: "Well, dear Universe," I think, "You've done it again; you've shown me your limitlessness."

It isn't just sound that can astound us, but also sights, smells, tastes, and textures – as well as the beauty of cultural diversity, which always serves to connect me to joy as I contemplate the infinite ways that life finds expression.

In addition to appreciating diversity, travel also provides a wonderful opportunity to appreciate the beauty of our common humanity. In doing so, we no longer feel alone. We can recognize inherent struggles that we all face, as well as values that we all hold (though in varying degrees and means of expression).

I've noticed that no matter what country you're in, everyone celebrates new life. When babies come around, everyone brightens and softens – the mood becomes light. Likewise, when there is a death, we become somber, honoring the person or the life of the person who has departed.

Regardless of where you go or what senses you ignite while you're there, travel offers your soul a chance to breathe and expand. It helps you see our diversity *and* our commonality as divine – and to connect with this Divinity…from anywhere in the world.

The pH of Our Soul

by Cindia Carrere

"Playfulness is absolutely necessary for your health and wellbeing – it's as important as the foods you eat and the thoughts you think."
- Denise Linn

Here's an incredible statistic: Did you know that there is 40 times more energy in empty space than in matter? Taking time out to play allows you to tap into the energy available in the spaces between the notes in your life's song.

Stress and overwhelm try to convince you that you never have enough time and that you can't afford to play, but play actually allows you to get *more* done in *less* time. Play sharpens your senses, dissolves blocks, and gives breakthrough results.

Biologically, pH stands for *potential hydrogen*, which has to do with the acid/alkaline balance in the body. An overly acidic condition is hard on your body, while an alkaline state promotes internal health and wellbeing. Soulfully, pH stands for *Playful Healing*. Resistance and stress are acidic, while creativity, intuition, and play thrive in an "alkaline environment." A diet of acidic thoughts, such as "you're not good enough" or "you have to be perfect to be loved," weakens the soul's health because they cause contraction.

Play is expansive and provides the freedom to make "happy mistakes." With room to explore, energy flows more easily through empty space than blocked matter. When you are no longer in resistance, ideas and solutions come in much faster.

Having fun is key to allowing health and wholeness. It invites you to be present and connects you with your bliss. When engaged in play, your abundance, love, and healing are easier to receive. Play also helps you to know yourself better, break old habits, and gain confidence.

Creativity and having fun let you release pain, refresh your mind, and renew your spirit. When you are aligned, you thrive.

Tune in to the sweet melody of your soul by creating space every day for playful healing. Flip the switch from struggle and dissonance to ease and flow, and reconnect with how inspiring and powerful you truly are.

Hot-Air Balloon Ride

by Aliza Bloom Robinson

Recently, I went flying in a hot-air balloon, a ride that took me up, up, and away to a brand-new perspective. Soaring above the Earth, I found peace and freedom. It was quiet – oh so quiet, like all the world was still.

We took off as the sun was coming up, and we flew with it. Up, up we went, with no sense of elevation change, then back down again. One moment we were dropping down over a river, the basket touching the water below us; the very next we were rising up again, and in only seconds we were soaring over 3,000 feet above the ground!

Looking at this balloon ride metaphorically, the sensation is like being lifted from the mire of our daily lives into a new perspective. Whether you are feeling stuck, struggling with a problem, or are simply bored, imagine in your mind's eye that you are being raised up in a hot-air balloon. Rise above your thinking mind, above all the challenges and distractions of your daily life. Imagine receiving a new, higher perspective – one that does not focus on small details, but rather a grander vision. One where you can see the beginning and also the end of your current situation.

As you are lifted, your awareness changes. From this bird's-eye view, the challenges become smaller, inconsequential even. From here you can see a new and greater picture, and you discover peace in your soul and in the world. Imagine hanging out in the heights until peace pervades. Return with a sense of clarity, serenity, freedom, wisdom, and a newfound connection with your soul.

Tune into Your Soul

by Alicia Isaacs Howes

You know how your favourite piece of music or a song can conjure up a sense of peace or joy, sometimes in just a few notes? Well, you can tune into your own soul's frequency in a very similar way – without a radio, iPod, or CD player!

I used to sing and hum a lot as a child. My bursts of vocal joy weren't always appreciated, however. I was scolded by a teacher for belting out "Zip-a-Dee-Doo-Dah" on the way to class and was mortified when my consulting manager asked me to stop singing in the break room, as it disturbed my colleagues. I understood their perspectives, but that didn't make it hurt any less. Gradually, I learned to suppress this impulse.

Years later, after a healing crisis sparked my personal healing journey, I was blessed to live in the countryside where I loved to walk in the woods every day to meditate. As I tuned into the rhythm of nature, I began to feel the urge to hum. One day, I simply couldn't resist any longer and my intentions burst forth in a song! I felt so free, with no need to monitor the volume or wonder what someone might think or say.

I began to sing my intentions every day, often surprised when the words would rhyme in the most beautifully fluid ways. My inner melody bubbled up more often, and I began to honour it instead of repress it.

You are pulsing with energy. When you hum or sing, you act as a tuning fork and channel a frequency through your cells so they can dance to your soul's rhythm.

Don't worry about how you sound, as that takes you away from your feelings, which are the language of your soul. Instead, focus on your intention, prayer, or the next notes in your heart. Let the words or sounds move up from your chest, through your throat, and into the air around you. Breathe them in, then breathe them out into your world.

Enjoy tuning into your soul so harmony can flow!

Set a Swing in Motion

by Monica Wilcox

Push . . . pull.

A swing is gravity experienced in the horizontal.

Push . . . pull.

A swing is a rhythm that beats beyond our culture, wealth, race, sex, weight, height, or ability.

Push . . . pull.

A swing is wind in your hair, flapping feet, arched back, grasping hands and an easy heart.

Push . . . pull.

A swing is a plank of joy.

We installed a swing between two oversized evergreen trees in a gap that begged to be filled with joy. Our kids took to it like ants to sugar. Then their friends showed up for a ride. Then the kids we didn't know started sneaking into the backyard to give the glorious 25-foot-long monster a try.

Now, I'm the one sneaking out each day. With the gentle thrust of my feet, I'm instantly transported into tender physical sensation. My mind clears of all the should-dos, could-dos, and didn't-dos. My breathing automatically slows as my legs take up a pace they acquired when I was four. I'm no longer moving through my backyard but existing *in it.* The birds venture closer than when I'm on my feet. The boughs of the trees are my umbrella, the ground my launching pad. Light and shadow splash across my skin. I am flesh in motion, mind at rest, soul surfacing.

Today, I watched one of our roofers sneak toward our swing. He was answering a call he couldn't ignore, and by the look he gave his co-workers, he was a bit embarrassed by it. He courageously took a seat and began to swing – allowing himself to feel giddy and joyful.

A swing in motion is like our soul: a steady, joyful energy patiently waiting for our embrace. Playgrounds are as numerous as coffee shops. Find your own swing to set in motion.

A Soulful Adventure

by Karen Gibbs

Sometimes our souls crave change – a new experience, an adventure, something to lift our spirits out of the mundane. I recently embraced this challenge by swapping suburbia for a home on wheels and heading off into the great unknown of Australia's magical Northern Territory.

Driving north on the Stuart Highway took me through arid countryside that wasn't as deserted as it first appeared. I saw kangaroos searching for food in the sparsely vegetated terrain. Further north, I witnessed majestic eagles perched on lifeless trees or scattering in flight just in time to avoid the passing vehicle.

It's a harsh country, but undeniably brilliant. The sky is the deepest azure, in stark contrast to the red earth as far as the eye can see. The beauty was indescribable, and somehow the vast emptiness filled my entire being. Looking out across the landscape brought a deep connection within me, a feeling of complete oneness with God.

Camping at the Mataranka hot springs enhanced this connection. The warm, crystal-clear water surrounded by lush palms offered an idyllic swimming experience. Two kilometers away, at Bitter Springs, the deep, flowing water meandered into the distance. Surrounded by a dense tropical woodland with abundant birdlife, I felt a deep sense of peace and tranquility.

Under the healing warmth of the sun, I floated down the spring, enjoying the passing scenery and the gentle chatter of birds. I could see right to the sandy bottom, six feet below, where the occasional boulder or fallen palm frond lay scattered on the pristine sand. The warmth enfolded my entire being as I allowed this new experience to renew and strengthen my soul.

As much as I (like many people) often resist change, I've found that it can delight the senses and reawaken the soul. If you're ready for some soulful rejuvenation, perhaps it's time to embrace an adventure of your own!

Chapter 5
Wellness & Self-Care

There's no doubt about it: most of us are super busy, and sometimes it feels like our world is moving faster and faster. Technology has made it possible for us to connect with each other in wonderful ways, but it has also made it harder to disconnect – since the online world never shuts off. No matter how long we've been away (five hours, five minutes, or five seconds), there will always be something new to see on our Facebook wall or to respond to via email. Because technology never takes a breather, sometimes we feel that we have to keep pushing ourselves to always be on, too. And if we aren't conscious of it, the more connected we become to the outside world – others, our work, and technology – the more disconnected we can feel from ourselves and our soul.

We've definitely fallen into this trap. After a decade of working for ourselves, we unconsciously got into the habit of working all the time and putting everyone else's needs before our own. We never wanted to say no to anyone, and we wanted to appear superhuman somehow. As a result, we ended up completely depleting ourselves physically, emotionally, and spiritually. It's only in the last couple of years that we've begun to take concrete, conscious steps toward loving ourselves again and really honoring our own self-care, which feels really good.

We know that we aren't alone in feeling overwhelmed with life at times, and so we're really excited to share this chapter with you. It includes many ways for all of us to take better care of ourselves and put our own care at the top of our to-do list. We've found that when we do this, we feel so much better and we have much more to give...to ourselves and also to others. It's our hope that you'll give many of these practices a try and feel yourself connecting with your soul in the process!

Start the Day by Connecting Within

by Christine Callahan-Oke

There's something powerful about nurturing my soul at the start of the day. It's like I'm saying to my soul, *I'm making you a priority.*

In the morning, I take time to connect within. It's become an essential part of feeling grounded, clear, calm, and like *myself.*

But it wasn't always like this.

Not all that long ago I was working part-time, writing, building a business on the side, and taking online courses. All of these were spread throughout the day and evening at no particular time, and it all felt so fragmented. I was disconnected from my inner wisdom and felt spread too thin.

Something had to change. I needed soulful *me* time.

A friend suggested I carve a bit of time out for myself each morning so I could begin the day in a heart-centered way. Then, whatever happened during the rest of the day, I'd know that I'd taken that time for myself.

I was excited to give it a go, not knowing the impact it would have. I took at least half an hour each morning for *me.* And it was wonderful! I started in the shower, thinking about things I was grateful for and speaking them aloud. Later, I gave myself time to meditate, write, walk in nature, or connect with my soul in whatever way felt right.

That time became so important to me that not only did I need to continue it – I needed to extend it! So I did. I was able to rearrange my schedule so I could do my part-time work in the afternoon and my coursework in the evenings. That left my morning time for *me.*

I now find that when I don't nurture my soul in the morning, I feel out of sorts. That's an important signal for me to be gentle with myself, regroup, and simply start again the next day. And when I do, I come home to *me.*

Create Your Sacred Spa Life at Home

by Jerri Eddington

Have you been sweeping self-care under the rug? Do you think you don't have the money to devote to yourself or the time to relax?

When it comes to self-care and relaxation, I resonate with John Holland's quote: "Taking the time to relax is my right – my gift to myself and my spirit."

Creating sacred self-care time is essential for you – both personally and in business. Without YOU, your business cannot survive – let alone thrive! How do I know? I ignored self-care for years until my body totally shut down. I literally couldn't walk across the room. I made a vow that if I ever regained my energy, I would never take the importance of self-care for granted again.

I decided to start my self-care in my master bathroom by creating a home spa, and my spa bath quickly became my new daily ritual. These are the steps I use to create a serene, spa-like atmosphere that recharges and revitalizes my soul:

- I clear any clutter out of the area and turn down the lights.
- While the warm water fills the tub, I light a lavender candle and turn on some soft, soothing music.
- I add Dead Sea salt to the water in order to release tension, tightness, and toxins.
- I add four or five drops of my favorite essential oil, "Joy," which has a high-frequency vibration and can quickly shift your energy.
- I use Yoga Toes® as a fun, easy way for me to relax and refresh my toes as I soak.
- I turn on a soft light that goes through the seven main chakra colors…to cleanse and clear the chakras.
- As I soak in the tub, I use this time to meditate and to connect with The Creator of All That Is. I gently place both hands across my heart space, the bridge between my physical and spiritual worlds, and know that all is well. And so it is.

Thanks to my daily spa time, I am embracing the importance of self-care and am connecting to my soul. I invite you to do the same.

Soul Clarity from the Fridge

by Ramona Remesat

I probably looked like a one-person circus act. Struggling to get out of a sweaty sports top with an arm that wouldn't bend must have looked comical but was anything but fun. Each time I tried to lift my arm above my head, or behind my back, searing pain would scream, "You have a frozen shoulder, silly: What are you trying to do here?"

When you go through a health challenge, it's easy to get down in the dumps; but my experience brought me one of the biggest blessings in my life: the ability to clearly hear the voice of my soul.

While struggling with my frozen shoulder, I got an intuitive nudge to change my diet, so I signed up for a 30-day raw-diet challenge. I went at it hard core, giving up all dairy, meat, grains, eggs, caffeine, sugar, and alcohol for one month. Amazingly, my pain and stiffness went away, and I quickly restored my range of motion. But what was even more amazing was the fact that I could suddenly "hear" my inner guidance (the voice of my soul) as if it were coming through in high-definition stereo! It was like all the wholesome food I was eating had magically tuned my antennae, allowing me to tap into my intuition on a level I had never before experienced.

I went into research mode, looking at the relationship between the foods and beverages we consume and how they impact us beyond just our physical bodies. I learned that substances like sugar, wheat, caffeine, and dairy severely impact our aura (the force field of energy protection around us), which then impacts our ability to clearly access our divine guidance. Being mindful of what you consume can help bolster the aura and enhance your ability to better tap into your intuition and hear what your soul is really saying to you.

Sit with this information. If it resonates with you, it just might be time to put down that latte and pick up that apple. Your mind, body, and spirit will thank you.

Believe You're Worthy of Love

by Brenda Reiss

After three divorces and several years of no relationships, I was forced to admit that, at my core, I didn't feel worthy of lasting love.

When I finally did attract a loving partner into my life, I thought I had healed this belief. Over time, however, I noticed an odd pattern: The more this wonderful man showered me with love, the more I pushed him away. I received a big wake-up call when he asked me, "Do you feel worthy of being adored, appreciated, respected, and loved?" Although my mouth said *yes*, I felt a heaviness tugging at my heart.

Shoot! I guess I had more work to do after all!

This awareness triggered a new stage of my healing journey. This time, I decided to approach it consciously – starting with simply naming my belief: "unworthiness." Next, I wrote down all the times it had shown up in my life: in all of my relationships with men, in friendships, and also with myself! As difficult as it was to confront this pattern, I decided not to judge myself or the belief. Instead, I saw that it wasn't here to punish me but to keep me safe. And over time, I began to convince myself that I *was* safe and that I no longer needed this belief's protection.

Then came the biggest step of all: loving myself for having this belief. After all, this belief had been the catalyst for deep emotional healing. This new perspective helped me release that old belief and embrace my worthiness…and the best relationship of my life!

Although it hasn't always been easy, this journey has taught me that I have a choice about my beliefs, and I have the tools to change them – and so do you! If you want to change your beliefs about love, worthiness, or anything else in your life, I hope you'll take your own journey of awareness, acceptance, transformation, and love. It's a wonderful way to connect with your soul – that part of you who always knows how worthy you truly are.

Walking with a Purpose

by Jaden Sterling

I wasn't surprised to learn that Ludwig van Beethoven often walked in nature with a notebook and pen, sketching ideas as they came to him. I, too, find this ritual incredibly helpful amidst the day-to-day noise and (oftentimes) confusion.

Much is happening as we walk and commune with nature. First, both sides of the brain are stimulated as our arms and legs crisscross. Second, the conscious thinking mind is occupied with the task of walking, which allows for an easier connection with the soul.

Walking with a purpose – with the goal of receiving soul guidance – can keep you fit and "in the know." This process is simple: grab a pen and a notebook. On the top of a blank page, write what you desire to know. Then go for a 20-minute walk.

While walking, as you notice ideas pop into your mind, stop to write them down. When receiving inspired thoughts, we often say, "I'll remember this," and we don't write them down. However, inspired guidance is tricky because it often leaves just as fast as it comes, which is why you will want to write it down.

Walking with a purpose to receive soul guidance is an efficient and wonderful use of time and energy. Now that you know this incredibly helpful process, you might find it useful to grab a notebook and pen and go for a 20-minute walk…*with a purpose!*

Take a 10-Minute Break from Technology

by Lynn M. Smith

Technology is a real asset, but could it be disconnecting you from your soul? Every time your phone rings or you receive an e-mail, text, or IM, your adrenal glands give you a jolt, sending you into fight-or-flight mode. Repeatedly spending your days in this state can exhaust you and rob you of peace.

I often recommend that clients disconnect from technology as a way to manage stress. And not just putting the phone on vibrate, either. A vibrating phone still triggers your reaction; and if you are in anticipation of receiving a call or text, you are still in that heightened state of awareness.

Peace, and connecting with what's within, happens in the silence. By just sitting in that space and breathing deeply, you can reduce your blood pressure and cortisol levels. But even more important than the physical benefits, unplugging can connect you with your soul.

In that stillness, your thoughts quiet. Serenity surrounds. Peace begins, and answers are found. Stillness is the best place to connect with your intuition. We all have an inner voice we can turn to, but that voice easily gets drowned out by our technological environment.

This doesn't mean that you have to eliminate technology from your life. All it takes is 10 minutes a day. Simply choose a place where you can be undisturbed, move away from your computer, and turn your phone off.

The next step is to embrace the silence. This may be awkward at first and you may get impatient, but trust the process. Let go of thoughts as they come up. Return to the stillness. Try not to judge yourself if you have trouble quieting. This is a practice. Give yourself permission to be imperfect.

After some practice, you'll start looking forward to setting technology aside, relishing that moment of peace in your busy day. You'll find that these sessions start to inspire you, to refuel you. The more you practice this, the more serenity you'll experience. It might take some effort at first, but connecting with your soul is always worth it!

Coming Alive Through the Rhythm of Movement

by Maura Smith

One of my favorite ways to connect deeply with my soul is through sports. Although I wouldn't consider myself an athlete by any means, there are certain sports that really make me feel alive. This aliveness, or higher vibration, is a signal that I'm one with my soul.

Where I live in Canada, our winters are pretty cold. Although a lot of people grumble about it, snowfalls are my signal to get out into the woods and head up to my favorite Nordic ski trails. I love feeling the fresh air, experiencing the rhythm of skiing, and being alone with nature. The gentle slopes of the trails wind this way and that, surrounded by forests of tall pine trees. With each glide of my skis, I feel in the flow, connected to the trees, and fully alive. Breathing in the scent of the evergreens and seeing the beautiful crystalline snowflakes around me is one of the most awesome sensations I've ever experienced.

I've had similar feelings of being fully connected and living through my soul in the summers when I'm swimming in the bay. When I get in that space, everything seems to merge together: the water, the air, my breathing, and my sense of presence. It's as if all that exists is a high vibration that runs through me. Each time I come up to take a breath, I feel the fresh water against my skin and glimpse the sun, trees, and water. As the rhythm of my movement blends in with the waves that wash over me, I know I'm fully alive.

If this type of experience calls to you, I invite you to engage in regular outdoor activities, too. The magic of sports is that you're embodying that which you are. Blending your movement with the sensations of being outdoors really brings the experience home – uniting body and soul in the joyful flow of life.

Mirror, Mirror

by Karen Hicks

It's wonderful to observe babies and toddlers watching themselves in a mirror. Babies reach out their hands to explore, eyes sparkling, smiling. They show genuine interest in the person looking back at them, and they may even start a conversation! Toddlers might do all of that, as well as prance, dance, and pose. So much acceptance and self-love!

Somewhere along the road, though, we lose that magical sense of self exploration. As pre-teens or even earlier, we begin to see ourselves through a critical lens. When we look at ourselves in the mirror, the first thought is often of what is wrong with the image. We start listing all the things we would change, the things that "aren't enough" (or are "too much").

Right now, go to the mirror and look at yourself. Notice what thoughts come to mind, and then come back to finish reading this piece.

If you had critical thoughts when you looked at yourself, here are two exercises that, when practiced daily, will help you find your way back to yourself:

1. On a mirror in your bedroom, post a baby picture of yourself. Each morning, say something nice – out loud – to the little person in the picture…then go to exercise #2.
2. Look at yourself in the mirror and notice one thing that you like, that you fully accept. Perhaps it is your chin, your ear lobes, or the curve of an eyebrow. Out loud, acknowledge this part by saying, "I like...." Focus on this part each day until you find another part you like, and so on.

Repeat at bedtime.

Do this every day, and after a couple of weeks, post another picture of yourself at an older age. Keep posting new pictures, and keep looking at yourself. Eventually, you will take in your whole face with acceptance and love. Look deeply into your eyes – for they are the windows to your soul, and your soul is waiting for your love!

Embrace the Innocence of Your Inner Child

by Radavie

Embracing our inner child opens the door to emotional and spiritual wellbeing, supporting us in moving toward higher consciousness. Due to parental and social conditioning, however, our innocence is often covered with defensive behaviors, protective personalities, and blame. So often as adults, we repeat thoughts such as, "If this had never happened to me, I would be…" We live in this longing, while blaming our past.

For me, the negative messages began almost as soon as I was born. My mother went through a difficult childbirth, and I had to be extracted by the midwife because of an unusual breach. We both could have died. Throughout my childhood, my mother often said, "You came to kill me."

The shame from my mother's repeated blame haunted me for years. My innocence was replaced with the thought, "I am a bad person." I emotionally withdrew from my family and wondered why I was born. With that, I walked away from my inner child, leaving her with my emotional wounds.

Years later, however, my inner child returned – appearing before me each day for several weeks, facing me with the saddest eyes I'd ever seen. I tried to lock her out, but she kept coming back until I finally got her message: She was a part of my soul that had to be integrated. She also revealed my soul's calling: to heal the wounds of others. But I knew that before I could fulfill this calling, I had to embrace the innocence of my own inner child.

As I embarked on my own healing journey, I developed close relationships with my clients' inner children. I came to know them for what they truly are: divine sparks and important parts of our soul's blueprint. These children showed me a golden key and gave me a message, pleading with us adults to release them from the entrapment of conditioning and return to the innocence that is our birthright.

As I discovered, both firsthand and through my work with clients, when we embrace the innocence of our inner child, we forgive more, we love more, and we heal.

Lifting the Sky: Meditation in Joyful Motion

by Jack V. Johnson

Thirty minutes ago, after Knocking on the Door of Life, I was Lifting the Sky and Flying. No, I wasn't hallucinating – I was practicing the ancient Chinese system of healing and energy medicine known as qigong (pronounced "chee gung").

I first learned of qigong in the early 1970s, when I began studying martial arts. Translated, qigong means the cultivation of the universal life energy through steady practice. Qigong practices can be classified as martial, medical, or spiritual, but they are all a form of moving meditation coordinating slow, fluid movements; deep, rhythmic breathing; and a focused state of mind.

Even though I initially encountered qigong in its martial form as t'ai chi, I've come to especially appreciate its spiritual aspect as a meditative practice harmonizing body, mind, and soul. As I flow slowly through each position, my breathing synchronizes with my movements and my mind naturally slows down. I feel the *qi* flowing in and through me, opening me to a calm centeredness and quiet joy.

Performing qigong as a spiritual practice doesn't mean there aren't benefits in other areas as well. The gentle movements allow me to practice even when I am in pain from the compressed discs in my back, while at the same time reducing my discomfort. If I am feeling stressed during the day, a few repetitions of the Centering exercise can bring me back to a more grounded state.

Qigong is a very flexible and forgiving system. If my knees are stiff, I can just crouch less deeply; or if my back is sore, I can spend extra time on the stretching movements. And even if I only have 10 minutes to practice, I can still walk away feeling calm, refreshed, and more in touch with the Universe and my soul.

A Day of Rest

by Cindy Jones Lantier

My husband and I both work hard. In fact, just a few months ago, I could be found working almost any time of day or night, any day of the week! It seemed as though there were not enough hours in the day for everything I wanted to do – including rest!

At the same time I was struggling with this, a Christian friend was exploring ways to bring more meaning to the Sabbath. Her talk about Bible study, simple meals, and family time sparked an idea: Why couldn't my family observe a Day of Rest, too?

When I mentioned it to my husband, he jumped at the idea, even though neither one of us had a clear idea of what this might look like for us.

I struggled for a few weeks with what our Day of Rest would look like – and why I wanted to observe it at all. Finally, a friend reminded me that a good farmer will periodically let his land lie uncultivated, simply because it needs to rest. People accomplish more when they rest regularly. Even our cats seem to understand the value of doing nothing, in service of being able to do more later.

At first, it was difficult to step away from the work, the laundry, the dishes. But now, we've found our groove, and the Day of Rest does what I'd hoped it would do.

Because I make it a point to rest and relax one day a week, I find I'm not only more productive during the rest of the week, but, come Sunday night, I'm actually eager to get back to my regular schedule.

The increased productivity and excitement about my work aren't even the biggest benefits. The most exciting part of the Day of Rest is the connection that I make with my expanded self – my soul. By taking time to care for myself, to honor my need for rest and relaxation, I feel as though I know myself better. I feel reconnected with myself. I feel at peace.

Take a Chocolate Day

by Jeanette St. Germain

Chocolate is a vehicle of present-moment bliss that invites an experience like no other. It is a sweet, silky trail of melted delight sliding gracefully across your lips. It is a moment of warmth that spreads instantaneously from the tip of your tongue, to the top of your head, to the curl of your toes. It is a sensual kiss for the spirit, a candied treat that offers a special kind of connection, a type of joy that has the ability to dissolve all distracting thoughts or rattled emotions. This velvety concoction can be shared with a lover, gifted to friends, or reserved for yourself. It is a magical blend of sugar, cream, and cocoa that not only engages all the senses but triggers the pleasure center of the soul.

Our day-to-day lives race along at a mile a minute with barely enough time to breathe. The responsibilities we shoulder are like revolving doors, circling between family, health, work, bills, and everything in between. We often struggle to find balance and to make a priority of the things that bring upliftment and rejuvenation. The sweeping tides of modern life can bring feelings of overwhelm or entrapment, especially when we choose to keep our thoughts cycling through various past or future scenarios, inquiring incessantly: "what if, when, where, why, how come, if only?"

When rough situations arise and feelings threaten to engulf, remember *chocolate*. Like a delicious rain falling on the parched sands of your spirit, let the sweetness of this confection help you shift focus, bringing your awareness back into flow with the precious *now*. Enjoy the tantalizing textures and edible intimacies of chocolate fondue. Awaken your inner child while decorating and drizzling a gooey hot-fudge sundae. Close your eyes and imagine the softness of a handmade truffle, the intoxicating waves of bliss that emanate as it gently melts in your mouth. Release all worries and burdens, and do what you must to reconnect with your chocolatey center, where all is right with the world.

The Great (Home) Escape

by Kimberly Brazier Flatland

As I reached in to feel the temperature of the water, its warmth began to wash away the busyness of the week. Inch by inch, the water called my soul. A soak in a tub filled with Epsom salt and lavender was the perfect way to begin my great escape: a solo retreat disconnecting myself from the world…in the comfort of my home.

Family away, friends alerted, and on hiatus from all social media. The glow of the candles ignited a reflection of how I could pamper myself with love and hydrate my soul.

After my peaceful soak, I prepared a warm cup of green tea. I was thankful that I had prepped the fridge earlier in the week with healthy food and drink, including a few of my favorite things.

As I settled into a large, comfy chair, I gathered my favorite pen and new journal. I began journaling – writing whatever came to mind.

Feeling calm and rested, I decided to end my night early. My body longed for extra sleep. As my head hit the pillow, I silently asked for guidance and direction in moving forward with my weekend.

After a restful sleep, my morning practice of meditation and affirmations seemed to permeate my cells.

Ready for the day, I ventured out to connect with nature. I chose a quiet country road near my home and began to walk. With each step, I released any mind chatter and practiced moments of mindfulness. A blue sky and slight breeze led the way. The smell of wildflowers filled the air. As one bird called to another, I realized I had walked for quite some time and distance. I took a step to turn around and there, in my path, was a heart-shaped stone. As I reached down to scoop it up, the sunshine broke through a passing cloud and its warmth reminded me of how beautiful this world can be.

Nearly 24 hours of bliss…and 24 more still to go.

Iron Yogi

by Sherry VanAntwerp

The "yoga flow" class was ending, and everyone around me seemed so calm and tranquil. As I sat on my mat, the prevalent thought in my head was, "I'm so glad that's over!"

I have to admit it: I am a yoga flunkie.

I wanted to love yoga. But neither Kundalini, Bikram, nor just plain old tree pose was working. How could I truly be spiritual if I wasn't a yoga aficionado? I mean, isn't that a requirement for being in touch with your soul?

Fortunately, before I descended too far into this yogic shame cycle, I realized that everyone is wired differently. Just because yoga didn't click with me didn't mean I couldn't find my zen somewhere else. And I eventually did find a place to get in touch with my soul: the weight room!

Yes, women can have the soul of an Iron Yogi just as easily as the guys.

Like yoga, lifting weights trains the mind as well as the body. It requires intense, singular focus. Your mind cannot be wandering while hoisting around potentially toe-crushing dumbbells. You must stay focused solely on the task at hand, in the now.

Weight lifting also demands an attitude of "can do." If your thinking slips for a second into the realm of "I can't," you most certainly will slip into failure. And for those of us who need stress relief, pumping iron can be an effective way to release a little aggression.

Through lifting I have learned that…

- my soul has a true warrior spirit.
- I am capable of doing much, much more than I imagined.
- consistency is key to spiritual, physical, and mental growth.
- I am in competition with no one; being better than yesterday is the goal.

If you also feel like a yoga failure, keep on searching for the activity that sparks your soul. Maybe you, too, are really an Iron Yogi trapped in triangle pose.

Rediscover Your Authentic Self

by Lacey Dawn Jackson

We all come into the world perfect – exactly as we are supposed to be. But all too soon, people encourage us to change – to be like others, to mold to someone else's ideal, or to tweak our bodies or personalities in order to fit into a box that is far from our original perfection. Working under the assumption that we can be improved, parents, friends, and society in general make suggestions or push us to change. Unfortunately, most of us give in, at least to some degree.

Rediscovering our authentic self and our original perfection is a process of stripping away what we have learned along the way. This can be messy! It can be the hardest job we take on! But as we continue to identify the roles, attitudes, and behaviors that do not resonate with our core, we chip away the pieces of ourselves that no longer fit. We start to lighten up. A new world opens up to us. We start to live authentically.

Taking time out is an important step toward finding our authentic self. When we separate from the noise that surrounds us, it helps us to become clear about what we want and who we are. When we embrace quiet time, we are able to put that monkey mind to rest and feel our true self, if only for a moment.

Getting out in nature is another way of coming back home to our authentic self. Five minutes of putting our bare feet upon the earth does wonders to bring us back to our inner truth.

We all come here for our own growth. It isn't what others think we should do that matters most, but what our own intuition prompts us to do. Others may not understand when we follow our inner voice. We may feel scared to follow it, but we must do it anyway. This voice will lead the way back to our true, authentic self, which will bring us immense peace and joy.

Slow is the New Fast

by Jane Duncan Rogers

Mind: "Get that thing done now! Hurry up, you've only got a short while to complete it. And then remember you must get the groceries, ring James, and complete your article before the deadline. And don't forget Anna's birthday, either!"

It was nearly lunchtime, and I already felt exhausted. I'd been having a "Lurching Day," one where there are so many things to be done, appointments to be kept, and conversations to be had, that I'd felt overwhelmed and exhausted.

The mind chatter was pervasive, criticizing, and relentless. But this time, instead of trying to get all the things done, I remembered the mantra that had just come to me in meditation the previous day:

Stop. Be Still. Listen. And Only Then Act.

In the middle of feeling anxiety and panic at the sight of my to-do list (which, as my mind reminded me, needed updating) and the hundreds of other things clamouring for my attention, I simply sat down, closed my eyes, and stopped.

I noticed my breath. I relaxed my shoulders. I felt the stillness around me that is always there – even when I'm being busy.

I turned my mind and heart inwards, tuning into my body and soul, going below the chattering surface of the mind. I listened with my ears, I listened with my heart, and I listened with my soul. In this gap, a thought popped up from a deep place:

Go even slower.

I recognized the paradox of slowing down when my mind was convinced that life would only work if I sped up. But I slowed down even more, as instructed. Immediately, I began to enjoy what I was doing again. Suddenly, I had the freedom to revisit my to-do list and reprioritize some tasks. And those that I did have to do still, I found myself doing in a place of relaxation and peace, leading of course to me being more connected, fulfilled, and happy.

I looked at the clock. More had been accomplished while going slowly than when I was frantically trying to get everything done. Unbelievable but true. Try it!

Love Your Body Now

by Rachel Kieffer

When was the last time you looked in the mirror and smiled back with delight – seeing yourself as inherently beautiful?

We live in a world that bombards women with messages that they are not good enough, beautiful enough, thin enough, young enough, or successful enough. We internalize those messages, and we direct them at our bodies: if only I lost weight, if only my breasts were bigger, if only I looked younger, if only my hair were a different color. Body hatred or its milder form, body dissatisfaction, seems to afflict almost every woman. It is important to look at those messages as what they truly are: lies.

The truth is that you are beautiful, your body is lovely, and every part of you is good and deserves to be loved fiercely and tenderly. Women's bodies come in all shapes, sizes, colors, and forms – and they are all magnificent. Your physical body is unique; there is only one of you in the whole world, which is cause for celebration. Your soul already knows this, and as a holistic nutritionist, I do my best to help your physical self know this as well.

I meet many women who want to make changes – and that is wonderful! It is a good idea to improve your food choices, to become more active, to increase your energy, to heal from what ails you, and to create a healthy body at a healthy weight. It is also okay if dissatisfaction with your body started you on a healing journey; but somewhere along the path you will have to learn to love your body, or any attempts to make healthy changes will most likely fail. Because why would you feel it is worth taking care of something you don't like? And what wouldn't you do to take care of something you cherish and love?

Wouldn't it be wonderful if the next time you looked in the mirror, you were able to see yourself through your soul's eyes – loving and accepting of exactly how you are? That's my wish for you.

The Conscious Plate

by Susan Mullen

We all embody three beautiful essences to help navigate our life: our mind, body, and spirit. We live harmoniously when our decisions are aligned with these three essences.

Right after my mother unexpectedly passed, these essences fell out of balance for me. I was suddenly acutely aware of the areas in my life that needed re-aligning, the most obvious of which was conscious eating.

Our bodies have an innate wisdom with their own voice and consciousness. With this in mind, I sat quietly, scanning my body and sensing which chakras felt heavy. Then, I asked one simple question: *What do you need from me?* I heard: *Integrity*. I instinctively knew that this was about eliminating the last few animal products from my plate.

I believe all sentient beings were divinely designed to live in the integrity in which they were created. So I researched the factory-farm machine, which manufactures animals for food, and found that it is steeped in cruelty. It was then that I knew it was time to honor my body's desire to up-level to my soul and choose cruelty free. In doing so, I instantly felt lighter.

To discover how your own food choices align with your body's wisdom, first investigate your plate. Imagine how many hands and processes this food passed through. Imagine the integrity of the life of the sentient being who sacrificed his or her body for you. Imagine the costs – to the sentient being, your body, and the earth – of participating in consuming this food.

Then, sit quietly and access your body's essence and voice. When ready, speak directly to your body, asking: *What do you need from me?* Depending on the answer, you may add more whole foods or reduce your intake of processed food, or you might find that higher-vibration food from a local farmer suits you better. Regardless of what specific choices you make, awareness is the first step.

I've found that when we raise the integrity of our plate to match our body's wisdom and our belief system, we can *feel* the difference! Not only does our food taste better, but we feel much lighter and in line with our soul.

Unmask Your Soul

by Cat Williford

We all wear masks. They develop when we feel threatened by something. While it is smart to stay safe, we often forget that the masks were just supposed to get us through a moment. When we continue to wear them, we surrender our authenticity to the inner naysayer's rules. Yuck, right? The fastest way to eliminate that voice is to remove the masks. It may seem counterintuitive – taking OFF the masks and exposing your vulnerability, which is probably the last thing you want to do – but this will reconnect you with your soul!

The best way I know to do this is through "The Authenticity Advantage" (a powerful set of tools that I've been using with clients and myself for 22 years). Grab your journal and a pen, give yourself a stretch of uninterrupted time, and go through the following steps:

1. Identify a situation or relationship that brings up your fears and the naysayer's voice. Ask yourself: "What is the fear or threat?" Don't stop at the first answer. Ask at least three times: "What about that feels threatening?" or "What fear is under that?"
2. Identify the mask you are wearing that keeps you feeling safe. Here's my list of the top nine masks women wear: Chief Operating Officer of Control, Smarty Pants, Super Woman, Over-Giver, Fairy-Tale Fine, Suck-It-Up-Buttercup, Man-Up, Schmoozer, and Prickly Pear. (See your fears under the masks?)
3. Next, name three aspects of your authenticity that will keep you safe and connected with your soul. Then, give the mask some props! Say, "Thank you, mask, for protecting me. Today, I choose to put you down." Then, let it know you will keep it close at hand in case you need it again.
4. Now, turn to your soul for guidance, asking it, "What do I authentically choose to experience in this situation or relationship?" (My favorites: love, serenity, confidence, gratitude, humor, ease, flow, and generosity.)
5. Set your intentions by developing a mantra or metaphoric image around the experiences you choose to enjoy every day.
6. Repeat as often as needed!

Divine Symptoms

by Nishaan Sandhu

Fatigue. Exhaustion. Lethargy. Depression. If you're experiencing these or any other physical ailments, or if you simply don't have as much energy as you'd like, you can look at your situation in two ways: You can see it as an affliction, or you can see it as a Divine Symptom – a message from your soul saying, "Hey, something's got to change!"

As with any medical condition, it's important to investigate environmental and physiological triggers, such as food sensitivities, toxins, and hormone imbalance. Although some of these triggers seem beyond our control, many factors *are* within our power of influence. Some of the deepest healings occur when we consciously shine light on our body-mind, emotions, and spiritual wellbeing.

Take time to ask questions about your symptoms, emotions, and soul lessons; and be open to receiving answers without reaction or judgment. Start with an honest exploration of your current situation – even symptoms that you may see as "negative" – by asking yourself:

- What causes stress, anxiety, resentment, and self-criticism?
- What people, tasks, or places do I leave feeling drained?
- Where do I expend physical, mental, emotional, and spiritual energy in ways that are not authentic?

It can be tempting to resist your symptoms or to judge them as "not right," "not normal," or "not me." But instead of fighting what is, you may be better served by surrendering – by accepting that *this is me…for now* and *this is normal…for today.*

Ask yourself questions that reframe your experience, honor the messages in your symptoms, and point to a healthier future: "Instead of resisting, how can I honor my symptom? How can I conserve and express energy I DO have? What would make me feel more satisfied and excited? How can I honor my body's wisdom and flow with my soul's longing?"

As your vital energy begins to align with your soul's evolution, you'll feel clearer, more radiant, and more balanced. A light will shine within you and radiate from you. And you will see your body-mind experiences not as curses or punishments but as Divine Symptoms.

Life Loves You

by Nancy Merrill Justice

For most of my life, whenever I looked out at the world, I felt detached – like I was peering through window bars, deeply embedded within a protective wall of fear. I felt like there was an unbridgeable distance between the "me within" and the world beyond.

A few years ago, however, this perception began to shift. It started while I was listening to Dr. Robert Holden, an author and coach who works in the field of positive psychology. He was discussing how the basic fear, "I am not lovable," is the primary cause of all suffering. The fear is not true; but if you believe it, consciously or unconsciously, it will cause you to contract inside to defend yourself. When I heard his words, I immediately recognized myself.

Listening to Dr. Holden introduced me to "mirror exercises," which are based on the affirmation, "Life loves you." The purpose of mirror exercises is for us to meet ourselves, let go of judging and rejecting ourselves, and connect with who we truly are. As Dr. Holden says, "At the deepest level, our purpose in life is to be a loving mirror to the world." Daily mirror exercises give us practice on *how* to love ourselves so that we can create a new world through our own new perception – one based on unconditional love.

After watching Dr. Holden's mirror-exercise video, I began following the action steps he suggested – in front of my mirror. I felt awkward initially, but very soon noticed subtle changes taking place within me. It felt good to be in a space of love and acceptance with my reflection staring back at me. My big breakthrough came on day three. I looked in the mirror and felt emotionally present – no distance between me and my reflection – and I smiled at myself for the first time! I had connected with my true self. I had connected with my soul on a level I had never experienced.

I highly recommend these exercises to anyone who wants to connect with their own soul, experience unconditional love, and know the profound truth that *life loves you!*

Hearing the Soul, One Footstep at a Time

by Ramona Remesat

Runners are a strange bunch. Anyone who has not laced up a pair of sneakers at 5 a.m. cannot fathom what prompts us to jump out of bed at such ungodly hours or compels us to run mile after mile in sub-zero temperatures. All I know is that, for me, running is my meditation. It's a way for me to stop the never-ending to-do list in my head, connect with my innermost self, and just BE.

There's just something about exercising out in nature that allows the mind to settle a little. It's as if among all the thoughts jostling for attention, a small space opens up, ever so slightly, allowing divine guidance to flow in. The key, though, is to pay attention enough to notice it, because it's often just a whisper rather than a roar.

No matter how it comes through, though, I always seem to get the best thoughts and ideas while out running – so much so, that I felt that I had to start bringing along a mini-recorder so I could capture them before they evaporated like my sweat. One footstep at a time, I've received creative inspiration, arrived at solutions to problems, and experienced wondrous "aha moments." How joyous!

No matter what I'm going through, I always seem to finish a run with greater clarity and a richer understanding of things. And the more I tune into the guidance that comes through, the more info I seem to get. Heart-healthy exercise combined with hearing the whispers of my soul is definitely a win-win for me!

Soulful Food

by Jenna Kelland

Food is an essential source of nourishment. Eating provides our bodies with the nutrients, vitamins, and minerals we need for physical survival. However, food also provides nourishment for the heart, mind, and spirit. Consider these easy ways to connect with your food before presenting it on the plate:

- Use your senses to explore the connections between nature and the food you eat. Listen to bees buzzing as they move from flower to flower, carrying the pollen that fertilizes pumpkins. Watch small seeds grow into fruit or vegetables. Smell the aroma of freshly cut herbs. Feel the dead leaves under your feet as they return to the soil in the cycle of life. Taste the tang of a tomato freshly picked from the vine.
- Reflect on the laws of economy in nature that guarantee that nothing is wasted, that everything contributes to producing the next step in the cycle. Insects, birds, and other animals help to fertilize flowers, spread seeds, and return dead material to the soil.
- Grow your own food. You can start small with a few herbs on your kitchen windowsill. Their fresh flavor will enhance your meals and remind you of the natural source of everything you eat.
- Eat local products where possible. Get to know where your food is grown and who is growing it.
- Join a community garden where you and your neighbors can share the work, your favorite recipes, and the bounty.
- Look for opportunities to become part of the food-production process by participating in community-shared agriculture. See the care and attention that goes into growing what you enjoy eating.

When enjoying dinner, reflect on how the food on your plate is there courtesy of the sunshine, the soil, and the rain. Each vegetable was grown in nutrient-rich soil, watered by rain, warmed by the sun, and tended by caring hands. Savor each bite as it nourishes your body, your heart, your mind, and your spirit.

Keeping in Touch...with Yourself

by Cat Smith

Every day has the potential to be beautiful and amazing! Some days might not feel this way, though, because we lose touch with our goals, dreams, and what's most important to us. This is becoming increasingly common in today's fast-paced, information-packed world, yet you can change this experience in your own life. I know because I was able to change it in mine.

While working in the corporate world, I had a calling to do energy work (natural healing techniques focused on working with the energy centers of the body to bring balance and wellness to people's lives). Yes, these are two extremes. It was difficult to go from the busyness and, on some days, complete exhaustion from my day job to focusing on others on a spiritual level in a calm, peaceful environment.

I realized I had the power to change the stress I was experiencing and work toward my goal of doing energy work full time, so I tried something new. I stood in front of a mirror to help focus my thoughts on ME.

I started doing a mini energy scan on myself. I cleared my mind, closed my eyes, and asked myself what my biggest pain or toxin was. The word "sugar" came to mind. Yes, I had been overloading on sodas, ice cream, and chai tea drinks at a popular coffee shop. I depended on this sugar to give me energy to get through my day.

I was amazed at how insightful this exercise was! It brought my main concern to light so I could focus on changing what was not working in my life. Now when I get stressed or upset, I do this mirror exercise and clear the energy blocks so I can have a beautiful and amazing day!

The great thing is that you can do this, too! As you do, know that energy moves with intention, so you can clear away any blockages by imagining blowing them away or destroying them. And remember: you and your thoughts create your own reality.

Of course, it's great to reach out to keep in touch with others. However, also discover the power of keeping in touch *with yourself!*

Begin with Kindness to Yourself

by Karen Gibbs

Even under normal circumstances, life can be hard enough; but when a catastrophe arises, it can feel downright overwhelming. Initially, we might react to adversity with strength and determination. Over time, however, our strength often erodes, leaving us feeling defeated. This insidious feeling engulfs us and saps our vitality. Before we realise it, we have lost touch with our inner being. We feel scattered and drained, disconnected from God.

I experienced this when a loved one suffered a sudden debilitating illness, which left him in need of long-term care. Although I always try to find the positives in seemingly negative circumstances, after several years in this situation, I felt that I had lost myself.

While assisting others, we often sacrifice our own wellbeing, putting ourselves last on the list without a second thought. It's strange that we don't extend the same level of kindness to ourselves as we do to others.

While caring for my loved one, it eventually occurred to me that as life becomes increasingly complicated, there is an even greater need to be gentler, kinder, and more understanding towards ourselves. We need to focus inwardly and strengthen our core being. Harmony within oneself is required before we can create peace for others.

Before facing this challenge, I had mistakenly perceived this concept as being self-centred. Through my experiences, however, I learned that when we take care of our spiritual wellbeing and connect with our inner vitality, we free ourselves. A strength is born within. We grow. We flourish. Not only do we survive, but we thrive. Problems become beatable, and we realise that life is what we allow it to be.

There is comfort and peace in the knowledge that when we begin with kindness to self, anything is possible.

The Path to Pilates Pleasure

by Lori Evans

One of my main purposes in life is to help people connect with, understand, and love their bodies. I've chosen to do this largely through the movement of Pilates because it provides an authentic and powerful connection to your soul.

I love sharing what Pilates truly is…and what it isn't. Pilates is often misunderstood. Some common misconceptions are that it's stretching, meditation, just for girls, easy, hard, only on a mat, or that it's just like yoga.

Here's what Pilates *is*:

- Pilates is a series of complex movements.
- Pilates is your own personal "body detective" – exposing imbalances.
- Pilates "reveals to heal."

It's through the struggle of understanding the method, the principles, the engagements, the breathing patterns, and the alignment, that you are forced to tune in to the rhythm of your body's own personal flow. It's like magic…as you focus your mind in the present and sync the breathing pattern to the choreographed movement, you naturally tune in.

The body and brain communicate effortlessly; and as the brain surrenders all thoughts and feelings to its soul, they connect…and your body becomes beauty in motion like a synchronized swimmer moving effortlessly through water.

If I could pop out of the page and instruct you, I would. Instead, allow me to teach you the technique of Spinal Breathing, which will connect your body and soul before any kind of movement.

To begin, take a deep, full breath through your nose, starting at the base of your spine (tailbone), then move the air along your spine all the way to the top (about the middle of your head). Then, with a little exertion, exhale through your mouth and move the air back down your spine.

That's it. Start there. Try it now for a round of 10. Feel your breath flow through your body…clear your mind…and connect with your soul.

Sacred Mirror Date

by Michelle Anne Gould

"I hate you! You are stupid, fat, and ugly!" The tirade of hatred being directed at me was incredibly painful, but I couldn't get away from it…because the critical voice was in my own head!

I couldn't just turn off these negative messages at will, so I decided to love, honour, and nourish myself the best way I knew how: by taking myself on a sacred mirror date.

Here's how the process works:

Set the intention to be loving, kind, and open to anything that comes up. While sitting or standing in front of a mirror, take a deep breath in for the count of four seconds, hold it for four seconds, and release it for four seconds. Repeat this breathing pattern until you are calm, relaxed, and centred. Tenderly look into the mirror. Look closely into each eye separately. Take your time with this.

Remembering that the eyes are the window to your soul, ask your soul to come forward through your eyes and show you the energy of love. Fill yourself up, from your head to your toes. Breathe this energy in. Bathe in it. Play with it. Soak it in.

If you are so inclined, call upon your angels, spirit guides, or higher self to support you during your mirror date. Embrace and feel all there is. Imagine a white light enveloping your whole body.

Continuing to breathe deeply, say aloud, "I love you, and I completely accept you."

For the courageous beginner: Look directly at a feature you adore. Say aloud, "Thank you. I love you." Next, choose a feature you *don't* particularly adore. Allow judgments and beliefs to surface. Say aloud, "I love you. You are perfect. I love that about you. I completely accept you."

For the bravest of them all: Look into the mirror and tell yourself seven things you are grateful for and proud of. Then, tell yourself something that you are not so proud of. Look into your eyes and tell yourself, "I completely accept you and love you." Repeat these affirmations until you feel the love with all of your heart.

A Sacred Place to Be

by Shelley Lundquist

In the past, in those moments when I felt out of sync, I sought the sanctuary of nature to soothe my weary spirit. Solace wrapped itself around me upon entering the protective shade of the forest's canopy, eclipsing the world outside. The sun-dappled leaves would dance on the breeze as the wind swirled around me, whisking my worries away as it breathed on by. With each step, I would feel myself more rooted, this sacred place always bringing me back to my peace.

Then there were the days when I was lost in life's minutia and could not escape to my sacred place. Sometimes days or even weeks would go by with my anxiety a daily accessory. I knew that I needed to find another way to contend with the turmoil inside me. I struggled to leave my woes behind, until I discovered that it was the struggle itself that kept me stuck.

When I found the courage to surrender and face myself, I learned to tune my awareness and to recognise what was missing when I felt fazed and out of alignment. When motivated by fear and misbeliefs, I could find no peace. When motivated by the truth of who I am and the guidance of my soul, I could feel the shift of energy as life began to flow, easily and effortlessly.

The more I was able to stay in the present moment, leaving behind the pain of the past and letting go of worry for the future, the easier it became to hold my balance. As I began to watch my thoughts and actions, and to check in with myself – asking, "Is this who I am?" – the more clarity I had in making choices. It is only ever *me* that blocks my connection to the Universe, and whenever I honour who I am, I am never out of sync.

What a blessing it is to now know that wherever I AM is a sacred place to be, and that is always where I will find my peace.

Heal Your Relationship with Food

by Rachel Kieffer

Our body knows exactly what food it needs to flourish, just like a plant knows to lean toward the sun for nourishment. But, somewhere along the line, we lost that connection with our body. Instead of using food for nourishment and energy, we began to use it to soothe ourselves, ease our loneliness, and numb our anxiety. We tried to fill a bottomless, empty space, which food cannot fill. We forgot to trust our soul and its connection to our body.

The path to a healthy relationship with food is manifold. There is no single "magic potion" that will solve all our food issues and repair our severed connection to our body's incredible wisdom. But we can start by taking two important steps in this direction by transitioning to whole foods and expressing our emotions.

Foods that are processed, refined, high in sugar, or full of additives and chemicals numb our body and create unhealthy cravings. But foods that are natural, high in nutrients, and full of life and energy will connect us back to our body's inner knowing – back to our soul. We crave what we eat; so the healthier our food choices, the more healthy foods we will crave.

Another important part of this healing process is to *feel* our feelings, rather than *feed* our feelings. It is not what we feel that is hard, it's the fear and resistance to feeling it that is hard. Allow yourself to be rocked by deep sobs. Allow yourself to laugh until tears run down your cheeks. Allow yourself to sit with grief until you feel undone. The feelings will flow over you like a river, cleansing and washing away old hurts and wounds. Underneath the pain, you will find a deep joy that you can only get to by being willing to feel fully.

These two steps will start you on your path to healing your relationship with food and help you connect with your soul at the same time! Once you begin implementing them, you'll begin to uncover your own compass to your most radiant life.

Rewriting the "Rules" of Self-Love

by Chrystal Kubis

Somewhere in our history and carried down for generations, the "rules" of self-love became distorted. Many people chose to live a life smaller than their spirit because it was deemed more acceptable. Well, times are changing…and so are the rules! Here are five new rules guaranteed to create a soul-soaring life!

- *Accept and own that you were born to shine!* Yes, you! Take a deep breath and begin to create a life that allows you to radiate in every way! Whatever you've been taught (or perhaps even believed) that does not allow your essence to emerge, kindly acknowledge it, release it, and carry on shining!
- *It's time to love ALL of you!* You, in your entirety, are 100% lovable and worthy of being cherished. Your inside, your outside, your crunchy parts, your smooth parts, your whole entire being. Take small steps or bold leaps to embody this truth from the inside out, and watch life rapidly change in your favor.
- *It's time to stop saying two things: "I'm sorry" and "I can't."* You are worthy of taking up space and never need to apologize for simply being. You are a walking miracle, built to dream and create. It's time to move confidently toward your dreams, believing wholeheartedly that you can!
- *Cultivate presence and acceptance – they are keys to freedom!* With presence, our moments can be cherished and our awareness begins to soar to new capabilities. Acceptance does not necessarily mean that you agree with whatever is happening; but once acceptance is present, resistance is replaced by freedom.
- *Create your own rules!* Leaders don't play by others' rules, they create their own. If you are complaining about status quo, quit following it and choose to lead instead! Your visions are uniquely your own. Consider yours as a responsibility, a soulful quest, and a joy to help create a better future for all involved.

When we rewrite the rules of self-love to include soul nourishment, our experiences of life are guaranteed to soar to new heights!

Healing the Overachiever

by Elizabeth Kipp

Hi. My name is Elizabeth, and I'm a recovering overachiever.

For years, I strove to reach one goal after another without ever allowing myself to celebrate accomplishments or even feel the satisfaction of reaching my goals. I was like a pole vaulter setting a goal for myself, such as jumping over a bar six feet off the ground. But just as I was about to clear that bar, I would raise it a little higher, just out of my reach, and reset my goal. Then, I would strive to clear that new bar…only to raise it once again before I could celebrate reaching the new goal.

This cycle provided no sense of fulfillment, only an unquenchable striving to get to the next higher, sought-after goal. Again and again and again.

Fortunately, I was eventually able to recognize that this was not a healthy pattern for me. And I was able to see to the root of this inner dynamic: I realized that it wasn't based on a desire to succeed or "better" myself; it was based on low self-esteem. My unremitting striving, attempts at overachieving, and constant resetting of goals were all just a series of misguided attempts to earn my way into a sense of self-worth. But my lack of self-esteem became a self-fulfilling prophecy, which led to an unending cycle of feeling that I was "not enough."

My recognition of this pattern marked the beginning of my recovery from this self-destructive behavior. With this new awareness, I began to evaluate not only my goals but also my motives for setting them. I allowed myself not only to reach my goals but to *celebrate* my achievements. I allowed myself to make mistakes without judgment. I learned to accept myself right where I was. I learned to value my own happiness and integrity above what I imagined someone else's measure of worthiness might be. I learned to give myself unconditional love.

And I finally learned what my soul knew all along: *I am enough.*

Be Your Soul-Soaring Self

by Annie Price

We are all individually unique *and* created from the same energy source. We show up here on Earth in many colors, shapes, and sizes – but there's only one *you*. While we may look different, underneath it all, we're much the same. Our physical self may be concerned with weight, but it's not an issue for the soul self. We can harshly judge based on physical appearance, and the subjective eyes of others can determine what's deemed beautiful and socially acceptable. Most often though, our worst critic is ourselves.

I've battled my weight for years – losing, regaining, and gaining even more as time passed. I'd felt that my worthiness was determined by how I "measured up" with unrealistic clothing sizes and numbers on the scale.

At age 10, I had my first experiences with overeating and using food as a comfort, gaining both weight and self-loathing. We'd just moved from our Nova Scotia farm with lots of physical activity, to a suburb of Chicago and much less activity. The adjustment was challenging for a shy kid, and I started 6th grade carrying a few extra pounds. On my first day at the new school, my teacher introduced me to the class. I'll never forget the kid who said loudly, "She's FAT!" I was completely humiliated as my worst fear was declared out loud for the whole world. So began my decades-long struggle with my body – with *me*.

It took a long time, but I eventually reached the point where I was ready to stop struggling. I decided to forget about "perfect" numbers and just go for what I could realistically maintain…*without* hard or painful processes. I was ready to be "Fearless, Fun, & Free" (which is what I call my new weight-release program). And most important of all, I was ready to love myself at the soul level – regardless of how much I weighed.

Now, I'm losing the weight for good, and it no longer gets to play an unhealthy, self-defeating role in my life. I've begun living a healthy, happy life – inside and out. I'm loving this new approach to my weight and my life, and I'm loving sharing this message: *Be your soul-soaring self, as you were divinely designed to be!*

Create Space for More of What You Love

by Ayesha Hilton

Most of us are so busy that we barely have time to stop and think or just *be*. Being busy has become a status symbol for many people. We compete about who is the busiest in order to create a sense of importance. Our lives are full of competing responsibilities and commitments.

Many times, this busyness causes us to lose sight of what our soul really desires. We agree to take on more and more without feeling into whether these are things in which we really want to invest our soul, time, and energy.

Connecting with our soul, or higher self, allows us to tap into that part of ourselves that knows what is best for us. You can honour yourself and your inner knowing by taking time to feel into an opportunity to see if it is right for you.

You may know immediately in your gut whether you truly want to do something. Or you may need some time, maybe a few days or more, to connect with your higher self to assess the situation.

When someone asks you to take on something new, stop for a moment before you automatically say yes. Let them know that you need to think about it and will get back to them. This may feel awkward at first, but as you practice this, it will become automatic to give yourself the time and space to consider an opportunity or request.

You may also like to reassess your current commitments to see if some have reached their "use-by" date. There is a time to let things go to make room for more of what you love. Write a list of all your current activities and see which ones make you light up and give you energy, which ones feel like a drag, and which ones you feel ambivalent about.

Start cutting back on those things that take energy away from you and focus on bringing more of those things into your life that enliven you and bring joy to your soul.

Chakradance for the Soul

by Sharyn Holmes

Last year, I returned to dance after many years off the dance floor. Truth be told, the dance floors of old were in smoke-machine-fogged and sticky-floored nightclubs. My return to dance, however, was in a very different environment – and with a very different intention. It came through the hugely transformative and healing experience of Chakradance.

It brings tears to my eyes to think about the experience I had during my first Chakradance workshop and to be able to share these special moments with you.

During the workshop, I travelled through my chakras – starting at my base, feeling Mother Earth and her grounding force. I then moved up to my joyful, creative sacral and reached my solar plexus to see golden soldiers steadfastly protecting me with their warrior strength. My dance became a march, and my warrioress rose up from within. But something held me back as I transitioned to my heart chakra. My lover-of-life essence had stalled and, like a butterfly whose wings have been rained on, I could barely raise my arms. Tears fell as I realised I had been holding back on what I most deserve: to live life with an open heart, to feel completely worthy and enough. As I let go of past burdens, my arms rose and encircled a huge, rose-quartz sphere. I had come home to myself. Finally.

As I moved through my upper chakras, colours merged kaleidoscope-like. I was amazed at what I was seeing and feeling. I felt compelled to hum and chant in my throat chakra. Intuition reigned as I saw a blinking purple eye at my third-eye chakra. The energy shifted, and I was bathed in a waterfall of light, taking me higher. I exhaled and felt completely realigned and connected with all that is as my soul heard these words, over and over: "We are one."

If you love meditation, music, movement, and embodiment practices, Chakradance is not to be missed. This powerful, soulful experience can take you to a whole new level of personal transformation and healing.

Make a Pact with Your Soul

by Ellouise Heather

When I became ill with Chronic Fatigue Syndrome (CFS), it felt as though I was losing my identity. It brought my life to a screeching halt. At first, it seemed as though there was nothing to do but sit and watch others' lives cruise into the fast lane.

Despite the debilitating symptoms of CFS, however, I soon began to appreciate that it gave me the time to reflect – time that others might not have had. Now confined to four walls, I realised that I had been so busy *doing* what I thought was expected of me (by those around me and by society in general) that I had lost sight of just *being*. As a result, I had essentially disconnected from the real me.

I concluded that one of the necessary elements for my recovery was to reconnect with my authentic self. I pledged to listen carefully to my soul's voice when it called out to me – a pact that would allow me to grow…and allow the stifled voice of my soul to fully flow, as though a dam had suddenly been broken down.

Ever since childhood, I had accepted the sickly feeling in the pit of my stomach as normal. Yet, as I learned to listen to my soul's whispers, I realised it was sending me profound guidance about whether I was on the right path. If I entered a room and observed that my gut feeling was peaceful, I would acknowledge confidently that I was in the right place. If symptoms of CFS flared up, I would listen to my inner voice to help me understand the message they were trying to bring to my attention through my body.

My new pact sent a clear message to my soul: I was ready to learn and intent on listening. It shifted my focus inwards, to my being, rather than to what I was or was not doing. I began to align with my true values and express my authentic self more freely. It is clear to me now that this devotion has cultivated the nourishment I needed to bloom.

Beauty Alchemy

by Amy Gage

"Beauty Alchemy" is consciously rising from the ego-mind's limitations into the soul's limitlessness. It is a choice and a commitment to see your body and life with new eyes and an open heart.

It's so easy to get caught up in limited ideas of who we are or who we think we need to be. So often, we have been conditioned and pressured to look at ourselves and others through the "ego lens," where we see ourselves as a body before being a soul. From a soul perspective, we remember that we are a soul first, having a physical experience. We remember that we are so much more than our body.

Eventually, the voices that say we have to be smaller or larger, darker or lighter, and less or more of who we currently are, start to lose power in our lives. We will start seeing that limited reality as nonsense as we tap more into our soul's sense. When we view our body from our soul's perspective, we feel love and acceptance for ourselves and others.

As I began viewing my body from a higher perspective, I identified less with my physical body and more with my soul body, which helped me have a healthier and more balanced perspective on my physical existence and my entire life. I began to trust that my soul was my truest form of beauty.

When we consciously rise into our soul's view of beauty, we assert our power to love what is. We start leading reality, rather than letting it lead us. We begin experiencing the magic of radiating soul beauty through our physical body and transcending our perceived imperfections.

Soul perspective is full of acceptance, honor, and compassion for yourself and others. The way you treat your body, feel about your body, and live your life will become more balanced, beautiful, and kind. This new perspective changes everything for the better.

We all have the potential to be beauty alchemists in our lives by allowing ourselves to embrace a beautiful soul perspective from the inside out.

An Authentic No is the Most Powerful Yes

by Karen Hicks

We are asked to give something of ourselves countless times each day. Requests come from our spouses, partners, children, co-workers, neighbors…from every direction. Perhaps the "ask" is to drive someone somewhere, to pick something up, to help with a school project, or to listen to someone's "I have a problem" conversation. The specific "ask" doesn't really matter; what matters is our response. In the absence of thoughtful inner dialogue, the answer to any request can be an automatic "yes." The more we say "yes," however, the more depleted we become.

Over time, if we continue to respond to every request with an automatic "yes," resentment often begins to creeps in. (One sign of resentment is the thought, "people always take advantage of me.") When resentment takes hold, we might find ourselves switching to an automatic "no." This can feel empowering, but it often doesn't feel as good as we thought it would. This is because resentment is the driver; it is not an authentic "no."

The good news is that it is possible to say "no" and to feel good about that response – no guilt, no shame, no judgment. How do we get there? By first saying YES to ourselves!

When someone asks you for something – time, effort, energy – first tell them you need a few minutes before you respond. Take this time to go inward and ask yourself, "Do I have this thing to give?" If the answer you hear is "yes," ask yourself, "Under what conditions?" Then let the person know how you can assist them. If the answer you hear is "no," respond with that. In both cases, there is authenticity and integrity in the response.

When we listen to our inner voice and let it guide us, we are filled up, not depleted. Our emotional and physical energy increases – along with our confidence. And once confidence is firmly rooted, resentment has no space to grow.

Through the practice of authentic response, we also teach those around us how to do it – kind of like paying it forward. We model for others that responding with an authentic "no" is actually a big YES to ourselves…and to our soul!

Love Your Body, Honor Your Soul

by Nishaan Sandhu

It's time to reframe how we see, appreciate, and converse with our bodies. Our bodies are not adversaries to be subdued or overcome. They are gifts. They are wise teachers. They are embodiments of soul.

Even when it seems that our bodies don't seem to be "cooperating," they are often exhibiting deep wisdom…and a knack for survival! For instance, if we don't eat, our bodies may hold onto weight – which is an appropriate adaptation and a gift in the face of actual starvation!

Challenges may arise, however, when we resist or ignore our bodies' wisdom. For instance, when we repress our hunger, we often end up opting for a quick fix (or "non-fix") such as sugar or empty calories.

Likewise, when we refuse to honor our soul's longings, we tend to rely on fast-acting yet unfulfilling substitutes (such as relationships that don't serve us…or never did). When you feel yourself looking for a quick fix in any area, this may be your wake-up call, urging you to examine your life, your priorities, and your soul's true desires – and to ask yourself some probing questions, such as:

- What are you waiting to let go of? Create? Do?
- What emotional and mental patterns hold you back?
- What if you could move through these blocks and start nourishing your soul?

When you listen to the longings of your body and soul, you will see that it is within your power to make time for movement and creativity that you love. You will begin to appreciate your wise body and greet your reflection with loving eyes. You will commit only when your heart says "yes" and say "no" when you want to say "no." You will start your morning with something that truly nourishes your body and honor your soul throughout the day.

You will love yourself wholly, humbly, courageously. You will honor your soul's gift of embodiment. And you will see your beautiful and unique body as soul's vehicle, brimming with purpose, creativity, and love.

Trust the Process

by Dana Ben-Yehuda

The phone rang and a low voice says, "I can't breathe."

"How do you mean you can't breathe?"

"It's hard to breathe. I don't feel good."

"Have you seen a doctor?"

"Yes."

"Can you breathe enough right now?"

"Yes…" Slowly, the story comes out…of being in school, not feeling good, coming home…and time passing. Years. I agree to work with him.

The young man comes to my office and sits with no form to his spine. Slumped. Quiet. Holding his breath. His head pulls in like a turtle, pressing down on his neck and throat. This cycle of fear and tightening makes it more difficult to breathe, the lack of breath causing more fear…

Slowly, quietly, we begin to work together. He starts to breathe more freely. Repetition helps; long-disused muscles need time to retrain and gain strength. Beginning to remember, coming back to himself. That's when I share one of the most important lessons I can offer: *Trust the process.*

In any transformation – physical, mental, or spiritual – progress may be slow. The changes may be too small to detect on a day-to-day basis. Or, like a caterpillar in a cocoon, they may be invisible from the outside, while inside, everything rearranges itself. Eventually, one day you reach a point of critical mass and suddenly there's a shift into a healing phase.

Have faith in the dark; that's when you're turning into a butterfly.

One day, the young man arrives looking taller. He has been studying, practicing on his own at home. The shift is happening. The weeks pass and he tells me about walking more in the afternoons. His breathing is better. Six months in, he walks in with a smile on his face.

After 29 Alexander lessons (a technique to release tension and increase body awareness), he has his final session. He's now standing tall, breathing deeply, and ready to embark on a new journey: going back to school to finish his degree. He realizes that this, too, will take time and that progress may be slow at times. But now he knows that he can and will succeed. And he knows to trust the process.

Chronic Pain and the Choice for Joy

by Elizabeth Kipp

As a chronic-pain patient, my physical discomfort was often so great that it precluded any trace of joy. Not only did I not experience joy in the midst of pain, though, my memory of past pain was so raw and vivid that I wouldn't allow myself to feel joy even when I *wasn't* in physical pain. What would be the point? Sooner or later, I'd be jerked back into the reality of pain – and the letdown would leave me feeling worse than ever. So I closed myself off even to the possibility of joy. It just seemed safer this way.

Yes, on one level this approach *was* safer: I didn't risk the disappointment of having something beautiful snatched away from me. But it also meant that I wouldn't have these beautiful experiences to begin with. I soon realized that my reluctance to experience joy had locked me in a self-imposed prison. There was plenty of joy around me; I just had to be willing to open myself up and take it in. I had to choose: remain a joyless captive with the pain, or experience the full spectrum of life – including joy, pain, disappointment, and beauty.

As I considered the options, I saw that by blocking out joy, I was robbing myself of opportunity, of possibility, and of experiencing the juice of life. If I wanted to experience all the colors of life, I had to choose to step fully into it – to play the "game" full out rather than standing on the sidelines as a spectator.

I dug a little deeper to further bolster my courage. I asked the Universe for strength and direction and was graced with an answer: "Turn to your heart." And when I looked into my heart, I found a fountain of courage waiting. Then I made my choice for joy. And I never turned back.

Trust the Magic of Your Heart

by Tanya Levy

It felt like too much to take all at once: I had just started a new job as a counsellor; I was caring for a toddler; and I had a terrible ear infection, which made me dizzy, exhausted, and barely able to walk. Despite all this, I ignored my own needs while I cared for others…until I couldn't. My body was failing me, and my soul was parched. My heart whispered – and eventually *begged* – for me to reach out for help. Reluctantly, I did. Slowly, almost out of necessity, I asked for and received support and made self-care a priority.

When we are going through a crisis in our lives, it can be difficult to listen to our heart's whispers and do what they ask. Just as importantly, we also need to let go of what no longer serves us and believe that we are worthy of new beginnings. This is what allows healing to happen.

Listening to our hearts allows us to give voice to our own truth and trust that, as we put one foot in front of the other in new practices and priorities that support us, our lives will improve. Trusting the magic of the heart is about finding what nourishes and fills our own cup – remembering that it is much easier to give when your cup is full!

As I began to reach out, accept support, and fill my own cup, my life transformed. I made healthier choices around eating, moving, resting, and helping others. I found time for the things I loved. I took time to breathe. I became a better parent, counsellor, and friend because I made self-care a priority. I looked for practices and routines that supported my newfound health. I sought out supportive people, places, and situations. As I listened to and trusted the magic of my own heart, I felt more able to shine in my own beauty. I birthed a life I love.

What are your heart's whispers telling you? Listen to them, allow them to guide you, let healing happen, and always trust the magic of your own heart.

Connecting with Your Soul Through Chronic Illness

by Tanya Penny

After sitting in the emergency room for six hours, I was told that I had Multiple Sclerosis (MS). As a 29-year-old marathon runner and avid hiker, I was completely shocked. At the time, I was an Occupational Therapist – someone who helps others with MS and other chronic illnesses. Now I was on the other side.

The truth is that this condition didn't come out of nowhere. I had suffered from anxiety, depression, eating disorders, and addictions for years, but this was the straw that broke the camel's back. I hit the lowest point of my life.

Over the coming months and years, I lost vision in my right eye, had a hard time finding words, and had difficulty walking. I decreased my work hours and struggled to do even normal day-to-day things like take my dogs for a walk, grocery shop, cook dinner, clean the house, and go out with my friends. I had always been a perfectionist and a "superwoman." Now, I felt like a useless failure, as my self-worth had always been tied to *doing* and staying busy – too busy to hear the voice of my soul.

At the time of my diagnosis, if someone had said that this was my soul trying to get my attention, I would have slapped them in the face – hard! But now this is exactly how I see it. Looking back, I realize that I'd been disconnected from my true self because of the overachiever part of me that pushed myself for fear of not being lovable or good enough. But this disease didn't allow me to keep pushing anymore. I was forced to slow down, surrender, and just be.

With all this time on my hands, I started to pray for answers – although I didn't even believe in God at the time! But I was in such a dark place that I prayed anyway – to whomever or whatever – and I started to listen. Eventually, I began to hear the whispers of my soul – that tiny voice I had ignored for so long. I cried tears of relief as I realized that I was not alone. The MS had helped me find my way back to my true self and also to discover and live my purpose of supporting others to do it, too.

The Soul and Your Fascia

by Daria Howell

Mid-afternoon and sitting down to write, I'm suddenly overcome with sleepiness. My brain is reluctant to focus. How grateful I am to be able to recall an excellent way to tune into the body-mind-spirit and enhance the flow of energy.

As a longtime massage and craniosacral therapist, I have a deep fascination with the body and its fascia (the network of fibrous tissue that holds all our cells together). Andrew Still, the father of modern-day osteopathy, calls this fascia "the seat of the soul" and has said, "The soul…seems to dwell in the fascia of the body."

So, taking my cues from John Barnes's myofascial unwinding technique, I take a deep breath and str-e-e-e-e-tch my arms and my head outward, away from the center of my body. Like magic, I feel some movement begin to happen all on its own. There's an electrical charge that's present in the fascia, and it begins to respond to the pressure of the stretch.

I allow my body to move and to flow, to go wherever it feels right, and to stop now and then to soften whatever restriction it comes across. It's a graceful practice, almost dance-like. In fact, it can be a lot of fun to play some gently lilting music while doing this unwinding process and turn it into a dance!

This practice is all about just letting go, flowing, not directing. Whenever the movement stops, I gently elongate outward, which triggers it to begin again. Aside from the initial stretch, all the movement originates from my fascia. Even though a few places may feel achy or sore, I can trust that this practice will never injure me. It's all about letting my soul take care of me.

I'm so thankful for this easy practice. I love knowing that all I need to do to connect with my soul is pay attention and flow with it.

In only a few minutes, I feel great – clear-headed and energized. What an elegant way to rejuvenate and be present for whatever's next, like finishing my writing!

Understand Your Cravings

by Rachel Kieffer

Most of us think of food cravings as the enemy. They derail us from our healthy eating plans. They take over and "ruin" our diets. We try to fight them, but they eventually win.

But there is a different and more empowering way to look at cravings. Your body is smart and has amazing healing abilities. Given half a chance, it will guide you to your most vibrant life. Cravings are your body's way of giving you important messages. Listen to them. Learn to understand and decode them.

A craving is often a signal that you are not taking care of your physical, emotional, and spiritual needs. You might need to slow down, rest, take time to nourish yourself, and get some alone time. You might need to talk to a friend, feel connected, and surround yourself with support. You might need to nourish your soul with meditation, connection to nature, or travel. You might need to love your body with a massage, a yoga class, or a soothing bath. When your needs are not tended to, cravings show up to compensate for what is lacking.

Cravings can also be a message that something is missing nutritionally. If you are not getting enough nutritious whole foods (such as a variety of vegetables, especially dark leafy greens; good quality fats; sufficient proteins; and the right complex carbs), your body will crave the most extreme form of what it is missing. Many women who go on diets that call for eliminating entire food groups and limiting the variety of foods they can eat will notice that their cravings intensify.

So the next time you crave ice cream, pizza, or potato chips, don't fight it. Instead, get quiet and listen to your body. Journaling can be a powerful tool in understanding your cravings and transforming them from foes to friends. Have a written conversation with them. Ask them what they are trying to tell you. You will be surprised at the gems of insight and healing that will come up when you truly listen.

Find the Courage to Express Your True Self

by Annalene Hart

"We need to learn to love ourselves first, in all our glory and imperfections. If we cannot love ourselves, we cannot fully open to our ability to love others."
- John Lennon

I still remember what my movement instructor said to me over 30 years ago: "You know more than you let on that you know." What a revelation! I felt the power of this statement immediately, but the process of fully embracing and expressing this truth in my life took much longer. My conditioning kept me playing small longer than I would like to admit.

I'm not quite sure what tipped the scale in favor of my self-liberation; perhaps it was just that it took more energy to hide than to express my true self. I finally realized that I just had to be me, and if I ruffled some feathers, well that was just too bad!

I had no idea that just being myself would seem like such a revolutionary act! But apparently it was, based on how much flak I took simply for not following the pack or adhering to the status quo of conformism. It's not that I was being a rabble-rouser; I was just being authentic. But time and again I got the subliminal (or not-so-subliminal) message: *just blend in and keep quiet, for goodness' sake!*

After years of dimming my own light, however, I wasn't about to shrink myself back down to Alice-in-Wonderland size in order to gain acceptance and validation. What I had to do was to accept, validate, and love *myself*. And that's just what I did.

When you love and accept yourself, it doesn't necessarily follow that others automatically will. Some people will be inspired to express their authenticity as well, while others may just try to knock you down to their size. In either case, remember that you're not expressing your authenticity for *their* sake – you're doing it for yourself and for your soul.

Find the courage to love and express your true self. Although the entire world may not thank you, *your soul will!*

The Wisdom of Self-Care

by Jenny McKaig

I asked my soul what I really needed and, as usual, it knew. The inner voice that replied was soft but clear: *space, self-care, and time to breathe.*

At this time, my life had become jam-packed with activities. I spent my days racing from one fitness class to the next, working long hours, and commuting an hour each way – often in rush-hour traffic, navigating my way around the other vehicles clamoring for space on the highway.

No wonder my soul was now asking – actually, *begging* me – for space in my life!

As I started to honor this request, my life began to change. I gave myself the space my soul longed for. I read. I got massages. I took breaks when I needed them. I took long, lavish bubble baths where I could breathe and *just be*. I softened to the rhythms of life and honored my needs.

As my self-care quotient rose, I began to notice positive changes in all areas of my life: my physical health, my emotions, and even my career. As I took the time to relax and nourish myself, I began hearing an inner calling to write – a passion that has now become my profession!

In any given moment, we have the opportunity to listen to what we need. Our souls whisper to us with wisdom; it's up to us to listen. For me, it was slowing down; writing; and creating a life of joy, peace, and passion. But self-care can mean many different things to many different people – and they are all perfect. What's most important is to listen to your soul, honor what it wants, and live your truth.

The Art of Date Night

by Dedra Murchison

"I have a date."

A rabid isolationist, I was looking for an out to what sounded like an evening of soul-sucking tedium. I had been looking forward to making my world-famous King Ranch Chicken and enjoying a quiet night alone with my art journal.

On the appointed evening, I stopped by my local Whole Foods and bought myself a bouquet of red and white roses that were on the verge of blooming. (I am not generally a fan of cut flowers, but these beauties called to me and insisted that we go home together.) I quickly assembled my dinner, and as it baked, I surveyed my dining room. It was covered in the remnants of my latest art project. If company were coming, I would have already cleared the table. So I decided that I would treat myself like company and cleared the table. I lit my favorite incense and dug out the candles and candle holders. I made up the table with a colorful scarf. I put the flowers in a make-shift vase from a recycled lemonade bottle and added them to the table. I used the good china, crystal, and cloth napkins.

I served myself dinner and settled in to eat while I warmed up dessert – my favorite pumpkin bread pudding from Trader Joe's. I sat down across from the mirror and decided to dim the lights and eat by candlelight. As I toasted myself in the mirror, I made a vow to continue this tradition.

The next morning, I woke up early with an extra spring in my step. I ran into my friend and she asked about my date, "So…did you get lucky?"

Yes, I did. I discovered the soul-expanding practice of dating myself.

Chapter 6
Creativity & Writing

We're both creative people. We love to play music, sing, and dance. We also love visual art. (In fact, for many years, our business centered around creating usable pieces of art: handmade journals, jewelry, decorated candles, scrolls, and many other creative products.) And most of all, we love to write.

We write as a way to communicate, to express ourselves, and to connect with readers. We also write as a way to connect with our soul. Oftentimes, we find that writing is more than just an act of creation – it's a process of self-discovery. We learn truths about ourselves that we weren't even aware of…until we saw them on the page we'd just written!

The same holds true for other art forms. As you dance, sculpt, or doodle, you might discover a deep well of emotion that you hadn't realized was in you. Perhaps you'll find yourself expressing previously unknown joy, sorrow, longing, or emotions that you can't even put a word to! Or perhaps you *had* been aware of your thoughts and feelings but hadn't been able to adequately express them…until you put pen to paper (or brush to canvas, bow to string, or tap shoes to dance floor).

There are so many ways to express yourself creatively. Even within a single creative outlet, there are endless variations. For instance, as a writer, you can connect with your soul through poetry, journaling, fiction, or any number of different styles and genres. In this chapter, we've assembled a wide variety of ways to connect with your soul through creativity and writing – including journaling, scrapbooking, knitting, coloring mandalas, making collages, and writing letters. We hope you'll enjoy exploring all the creative options available to you and discovering which ones feel right…and bring you closer to your soul.

Inviting the Muse: Inspiration is Waiting for You

by Cindie Chavez

"If someone should ask me, 'What does the soul do?' I would say, 'It does two things. It loves. And it creates. Those are its primary acts.'"
- Sue Monk Kidd

For years, I was an art instructor. I taught kids at Jewish summer camp how to make candle holders and pretty tchotchkes to take home to mom and dad. I taught adults who had never held a paintbrush before to paint intuitively, creating beautiful paintings and healing their souls in the process.

One thing I heard often from adults that I never, ever heard from a child was: "I need to wait until I'm inspired."

The children never had a need to wait when art supplies were available. In fact, many times I had to convince them to hold their horses until they had a bit of instruction on the project at hand. Inspiration was never an issue for them.

I have been that child artist who was always inspired and couldn't get enough of creating. I have also been the adult creator waiting on inspiration.

One day, I was teaching an adult class and one of my students stood at her painting station for what seemed like forever just staring at her supplies. "How are you doing?" I asked. "I'm waiting for inspiration," she answered. And out of my mouth came some wise words that took even me by surprise: "NO! Inspiration is waiting on *you*!"

Over the years I've reminded myself of this many times. I merely have to invite my muse. (She loves to be invited with a pen in my hand or some silk thread on my knitting needles.) She arrives quickly, full of creative spirit. I no longer wait to be inspired but remember that inspiration has been waiting on me all along.

To love and to create – the soul's primary acts. How will you invite your muse today?

64 Shades of Magic

by Michelle Radomski

When I was five, my life was gray.

I was afraid to move, afraid to breathe, and afraid to share my voice. I dimmed my light and kept my color hidden deep inside. I lived my life in the shadows.

And then I received my first box of 64 crayons.

To me, those crayons were so much more than sky blue and carnation pink. They were unlimited passports to a world where silver-winged angels danced on lavender clouds, and mulberry-striped horses lived in rainbow-painted houses filled with love.

Crayons were magic. With them in my hand, my soul came alive.

When I turned 13, however, I put the crayons away. My heart, my dreams, and my self-expression were put on hold as I desperately struggled to fit in and find anything that felt like love.

The color was gone. The gray returned.

Many years later, I became a graphic designer. I worked with color every day. And still, my soul remained gray…until the day I created and colored my first mandala. In that moment, I remembered the magic of color as I (once again) heard the whisper of my soul.

Today, mandala coloring is sweeping the globe. People are stepping away from their computers and silencing their phones. They are picking up markers, colored pencils, and their very own boxes of 64 crayons.

They are transforming their minds and their hearts, reducing their stress, relieving their pain, and remembering their dreams. And, perhaps unbeknownst to them, they are connecting with their souls.

There is something magical that happens when we use our own creative genius to apply color to paper. Time stands still. Our hearts open. Worries fade. Stress melts. Our chattering minds quiet as we watch patterns unfold and focus on what color goes where. And in the quiet, we hear the whispers of our soul.

Now it's your turn. I invite you to color a mandala. Remember your voice and awaken your soul as you connect to your very own 64 shades of magic.

Write Yourself a Love Letter

by Stacy Carr

Have you ever received a love letter – with each word tenderly inscribed by your beloved just for you? Did you begin to glow as you read it, feeling cherished and adored?

Think of how amazing it would be to collect your mail tomorrow and find a surprise love letter telling you just how wonderful, special, and lovable you really are? What if you didn't have to hope for that letter but instead wrote it to yourself?

Let's admit it, this idea might sound silly. However, words are so powerful, especially the words we tell ourselves. The act of taking time to think of yourself, hold yourself tenderly in your own heart, and express how much you love the person you are is such an incredible gift. It is also wonderful to realize that you don't have to wait for someone else to express it!

Before you begin, imagine the love letter you've always wanted to receive. Go all out and gather everything you'll need to make it absolutely perfect. Buy a beautiful stationery set or pens in colorful ink. Sit down in a quiet place, and begin by thanking yourself for the amazing person you are today. Remember how much you've been through. Think of all your favorite traits, physical and otherwise. Don't allow negativity to enter your mind. If this is difficult, you can start small and simple and work up. Simply begin with a sentence or two about your favorite feature or a quality that makes you feel proud. Then use this as the basis to write more over time.

Loving yourself and expressing that love is such a beautiful and easy gift you can give to your soul. After you have finished, read your letter and then put it away to read again when your heart and soul need nourishment.

Practicing self love is one of the best ways to feel whole and joyful every day, and it will shine outwards and attract love back to you!

Create a SoulCollage®

by Maria Angela Russo

I embrace the philosophy that the soul is individualized pure consciousness, that only goodness and beauty reside within us all, and that we must align with the essence of our souls in order to fully experience life on Earth.

A few years ago, while in search of new ways to make that soul connection, I met a SoulCollage® facilitator. She explained that SoulCollage® (founded by Seena B. Frost in the late 1980s) is a spiritual process for accessing our intuition through imagination and images cut from magazines. This practice engages the spirit in profound ways, leaving the ego behind, encouraging self-discovery and a connection to our inner voice.

At the first workshop I attended, our facilitator directed us to go to the "image garden," a table covered with hundreds of pictures. "Pick two or three images that jump out at you," she said, adding, "Drop all expectations; the images will call to you."

When I saw the image depicting nuns, I knew what she meant, as nuns have played significant roles in my life. Not knowing what kind of collage would emerge, I paired them with a young girl meditating in the lotus position. I chose a background and a beautiful butterfly and pasted the images on a card that began to speak from somewhere deep inside: "I am one who has transformed from religion to spirituality."

I learned more in subsequent workshops, including such things as how the cards fall into suits, the meaning of transpersonal cards, and the many ways to do readings.

Making SoulCollage® cards is fun, and now I have a deck that is the "Story of Me" – a multi-card mirror of my self and my soul that allows my inner wisdom to be expressed. Journaling about each card helps me discover all that the cards have to say.

The ultimate gift of SoulCollage® is learning to consult the cards in order to access inner guidance for navigating through life transitions or addressing life's questions. It is transformative and has deepened my relationship with myself. I hope that it will do the same for you.

Morning Conversations with God

by Bree Orata

Have you ever wished you could have a heart-to-heart, no-holds-barred conversation with someone – especially if that "someone" was God? Well, you might be able to fulfill that wish more easily than you think…through journaling!

I have been doing this since high school. Back then, I would write during the final 15 minutes of each day. While it sometimes felt like a monotonous exercise, those minutes before the bell rang allowed me to savor my adolescent experiences.

As an adult, I learned about a different type of journaling through Julia Cameron: Morning Pages – three pages of uncensored writing done first thing in the morning. The beauty of the Morning Pages lies in the freedom to write whatever is in your heart.

My own pages have revealed *me* to me, and this practice has transformed my relationship with my self. The thoughts that I refuse to acknowledge publicly due to fear have been given space to unleash themselves. Frustrations have been vented and released, and ideas that seem too good to be true are dreamed up. This is my chance to write it all down without judgment.

For me, the Morning Pages have been a time of meditation; quiet self-reflection; and, most importantly, a moment to talk to God. As I write, I speak to God and He speaks to me. Sometimes I talk and He listens; sometimes He talks and I listen.

Through this process, I have experienced an awakening like never before. I have learned to trust in the goodness of God to lead me exactly where I need to be. I have learned to listen to the wisdom of my soul and my heart. I now know without a doubt that God does answer prayers. (Besides, what is prayer if not conversation with the Creator, the Source?) My pages have taught me that if we seek, we shall find. Help is always close at hand. We are never alone.

I invite you to have your own conversation through writing Morning Pages. Give God a chance to speak to you. You may be surprised by what you hear!

Finding Forgiveness Through Unsent Letters

by Cindy Jones Lantier

Forgiveness is a big issue.

But here's the thing: Holding grudges or needing to forgive someone rarely impacts the person we are at odds with. The situation doesn't change just because we resent the outcome. Yet we are left with stress, anger, and maybe some physical manifestations of these now-toxic feelings.

Forgiveness does not mean that we condone the actions of the other person. True forgiveness does not turn us into victims; it actually empowers us. It is a declaration that we are not going to let that person have control over us any longer. They do not get to continue to influence our moods, emotions, or actions.

This all sounds good, but how do we actually do it? How do we forgive someone who hurt us – and sometimes hurt us badly?

For me, it happens through unsent letters.

When I need to forgive, I spend time alone with my journal. I write about the person, their actions, and the situation. Without excusing their behavior, I try to see them with compassion. I try to remember that they, too, have probably been hurt. They may have been acting out of their own sense of survival.

When I've explored the event as fully as I can, I turn to a clean sheet of paper. I write a letter to the person, telling them how I feel about them and their actions. I let it all out; there are no sugar-coated euphemisms here! I may cry. I may curse. I may have contradictory emotions. I simply express myself fully.

When the letter is finished, I read it over once. I often destroy it, to release the pent-up emotional energy. Sometimes I have to write more than one letter, but with each note, I can feel the shift in my emotions; I can feel the toxicity leaving.

It's difficult to be connected with your soul when your feelings are toxic. Getting them out – with acceptance, compassion, and an eye toward forgiveness – can be very healing for your psyche and your soul.

Click, Clack: Soulful Knitting

by Janice Lawrenz

There is something very soul connecting about having a pair of knitting needles in your hands – hearing the soothing sound of the repetitive and rhythmic *click, clack, click, clack* of the moving needles and feeling the smooth texture of the yarn as it passes through your fingers. Many people have likened the knitting process to a type of meditation. While you knit, it is easy to get lost – focusing on the stitches and the pattern. In our fast-paced world, it allows you to slow down and be mindful. Time slips by. You feel total bliss – creating something beautiful and receiving spiritual and mental benefits: building your confidence and pride at a job well done and satisfaction in seeing your creation coming into being.

I have been knitting since I was seven. I've created sweaters, vests, bonnets, booties, baby jumpsuits, pants, and toys. And lately, I've used my knitting skills for charity. My favourite charity is "Wraps with Love" – which connects people in knitting 28 large squares, which are sewn together as a blanket. The blankets are pooled at a central location, then distributed locally and overseas.

I love being able to use my knitting to give back to society, but there are other benefits in knitting for charity. These include:

- Relaxation
- Using a God-given skill
- Learning a new skill
- Persisting at something and building confidence in yourself
- Connecting with your heart and soul
- Connecting with likeminded people, sharing a common interest
- Having a true sense of purpose

If you are interested in knitting but are worried that it's too complicated, fear not! The basics consist of learning only five skills: casting onto a knitting needle, mastering the knit and purl stitches, casting off, and interpreting a pattern. Once you learn these basics, in hardly any time at all you can start enjoying the meditative bliss of the process, appreciating the satisfaction of a job well done, sharing your talents with others, and connecting more deeply with your own soul.

Sensing Soul Connection: The Emerging Artist

by Aprile Alexander

Artmaking can be a wonderful way to go more deeply within. Soul doesn't mind if you can't draw a straight line. Soul doesn't think your stick figures look ridiculous. You can "come home to Soul" through artmaking by having fun, experimenting, and even making a mess creatively.

Although I am a professional artist, my favorite way to sense my connection with Soul through art is to sit in bed with an unlined pad and kiddie crayons and just scribble, using my left hand. (I'm right-handed.)

Right-handed people can easily tap into their intuitive, creative right-brain hemisphere by drawing or writing with their left hand. If you're left-handed, using the right hand can create a similar change. Utilizing your "other hand" can deactivate the inner critic, also.

If you'd like to express your creativity (and "become like little children"), you might be inspired to try this process.

First, enjoy wandering around your home collecting pens, markers, colored pencils, crayons, paints, or anything else you can draw or paint with. (Yes, even ketchup works, but maybe not in bed!) Next, gather used envelopes, cereal boxes, old telephone books, magazines, greeting cards, or scrap paper of any kind – anything you can draw or paint on. Then, choose somewhere you can relax. Put your paper or cardboard onto a stable surface, pick up your marker (or paintbrush, crayon, ketchup, or whatever takes your fancy) with your non-dominant hand, and start moving it over the page, letting it go wherever it wants to.

Abstract is good! Stick figures are fabulous! Weird color combinations are a delight! Wonky shapes that don't make sense are perfect! Keep your hand moving over the paper, choosing colors at random.

Do one or more quick drawings, or keep going over the same artwork, layer by layer. You can add words, more colors, or whatever you're inspired to do. Just be yourself. Mindfulness helps: be a relaxed, happy, little child – totally focused on the joy of putting colors on paper.

Sooner or later, I believe that you will notice yourself moving into a new space of awareness, which may be a sign of your connection with Soul.

Poetic License for the Soul

by Ellouise Heather

Looking through the misted glass to the ominous clouds above, I sipped on the cappuccino that was the stopgap measure for another sleepless night. I sighed, feeling isolated in the bustling morning rush of the coffee shop, a feeling with which I was becoming all too familiar. I felt that no one understood what I was going through, but how could they when I didn't quite understand it myself?

I took out my little notepad, which had taken up residency in my handbag over the past few weeks. I had decided to start writing again, something that I truly love but had let fall to the wayside for "more important" aspects of life for many years. So I had started to carry a notepad and pen with me whenever I left the house, should I have a moment in my day to write. I did not expect what I wrote to be good, and I had given myself permission to write for as briefly as I felt. As it turned out, I was finding it easier to write in short poems because there was no pressure for it to be an epic novel worthy of awards.

So far, I had written plenty of poems telling fictional tales, but none reflecting my feelings. Or so I thought. As I flicked through the notepad, I took in the many metaphors peppering my imperfect poems and realised that my quiet inner voice had been attempting to grab my attention. As I finished reading, I began to feel a surge of inspiration and reached for my pen.

And I wrote.

I absorbed each penned word, and by the end I had a lump in my throat. The page began to blur, and I realised I was shedding tears of relief. It was then that I recognised that writing poetry was like having a direct line to my soul. Abandoning it all those years ago had been a disservice to myself. In that moment, I decided to let go of regret and to whole-heartedly embrace my rediscovered poetic license.

Engage Your Own Soul's Movie

by Murray James

Have you ever come away from a movie inspired by the qualities of one of the characters? Often, the hero or heroine overcomes great hardship and struggles to rise above the odds.

One of my favourites is Scarlett O'Hara, in the 1939 classic *Gone with the Wind*, who raises herself from her impoverished circumstances with tenacity and guile.

Another movie that touched me is *The Railway Man* (2012), the real-life story of Jeremy Irvine. This hero is able to release the abuse he suffered in a World War II concentration camp and go on to meet and eventually forgive the enemy who tortured him.

Jimmy Stewart's role as George Bailey in *It's a Wonderful Life* (1947) is another inspirational character. In a moment of suicidal despair, he unexpectedly learns about the life transformations that have been experienced by numerous people in his town due to his actions over the years.

All of these inspiring stories can resonate within our own life and our soul's journey. My suggestion is that we can bring these characters to life and into focus in our own inner story.

To do this, set aside a reflective time and bring to mind the fascinating, uplifting characters that you find appealing. For example, it could be Atticus Finch in *To Kill a Mocking Bird* (1962), who displays integrity and broad-mindedness, or the resilient and intelligent Jane Austin in *Becoming Jane* (2007).

Choose one or two movie characters who speak to your soul. Write down or think about the storyline. After some quiet reflection, imagine yourself interviewing these people. What might they say to you? Let them speak to you, and even ask *you* questions. Then, identify those characteristics that are indeed residing within you.

Write or record your response, then do some free-flow journaling. Use your affirming voice to honour these positive qualities within yourself, especially the ones you may have neglected. Finding and celebrating this, you can now start broadcasting on your own screen these very aspects of *your* wonderful life.

Harnessing the Power of Spiritual Love Letters

by Tia Johnson

There is just as much power in the written word as there is in the spoken word. When we write and speak from the heart, that power becomes magnified. I learned the power of my written words when I found notes I wrote years ago.

After my grandmother died from cancer and my Pop-Pop died from a broken heart, I underwent a two-year healing journey from 2008-2010. I wrote often about my thoughts and feelings; however, what I didn't realize was I actually wrote spiritual love letters that were packed with healing beyond measure. Reading the notes, even years later, provides emotional and spiritual relief that can only be found in words that come straight from the heart.

If personal notes about one's thoughts or experiences compiled together can be called *memoirs*, then personal notes about one's healing process can be called *spiritual love letters*. Spiritual love letters can be an eternal source of internal healing. After all, the cornerstone of spiritual healing is love and a calling out to Spirit for spiritual assistance.

Writing a spiritual love letter is a means of reconnecting us with the divine love and strength that resides within each and every one of us. It is a kind reminder of the insurmountable love, support, and strength that is around us when we experience unfortunate situations.

I highly encourage you to write to your higher self and the people you love. Write a spiritual love letter to yourself, put it in a time capsule, and read it at a later date. Write another spiritual love letter to yourself, mail it to yourself, and know that love is coming your way. Write a spiritual love letter to someone you love without telling him or her. Write a spiritual love letter to Spirit, burn the letter, and watch the smoke go to Heaven.

The written word can be a powerful vehicle for spiritual healing, soulful connection, and love. And it always feels good to spread love as often as possible, because we never know who it may help.

Write to Feng Shui Your Soul

by Laura Probert

"I write to feng shui my soul."
- Laura Probert

Writing, in all its forms, is a direct path to your soul. Whether it's a poem, a journal entry, a blog, or a letter, your words move the precious things from inside to out, and the voice of your soul can be heard – even if it's just you who's listening. Are you listening when your soul speaks?

I began writing in my teens as a way to connect to my deepest desires and dreams. As an adult, I ached with a need to tell my stories and began to transform my fears and heal my life when I started writing those stories down. Writing is a necessary part of my life, a powerful way to clear a path for divine flow and creativity.

People think you have to be creative to be a writer or an artist. I think that when you write, you clear a path for creative inspiration. Writing without rules, without agenda, clears out the thoughts, plans, and judgments that get in your way. Writing becomes a healing tool, a tool of awareness, that can shift your thoughts and beliefs, which can ultimately change your life.

Try it now. Grab a notebook, a pen, and a timer. (I use the timer function on my iPhone.) Set your timer for five minutes and answer the question: *What do I love to do so much that it makes me lose track of time?* Try to write without stopping until the timer goes off. Don't worry about spelling, punctuation, or finishing sentences. No rules – just write.

Writing about the big, important questions makes you aware of what matters. With awareness you can choose new ways to think, believe, and act. It's through this aware action that your life can change and become everything you desire.

What are your big questions? Make a list and try writing about each one for at least five minutes. Allow yourself to hear your soul's whispers and see where they take you!

Accentuate the Positive with Constructive Creativity

by Susan Huntz-Ramos

I have found that drawing has immense healing powers. Many times when I've been stressed out or dealing with anger, I'll sit down to write but find my mind drifting…and I start doodling on my paper instead. I drift into a zen-like state, and before I know it I've filled almost the whole page with my doodles. (I can't draw people or animals well, but I can doodle lots of fun stuff!)

Years ago, after learning how our thoughts become things and how we attract what we focus on, I realized just how vitally important utilizing our creative imagination can be to our health. Without a healthy outlet, stress can build up, leading to anger and to illness. Especially when you are in a difficult place in life, constructive creativity can help you to accentuate the positive, making your difficulties a little easier to navigate.

It doesn't matter if you're a master artist or can't even draw a straight line. What matters is finding the element that "soothes the savage brain" in you. Make time for yourself to sit and do the thing that relaxes you: doodling, drawing, painting, or even cutting pictures from magazines to make a collage. Get your hands off the electronics and instead reach for some paper, pencils, crayons, paint, chalk, markers, scissors, and glue. Don't be afraid to get messy! Don't be afraid to erase or start all over again. And don't feel that you have to be "perfect" or create a masterpiece. Just create something that makes YOU smile, that makes you feel good.

Your constructive creation doesn't have to make sense to anyone else. Just you.

Releasing Anxiety Through Art Journaling

by Gina Karas

As an artist, I both love and hate the freedom of an empty canvas. I love being able to create anything that I want, but I hate the anxiety of choosing what to create and worrying about what others will think of it. Anxiety has been my biggest obstacle, but the freedom of art journaling has helped me immensely.

Art journaling is a form of journaling that brings additional elements to the page besides just paper and pen. My basic art journaling supplies are: a blank art journal, acrylic paints, gesso, paintbrushes, sponge brushes, molding paste, stencils, glimmer mists, acrylic and rubber stamps, ink pads, paper towels, baby wipes, and my creativity! I love being able to experiment with different mediums – knowing that it's all okay!

Art journaling forces me to disconnect from my anxiety and connect with my creative soul. The blank pages fill up with colors, textures, and quotes. The anxious feeling of heart-pounding dread disappears with each brushstroke. Creating in my own private space allows me to escape and create a world of my own. Whether I choose to share my creations with others is entirely up to me. That freedom empowers me even more.

Life gives us an empty canvas. It is up to us how we wish to color our world. I hope that you will join me in my artistic, personal-growth journey and let art journaling heal your soul.

Journaling for the Grieving Soul

by Dortha Hise

From July 2012 to May 2014, I lost 28 loved ones.

This experience of loss, grief, and awakening began with the unexpected death of my mom. Understandably, I felt heartbroken – but not because I was incredibly close with her; rather, because I was *not* close with her, and I felt uncertain about my grief process. I didn't feel like I knew where to turn or how to move forward. So I made a special trip to a stationery store and picked out a journal, which I intended to use especially to journal about my mom.

Some days I felt like I was reiterating the same thing I had written 10 times before – and that didn't matter. Other days, I felt as though I'd made real progress along my grief journey – connecting thoughts, ideas, and various feelings that I hadn't previously been able to put into words.

I had never considered myself a writer; but during that two-year period, as I lost more and more of my loved ones, I journaled as often as I could – a practice that I found deeply cathartic as I traversed those many deaths. Journaling about my feelings over these losses enabled me to process my grief in a healthy manner.

Just as I was finding my written voice, however, I all but lost my speaking voice: I was diagnosed with a neurological condition that presented itself as a vocal disorder. This condition rendered the sound of my voice lower than a whisper. Never was my journal more important to me!

Over the past few years of having this condition, I've really embraced the fact that although I now have a tiny voice, I have a big message to get out – which I've done through the powerful written form. I continued to journal about my experiences and ultimately wrote and published a book about my journey.

Not only did journaling through my grief allow me to process my losses, but it enabled me to find a new voice…and a deeper part of my soul.

Scrapbooking for the Soul

by Janice Lawrenz

Scrapbooking is a craft where you can easily connect with your soul on whatever level you choose. Depending on your mood and the subject you want to focus on, you can create a scrapbook that expresses your creativity and brings together important elements from your life.

Why do people scrapbook? There are many possible reasons:

- To create a legacy for their children and grandchildren
- To note their children's milestones from birth onwards
- To record their own engagement, wedding, honeymoon, and other important life events
- To heal from the loss of a loved one
- To recount stories and memories
- To produce a special gift for someone

I currently have a number of scrapbooks in process: my son's milestones, my holidays, and a book of memorabilia of my family history.

Although many people now use digital scrapbooking, I still prefer the traditional way. There is something to be said about the awareness, excitement, and sensitivity I feel as the pages are created. It gives me great joy and pride to see the pages become real. I love picking the colours and textures of the paper and cardboard, touching the lumpy and smooth elements, cutting and trimming, choosing photos/images, measuring the journaling space, and coming up with a title. I arrange everything on the page until I am happy with the look, balance, flow, and harmony of the bits and pieces. It is like putting jigsaw pieces together to make a final picture. I allow the features to speak to me on a deeper level.

The process gives me total freedom to decide what I want to place on my pages. It is relaxing, allowing me to zone out and be blissful. My journaling on the pages gives me the opportunity to write creatively, express my feelings, and feel the lift of connecting with all the elements on the page. It is also an avenue that allows me to be truly authentic and grateful on a deep spiritual and energetic level.

The Magic of Ink on Paper

by Cindie Chavez

As a coach, I've been known to ask "If you had a magic wand, what would you wish for?" And, like many coaches, I often encourage my clients to write down their goals.

Why is it so important to write these things down? It seems that written goals have a better chance of being realized. A Dominican University study has quantified this, showing that "Those who wrote their goals *accomplished significantly more* than those who did not write their goals." That alone might be enough motivation for most of us to begin writing down our goals; but there is another, more inspirational, reason for me.

I remember blowing out the candles on my birthday cake and making a wish, and I remember wishing on stars. Maybe you remember these rituals too, or maybe you had other wishing rituals while you were growing up. I believe that wishing rituals came easily to me as a child because children are so connected with their souls. Our wishes reflect the deepest, most authentic part of us.

As a child, the magic of wishing was often provided by an adult (possibly wearing a Santa Claus costume), but as an adult I get the thrill of bringing my own magic to bear on my wishes.

That magic begins with two very non-magical items: pen and paper.

When we write down our goals, we have already begun to bring them out of the metaphysical realm – the realm of thoughts, ideas, dreams, and wishes – and into the physical realm: real ink on real paper.

The simple act of bringing your soul's whispered desires from deep within into the physical world as ink on paper is the beginning of magic – and of wishes coming true.

What wish is your soul asking you to write down today?

A Soulful Hobby

by Polina Blair

Having a hobby is a great way to connect with the soul. My hobby is making jewelry. When I get in the flow of the creative process, I feel joy, satisfaction, and peace.

It started when my son was a toddler and we went to a craft store to look for craft ideas. I came across a jewelry-making starter kit and decided to try it. As soon as I had a chance, I put together a necklace. It was really enjoyable and brought me a sense of satisfaction.

First, I made jewelry on my own. As time allowed, I started taking different classes to improve my skills. Soon, I gained enough experience, skills, and confidence to make jewelry as gifts for family members, friends, and co-workers. People really seemed to like my jewelry. I received a lot of positive feedback, which made me feel appreciated.

I also joined a local Rock & Gem Club, which was a great way to connect with people with similar interests. Not only did it allow me to advance my jewelry-making skills, but I also studied and collected rocks, minerals, and fossils. My interests rubbed off on my son, who is now a club member. We've gone on several field trips together and have created wonderful, shared memories.

Because I enjoy jewelry making, I thought that teaching this skill to other women could become a good way to share my interest and introduce others to a wonderful creative activity. I checked with my friends to see if they would be interested in attending a jewelry-making workshop and received quite a bit of interest. I am grateful that my first workshop was successful, and class participants asked that I consider hosting more classes. Though I work full-time, I continue to teach jewelry-making workshops when time allows.

For me, an unexpectedly discovered hobby became an outlet for creativity and an opportunity to connect with other people in a meaningful way. Most importantly, it made me feel good about myself and closer to my soul.

Writing to Listen

by Rachel Cohen

Accessing the divine guidance of your soul is easier than you may think. You can tap into this wisdom any time you want through a process I call "Writing to Listen."

All you need for this practice is uninterrupted quiet time and a journal/notebook and pen or a computer.

Here is how this process works:

- *Set up your space, physically and energetically.* Clear a space for yourself that is clutter-free and clean. Surround yourself with inspiring things – fresh flowers, meaningful pictures or artwork, candles, crystals, items from nature, or anything that feels yummy to you. If you don't have the items you want, you can visualize them around you.
- *Begin to tune in.* Relax, close your eyes, and take some deep breaths into your belly. Feel your feet or behind planted firmly on the ground. Set an intention that you will open to receive information easily and effortlessly.
- *Ask for guidance.* Call in your soul, your spirit guides, and/or your angels. You may feel the presence of one or many, or you may not sense anything different. Whatever you do or don't experience, know that all is well. Continue on.
- *Begin to write.* Listen deeply, put your pen to the paper or your fingers on the keyboard, and follow words as if you're following breadcrumbs on a path.

There is no wrong way to do this. At first, it may feel like you are making up words, which is okay. Trust the experience you are having. Over time, you will grow accustomed to what it feels like to connect with your soul and your guides in this way and how it feels for words to come through you. Remain open to the inspired messages from your soul during this process. And most of all, have fun with it!

Pictures of Possibility

by Laurie Seymour

Remember the imaginary worlds that you used to create as a child? Each image connected you to possibility: you could be a world-changing hero, fly without wings, or communicate with animals – or all three!

Pictures provide glimpses of your vast untapped potential. They transcend language or cultural barriers. They are connectors, a means of communicating with dimensions of existence that transcend the ordinary. By using pictures for self-dialogue, you have a vehicle to access universal energies that can fuel your actions. If you are creating a new business, career, relationship, or living situation, you can use pictures to access direction from your deepest self. Try this:

- *Take some time to sit quietly with whatever you are considering, noticing the ideas that catch your attention.* Allow an idea to become a picture in your mind's eye and then flesh out the details. Get up close. Then step back for a wider view.
- *Notice how you feel.* Connect the sensations with your pictures. Ask yourself questions about your responses to the pictures: *Where does your energy get stuck? Where does it flow easily? Have you dismissed the picture as impossible?* Pay attention to what feels "right" to you, making notes of ideas, insights, and any direction for your next step. Continue to create and refine your picture(s) for as long as you need.

Creating a picture of your desired outcome sets a powerful dynamic into motion. People, situations, and resources seem to come out of the woodwork to bring your picture into form! Allow your picture to change as you take action. Different elements will surface. Continue your self-dialogue, refining your picture and receiving new insight.

Creating with pictures takes time, attention, and a willingness to explore the unknown…which can be your best ally when you are considering a new direction in life! It builds an intimate relationship with the part of you that lives beyond what you already know. It connects you with the magic of your soul's expression. And it reminds you that anything is possible!

Messages from Doodling

by Laura P. Clark

There it was: the mighty mitochondria, powerhouse of the cell, being created by my doodling. Not just once but dozens of times, doodled all over my notes. I was not, as one might think, in a biology class but an English class in college.

Like so many others stepping into adulthood, I had low self-esteem and even less confidence. As I doodled, only half listening to the lecture, I had no idea that my soul was speaking to me through my drawings. It wasn't until 20 years later that I understood the powerful message that these images were trying to deliver: "Like the cell's mitochondria, I am powerful beyond measure."

Since these first doodles, I have received many more powerful messages, and I now see what a soulful process doodling can be. It brings you to a place of quiet centeredness. It allows your mind to wander and become curious. It allows you to empty your mind of all thoughts that do not serve you. And it brings forward soulful messages from deep within that *do* serve you.

Even those who struggle with their artistic side can doodle. It can be done anywhere, anytime, with no supplies other than paper and a pencil or pen. You simply allow the pen to go here and there with no apparent rhyme or reason.

But the real art of doodling is the interpretation of the images you've created. With practice, this art becomes a wonderful way to connect with your soul and see what it wants you to know. From your doodle interpretations, you can get a glimpse into your subconscious, gain confidence, see how obstacles can become opportunities, or receive any number of soulful messages.

So give it a whirl today! Doodle for five minutes. Then look at your creation and ask yourself: "What does my soul want me to know?" There, in your doodling, will be a message for your powerful self to see.

Non-Scary Poetry Writing

by Aprile Alexander

Years ago, I felt very far from Soul. Then one day, while living in the Blue Mountains of Sydney, Australia, I was led to follow a wilderness trail. I found a sunny rock and started writing snippets of non-rhyming poetry for the first time ever. Within a short time, I felt a miraculous connection to Soul.

I invite you to gather something to write with (such as a pencil, pen, marker, crayon, or a paintbrush) and something to write on (such as a the inside of an old envelope or even a paper napkin), and find a safe place in which to write.

If you think that you can't write poetry, aren't good at English, or can't spell, please gently put those beliefs aside. Anyone can do this. Simply decide to be kind to yourself while you write.

When you are ready, take a couple of deep breaths. You may like to pray or meditate for a few moments.

To connect easily with your creative, intuitive brain, take your writing instrument in your non-dominant hand (seriously, this will work!) and lovingly give yourself permission to write "kiddie stuff." Play with letters on the page, as though you were a little child again learning to write your ABCs, but with your "other" hand.

Then take a couple more deep breaths and ask Soul, "What shall I write?" One or more words may come to you. If not, then choose a word or phrase, such as: "Love," "Cats," "Sadness," "My horrible job," "Beauty," "How can I reach out to my kids?" or "What's my next step in life?"

Let the words appear on the paper. You might sense that the words are being "fed" to you. Or you might feel that you are making it up. It is all just right, so keep your hand moving over the paper until you feel led to stop.

Your poem might be one line or many lines. It might even be just one word. You are connecting with your inner poet. You will know. Soul will guide you.

Create a "Life MAP"

by Mariët Hammann

I came into this life colorful and whole, living with curiosity, wonder, and boundless creative expression. I was living my authentic purpose, and I had a "life map" that would help me continue doing so.

Or so I thought…until the day I woke up to find myself totally out of sync, directionless, overwhelmed, and without a map. I was overweight and unhealthy, exhausted and depleted, withdrawn and unhappy. It felt as if the world was moving to a different beat than mine and that my life was missing its purposeful brilliance. I was just going through the motions.

I realized that something needed to change. I needed my beat back. I needed direction. I needed my map-less life to be one of full-color meaningfulness. I needed to get in touch with my lost, scattered parts. I needed my soul to speak its truth. And for this to happen, I knew that I would have to slow down.

So I did. I slowed down enough to hear my soul whispering: "I want to dance, create, and color your brilliance alive." With these words, my heart sparked, my mind paid attention, and my soul connected. My soul sent me on a journey of self-discovery through color, food, and creativity. My soul purpose was reborn in its brilliance, and I discovered an authentic "Life MAP" (Movement * Art * Plenty of Color) to guide me.

I invite you to create your own Life MAP. To start, answer the following questions from each of the three categories:

- Movement: *At what pace do I need to move through life at this moment? Where is my life missing a beat? What movement will spark my brilliance?*
- Art: *What symbols am I noticing around me in my life? Which stories keep showing up? How do I express my brilliance?*
- Plenty of Color: *Which colorful foods will nourish my whole self? What does "living my color brilliance" mean to me? What color will support my brilliance?*

I hope that these questions – and, more importantly, your answers – will help you develop your own Life MAP, rediscover your spark, and reconnect with your soul.

Sleepless Inspiration

by Susan Huntz-Ramos

You would think that during my nearly four years of being a full-time caregiver for my father-in-law, I would be exhausted enough to sleep through the night. Being a 24/7 caregiver, there are periods of time when night and day seem like one big blur. Even during those periods when Papa would sleep through the night, I'd often find myself wide awake in the wee hours of morning. On a positive note, that's when some of my best ideas would come to me!

Often, I would lie there tossing and turning, finally falling back to sleep just before sunrise. By morning, I would be so busy getting our youngest teen up and off to school and Papa up and ready for the day, that if I did remember any of those great ideas, I would end up forgetting nearly all of them before I had a chance to write them down. Until...I rekindled my old passion for writing and drawing.

Because I wasn't always able to get back to sleep – and not being a fan of reading to fall back to sleep – I often found myself writing or drawing. I began to look forward to those middle-of-the-night creative times. Writing and drawing became a form of meditation for me. Pouring my thoughts out on paper always reconnected me with my inner peace.

When I look back at my pieces, I am often amazed that by allowing the creative process to flow without any specific agenda, I was able to release stress, worries, and other feelings that weigh me down, while producing writing or art that leaves me in awe of myself and my abilities – inspiring me to do more!

Although my creative inspiration often arrived in the middle of the night, yours might come at any time of day or night. If the idea of meditative writing or drawing resonates with you, then you should give it a try – and see what inspiration flows from your soul onto the page!

Chapter 7
Meditation

There are many different definitions of meditation, but perhaps our favorite is how a woman from one of our meditation classes once described it: she said it felt like coming home. That truly is the goal of meditation: to come home to yourself, to your soul, to the Divine. And just as there are probably multiple ways to get back to your house, there are numerous meditative paths that can lead you to your soul-home.

Most forms of meditation involve focus. The object of the focus can vary greatly. In some forms, the meditator stares at a candle. Other meditations involve focusing on a word or phrase. A wide range of visualizations involve focusing on an inner journey – seeing a scene in your mind's eye. Other meditations involve body awareness – such as focusing on your breath or your heartbeat. Regardless of the focus, almost all meditations can induce feelings of calm connectedness, which often remain long after the meditation sessions have finished.

Over the years, we've tried many different types of meditation, including breath counting, guided visualizations, chanting, entrainment, and even a meditation game on Wii (where you sit on a board and strive to maintain balance [or, perhaps, practice *non-striving*] as you stare at a flickering candle on the TV screen – there's even a point system!).

This chapter features numerous meditation techniques – from ancient practices to modern meditation apps, as well as meditations centered around nature and animals, meditations to help you connect with the spirit of abundance, meditations to help you connect with the Divine, and numerous ways to get centered and find peace – even in the middle of the busiest days. We hope you'll give some of them a try – and find at least one technique that helps guide you home…to your soul.

Expand Your Joy

by Alicia Isaacs Howes

I used to believe that my soul was something far, far away in the distant heavens – and that in order to connect in a meaningful way, I needed to be very calm and in a sacred space or have a trusted spiritual advisor do it for me. Sound familiar?

What I've come to realise, however, is that we carry our soul's light in every cell of our bodies. So wherever we are, our soul is right there, too! It's wonderful to have special time to go within, but it's not a prerequisite for making a soulful connection.

As the best word to describe the soul's essence is *joy*, here's a simple practice to connect with your soul's energy whenever you wish:

1. Bring your attention to your inhale and exhale for one, two, or three breaths. As you do this, imagine a sphere of light expanding from your heart, surrounding and holding you.
2. Ask: "As I now connect with my soul's wisdom, how can I allow for more joy in my life?" and become present to the answer, no matter how it comes to you. The answer may show up as an idea or sudden insight, a feeling, an image, or a symbol. It can be words you hear inside or a knowing of what you can start, stop, or do more of so more joy can flow through you. If your answer doesn't come to you immediately, don't worry! Your soul's whisper may show up as a chance meeting, an overheard conversation, a random page in a book, an invitation, or an unexpected opportunity that answers your question more perfectly than you could have imagined!
3. Express thanks for the response to your request and for being fully supported in noticing, understanding, and taking inspired action on it.

When you allow for more joy, you naturally deepen your soul's connection. Enjoy this meditation as often as you'd like, and feel free to change the question if you'd like to explore other areas of focus and guidance.

And don't forget to take action on your answer. That's how you can experience increasing levels of soul awareness; conscious co-creation; and, of course, joy!

Mending-the-Heart Meditation

by Jody Rentner Doty

There are times in life when your heart is heavy. You may have experienced a loss, a breakup of a relationship, or you may just need a boost to your self-affinity. The following is a guided meditation for the heart. You may find it helpful to have someone read it out loud, or you may choose to record it to play during heart-challenging times.

Begin by taking a few deep breaths, inhaling and exhaling slowly, stilling your mind, and quieting your body. Invite into your mind's eye a vision, a symbol of your heart, to appear before you. Admire your affinity. Ask your higher self for a word or two to describe your heart, paying attention to what your heart is telling you.

Place your hand over your heart and feel your pulse, your heartbeat. As you breathe in and out slowly, release anything you are holding onto that causes you pain, heaviness, or sadness.

Use your breath to let go of any hurtful words, other people's energies, painful memories, trauma, or hate. As you do so, recite these words: "I breathe in me, my highest vibration of love. I accept the transformative power of love and choose to heal and release any and all chains, protections, or barriers to loving myself as I am, right now, in this moment. I give myself permission to let go of anything that keeps me from experiencing love in my life."

As you slowly inhale and exhale, imagine releasing to the Universe any heartache, pain, words, or images that no longer serve you. Fill in any empty places within your heart with your highest vibration of love. Wrap yourself in a blanket of self-love, tucking it in around you. Let the energy fill every cell of your body.

When you feel whole and your body is filled with the loving essence of you, open your eyes. Sit for a time in the stillness of you. Shine your soul. Bless your heart, truly and completely. Know that you are wholehearted and loved.

Soul Technology

by Ashton Aiden

If there's one thing I've found in my own endeavors to nourish my own heart and soul, it's this: I will never be at a place where this journey is over and life has ceased to distract me from myself.

Staying connected with my soul, my heart, and that which gives my life peace is something that I must practice daily, from moment to moment. Regardless of where I am and how far I think I've come, it will always be necessary for me to *choose* the joy of my soul over the activity of my racing mind – again and again.

I learned very early in my life that I had a highly overactive mind. This became most apparent in my early 20s from many failed attempts to meditate. I just couldn't do it. I couldn't relax and let go of the mental stream. I was completely, hopelessly plugged into the matrix.

My ability to unplug and let go came to me finally through a very peculiar technology known as brainwave entrainment. Through this technology, the brain is effortlessly led into immersive states of consciousness by mimicking the brainwave patterns of profoundly deep meditation. It's sometimes called "the lazy man's way to meditate," or "meditation on steroids." For me, I don't mind taking the easy way, so long as it gives my mind that extra push to let go and rest in stillness.

So, I connect with my soul while sitting in an ordinary, comfy chair, in a quiet corner of my room, listening to a peaceful soundtrack with headphones on. The sound of birds chirping, rain falling, or a gentle creek in the background guides me into deeper and deeper relaxation as I feel my body letting go, and my mind beginning to commune with peace.

But the *real* magic is not in the technology itself. It is in realizing that all I must do to connect with Divinity is let go. In any of these sincere attempts to reach out to my soul, I discover it patiently waiting for me, reaching out to meet me halfway.

The Zen Lane

by Gia Reed

Meditation isn't always about being in a totally quiet, controlled environment or sitting in the lotus position. Sometimes it's about listening to your inner voice, expressing your love and gratitude, and connecting to the Divine within you. One of the places I can slip into an alpha state and really connect with my soul is…in the car! Yep, you read that right: in the car.

A number of years ago, I faced a very long daily commute in heavy traffic – rush-hour-encompassed horn blowing, hand flailing, and hollering complaints at my fellow drivers. Prying my fingers off the steering wheel had become a daily habit!

Once I realized how much time and energy I was frittering away while on the road, however, I made a conscious decision to move into the "Zen Lane." I began using my commuting time to center myself and do my "I AM" affirmations. I talked to the Divine and shared my thankfulness. I smiled. If someone cut in front of me, I wished them a safe journey. Delays? No problem – more time to get my thankfulness on!

It's been years since I made these changes, and they still have an amazing impact not only on my own life but also on the lives of my passengers. Last week, my daughter and I pulled up to a drive-thru line behind an open Jeep with several very young children in the front and back seats. In the past, my first reaction would have been to start a rant about bad parenting and children being protected and safe. Instead, I got very quiet, and after a moment my daughter turned to me and said, "I'm sending positive energy to that Jeep to protect them on their journey"…exactly what I had been doing!

These days, instead of grumbling about traffic or a rush-hour commute, I always cherish my time in the Zen Lane. How amazing is it that something I once dreaded has become one of the best parts of my day!

Inner Forest Meditation

by Allanah Hunt

I invite you to go on an inner journey with me. Close your eyes and imagine that you're walking with me in the coolness of the forest. Surround yourself with the sounds of nature as we stand protected and sheltered by the branches above, welcomed by the birds, and whispered to by the gentle breeze. Breathe in the freshness, the sense of life all around, and surrender to the peace that exists in this moment.

Stop for a moment and become aware of yourself. Feel your breath as it tickles your top lip. Hear the beating of your heart. Deliberately slow your breathing until you feel your heart and breath in alignment, slow and steady signs of life. Focus on the stillness of your soul as it matches the quiet aliveness of the forest.

Keeping your connection with yourself, project your attention outward toward the trees around you. Feel the slow and steady beating of their hearts; understand the permanence they offer, the sense of time without time. Know that they have been here far longer than you and will continue long after you have gone. Find comfort in their girth, their solidity, and the majesty of their height. Allow your soul to connect with theirs, and know peace in this moment.

Whatever troubles you today is temporary. Just as a tree can lose a branch yet continue to stand, damaged but still strong and beautiful, so can you. Bring your pain to your centre. Sit with it. Feel it join and be swallowed up as it beats in time with your heart. Know that your heart will continue to beat, your breath will continue to flow, and that you will still be here long after the pain is gone.

Take strength from the trees. Imprint this memory on your soul and take it with you. Come back to this moment any time you choose, and walk again with me in this inner forest.

Busy-Day Soul Connections

by Cat Williford

Remember the American Express slogan, "Don't leave home without it"? Here are my busy-day "Don't leave home without them" soul connections to ensure all-day connection with the Light of Love inside:

1. *Greet your soul in the mirror each morning.* It doesn't care about the pillowcase creases on your cheek, crusty eyes, or bed-head hair. I smile from my heart and say, "Hello, Joyful Light. We have a lot on our plate today. I know I will do better with it all when I am connected with you!" To maintain this connection, I have two daily reminders set on my phone at my busiest times. One is to "Breathe," and the other asks, "What am I grateful for right now?"

2. *Even when I'm squeezed for time, I use my go-to meditation.* Because it is only five minutes, I do it twice more during the day – usually when the Breathe and Gratitude reminders chime! Here it is:

- Close your eyes, inhale slowly through your nose and exhale slowly through your mouth three times, keeping the tip of your tongue on the roof of your mouth. Use your exhales to release any tension you find as you move down your body.
- Notice the sensations behind your eyes, what you hear, and how tight or loose your jaw is.
- Become aware of your neck, shoulders, arms, and hands, noticing the sensations along the way.
- Focus on your chest rising and falling with your breath, your belly's fullness or hunger; notice the weight of your body on your buttocks. Feel your thighs on the chair and your feet on the floor.
- Place your hands on your heart center and whisper to yourself: "I love you, [your name]. I love you, [your name]. I love you, [your name]."
- Take three gentle breaths and open your eyes.

3. *Claim three experiences you choose for the day.* (My favorites are: love, ease, flow, fun, and accomplishment.) Write them in your journal, in your calendar, and at the top of your to-do list!

Even during the busiest of days, these simple steps can help you connect – and stay connected – with your soul.

Bubbles of Light

by Courtney Long

Who said that blowing bubbles is just for kids? Bubbles are a powerful spiritual tool for relieving stress and tuning into the voice of your soul. After all, your soul is pure light – and what's lighter than a bubble?

"Bubbles of Light" is a fun meditation technique that helps your conscious and subconscious mind to release fear and open to the expansive wisdom and love of your soul. Use this technique when:

- Daily stresses have piled up, and you feel heavy or weighed down.
- Self-doubt rears its ugly head, especially when making a decision.
- You want to hear your own truth amidst others' opinions.
- You feel scattered or unfocused, and you long to feel happy and free!

Here's how it works:

- Close your eyes and take a few deep breaths to relax and let go of stress. Imagine several bubbles of light floating next to you. Place any stressful situations from your life into those bubbles and watch them float away. Notice yourself feeling lighter already!
- Next, imagine pulling your ego and all fear out of your body and placing it into another bubble next to you. Place your hands on your heart and notice the light glowing from within – from your soul.
- Then, imagine a sparkling white bubble of light all around you. This raises your vibration so you can easily hear your soul. Ask your soul a question, such as "What do I need to know today?" or "How can I experience love today?" Breathe deeply and notice anything that comes to mind – images, feelings, words, or a "knowing." Continue to ask your soul questions and patiently allow the answers to arise. Trust the guidance that comes. (Don't worry if "nothing" comes. An answer may come later in the day when you least expect it!) When you feel complete, thank your soul and ask for continued guidance throughout the day.

Fun option: Buy or make a bubble-blowing kit, and play to your heart's content.

Enjoy the lightness, joy, and wisdom of your soul!

Four-Directional Meditation

by Linda J. Dieffenbach

Nature has always been my refuge. It is the place I turn to that calms and grounds me, that brings me peace. The wind, the trees, and the water are my confidants. Amidst the chaos of life, here, in nature, I find myself again. I find that even when I cannot physically be in nature, connecting with nature spirits and the four directions helps me reconnect with my soul's wisdom. Through this practice, you, too, can connect and listen to the wisdom of your soul.

Begin facing the east. You may sit or stand – whatever is most comfortable. If you are in nature and choose to keep your eyes open, relax and soften your gaze. Take a couple of slow, gentle, cleansing breaths as you ground your energy into Mother Earth. Feel her holding you to her, supporting you.

Focus your attention on the east, the place of the rising sun, the place of new beginnings. Here, connect with the spirit of the great eagle, inviting him to lift you into the air with mighty wings. As you soar through the sky, look out at your life through far-seeing eyes. See the big picture of your soul experience in this lifetime and beyond. Witness.

Turn to the south, the place of fiery youth, abundance, and growth – the place of truth. Here, connect with the spirit of the wolf. Walk with him and listen to the passion and truth of your soul.

Turn to the west, the place of the setting sun, the place of healing, strength, and introspection. Here, connect with the spirit of the bear. Follow her into the deep, dark, still places within and draw upon your infinite, internal wisdom.

Turn to the north, the place of the wisdom of the ancient ones, of those who have come before us. Here, connect with the spirit of the buffalo. Follow her as she leads you to the realm of the ancient ones. Listen, knowing that this eternal and ancient wisdom comes through your wise and eternal soul.

Offer a prayer of gratitude.

Meditative Dishwashing

by Anne Aleckson

When I found out all the things a daily mindfulness practice could do for me – such as training my brain and improving my memory, helping me gain better control over emotions, increasing my capacity for compassion, and even helping to manage pain – I knew I had to find a way to practice mindfulness every day. But how could I squeeze yet another activity into my already jam-packed to-do list?

The answer came at the kitchen sink.

I could use the time that I was washing the dishes for practicing mindfulness rather than spending that time letting my mind worry about the future or ruminate over the past.

I invite you to join me in this practice. Here's how to do it:

Once the sink is filled with warm, soapy water, put your hands in to the bottom, close your eyes, and take a few deep breaths in and out. While you are breathing, become aware of the water – how it feels and how your hands feel in it. Keep your focus on what you are feeling in your body, particularly in your hands as they become one with the water. Now, start doing the dishes with awareness. Notice what you are doing. Be aware of what each dish or utensil feels like. Look at each item with a new interest and awareness. If other thoughts come into your mind, just notice them and bring your focus back to the job at hand until it is complete.

Without taking any extra time out of the day, this mindfulness practice brings a triple benefit: the dishes are done, we feel relaxed and stress free, and (as I discovered through my daily practice) we are building a stronger connection with our soul.

Flow Through Fear to Return to Your SoulHome

by Helen Rebello

Connecting with your soul sounds so beautiful doesn't it? So beautiful. So simple. And yet this seemingly simple concept has multiple facets – offering potential, promise, and excitement, but also trepidation, resistance, and fear. These emotions aren't good or bad, right or wrong; they just *are* – and they arise when you contemplate any change, even something as beautiful as connecting with your soul.

Of these emotions, fear can metaphorically paralyse you – undermining you by sending "danger whispers" of warning to discourage you from exploring anything that might change the status quo. When fear arises, I invite you to thank your inner safety guide for trying to protect you, and lovingly reassure it that all is well. Then gift yourself the following focus so that you can flow through fear to return to your SoulHome.

To begin, get comfortable in a safe, quiet space. Close your eyes and softly bring your awareness to your breath, which will start calming your system and settling your mind.

Next, imagine that your skull is a wonderful, cosy cave – your eye sockets are the cave's entrance, and the back of your skull is the back wall. Imagine softly burning candles, sumptuous cushions, and calm music, which draws you into this peaceful, restorative sanctuary. Visualise yourself entering the cave and resting at the back, feeling safe, secure, and settled.

As you relax, allow yourself to start softly merging into the back wall, moving away from the busyness at the front, into a deeper, quieter, larger space. Notice that as you drift further back, your sense of self starts changing – becoming stronger, larger, more confident, and deeply peaceful as you come into connection with your highest self: your soul.

Rest here, in this beautiful space, for as long as you desire – knowing that you have returned to your SoulHome.

When you are ready, softly bring your awareness back to the room and to your day, free from fear and deeply nourished from connecting back to your soul.

Welcome home.

Playful Pet Meditation Journey

by Andrea Bryant

Winter has truly set in. It's wet and cold and everything looks dreary. My pet rabbits and I have a bad case of cabin fever. As I head into the spiral of frustration, I stop myself.

What can I do to uplift myself? I dream of how wonderful it would be to watch my bunnies running and jumping with joy in the garden.

I am enjoying the dream so much that I realise I need to make it bigger and better! I will go on a playful pet meditation journey with my bunnies. I get excited just thinking about it. I settle into a comfy position close to my bunnies. I close my eyes and take some deep breaths.

I imagine myself on a beautiful paved path. My pets are standing by my side, and I can see the excitement in their eyes. We start to stroll down the path. I can hear birds chirping and the rustling of leaves. The bunnies' noses are twitching at all the wonderful smells. My pets are radiating joy at going on this adventure with me.

A beautiful clearing appears in front of us. It is filled with wildflowers and luscious, green grass – a delightful sight for rabbits! We are all alone. The area is just for us, to play and frolic and enjoy being together.

We all run joyfully into the clearing. Playing, jumping, and twisting with glee. Exploring the wonderful grasses and flowers. Taking time for nose kisses and snuggles. Then more play, digging, and being silly.

My soul remembers how fun it is to play. How important it is to be present in the moment and enjoy life as it unfolds. Winter is a long-forgotten memory.

Declutter Your Mind

by Holly Worton

Several years ago, I joined a group where I began a daily practice of meditative spiritual exercises. Like many people, I struggled to concentrate on my exercises due to the never-ending stream of thoughts trailing through my mind. The moment I would close my eyes, my mind would start racing with thoughts about projects and items on my to-do list.

Around the same time that I joined the group, I read David Allen's *Getting Things Done*, a book that emphasizes clearing the mind by writing down tasks to be done – rather than allowing them to keep swirling around our heads! I decided to combine Allen's advice with my new spiritual practice by creating a mind-decluttering pre-meditation exercise. I would sit in my meditation area with a notepad and pen by my side, and whenever anything popped into my mind, I would open my eyes and write it down. Once I had made the note, I returned to my meditation, continuing until my mind was quiet.

Because I was just beginning to implement a system for my to-do list and projects, I still had a lot of mind clutter related to tasks that I was afraid of forgetting. Eventually, however, my mind was cleared of these task-related thoughts, and my spiritual exercises became much easier to perform. To this day, I often sit down for a few minutes of mind-decluttering meditation to clear my mind of anything else that hasn't been put in my system for tasks and projects.

It can be really challenging to meditate or perform other spiritual practices when our minds are cluttered with items from our to-do list. With just a few minutes of preliminary mind-decluttering meditation, however, you can free yourself of those swirling thoughts, help yourself get organized, and more easily connect with your soul.

Living from Your Soul

by Autumne Stirling

For many of us, the morning begins with an alarm – radio static or, even worse, harsh buzzing – jarring us awake. Days are long, stress-filled, caffeine-fueled ordeals. We rush from one activity to another, barely fitting in a quick processed meal.

Our society has established that working hard and making money are priorities, regardless of the consequences. Many are employed in positions they do not enjoy, working long hours, resulting in little satisfaction and limited time with loved ones. After work, perhaps they "reward" themselves with technology, unhealthy food, or unhealthy behaviours in an attempt to relax.

Why is work, wealth, and success deemed so important, when they frequently have such negative impacts on our health and happiness? What has happened to the concept of balance? Why do we believe the myth that financial success is superior to moral success? After breathing our last breath, we only carry forth our souls. Why then, are soulful living, love, forgiveness, humanitarian aid, equality, and happiness not at the top of our agendas?

Soulful living has changed my entire perspective on humanity and the way I choose to live. Extracting myself from the chains of survival mode, I recognized that I was merely existing rather than living from the soul.

Living from the soul means that we live in a way that supports the growth and nurturance of our spirits. To me, this includes purposeful breathing – not for survival's sake but actually sitting with the aim of just breathing, noticing the expansion of our chest and diaphragm, feeling the circling of the "oracle breath" moving up and down our spines. This practice may inspire us to use our bodies to consciously move, connect in conversations with people (as opposed to "engaging" with technology), and spend time getting reacquainted with nature.

When we shift from survival-mode living to soulful living, we experience rewards that go far beyond money or status. When we are truly living from our souls, we are able to be present in the moment, feel constant gratitude for our blessings, and love ourselves for exactly who we are.

Reiki Meditation

by Sandy Jabo Gougis

Reiki is most often translated from the Japanese as "Universal Life-Force." The "ki" in Reiki is the same "ki" in aikido, the "chi" in t'ai chi, and the "qi" in qigong.

We all have Reiki. It's the energy that animates living beings. Unlike the martial arts, however, Reiki energy is a purely healing frequency. It can be used by anyone, and it can do no harm.

The founder of the Reiki healing system, Mikao Usui, taught his students this simple Gassho Meditation for connecting with their inner knowing – their souls.

Gassho literally means "two hands coming together." It's formed by placing your hands with palms together, in the prayer position, in front of your heart chakra. All 10 meridians in your body are aligned through the connection of your hands.

It is easier and better to meditate with a straight spinal column, keeping your head still. You may sit in a straight-backed chair or on cushions on the floor.

Sit down, close your eyes, and focus your attention on the point where your middle fingers meet. If you have been trained in Reiki, begin the flow of energy. If not, observe how the energy manifests in your body. Let go of everything else. When your mind wanders, acknowledge the thought, let it go, and return to the point where your middle fingers meet.

If you find it uncomfortable to hold your arms up, simply let your hands (kept together) slowly drop down onto your lap, finding a more comfortable position to continue the meditation.

You may observe energy in the form of heat, cold, or images. This is your soul speaking to you through Reiki. Don't get attached to a result. Keep your focus on the tips of your middle fingers.

If you need to adjust your posture, move slowly, deliberately, and consciously. Respect your body's signals, and never ignore pain.

If meditation is new to you, try this practice for five minutes. Eventually, see if you can build up to 20 minutes each day. Allow the loving wisdom of Reiki to be the bridge to your soul.

Cosmic Aum Activation

by Akasha Rainbow

The sound our soul makes is the Cosmic Aum. We can hear it with our temporal lobes when all other sounds, including our thoughts, emotions, and bodily tension, drop away. It is ever present in our minds, and, when we listen, it awakens us to the consciousness of our fifth-dimensional soul-self and brings us into ecstatic union with the divine within. As we focus on the frequency of our soul for the first time, we may begin to feel the life-force flowing in our bodies; rising up our spine; uniting our hearts, minds, bodies, and soul in spiritual and physical ecstasy.

To identify with our soul, first we must identify our thoughts, which merely come from us but are not who we are. Listen. If you hear worries about your life or livelihood, tell yourself you are safe. If you hear worries about love, relationships, and belonging, tell yourself you are loved and loving. If you hear memories, let yourself live in the now. If you hear judgments, analysis, or the beginnings of plans, tell yourself it is time to relax. If you hear music, see flashes of images, or feel urges for creativity, tell yourself that there is time for everything and you are totally okay. Keep doing this, and spaces between the thoughts will open up.

At first, you may think this is silence, for you are not hearing your mind speak. Yet, if you listen, you will hear a faint crackle of static. As you listen, the static will grow. If we focus on the static, our concentration will grow into *samadhi* – an ecstatic union with the divine soul within.

It is now, and only now, that we will hear the thoughts of our soul burning within us. Our heart will feel very hot, as if it were the core of a star, and you will feel as if you're beginning to spin. Let yourself burn in the bliss of being, now and forever, who you truly are: a soul in infinite, fiery flight across the night sky of eternity. This ecstatic union with your own soul as an expression of the Divine Cosmic Heart is the bliss of being that we were all born to as our birthright.

Cultivating You: A Perfect Seed of Love

by Jan Deelstra

Rituals bring us to a place of being present – to a creative space where manifestation and self-growth take root. The use of rituals is a daily thread in my life's weave, and a mainstay in my repertoire is *Seed of Love.* This ritual is born of an understanding that, just as a seed eventually grows into the exact tree it is meant to be, each of us is also a perfect seed.

Contained within the seed that eventually grows to be a magnificent sequoia, for example, is the knowledge and the blueprint, which, when nurtured, will take root and stretch toward the light, growing to perhaps over 250 feet tall. Likewise, within you is the seed of your perfection, which, when nurtured, matures into the exactness of your unique possibility.

You may create your sacred space for cultivating your perfect seed anywhere you desire. If you are visual, you may hold a sacred nurturing space in your third eye, or you may prefer to hold space in your heart chakra. Alternately, this ritual can be practiced at an altar by placing organic objects with intentionally infused energy. All that is required is a focused intention to nurture your seed into what it already is: *your limitless potential.*

To perform this ritual, simply get quiet and *see* the seed of your perfection within your mind's eye or your heart. As you hold the vision, anticipate that this sacred seed will grow into whatever you consciously intend it to become. See yourself sprouting from the seed, budding into your optimal self. The seed contains the knowledge for how to ripen into the highest version of you. All you need do to fertilize your inner seedling is nurture yourself with self-love and full acceptance.

Seed of Love is not only a ritual of holding sacred space for enhancing the self, it can also be extended outward to support others. To do this, simply direct your benevolent intentions of highest good to specific people or to the masses. Either way, the expressed intention is an affirmation that you are a perfect *seed of love.*

Accessing Abundance Consciousness

by Sheelagh Maria

Mass consciousness is often considered fearful and limiting. There is, however, an abundance of loving, rich, and prosperous consciousness that we can tap into and duplicate. Rather than getting sucked into the consciousness of scarcity, we can access the consciousness of the rich!

To celebrate your natural birthright of abundance, simply take some time to go into a relaxed state. Now pick someone whose presence embodies abundance, prosperity, and success to you. In your mind's eye, "see" this person in all their glory, smiling and loving life. Simply reach out with your mind and "lift" the wonderful abundance and prosperous part of their energy into your own energy field – almost like lifting a hat off someone's head and placing it on yours for a time. (And don't worry about this person – abundance is infinite, so by tapping into their energetic supply, you are in no way depriving them of anything!)

Next, visualise the energy of abundance and success soaking into your mind, body, heart, and entire aura. Feel yourself getting lighter, stronger, clearer, and more connected to the endless stream of abundance that flows throughout creation. Smile, and know that you can do this as often as you wish.

As you go about your day and your week, affirm: "I am abundant. There is so much abundance around me." Affirm this no matter what your external experience may be. Focus entirely upon nature's abundance: flowers, trees, wildlife, smiling children, the warm sun, the cleansing rain, and all other examples of abundance you encounter. The more you do this, the more abundance *becomes* you. The consciousness of abundance becomes your *tone*, which is loudly heard by the Universe, which will send much more your way.

Remember that you yourself contain infinite abundance – you *are* infinite abundance; so by connecting with this source, you are connecting with yourself, your truth, your soul.

Motion Meditations

by Amy Gage

Motion meditations are sacred meditation rituals conducted while in motion of any kind. Engaging the conscious and subconscious mind, while adding physical motion, creates a powerful manifesting dynamic. For me, motion meditation usually includes music, which has a way of absorbing us, taking us to its level of vibration, and enhancing the meditation experience.

One of my favorite motion meditations is to dance barefoot in my backyard, preferably under the moon. I also enjoy swinging on the swing set in my backyard, often while listening to music. I generally do this for at least 15 minutes, sometimes for up to an hour, if possible. It's a very potent healing and regenerating process. If I have been swinging a lot, I walk around my yard or dance barefoot afterwards, to help ground me back into my body. Sometimes, I go into this practice with a focused intention. Other times, I just go with an empty mind to be filled with a message from my soul.

Motion meditations can be even more potent if they're done with others – even if the people are in different places! For instance, even if you're not in the same physical location, dancing with someone else while focused on the same intention can be very healing. This can help to process grief to a more manageable state. It can bring anger, guilt, shame, or victim energy up and out, transforming it into a new state of nourishing energy, no matter how painful and immovable the energy once may have seemed to be. And, like all motion meditations, it can be a way to connect with the Divine.

Feel free to create your own motion meditations. Trust yourself and the messages you receive. Surrender to the experience. You will find your own rhythm and, in due time, you will find your own authentic, powerful dance with the Divine.

Body-and-Soul Connection Meditation

by Nukhet Hendricks

It was one of those days. I was continually running into everything in my way: doors, tables, chairs…pretty much anything solid! I felt like my soul had "left the building" – that it was entirely disconnected from my body.

Fortunately, this is a fairly rare experience for me these days. There was a time, however, when I my soul was "checking out" nearly every day. In some ways, it was much easier that way, not having to feel every single feeling that people around me were feeling. Living on "autopilot" was hardly a fulfilling life, but I didn't know how to stay one with my soul, keep my soul in my body, and still be around others without feeling everything they did. Eventually, however, I found out that the reason I felt this way was because I was an empath. I also learned that there were ways for my body and soul to stay connected (even around other people…and furniture!), such as through the "Body-and-Soul Connection Meditation."

Fortunately, I was able to remember this tool on the day when I kept having all those "hit-and-run" encounters! Before I ended up completely black and blue, I realized that it was time for the meditation.

I laid down and let my body completely sink into the floor. I just let it go completely limp and started to converse with every single part of my body, asking them all to release the tension they were holding. Once I felt completely relaxed, I started to converse with my soul, inviting her to pour her loving presence into every single part of my body – my toes, feet, legs, womb, torso, heart, arms, fingers, throat, eyes, third eye, brain – until I began vibrating with exquisite energy, feeling my body and soul connected once again. When I opened my eyes, I knew my soul was back at home.

Connect to Infinity and Beyond

by Alicia Isaacs Howes

As an infinite being exploring the finite realm called Earth, you can never be disconnected from your soul. The illusion of that, however, certainly exists! It often shows up as not feeling good enough or having a sense that you don't belong or have been left behind, forgotten, abandoned, or sent here as punishment.

If you ever feel stuck or limited, do the following exercise to help you expand back into the eternal flow of energy that runs through you, to you, in you, for you, and as you!

1. In your mind's eye, get an impression of an infinity loop (∞). Place your finger on the very far left of the left loop. This represents Source, or the God of your understanding.
2. Imagine tracing along the bottom of this loop towards the intersection or midpoint. This represents your soul.
3. Follow the loop from your soul and move up along the top of the right-hand loop until you come to the farthest point on the right. This represents you in your physical form. What you've traced so far represents the eternal flow of energy from Source to your soul and then to your human self. This energy – which can take the form of intuitive guidance, wisdom, gifts, love, and more – allows you to explore creation in your human form.
4. Next, follow along the bottom right of the loop back towards the mid-point and up along the top left loop. This section represents the energy that flows from your human self to your soul and then back to Source – energy that pulsates with your every breath, experience, exploration, and ever-expanding wisdom.
5. Continue to trace the endless flow of energy – from Source, through your soul, to your human self, and back – as you say (silently or out loud) this truth: *As I evolve, so does my soul. As my soul evolves, so does Source.*
6. Repeat until you feel a sense of relaxation, expansion, or inspiration. It may take a few minutes at first but, with practice, you can feel this infinite connection in the blink of an eye!

The Stillpoint Meditation

by Sandy Jabo Gougis

Meditation is a profound way to connect with your soul. It's not about forcing the mind to be still. It is about allowing the thinking mind to rest. In "The Stillpoint Meditation," you'll use your breath as a meditative focus. The Buddha recommended the breath because it's always with you and always in motion.

To begin this meditation, start by finding a comfortable and stable seat. (If you lie down, you may fall asleep!) Keeping your spine straight helps you stay alert. If you can, keep your eyes open. With your head straight, allow your gaze to drift down to the floor in front of you. Don't stare, but just let your vision rest lightly.

Begin by taking a few deep breaths. Feel where you notice the breath moving in your body. Perhaps you feel the rise and fall of your chest. Maybe you feel the expansion and contraction of your belly. You might even feel the air passing on your upper lip. Take a few moments to connect deeply with your breath.

Once you have a bond with your breathing, allow it to drop into its own natural rhythm. Stop taking deep breaths. Just let your breathing happen all on its own. Your thinking mind is now the observer, noticing your breath.

You might think in words to yourself: "Breathing in. Breathing out." Or simply "in" and "out." Or you might let your breathing occur with no labeling at all. Use whatever technique feels comfortable for you.

As you breathe, notice the natural pause that happens at the end of each out-breath. This is the stillpoint. All of the processes in your body are at their slowest during this sacred, biological pause.

Focus on the stillpoint between your breaths. Experience that vastness. That open expansiveness is the very essence of who you are: your soul.

Thoughts will still arise as you meditate. This is normal. Notice the thoughts, and quickly allow them to pass. Return your attention to your breath and the stillpoint. Savor this connection with your soul.

Stop, Breathe, and Reconnect

by Kate Whorlow

Whether you are a work-at-home parent, work in a busy office, or run around all day doing errands, there will likely come a time in your day when you feel a bit frazzled and overwhelmed – needing just five minutes of peace so that you can clear your head and reconnect with yourself.

Below is a short and very effective revitalising technique to help you to get out of your head, away from the day's busyness, and back to *you*. Leave frustration and overwhelm behind, and enter your place of peace. Just by giving yourself a few minutes to breathe and centre yourself, you can emerge calmer, clearer, and better able to move forward to your next task with ease and grace.

Firstly, find a place where you won't be disturbed for at least five minutes. Sit down if you can. Close your eyes, place one hand over your heart, feeling your heartbeat and listening to your breath. Focus on breathing in for a count of three and out for a count of three. By focusing on your breath, you are calming yourself down and allowing your mind-chatter to subside.

Next, imagine your energy literally leaving your head, travelling into your chest and settling within your heart. Within this space, it is calm, with comfy seats and soft music playing (or the sounds of nature). You feel safe, nurtured, and at ease. There is only love in this space. You are able to connect with your true self here, feeling deep serenity and bliss. Stay here as long as you need to.

When you feel that your breathing is deeper and your body is relaxed, gently bring your attention back to your surroundings and open your eyes. You can stay in this centred, connected space all day if you wish, or repeat the exercise as often as you need to.

By coming from a place of love, tranquillity, and self-connection, you will attract more peace and positivity into your everyday activities.

Reaching Your Soul's Wisdom

by Linda J. Dieffenbach

Have you ever noticed how busy and noisy the world can be? It is full of activities, distractions, responsibilities, and demands. It is overwhelming sometimes!

There are days that go by so quickly that I barely catch my breath; and when I look back, I cannot figure out where all the time went. I get caught up in the rush and distraction and end up feeling exhausted and completely disconnected from myself.

In these moments, I often feel an overwhelming need to simply stop, breathe, and reconnect with who I am. I yearn to find that quiet, wise, and peaceful place within. I have found that my heart center is a powerful gateway into that stillness. I love to go inside and sit there, soaking in the loving heart energies that fill me, soothe me, and nourish me.

Here's how you can enjoy this experience as well:

Find a comfy place to sit and close your eyes. Take a couple slow, gentle, cleansing breaths, allowing your body to relax and bringing your mind into the present moment. Bring your attention to your heart chakra, in the center of your chest. As you focus there, feel your heart chakra gently relax and open. Visualize a door opening. Enter there.

Visualize a corridor that you follow until you come into the center point (in your body, this is just in front of your spine). Here, you enter a chamber or room where you sit in the center and relax. As you enter, you notice a surge of gentle yet powerful energy emerging and flowing from the center of your heart. Breathe. Feel the energy of your heart filling and surrounding you. Allow yourself to receive this gentle, loving energy as you come into deeper stillness. In this quiet place, you come into full and deep awareness of your connection with your soul. Sit here, feel, receive, and listen for as long as you wish.

When you feel complete, release your focus and open your eyes.

Kundalini Tree of Life Activation

by Akasha Rainbow

The seed of your soul, from which your body grew, cannot be touched. The life-force within us is immortal and ever sprouting. Whatever path you walked in the past, whatever branch fell or fruit grew from your seed, render it unto the immortal within you. Drink deep in every moment from the ever-expanding essence of your soul-self that aches to fill you in consciousness and bloom.

Feel the cool breeze now on the nape of your neck at the top of your spine, where the wind whispers the secret longings to you of your long-forgotten soul. Let your skull weave ever so lightly, side to side, as if succumbing to the ecstasy of the words of your highest beloved's adoration for you spoken breathlessly upon your ears.

Let that willingness to move together seep into your shoulders now, and feel no limitation as your upper body makes an infinity sign, one shoulder drifting down as the other shoulder rises, ever so gently, so full of the promise of the harvest of tomorrow. There is no need to rush. Feel the energy of love move into the breast space of your heart now as your upper spine pulses, ready for your true love's eager touch.

Drink her in. The tendrils of your soul reach to you from the farthest corners of the universe. She comes to you as whispers, as aching, as the deepest yearning for a bliss you already know intimately as yours. Let the blood rise to your cheeks, and your eyes drift up, knowing your true love already has you in her embrace and always has.

Love yourself as your love's greatest longing and your greatest fulfillment. In all your incarnations, all you have sought is an awareness of yourself, in the here and now, as the great one, as the Infinite Divine. Let that search be over. Let the keys of Shambhala open within you now, and be open ever more. Make the room warm and the house fit to accommodate the vastness of your mighty soul, and embody these words:

I am God.

I am nothing.

I am the second coming.

I am here and now.

I am everything.

The Mighty "I AM" Soul Connection

by Rev. Kathryn Morrow

Where is our soul? How can we communicate with our soul on a conscious level? How can such an important part of who we are sometimes feel so far away and disconnected?

There are many ways to connect with our soul. One has been whispered to us at birth, and our life's journey is to remember it. This secret has been taught by our greatest teachers and modern-day scholars. It has been protected deep within us and held safely in our holy books:

And God said unto Moses, "I AM THAT I AM." [Exodus 3:14]

The secret in this simple statement opens the door to the most divine part of who we are. To me, I AM means pure being, life, awareness, and the indwelling Christ.

When you say I AM THAT I AM, you are declaring yourself in the present tense. You are now conscious of being the creator of your life. Whatever you attach to the I AM you become.

Speaking these words out loud awakens a deep conversation within the depths of who you are. Our soul communicates through the vibration of our voice. We receive and comprehend this voice through our feelings. Our feelings bring understanding to our minds.

Let's try this together: Following your breath, breathe in and out gently. Now speak, "I am now connecting consciously with my soul through my I AM Presence." Allow your breath to show you where that is in your body. As you feel where that is, breathe gently into that space asking, "Please allow my I AM in me to awaken my soul connection for my highest potential." Breathe in and breathe out.

The soul dances in the I AM Presence, where it sends us health, love, prosperity, joy, peace, and anything else we ask for in any area of our life. It is our job to expand our awareness, open our voices and our souls, trust in our I AM Presence, and be open to receive all that it will bring.

This path of knowing the divine secret allows us to walk boldly in confidence, knowing: I AM THAT I AM.

Transpersonal-Energy Meditation

by Tracy Una Wagner

A wonderful way to connect with your soul – and to expand it – is to practice Transpersonal-Energy Meditation. The Transpersonal Energy System is the energy field that goes beyond our physical bodies. Accessing this energy allows us to combine the energy of Mother Earth and the Divine Universe, blending them together for a deeper, more grounded connection with the soul.

To begin this meditation, imagine a beam of light (of any color) going from the center of your chest down, down, down until you begin to feel energy shift and get thicker – around six inches below your feet. Let your beam connect with the energy known as the "Earth Star" chakra, and allow this chakra to bring the energy of Mother Earth up into your body through your beam of light. You'll begin to feel calmer, more centered, and more balanced. Let this essence fill your chest and begin to flow out to the rest of your body – your organs, muscles, bones, and cells – filling you with the wisdom and grounded harmony that is Earth.

Next, from the center of your chest, send out another light beam (which may be of the same color or a different color from your other beam). Send this light up, up, up, and out of the top of your head, into the sky until you begin to feel another shift, or mass, somewhere around 12 inches above your head. Unite your light with that of this chakra, known as the "Stellar Gateway," which is the bridge between your physical and your spiritual BE-ing. Bring the cosmic energy down your light beam and into your chest. Fill your chest with the lovingly pure Divine Essence, allowing it to mingle and merge with the Earth energy still flowing into your body.

When you feel grounded and full, thank the Universe and all the BE-ings who have sent you messages. Then slowly bring your light beams back into your body and into your heart space. Place your hands over your heart, feeling the full effect of your soul expanded, open, and grounded.

Call on a Dolphin

by Nukhet Hendricks

I am a product of the sea, born and raised along the shores of the Mediterranean. Currently, however, I live in Fargo, North Dakota, miles away from the salty water. I never thought I would end up living so far away from any ocean beach, but here I am. My husband, the love of my life, and I built a life here together. We both know that we are going to spend the rest of our lives by an ocean beach starting in the not-too-distant future, but Fargo is home for now.

I am at peace with my current home because I've found a way to satisfy my soul's yearning for the sight of the ocean as it shimmers under the sun, the smell of the salty air as it swirls through my nostrils, and the feel of the water against my skin. It wasn't always like this, however; there was a time when I felt that if I didn't get to an ocean beach in a hurry, I would go out of my mind! Nowadays, though, when I have one of those difficult days, I do my "dolphin meditation."

I begin my meditation by getting comfortable and silent. After a few deep breaths in and out, I travel to my safe space: a beautiful beach by the ocean, surrounded by palm trees. I call out to my dolphin guide, Tulu, who always shows up. He first delights my senses with an incredible dolphin dance, jumping up high and diving into the water, and then invites me to hop onto his back. I hop on and surrender myself to the water as it gently envelops me, and Tulu takes me on the most exquisite underwater journey. (In this meditation, I have no trouble breathing under water!) I feel the ocean embrace me; every single cell of my body soaks up that delicious, salty water. This journey deeply connects me with my soul. Once I feel completely one with my soul, Tulu brings me back to the shore with another dolphin dance, saying "so long…" until the next time.

Our Wandering Mind

by Katie Power

Have you ever been stuck in a dull conversation and felt your eyes glazing over while your mind went astray? Our minds are amazing – they just love to wander into the ether, especially while doing boring stuff like daily chores, long drives, or...*hey, wake up!!* (Whew, I thought I lost you there for a minute.)

Anyway, where was I? Oh yes, with all of the tedious, mundane, and *boring* stuff going on down here on Earth, it's no surprise that we often like to leave our bodies and go off exploring other dimensions. (Or maybe that's just me?)

Anyway, to help me stay grounded, a few years back I started practicing the art of mindfulness. The problem was, whenever the opportunity came up to be mindful, my soul was already happily skipping off on its own little adventure. (What can ya do?)

I decided to try a different approach: the age-old practice called meditation. Apparently, the goal is to quiet the mind, focus solely on the breath, and disconnect from the world. (Piece of cake, right? After all, I pretty much had that last part down already!)

With nothing to lose, I gave it a try. I dimmed the lights, sat up straight, closed my eyes, took some deep breaths…and, as if on cue, my stepdad burst into the room, made a scene, and started yelling to the family that I'd gone mad. An inauspicious start to my meditation practice, but it did improve. (Somewhat.)

Nowadays, I still practice mindfulness and meditation. However, I also embrace the fact that my mind likes to roam to far-off places and ponder things without being bogged down by every last prosaic detail of earthly life. As it turns out, this is part of how I access the wisdom of my soul.

Well, I see you've managed to stick with me till the end – congratulations! I hope my story has inspired you to try meditation or other mindfulness techniques, while still honoring your mind's desire to wander from time to time! And above all, keep smiling, stay true to yourself, and don't take life so seriously!

Reigniting Your Inner Sun

by Karrol Rikka S. Altarejos

Within each and every one of us lies a personal sun, an inner spark to light and guide us. Its radiance is so bright that one can gather and pool one's strength there to call upon when reserves of energy are low. Physically found in the core and energetically located in the third chakra, power and empowerment stem from this source in our being.

My path to reigniting my own inner sun began when I placed awareness on a limiting belief that those around me were more important than me. I was giving away my own energy in pursuit of the happiness of others. In moments of stress, I felt drained and anxious, losing both confidence and focus. Energy leaking though my solar plexus and neglect of self-care became apparent as my body expressed signs of fatigue. My "glow" was seriously undernourished.

I sought out experiences to enrich body, mind, and spirit; and I found balance through this exercise taught to me by a beloved mentor:

Taking a few moments out of my day, I visualize the sun's amazing brilliance, its rays and heat emanating support and life-sustaining power. Recognizing this beautiful star as a representation of a source of strength, I call back energies of love, happiness, and all that I have given away to others. Allowing that sun to shine, I bring the energy through my crown and into my body, and let it rest in my third chakra to replenish my soul.

Through this exercise, I have nurtured my inner light and, in doing so, I have begun to embody more and more of my true self. From this space, I once again feel my soul's motivation. Finding harmony between self-care and care for others encourages radiance to flow forth from my being and empowers me to better serve the world, as I share the best of what I have to offer.

If you were to reignite your personal sun, what energies would you invite back to nurture your soul?

Connecting with Your Divine God/Goddess Within

by Linda J. Dieffenbach

Some days, I am fully aware that I am a Divine Child of Light – a Goddess in human form, enjoying all the joys of the human experience. Other days? Well, let's just say I forget. I get lost. I feel disconnected. I even get a little cranky. Have you ever had that problem? If so, you might find this practice useful.

Stand with your feet about shoulder width apart, planted firmly on the ground, with your knees slightly bent. Open your hands with your palms facing forward and slightly upward.

Feel the energy of Mother Earth rising up into your body, through your feet and up through your root chakra. Feel the energy continue to rise up through your body and each of your chakras, flowing gently yet powerfully, filling your entire body and energy field. Feel the powerful energy flowing through you and around you.

Continue to feel the energy of Mother Earth flowing through you as you simultaneously feel the energy of the Universe flowing down through your crown chakra and into your body through the top of your head. Feel this energy flow down through your body, through each of your chakras, flowing gently yet powerfully, filling your entire body and energy field.

Continue to stand in this space, allowing the ascending energy of Mother Earth to flow through you while simultaneously allowing the descending energies of the Universe to flow through you. Your spine may soften and your body may begin to sway gently as this energy flows. Allow this. If you feel unsteady, sit, but maintain the flow of energy.

Feel the power, grace, connection, and flow. Feel the Oneness. Know that this Sacred Divine Energy that is flowing through you IS YOU. Know that YOU are a Sacred Being. YOU are a Divine Child of the Universe. Feel your power. Feel your true Divine God/Goddess energy flowing through you. Embrace it. Own it. Know that this is your true essence.

Speak these words: I AM.

When you feel complete, release your focus and open your eyes.

The Experience of Ecstatic Meditation

by Leah Grant

You don't know what a meditation will feel like until you try it. Sometimes you're pleasantly surprised, as I was the first time I experienced Ecstatic Meditation – a combination of music, movement, guided visualization, stillness, mantra, and vibrational transmission. The reason I was so surprised by my first experience is that I channeled the recorded meditation myself! When Spirit uses me as a messenger, I usually have a pretty good idea of what I've been guided to create. But being on the "other side" of this final product was a completely different experience.

The session began with 20 minutes of music that vibrated to each element – Water, Earth, Fire, and Air – providing the backdrop to move and release energies and emotions stored in the body. As I listened, my body started to glide, as though in glistening water. I allowed tears of sadness to fall, and I felt the heaviness of guilt flow out of every cell. I stomped the ground to transfer these released emotions into the earth. I then found myself punching and kicking, driven by the fire of anger. When the fire burned out, I was left feeling as light as air, happily dancing in circles, and experiencing pure joy.

Feeling both relaxed and amped up from the release of negative emotions that had been stored within my body, I surrendered to the instruction to lie completely still on the floor. A guided meditation opened my heart chakra as my breath fell into a soft rhythm. This was followed by high-vibration music accompanying a melodic voice singing a hymn-style Sanskrit chant. The angelic combination of tone and pace lulled me into a trance-like state in which I felt engulfed in love. My body felt weightless. My mind ceased to chatter. My heart expanded.

When the music stopped, I let myself linger in the cocoon of safety and joy a bit longer before moving into the rest of my day. Long after I'd finished the meditation, I continued to feel connected, receptive, grounded, and light.

I invite you to have your own experience with Ecstatic Meditation – or any other meditation you feel drawn to. Approach it with an open heart, mind, and body – and you, too, might find yourself pleasantly surprised by your own experience!

Sacred Heart-Chamber Ritual

by Jan Deelstra

The regulation red-and-black deck with the royalty of kings, queens, sly one-eyed jacks, and prevailing aces were spread in formation across the gray Formica kitchenette; the chrome-legged chair squeaked under the strain as my mother considered the messages: Red was good; black, not so much. Regardless of how short or long the distance, before we left the house on any occasion, she read the layout to predetermine our chances for surviving the trip. My mother concentrated on the messages and trusted the guidance of the cards decades before the New-Age tarot trend.

As is true for most adults, I blame my mother for my shortcomings and credit her for my more acclaimed characteristics. As far back as I can recall, ritual has been a cherished part of my daily life. For that, I credit my mother. You might say that rituals are in my blood. Our ancestral line of pioneering women sought escape from religious persecution and practiced healing rituals of nature behind thinly veiled half-smiles. (You know the kind, like Mona Lisa with a secret…or a tart lozenge tucked center in her tongue fold; I'm never really sure.) Ritual is ingrained. It's my go-to when I need answers or peace. It's private time when I need connection to my soul.

A ritual I practice often is one of going into the sacred heart-chamber where the source of wisdom and connection reign. It's a practice that takes me to where my Goddess-Source energy resides. It is also the home of my authentic spirit voice. Closing my eyes, I go deep into the original intelligence, the intellect of the heart. My chamber is divine, ornate, and blissfully peaceful. It is where my inner goddess, my inner child, my soul connection, and the wisdom of the ages merge.

I ask any question and *feel* the answer. There is no deception here. I know the truth by the way it feels. Like my mother before me, reading cards for the signs, connecting with my inner soul prior to taking any action enhances the experience with the juiciness of spirit.

Meditating on Beauty

by Cindy Holtfreter

When you think of beauty, what is the first thing that comes to your mind? It may be a physical object, a piece of art, music, a view out your window, a vintage car, a piece of jewelry, a person, or a special place. What is it that you think is beautiful?

Now imagine that whatever you labeled as "beautiful" is right in front of you. Take a few moments to get present with that beauty. As you become more connected with the beauty, start to notice your breath and see what happens as you slow everything down just a little bit. Using your imagination, move in a little closer and start to close the distance between you and beauty. If beauty is an image, see yourself stepping into it. If beauty is an object, reach out and touch it. If beauty is an experience, fully sense it – as if you were in the midst of it right this very moment. Allow yourself and the beauty to become one.

Start to identify the qualities and attributes you see and sense. What is drawing you in and why? What is subtle and not easy to notice? What are you feeling? What emotions are being evoked by beauty? What is true about beauty and also true about you? In this quiet moment, what is beauty saying to you?

Allow yourself to be present and connected with beauty. With each inhale you take, breathe it in as love and truth. With each exhale, let go of anything outside of that connection until you feel complete, connected, and full of your beauty. In this divine connection, what are you experiencing? What is now possible? Once you are complete, speak this blessing:

May beauty catch my attention, reflect and remind me of who I am and that I am always connected with my soul. May beauty continue to nurture and expand my soul, speak to me, and lead me on my soul journey today.

Remembering to Breathe

by Tae Lynne

For the longest time, I felt as though I had no connection with my soul. I was caught up in surviving, rushing to check things off my list and make it through the day. I was so busy that I often forgot to breathe, which I didn't even know was possible.

I learned that when we don't slow down enough to breathe properly, the frantic, tense air gets trapped inside our bodies and can show up physically. For me, forgetting to breathe resulted in a bloated belly and tense face. People began asking me "Are you pregnant? What's wrong? Are you stressed out? You look upset."

I knew that I needed to find a way to slow down and breathe again, and so I began to meditate.

For a while, I practiced meditation first thing in the morning. Over time, however, I realized that I needed help remembering to slow down and breathe during my busy day. My solution was a meditation app that I could carry with me.

Now when I feel myself heading into a tailspin, I open up the "Stop, Breathe & Think" app on my phone. You can do this anywhere and anytime, even in your car after a stressful day before walking into your home and taking it out on your family (guilty)!

The mindful breathing track on the app has especially helped me while sitting in traffic jams. When I feel myself getting stressed or worried, focusing on the guided breathing helps me to stay calm.

By taking this time to slow down and meditate throughout the day, I've found that I'm remembering to breathe much more easily. I also feel much more relaxed and present to what my soul is trying to tell me.

Meditation slows down the breath; the body; and eventually, the mind. Learning to sit quietly with your thoughts can be difficult for those who've never tried it. I invite you to give a meditation app a try!

Heart-Space Centering

by Beth Shekinah Terrence

Living in our busy, modern world, it seems easier to be disconnected from our soul than it is to be connected. One of the biggest challenges I have found is a tendency to act from the mental plane rather than from the emotional/spiritual plane. When we're centered in our minds, we can get a lot done, but there can be a disconnect that comes along with that. We may override the feelings and wishes that come from our own sacred center, relying instead on what others suggest is a good path for us.

Learning to shift from the busy mind into the still, quiet space of the heart is a gateway to connecting with our soul in any given moment. As we cultivate this skill, we receive the key to opening the door to our deepest essence, no matter what is arising in our lives and in our world.

You can make this shift through this simple practice of "Heart-Space Centering":

Find a comfortable position, sitting or lying down. Begin with some deep breaths, breathing in and out for a count of five. Then, allow your breath to return to a natural rhythm. Place your right hand on your heart space in the center of your chest. Allow your left hand to open and rest on your lap or thigh.

Bring your awareness into the heart space. Notice how your heart feels. Is it open or spacious? Is there resistance or constriction? Simply notice. There's no right or wrong, no needing to get anywhere. It's simply a time to connect with your soul through the space of the heart. Do you notice feelings or emotions bubbling up? Any images or words? You are just breathing, being with your heart, and listening to your soul. Finish by gently rubbing your heart space a few times.

Start with practicing this for five minutes per day, then move to 15 or 30 minutes. Explore what's possible for your life and your dreams when you regularly shift to your heart space and connect with your soul.

A Group Meditation to Raise the Vibrations

by Helen Clear

I believe that we are here on this planet at a time when it is undergoing massive evolutionary expansion. We each have our own unique process of soul embodiment and ascension. Yet, we are never alone. We are connected and supported beyond our comprehension.

To help us all access the evolutionary energy available to us, I would like to invite each of us to participate in a group meditation – a celebration of unconditional love. When we consciously come together, we can lift not only our own vibrations, but the vibrations of the entire planet.

This meditation is a huge, joyful gathering that meets any time in any place – wherever we happen to be at the moment. (Let's not allow the illusions of time or space to limit us!) During this meditation, we are invited to consciously love ourselves, each other, and Mother Earth. This is an opportunity to celebrate with each other and open our hearts as wide as possible. We will welcome in spirit, our universal healing teams, our archangelic lineages, and our guides and angels…and connect with our own souls and our own divinity.

In coming together, we will change the course of history. The evolutionary process is already underway. We have the choice to do something with full intention and commitment. So join us. It's like a big town-hall meeting of our hearts and souls, with the intention to raise the vibrations of ourselves and our world with unconditional love. We can do this! We are powerful beyond measure.

This is a sacred time. Come with a sacred intention. Each and every moment of our lives is sacred, but perhaps we haven't allowed ourselves to know that. Let's explore the depths of unconditional love. Be ready to consciously infuse yourself with love to the very core of your being, into your bloodstream, and through all the layers of your essence. "All you need is love"…unconditional love. Give it a try. It is a beautiful entry point to your own soul. Your soul's deepest desire is to be loved and supported. So let's feel it. Let's do it! Let's raise the vibrations!

Chapter 8
Angels, Spirit Guides, & the Ethereal

We love knowing that we're never alone in this world and that we are always supported by much more than we can see. Over the last several years, we've received signs from our angels, felt immense love from the Universe, and connected with loved ones on the other side – something we weren't even sure was possible until we experienced it firsthand. Each of these moments helped us open our hearts and minds more and look beyond what was right in front of us – to trust in something that we couldn't even see, to have faith, and to connect with our soul in ways we never would have imagined before.

We both tend to lean toward the skeptical side, and so believing in and accepting all of this magic didn't necessarily come easily to either of us. Thankfully, however, our angels, spirit guides, and loved ones on the other side were persistent and helped us see that life truly does go on after our time here on Earth ends and that our soul is eternal and part of all that is.

You may already be open and aware of all of the infinite goodness that constantly surrounds you. If so, that's wonderful! We are so happy that you're also able to experience it and hold it close to your heart. If you're just starting to open up to the possibility of this magic, that's wonderful, too! It's our hope that the pieces in this chapter will support you in that and help you see how vast and miraculous our universe is.

Like always, please take into your heart what feels right and leave behind anything that doesn't. There are so many beautiful ways to connect with our soul, and those outlined here highlight connecting in ways we can't necessarily see but can truly feel. We find that truly fascinating, and we hope you do, too!

What is the Soul?

by Sandy Jabo Gougis

One way to connect with your soul is to ponder this question: *What IS the soul?*

After more than 17 years of meditation, I still can't answer this question definitively, but here's what I intuit to be true: My soul is that part of me that existed before I was born and will continue after I die. More than that, it's my best self.

Perhaps it's easier to say what it's *not*: It's not my personality. It's certainly not my body. It's not my collection of likes and dislikes formed over the last 50 years. (What's 50 years to an immortal soul?) It's not my political views or even my religious beliefs.

My soul is the deepest part of me, that vastness that dwells below consciousness, beneath the chattering mind.

As a Zen priest, I would call this my Buddha-Nature. My Christian sisters and brothers would call it their Christ Consciousness. As limited as language is to describe something this expansive, these terms both point to the same thing: Our souls are so much grander and holier than we can imagine.

When I allow my soul, my Buddha-Nature, to shine through, I show the world my best self. When you connect with your soul, others see that in you.

So, what is the soul? It is "yes" and "thank you." It is the unity of all things. It is the stillness between my breaths. It is small enough to fit in the spaces between subatomic particles and as large as the universe. It is part of something greater, which we may think of as the Divine. It is the union of all opposites.

My soul is that part of me that knows there is no separation between us. It's the part of me that exists beyond time and knows that "this too shall pass." My soul abides in acceptance of what is, moment to moment. And when I connect with my soul, embracing its loving wisdom, I am at peace.

Coming Home

by Nita Chapman

In 1989, I was living in South Dakota. I had a wonderful job as a psychiatric nurse and lived in a beautiful home. One day, I heard a quiet voice inside my soul say: "You need to be in New Mexico." Having never been to New Mexico, I was puzzled, to say the least. I dismissed it and went about my life.

For five years, that persistent voice kept telling me to go to New Mexico. In 1994, it was so loud and frequent that I could no longer ignore it, so I decided to take a risk and bought a plane ticket to Albuquerque to appease it.

My medical director thought that I'd lost it and said, "Nita, you're 46 years old and have a great job, friends, and stability here. Why would you even consider leaving?" It seemed crazy to me, too; but that voice was so persistent, and I just had to see for myself what New Mexico had in store for me.

When my daughter and I deplaned, she took my arm and said, "Mom, it feels like home." And it did. Even though I had never been there, it smelled so familiar and the energy felt so welcoming. During our four-day vacation, we did some sightseeing and I got a job at the psychiatric hospital. Even though I had only been there for a few short days, I knew that this was where I needed to be.

Six weeks later, my life looked very different. I had quit my job in South Dakota, sold my home, packed up, and moved to New Mexico. I've lived here ever since and have loved every second. I live in the beautiful red-rock mountains, which is as close to Heaven as I can imagine.

I listened to that quiet voice, which some would call the voice of my soul, and allowed the Divine to lead me home. And even though it sounded completely nuts at the time, I am so glad that I listened. It was the best decision that I've ever made.

Unlock Your Intuition

by Veronica Mather

Have you ever met somebody or walked into a situation and had an overwhelming feeling that something wasn't quite right? Did you pay attention to this inner guidance, or did you dismiss your thoughts and feelings because there was no logical reason to justify why you felt that way?

There have been times when I have regretted not paying attention to my soul's wisdom. Deep down, I knew certain people did not have my best interests at heart, but it didn't feel right for me to judge them on a "gut feeling." Eventually, these individuals showed their true colours, leaving me disappointed in myself for ignoring the warning signs.

Intuition is an amazing ability that we all possess. And although we are born with intuition, we can further develop it through trust, awareness, and practice. The next time you meet somebody for the first time or you are required to make a decision, utilise your intuitive instinct. Before your mind begins to analyse and interfere, consider your initial feelings – and ask yourself these questions:

- *How did you feel?*
- *How did your body respond? Did you feel sick, stressed, or resentful?*
- *Was there a dark feeling of dread that you couldn't shake?*

Be mindful that there is a difference between a warning feeling and learned fear. Earlier life experiences – such as those that may have left us embarrassed or feeling like a failure – can sometimes overpower our intuition. Also, remember that intuition can also reflect positive feelings, such as the moment when you felt instantly comfortable with your new acquaintance, or the thought of undertaking an activity generated excitement and enthusiasm. Keep a journal of the decisions you make using your intuition. Reflect back on the choices you made. Did you follow the correct path? Were your feelings accurate?

Time spent developing your intuition and reflecting on your progress will ensure strengthened ability and accuracy. So many answers that you need for your life's journey can be found within. Intuition is the key to unlocking your best pathway forward.

Dreaming on the Soul Bridge

by Cathleen O'Connor

After a day of non-stop problems – my computer mysteriously deleted much-cherished photos, ate the beginning draft of my foray into women's fiction as well as a blog piece due the next day, and then proceeded to sound like a jet engine on the way to take-off – I looked forward to a good night's sleep.

I set an intention for my dreams, asking my angels and guides to help me find what I had lost during the unexpected technological mayhem of the afternoon and, surrendering my worries to my angels, I drifted off to sleep.

Once I fell deeply asleep, I stepped into a world filled with magical symbols. I kept dreaming of nested Russian dolls, one inside the other. In the dream I kept opening one doll to find the next and then the next, while still not getting to the bottom.

I woke up around 5:00 a.m. puzzling over the dream but trusting that the answers to my problems were hidden within the symbolism of the images and actions I was shown. And that's when it hit me – hidden! The dolls were hidden within each other.

I literally jumped out of bed, rushed to the computer, and turned it on. It booted up normally, and I began my hunt for the nested, hidden files. Ten minutes later, I found all my missing material that had somehow ended up hidden within other files and folders. I may never know how they got there, but I was so thrilled to have them back and my work saved that I could have burst into song!

That night, my dreams provided the bridge between my ordinary waking reality and my true reality as a spiritual being who is always connected with my soul's wisdom and knowledge.

I now know that whether I am solving a pressing problem, releasing emotion, or even flying in a world without limits, I am profoundly embraced in a divine, soulful communication at night. As I go to sleep each night, I can't wait to connect again with my soul and discover the love, light, and healing in store for me.

The Angels Have Your Number

by Pam McKinney

A few years ago, when I was still in the beginning stages of "waking up" to my connection with Source, I started seeing 5:55 on my clock almost every day.

I knew this meant something, but I wasn't sure what. A friend referred me to a book by Doreen Virtue, *Angel Numbers 101*, which contains messages from our angels corresponding to numbers 0 through 999. From this book, I learned that 555 indicated that a big life change was upon me. This was so amazing to me – that I could get messages from my angels through my clock!

After that, I began seeing series of numbers consistently. No matter where they showed up, I recognized them as messages from my angels. I always thanked them for sending me what I most needed in perfect timing.

I keep a small calculator on my dresser. I rarely use it, but when I began using a new essential oil diffuser that sits next to it, I started noticing numbers on the calculator readout that changed periodically. Then I really started to pay attention! Sure enough, almost every morning and sometimes again in the evening, the number sequence on the calculator changed – more messages from the angels!

For over a year now, I've been excited to check my angel messages each morning and again before I go to bed. Sometimes there is a message, sometimes not; but every day I can be assured that my angels are watching over me and sending me hope and love.

It's so exciting when you fully realize that you're always being cared for, watched over, and loved beyond measure and that angel messengers are there for you whenever you ask them for help. There isn't anything too big or too small for your angels to handle or help you with – you just have to reach out to them, ask for their assistance, and then stay open to receiving the messages…sometimes in unexpected ways.

Once you start paying attention to these messages, you'll see that your angels have your number, too!

Astrology and the Soul

by Cathie Bliss

Who am I? Seriously, who is the "Real Me"? How can I find myself? What is my purpose?

A fascinating way to gain clarity on these questions – and many other profound matters in your life – is through astrology. I'm not talking about the entertaining column in your favorite magazine, but an astrology that reveals the depths of who you are and why your soul chose to be born in this time and place.

The little bit I already knew about astrology gave me hints as to why my kids were so different from each other. I wanted to learn more! How could astrology help me know and encourage the souls of my children and better understand my own life purpose?

Right away, I learned it's a myth that astrology is all about predetermined events. The planets don't control you or cause events to take place. Rather, understanding planetary energies and cycles allows you to best express your soul's potential in alignment with universal timing. The planets mirror back to us what is within us.

Your unique natal astrological chart is a map of the sky at the time you were born. When we incarnate, our souls have already chosen to experience certain events in this lifetime, known as fate. Your chart also illuminates portals of destiny, where you have free will and high-voltage potential.

The birth chart allows you to see your inner nature, to know yourself beyond ego and personality. It is a frame of reference for your purpose, as well as the unveiling of your soul's intended timing.

As I studied with Soul Contract Astrologer Robert Ohotto, I learned that astrology facilitates soul dialogue. By understanding the inner language of your soul, you know which life choices are true for you. And as you consciously implement and live those choices, doors open to new avenues of expression. This power to live an inner-directed life will propel you toward your highest destiny and wholeness of being.

Whether you choose to work with a professional astrologer or study on your own, astrology is an incredible way to learn more about yourself, your family, your life purpose, and your soul.

The Akashic Records: An Etheric Library of Wisdom

by Patricia Missakian

The Akashic Records are a database of all thoughts, experiences, and lessons people have had throughout their many lifetimes. These Records contain information about the past and the present, as well as possibilities for the future.

Imagine the Records as an etheric library in a parallel reality. When you work with the Akashic Records, you are aided by your Akashic Records' guides, who help you find and decode the information you are looking for in order to move forward in your life towards what you want to manifest.

Each soul has its own Akashic Record, and there are collective Records of all souls and all journeys. That explains why the Records are everywhere, whether in a planet, a crystal, a plant, or inside a person – an infinite wealth of information!

There is so much to explore about the wisdom of your soul in the Akashic Records. I love teaching my students how to access these Records so they can tap into their own wisdom of skills mastered in their past lives. My guides from my Akashic Records have taught me a particular method for opening and reading the Akashic records. The advantage of this technique is that it is very grounding. This is important because while you're deeply connected to the Divine and developing your eighth chakra (which is used for reading and decoding the Akashic Records' data), you are still very connected with the earth. This creates a grounded channeling that allows you to manifest while you are deeply in tune and connected.

I believe that the Akashic Records are a key piece to support the transformation the Earth is passing through, and every day more people are being called to work with the Akashic Records.

When the student is ready, a teacher shows up. If you are interested in learning more about how you can tap into this infinite source of wisdom, set the intention that the right teacher or method to access the Akashic Records will show up for you.

It's All in the Cards

by Ramona Remesat

If you head to the New-Age section of any bookstore these days, chances are you will find one of the most amazing tools for connecting with your soul. There, wrapped in their lovely cellophane packages, are decks of angel oracle cards.

Oracle cards have been used as a divination tool for centuries, and my take on things that have endured through the ages is that *they work!*

There will never be a shortage of people who want to know how a situation or decision may play out. Hence, there will always be tools to help them arrive at the answers they seek. I'm sure you, too, have wondered at one time or another if you should take a new job, move to a new home, leave a relationship, or trust your gut instincts about something.

While we all have inner guidance that can show us the answers to these questions, when you are really in turmoil and struggling for clarity about something, it can sometimes be difficult to tap into the whispers of your soul and spiritual helpers that guide you in the right direction. So that's when a tool like oracle cards comes in handy!

The messages that the cards reveal are completely separate from our thoughts, feelings, and innermost wishes, which makes them easier to trust. I have found that whether I draw several cards or only one, the messages that come through are always exactly what I need in that moment.

Why not add working with the cards to your daily routine to support you in connecting with your soul? Just as you may perhaps read your horoscope to find out what lies ahead each day, why not select an angel card first thing in the morning and see what angel guidance is coming your way?

The angels' messages are always loving, guiding, and supportive. And I can't think of anything better to wake up to than that.

Give Your Soul a Name

by April Williams

It is safe to say that I, April, am more than just my name. I am a body that makes meticulously morphed actions. I am an awareness that takes in all the sensations that surround me. I am a mind that analyzes and creates the narrative of the grand novel of me.

While my name does not define who I am, it gives others a way to communicate with me and write me into their own personal story – a character in their own book of life. Of course, there are ways to identify each other without actual names; but those, too, are just other ways to use a system of classification to make sense of all that surrounds us.

While none of existence was ever meant to be defined, our definitions and labels have given birth to the world we live in, our identities, and the societies our identities play in. So why not give an official birth to your soul by giving your soul a name!

Open up space in your story of life for another character, and watch as a stronger connection is created.

Meet my soul, Sunshine! She is bright and playful and gives off an inviting yellow hue filled with the warmth of a loved one's embrace.

Even if you feel silly calling your soul a name, the process of tuning in and noticing all the possible labels your soul adheres to will in itself bring you closer. For now, when you see, feel, hear, taste, smell, or encounter any sensation that aligns with your soul, you will be reminded of it, comforted by its presence, and able to acknowledge it as a part of you. You will naturally form an everlasting connection to that very important piece of you that yearns to be seen: your beautiful soul.

Angels and Rainbows

by Nukhet Hendricks

I was so tired of feeling afraid of dying when I was on a plane; yet here I was, on a plane for another ride. The fear was so strong that it felt overwhelming, crippling, almost debilitating. Worst of all, it made me feel disconnected from my soul. I didn't know what to do.

Then I considered an approach that was completely different for me: simply surrendering to the fear and not trying to make it go away. I'd never done this before because I had always thought that surrendering meant giving up, but I tried to look at it in a new way – as simply letting go of the struggle.

It seemed worth a try, but there was one problem: I didn't know *how* to surrender. So I did something I *do* know how to do: I turned to the angels. I called on all seven of the archangels. I asked them to surround the plane and keep us all safe with their colorful energies, just like the colors of the rainbow. It felt good; I felt the air fill my lungs again for the first time since I'd boarded the plane.

We took off, and when we finally reached cruising altitude, I realized I was not clutching the arm rest. I felt surprised and delighted; then I felt an inner nudge to turn my head to look out the window. First I noticed the beautiful, white, fluffy cloud traveling alongside the plane; then I noticed the shadow of the plane reflected on the cloud. "What a perfect vision," I thought. And then I saw it: the perfect rainbow circling the perfect reflection of the plane!

At that precise moment, this incredible message from the loving angels reconnected me to everything divine. Since then, whenever I feel fear clutching my heart, my breath getting stuck at the top of my lungs, or my soul starting to leave my body, I call in the angels and ask them to surround me. Within minutes, I am back to breathing fully, feeling loved and blessed, surrounded by the beloved archangels. They connect me back to my soul with their colors of the rainbow…and their divine love.

The Mid-Night Cleanse

by Karen Packwood

One night, I was awakened by a refreshing gust of ice-cold air blasting through my window. I had fallen asleep with the brilliance of the full moon bathing me in its majesty, as if I were a precious gem about to receive the deepest healing. But now the sky was a calm, deep black, with just a few stars twinkling. I rested in the protective arms of the night. The church clock struck 3:00 a.m., each chime ringing magically through the stillness. Just then, the hooting of a solitary owl rang out, calling me. "Come fly with me," it invited, "Let's swoop and soar. Let's explore."

So I did. I imagined myself flying above the trees and amongst the stars. From such a height, I was able to look down with the piercing accuracy of an owl's vision and see myself lying in bed, as if viewing myself for the first time. How sweetly precious I looked. How fragile yet so strong within this fragility. In that one tiny being, I saw the exquisite glory of the world reflected, feeling a sense of oneness with all that exists.

Eventually, I let myself float back into my body, feeling the clean energy of the night sky, the clarity of the owl's vision, and the magic of the church bells becoming one with the truth: *I am, just like you, a truly precious gem that needs to be held tenderly and treated lovingly each and every day.*

Now, each full moon, I imagine myself soaring through the night sky, resting on a star where I take time to remind myself: *I am precious. I deserve only the best for myself. I am a vital part of this world.* I let the moon cleanse me and reconnect me with the purity and love at the heart of my soul, knowing that the sacred beauty of this moment will last and be passed on throughout the whole world for eternity.

I invite you do the same – to take yourself on the magical journey of a mid-night, moonlit cleanse.

Make Friends with Your Chakra Guides

by Qatana Samanen

Your soul holds all the guidance and loving support you seek, and it longs to share these gifts with you. You just need to reach out and ask.

One way to connect with your soul is through the portal of your seven chakras, inviting a guide to come forth from each one. As you make friends with your chakra guides, you discover all the wisdom and love that's been waiting for you. You find strengths you didn't know you had. You view the challenges you face from a fresh perspective, empowering you to create a life of greater joy and peace – the life you long for.

How do you do it? First, allow yourself to enter a state of deep relaxation. Then ask within, "Where do I go first?" Listen and discover which chakra is calling you. Turn your attention there.

When you're ready, invite the guide of this chakra to be with you. Then just wait.

Your guide may come immediately, or it may take a while to appear. Once in its presence, welcome it and thank it for being there. Spend time observing what you notice about your guide and how you feel in its presence. Share these observations and notice your guide's response. Begin to feel the connection that's already developing.

Then ask your guide, "What have you come to show me or tell me?" Wait receptively for any awareness that comes to you.

Be very open to whatever your guide offers. If you have any questions or concerns, share them openly, entering into dialogue with your guide. Through this interaction, you will receive exactly what you need. Feel free to ask your guide for help with any challenges you're facing. Always express appreciation for the gifts your guide has given you.

What a relief to learn there's a resource within that you can trust more than the one who's usually running the show! How wonderful to discover that your guides can provide you with wisdom, strength, loving guidance, and support any time you want!

Receive Direct Messages from Your Soul

by Rozlyn Warren

I love channeling information directly from my soul…without concern that my ego is sneaking in its desires. When I use the word "channeling," I mean that I step outside my human personality, ego, and mind chatter and become a clear channel to receive direct messages from Inner Guidance. This form of connection is both a spiritual practice and a skill that can be developed.

I began using this process as a teen, and it has never failed me. I used the name of my religious icon at the time because that was the breadth of my knowledge of Spirit. Today, I channel Sophia (which means Wisdom), the name for the group of non-physical friends who communicate with me most intimately. I asked for a name to make the relationship even more intimate, and they graciously agreed.

Here is the spiritual practice that is the basis for my connection, which you can also use to develop an intimate, loving, guiding connection. Using a journal, date the page and continue in this format:

- Write your name, and then ask to connect with Inner Guidance (e.g., "Sophia, may we chat?").
- Write your Inner Guidance's name. (For me, this is Sophia. Use whatever is comfortable for you: Inner Guidance, God, Universe, or whatever resonates with you.)
- Write whatever comes to you. At first, it will feel like you are just making things up. That's fine; your imagination is the bridge to your intuition and Source.
- Next, write your name again and continue the conversation, going back and forth with your Guidance.

When you begin the practice, wait a day or two to read what you have written. You will be amazed at what you discover. As you learn to trust the connection, you will be able to receive and believe messages as they are shared. Will you channel Sophia? This is doubtful. You have your own group of non-physical friends guiding you, but you will be connecting in a more conscious and deep way. Will they give you a name to call them? I don't know…ask and see what happens!

Stay Open to Soul-Stirring Signs

by Annie Price

We're not always mindful of heavenly signs assisting us along our soul's path. Maybe this is because a stirring sign isn't always a grand event. Often, it's a simple heart-knowing occurrence, a pattern unique to us. It might be a song repeated throughout our day. It might be a phrase used by someone who's totally unaware that it's reached us in a special way. Or it might show up as a comforting signal from a deceased loved one, something that leaves little doubt of the sender's identity. It could be something big and elaborate or something as simple as a bird's song.

During a turbulent time in my life, I'd often wake up hearing the call of a mourning dove. It wasn't so mournful to me, though! It was a reassuring sign telling me, *Hang in there – everything's going to be okay.* To this day, I feel a sense of calm whenever I hear the mourning dove's song.

Sometimes, we get a sign for someone else who isn't able to receive it. Years ago, I had an unusual experience that I later realized was a sign meant for my friend, Dave. He'd lost both parents within a short period of time – his mother died of cancer, and three years later his father died unexpectedly. Dave was particularly close to his mother, and he was in a lot of emotional turmoil following her death. One day, while I was helping him go through boxes of her belongings, the phone rang. I answered it and heard a familiar, sweetly high-pitched female voice say only, "Hello," and then the line disconnected. I knew who it was. When I described what happened to Dave, he got a strange look on his face. I think he knew who it was, too – his mother's way of letting him know she was there for him. All these years later, I still have her Corningware casserole dish, and I'm reminded of this special sign every time I use it.

Soul-stirring signs are happening everywhere, all the time. I believe if you ask for the signs, you're sure to receive them. Stay open to the possibilities, and you'll get to experience your own unique soul signals.

Becoming BFFs with Your Soul

by Astra Spider

During my life's work as a shaman, the Universe has shown me that our souls hold all the wisdom we need. With this in mind, I know I want my soul on my side! And, in this particular lifetime, I want my soul and I to have FUN together! I am so over my past lifetimes of struggle, strife, and poverty. I embrace them for their lessons – and I release them.

This is the lifetime for happiness, vitality, abundance, peace, and freedom. And who better than my soul to show me the way? We've been through so much together. We've laughed, cried, loved, lost – even died together. And together we were born again.

How amazing to have a built-in "Best Friend Forever" – literally forever! – who knows me like the back of her hand.

As my soul and I travel together through this lifetime of awareness (apparently that's what we're calling it – the "Lifetime of Awareness" – cool!), we get to *consciously choose* what we create. We get to laugh, eat midnight snacks, and sleep till noon. We get to cry cleansing tears. We get to choose peace. And we get to sing. YAY!

Astra to Soul: "Oh, Soul, thank you – I love you so much!"

Soul to Astra: "Oh Astra – we are so lucky to have each other, live together, love together. Always. Thank YOU!"

We hug.

How does it feel to hug my soul? It feels like a warmth flowing through my heart. It feels multi-colored. It feels like snuggling a giant lion. It feels rich, full, and whole. Hugging my soul...I AM home.

You, too, can be BFFs with your soul!

How?

Connect with that part of you that is magic, eternal, wise, and free. Breathe into this connection. Invite your soul to be part of your life, of your decision-making, of creating all that you desire. Invite your soul to be your partner in your dreams made manifest.

You and your soul were made for each other. Together, you are perfect. Together, you are DIVINE!

Connect with Your Eternal Star-Self

by Akasha Rainbow

To help remind me that I am a soul and not a body, I like to go outside on a clear, moonless night and look up at the sky and see the infinitude of stars. I find a star that seems distant and faint and then focus even beyond that, into the depths of darkness and seeming nothingness, knowing there are stars even beyond that.

There are stars so far off that they are in another dimension – stars that are the homes of our eternal souls. These stars encode our many lifetimes across the galaxies, dimensions, universes, and time-frames. We exist now in all places, and we exist now in that higher-dimensional star, even though its light does not reach our physical eyes.

That star, beyond the veil, is our higher self. We are infinite – nothing that troubles us here on Earth is of any consequence to our star-self. It is all a game for our amusement and for our ever-expanding higher self, even if the play may seem harrowing at times. And yet, when we align with the frequency of our star-self, we feel in our bodies who we are. We feel like love, and we pulse energy through our third eye to turn it inside out. We experience knowing ourselves as that ever-burning, ever-infinite, and ever-shining star – sending our love across the far reaches of creation, incarnating, even now, as a speck of stardust on this beautiful divine Earth.

Look up at the vast sky and connect with your eternal star-self. Feel who you are when you feel love pulse through your body, and follow that frequency in your life, because it is the frequency of who you are as a soul. This star is the beacon to call you home, beyond the veil, beyond the darkness, to the powerhouse of the sun that lights your higher self and manifests the possibilities encoded in your soul here on Earth.

You are infinite.
You are one.
You are holy.
You are everlasting
and eternal.

Resolving Problems with Your Guardian Angel's Help

by Lumi Vasile

Several weeks ago, my daughter came for a visit. She needed some guidance, as she had a proposition for a new job and wasn't sure whether or not she should leave her present job. We talked for a while, and then I reminded her of an exercise we once did in an angel workshop some years ago. She was eager to give it a try.

I asked her to close her eyes, take some deep breaths, inhale pure white golden light, and exhale all the worries and confusion she felt. Then I asked her to call in her guardian angel and feel her presence in any way that was significant to her. When I sensed that she was relaxed, I asked her to open her eyes and start writing to her guardian angel about her issue.

When she finished writing, I asked her to close her eyes and again feel the presence of her guardian angel, then open her eyes and start writing as quickly as she could, without analyzing the words that came into her mind, until she finished.

When she first read the words, she thought that it made no sense; but I reminded her that Spirit has its way to give messages and she should look again at the words, phrases, and the drawing she was given and allow herself to receive their hidden message. And then she suddenly exclaimed, "Now I understand! I know what I have to do!"

Later on, she followed that guidance and inspiration, and the results were beyond her beliefs.

Now, why am I telling you this story? Because you, too, can do the same. Just follow the steps described above, and you will find the guidance, inspiration, and release that you might need in a difficult situation.

And remember, all is possible when you connect with your soul and allow Spirit to be your guide!

Soaring with My Soul

by Sharon Rothstein

When I feel like I am in need of a bit of divine perspective, I like to imagine that:

I soar like an eagle with my soul, on a magic-carpet ride of possibilities. I lift off and glide with my creator, my own soul connection and knowing, void of burden, likened to personal freedom.

I look down on the perspective of my human existence from an aerial view, my view from innate wisdom. I become far greater than the small earthly being with which I generally associate.

I fly in the present moment, a place where I more often choose to be. I uphold my personal power and soar above the clouds, the stars. I take on a lighter demeanor.

My wings carry me to greater heights of personal awareness and a most precious gift called my life. My life is not small, in fact, quite large from this optimum view. I am important, I matter, and my contribution to society is necessary.

Through rising above past or future, I relax and let my now take care of itself. I am alive, awakened, and feel the gentle breeze. My ideas begin to flow more readily. From up here, such clarity appears. I know how I am doing. I am shown that something that I need to know. My next steps are provided. My true essence and value are revealed in this present moment of flight.

As I take a break from my judgmental perspective, life remains peaceful in the present, soaring with my soul. Letting time unfold, free of self-imposed stress. No worries, I step back and wait for guidance for my next approach. I take charge and proceed with easy living.

When a moment of imbalance arises, I get quiet and relaxed. I become present and soar with my soul again. Greater confidence and relief are now restored, and I have enjoyed yet another time of soaring and have gained insight into me.

Lucid Dreaming for Soulful Awareness

by Laura P. Clark

Remembering dreams is an art and a skill to be cultivated. Through dreams, our subconscious brings us messages that we would otherwise not see. One of the most powerful types is known as *lucid dreaming*, which is when, during a dream, you become aware that you are dreaming.

This experience opens up a whole new realm of dream-state, allowing you to bring your waking consciousness into a dream. By having lucid dreams, you can explore your dream-state with complete clarity. You can use all of your senses as you would in your awake-state. And, even though you are dreaming, it actually feels real.

Lucid dreaming has many advantages. It helps you overcome fears by facing them. It allows you to tap into your inner creative genius. And, of course, it allows you to fulfill fantasies of doing things that you are physically incapable of doing.

The first step of lucid dreaming is to remember your dreams. Everyone dreams, but remembering them is often difficult. To facilitate this process, keep a pen and paper next to your bed; and when you wake up, write about your dreams. If you don't remember them, write about your feelings and any images that pop into your mind. As you do this, you'll begin to remember more of your dreams.

Once you begin to remember your dreams, you can train yourself to induce lucid dreams. A great way to start this process is to simply be more aware during your day. Stop, look, and listen! Look at your environment and examine your own awareness – bring the awareness of a sacred observer to your surroundings. You may begin to notice when something is not as it first seemed to be. Keep investigating. This may be a sign that you're actually dreaming!

Someone who has lucid dreams has a much higher level of awareness – not just while sleeping but also during their waking life, which is one of lucid dreaming's greatest benefits. So, go ahead and bring a soulful awareness to your day *and* to your dreams – and find a deeper understanding of who you are in the process.

Sacred Spirit Journeys

by Marianne Soucy

My favorite way to connect with my soul, as well as to receive guidance and insights, is through sacred spirit journeys. So, as I prepare to write this piece, I connect with my spirit guide.

Preparing for the journey is an important step. I am sitting out in the garden – a sunny afternoon. I take a deep breath in, and on the exhalation I relax into being here now. Being present where I am. Filling out my body with my awareness. Letting everything be okay just the way it is. Butterflies flying around me, birds singing. A dewdrop lingering on a blade of grass, shining green or red, depending on the angle I look at it from. The old apple tree behind me beginning to get leaves.

As I begin the journey, I sense my spirit guide close to me. He says:

> Connecting with your soul is what you do every time you journey, every time you connect with us; for what we do is gently guide you closer to seeing, experiencing, and expressing the real you, your soul, your authentic self.
>
> A powerful way to connect with your soul is to go into your heart – that's where you'll find me, and that's where you'll find the path to expressing your gifts and shining your light.
>
> The path to your soul is not a journey you take alone; it is best taken with us – your heart guides – by your side, for we know your heart and soul. We are not stuck in the separation between past, present, and future – no, we live in the eternal Now, and our job is to guide you to the Now – to the present moment where you'll discover infinity as yourself, as your true nature.
>
> Just call on us and keep us in your heart. Live from the heart, and your soul will shine through everything you do.

I give thanks and end the journey.

These sacred spirit journeys are always so soul nourishing for me. I invite you to take a journey of your own and see what happens!

Connecting with Fairy Magic

by Sheelagh Maria

Fairies (or flower beings) are the devas of the plants and flowers that grace our beautiful planet. They are light, magical, and always happy to help us. When the fairies work with nature, they meditate consistently on the shape and form of the flowers they are overseeing, in order to bring into reality the beautifully consistent shape of the blooms they protect. The fairies can also work with people; however, because of their light and pure energy, they can only work with those whose energy is high and clear. So ensure that you are feeling playful, calm, and aligned with inner peace as you strive to connect with them. Going for a walk in nature or simply opening a window and invoking them before you sit to connect works beautifully.

As with any kind of energy work, see yourself surrounded in a globe of white light before you begin. Breathe this white light in, open your heart, and smile. Then, with an open, loving heart, say out loud, "Dearest Fairies of the Flowers of the Light, thank you for sitting with me, infusing my aura with joy, and helping me to manifest in my sacred life." If you'd like, you can ask them for a specific form of manifestation (such as money or experiences) or seek their aid in connecting with your soul.

The fairies often appear as specks of brightly coloured light out of the corner of your eyes. They will stay with you if your energy is high and will show you signs – often feathers or brightly coloured stones or birds – to signify they are really there. Whether or not you feel their presence or see outward signs, know that they are with you and your prayers are heard. Smile, sit with the fairies' energy, and feel yourself receiving your desires – while enjoying the energy of anticipation. Feel how magical and grateful and appreciative you are for this experience of connecting with the fairies and aligning their magical energy with your own soul.

Intuition Versus Intellect

by Kristin Schmidt

All of us are gifted with intuition. That "knowing" is our soul whispering our truth. We only need to stop and listen. But all too often, we ignore our gut feelings or rationalize them away. Our intellect tells us that our intuition is wrong and that only hard, cold facts are valid. Even when we do acknowledge our intuition, fear often makes excuses about why we shouldn't act on it, and we end up losing faith in our intuition, in ourselves, in our dreams, and in our soul.

This is what happened to me.

For a long time, I kept hearing intuitive whispers telling me to share a message that "pretty is an inside job." I wanted to show the world that "pretty" isn't just about superficial living – it's about giving to yourself, being who you are, and allowing the best in all of us to be expressed. My soul urged me to create a community around this premise, but my intellect told me that it didn't make sense, it was too complicated, I didn't know how to make it happen, and it just wouldn't work.

So I gave up on my dream.

But my intuition didn't. It kept up its whispers to me – night and day – until I finally revisited the idea. My soul showed me inner visions of reaching out to women who were lonely, without hope, or simply in need of a friend. I was filled with a desire to share hope and love, to reach one heart at a time until we became thousands of hearts sharing in this vision.

Again my intellect rebelled, but this time I chose to follow it. I stopped worrying about *how* to do it and simply *began*. In that moment, it happened: people showed up to help me with my dream. Things started moving quickly. Before long, my intuitive flash had become a reality – an amazing community of women all over the world supporting each other, bringing pretty back to each other and to ourselves.

No matter what your intuition may tell you or how much your intellect might resist, I can tell you what I've learned from experience: When you listen to your intuition and follow its calling, you honor your soul and live your dreams.

Walking with Your Soul-Partner

by Scott M. Dehn

As I look back, I see that my soul-partner was always with me, from birth. But in my youth, I was unaware of this sage within me. I was wrapped in the mistaken distinction that I was walking my road alone, believing what I had heard for so many years from my parents, teachers, and friends: "No one is going to help you but yourself."

Because of my limited understanding and emotionally insecurity, I took the straight road carved out by so many of my peers: marrying, then starting a family too young while I pursued growing my career. Unlike my soul, my marriage didn't stand the test of time, and I ended up feeling more alone than ever.

After further trials and disappointments, I asked God to help me. The answer to my prayers came from a voice deep within me: "You are not alone. You have an eternal companion: the soul."

This voice seemed to represent all accumulated knowledge and wisdom. I felt the presence of this ancient sage pulsing in my being, the words indelibly etched in my heart.

"But why do I need a partner?" I wondered.

"I am with you, Scott, to help you, guide you, teach you, offer divine comfort, and love you unconditionally as together we travel this path back Home."

"Home?" I asked.

"Back to the Source, dear Scott. It is a journey of awareness that you come to realize – the Conscious Path of all that you need to experience and learn, my love."

At that moment, everything clicked into place in my awareness, like a perfectly fitting mosaic, coming together to complete a story that had begun years ago. I learned that I was never alone. I *did* have a travel partner – one that came from an eternal source, one that offered steadiness on the most unsure roads, a guiding light that I could rely on even while walking through the darkest tunnels.

From this new place of understanding, I now reflect often on my journey with my partner – my soul – as we walk together on this path that I have learned to cherish and share.

The Wisdom of Lemurian Crystals

by Patricia Missakian

The Lemurians were a civilization deeply connected to spirit and the Earth. They knew Lemuria would sink, and they discovered a way to keep their knowledge for when the world was ready to restore oneness: they stored it within Lemurians crystals and placed them deep into the earth to emerge when the time was right. When you look closely at those crystals, you will see the bar codes where this information is recorded.

Here is a simple method for you to reconnect with the wisdom of Lemuria. For this exercise, you will need a Lemurian crystal. You will also need an open mind! (Through my experience of teaching these techniques, I've learned that doubt is my students' worst enemy.) Set the intention to receive information about your past lives and connection with Lemuria. Be open to letting the information come to you. Do not force it. Simply be in the present and have fun!

Once you are ready, sit upright with your Lemurian crystal on your left hand. Clear your mind of any thoughts, worries, or things to do later on. Be present with your breathing. As you breathe, visualize the light within the crystal coming to you through your breath. Let the light go through you. Find anything you are ready to release in your body, and release it as you breathe out.

Repeat two times.

Next, bring the crystal to your heart and let it exchange energy and wisdom with your heart. You will notice that the crystal has what resembles sidebar lines along its body. Slowly move your thumbnail up the etchings one by one. Ask to receive the messages it has for you. Be open to receive the download. Remember to let the information come to you in the way it wants to come to you.

When you feel complete, take a few more breaths, thank the crystal for all the wisdom shared, and open your eyes.

The Grief Connection

by Cathie Bliss

I didn't know if I still wanted to be here. I existed in fog and functioned on autopilot. My mom had died without warning. Six months later, my angel of a daughter, Cailen, unexpectedly passed away. I felt like a tangled ball of yarn with lots of loose ends, and I felt that if anybody pulled one, the world would certainly fall apart.

Grief trapped me in hell. I wept. I had constant migraines. I had to remind myself to breathe. I couldn't get out of bed. I thought the pain in my chest was a heart attack. Occasionally, I'd feel a little better, but not for long. The grief roller coaster would start up again.

As I surrendered to the darkness, I found small ways to be present. I wrote short poems. I prayed for trust, joy, and renewed purpose. I read for inspiration and to learn how others survived tragedy. The healing words, "Infinite Love and Gratitude," became my mantra. I talked to Cailen in Heaven and a few wise souls on Earth. Gradually, through the shadows, a light began to glow.

Once I could breathe on my own, there were so many revelations. I discovered that grief is a sacred time, a spiritual journey. I realized that grief has purpose: it's a process of soul growth. It's a place to explore what matters and what doesn't, to recall why we were born. My soul remembered faith.

I learned that love truly is eternal; we can continue relationships with our loved ones in Heaven. My gratitude for the time we were together on Earth continued to deepen, and our hearts remain close. My soul expanded.

It's choosing – not once, but over and over again – which loose threads to weave into a new tapestry and where to add anew. As I did, Light entered my soul.

Author Tom Zuba writes, "Healing from the death of someone you love…is hard, hard work." He is so right. Do not search it out; grief will find you in its own time. And when it does, surrender to the journey. Try to remember that the tangled-dark-messy-hellish ball of yarn has deep, loving, soul-expanding purpose.

Remembering the Divine Partnership with My Soul

by Sharon Rothstein

I must now remember that I am in divine partnership with my soul, an agreement made before my entrance into this human body. I now have memory of where I came from, why I have come, and what I am here to do. I came from Spirit, and someday to Spirit I shall return.

My contentment resides in remembering that I was put here to experience an earthly adventure, one that my soul and I set out for – a life of joy and personal growth. Every day of this soul partnership is a day of opportunity, a way to connect with my greater half, to share the responsibility and fulfillment of my choices.

I was told to go forth and enjoy, to enhance and develop my senses. To see the beauty before me. To taste the riches of accomplishment. To stop and smell the roses, not taking time for granted. To hear my spirit's call through helpful ideas and insight. To touch the heart and soul of others. Yes, I remember now!

Peace of mind is directly proportionate to remembering my soul's participation, ensuring more playful, easy, wondrous experiences for me. A life that would seem more difficult if it were up to me alone.

Worries and concerns are lifted from my incorrect perception as I unlearn false perceptions of the past and remember my truth. I am shown the miracles that are mine to be realized, the hope that is before me, and my faith is restored.

At times it seems that I am magically powerful. I simply ask my soul for my greatest desires, and they appear in divine right timing. I trust that if a request does not manifest quickly, spirit has prepared a better plan.

Remembering, I am home again – living in two worlds simultaneously: I am spirit and a human being.

Embodying Your Sun and Moon Sign

by Milada Sakic

Since I can remember, I have always looked for ways to connect with nature and the cosmos.

When nothing around me made sense, the astrological Sun and Moon always held so much natural wisdom. However, even as an astrologer since the age of 16, I used to deny my Sun sign in Taurus by saying: "I am not your typical materialistic and conventional Taurus, concerned so much about the physical realities of life (food, shelter, physical body, and money); I am more spiritual." I always seemed to relate more to my Moon sign in Aquarius – the non-conventional, liberal, and "interested in New-Age philosophies" kind of person.

For years, I was convinced that the Moon – representing our emotions and our needs – was more important. It took having two children, a busy corporate career of 16 years, and two physical and emotional burnouts to realize that nurturing both our Sun and Moon energies is essential.

The Sun symbolizes our vibrational essence, our relationship with masculine energies (e.g., ego), and who we are becoming on the journey. The Moon represents our vibrational mood and our relationship with feminine energies in our psyche (e.g., our soul). I have experienced that denying either one of these two greatly affects our general sense of physical and emotional wellbeing.

The conventional and calm Taurus energies bring me into my body through walking in nature, using essential oils, consciously cooking, or enjoying a good meal. And the non-conventional Aquarius soul signature inspires me to always emotionally reinvent myself – to seek inner freedom, forward movement, and progress.

I am finally at peace with my Taurus Sun, and connecting with its consciousness every day helps me honor my natural rhythms to find the inner peace and tranquility that most Taureans crave.

Regardless of the level of your knowledge of astrology, exploring the energy of the sign archetypes will help you gain so much wisdom in achieving wellbeing.

Setting Dream Intentions

by Gretchen Duhaime

When you woke up this morning, did you remember any dreams?

Dreams are often direct guidance from your soul. Whether you are a prolific dreamer or you're in the midst of a dream-recall dry spell, you can get a message from your soul tonight in three easy steps:

1. *Be specific.* If your intention is to find your purpose, break it down into a smaller, specific, question. Instead of asking, "What's my calling?" try asking "What one action can I take tomorrow to help me find my calling?"
2. *Place your order.* Write down your question on an index card or small piece of paper. I also write it in my journal. (You'll see why in step three.) Place the paper under your pillow. I like to think of this as placing my dream order, just like putting out a room-service breakfast order at a hotel.
3. *Write down your dream memories and emotions.* When you wake up, write down your emotions. (That's why I write my intention in my journal before I go to sleep.) How you feel when you wake is the biggest clue to the meaning or message from your dream. Then write down any dreams or snippets you recall, even if they don't seem to relate at all.

Sometimes you'll get a very obvious, direct answer to your question. If you asked what one action you can take to find your calling and you dream about interviewing for a new job, it might be time to start looking. But what if you dream something that seems random and unrelated? Trust me, your answer is there, just not so literally. You can ask a friend what associations they would make about your dream, but always remember that *you* are the final authority on what your dreams mean.

Tapping into Heaven's Consciousness

by Sheelagh Maria

What does *abundance* mean to you? For most people, it means money – and oftentimes, this thought is accompanied by the feeling of not having enough. This very thought/feeling/energy of lack is exactly what prevents the Universe from providing the very abundance that most of us desire. The good news, however, is that we all have access to infinite abundance! To receive it, we must be open and willing to tap into Heaven's consciousness.

The first step to doing this is to realize that Heaven is not "up there" somewhere far away – it is inside your own energy field and in the world all around you. Heaven is as available as your next breath. When we tap into Heaven's consciousness, we can receive anything we are a vibrational match for.

Once you realize this, the next step is to look at everything you already *do* have an abundance of. This may be a supportive family and friends, patience, or knowledge. It may be something tangible or something you could have access to if you wanted it (such as parental or sibling support). Feel a deep appreciation (even deeper than gratitude) for what you already have an abundance of. Send this appreciation into your heart, hold it there, and consider exactly how this abundance blesses or has blessed your life. Smile. Allow your appreciation to deepen within your heart, and then send this beautiful energy out into the ether. See it floating like a feather on the breeze, merging with the euphoria that is consciousness.

Next, bring that loving energy back to you. You could visualize this as soft-pink energy flowing through your heart, like a wave of love. Breathe this beautiful pink energy into the whole of your body and aura. Smile and savour it. Really *feel* how loved you are.

For the next two days, continue to feel this loving energy and see your life through the eyes of love and compassion – for others and for yourself. Know that Heaven loves you, that everything *is* working out for you, and that you *will* receive everything you desire.

Singing with Your Angels

by Lori Kilgour Martin

On the first day of kindergarten, I was afraid to go. I sat on the front lawn, in silence and alone, unable to move. My mother had to come out to get me. She took me by the hand, and we walked together, slowly, one step at a time, until we reached the school.

A lovely woman was there to greet us. She was my first teacher. The softness emanating from her bright eyes, and her gentle presence eased my mind. The classroom door opened, and I was greeted by my schoolmates' smiles. The sun shone through the windows onto the walls, which were painted yellow and covered with pictures of butterflies and all things joyous.

Perhaps the greatest joy of all my early school days came when it was time for music. At first we were introduced to simple instruments: cymbals, triangles, little drums. Later, we learned to sing lullabies and Celtic songs. (The lullaby "All Through the Night" was my favorite.) When singing, playing, or listening to the music, I sensed a gateway opening up within me – a luminous light flowing through, a welcome meeting with my soul. I felt connected – at once uplifted and soothed by the melodies. Those songs, tucked inside my heart, continue to reassure me to this day.

In the years since then, I've continued to feel the angels sing with me and through me. A wondrous ensemble, they sing with you, too. Whether you sing, chant, or hum, radiant rays of golden, angelic light form a bright cocoon around your body, bathing you in warmth. The finely tuned vibrations, interwoven with God, carry unique energies. The sparkling facets of your soul are gently gathered together, bringing you into a renewed state, stronger and completely aligned with the Divine.

The angels invite you to enter your sacred sanctuary of song today. Allow their iridescent wings to enfold you. Mother Mary shares this message: *Your voice is glorious. Sing, dear one, sing. Your every note is heard, and all are infinitely blessed. For you are an exquisite expression of God, treasured and held in loving care.*

Sleep my child and peace attend thee, all through the night...

Your Soul Longs for You

by Sophia (Translated by Rozlyn Warren)

Your soul longs for you – longs for connection, for oneness. When you decided to come and play in this time-space reality we call Earth, we – the greater part of you, the part called "your soul" – remained behind with your guardians, guides, and helpers.

We did not grieve this "separation" because we know we are never really separate and that the "Earth Adventure" begins with you *feeling* separate so you can freely discover new things, have experiences, and create based on your newly discovered desires. This is very exciting and pleasing to us; it is the very reason for the "Earth Adventure" – that and to have fun, of course!

We do grieve (as much as it is possible for us to grieve, which isn't much, but still…) that *you*, even for an instant, feel we have abandoned you! *Never!* We are breathing you, beating your heart, laughing your laugh, crying your tears.

We desire that some of the ways to connect with your soul that are presented in this book will feel light and true for you and that playing with these practices will allow you to drop, even for a moment, the illusion of separateness and sink back into oneness with your whole self – for this is the final part of the Earth Adventure: letting go of the separation and returning to yourself – to oneness with you and with All-That-Is.

If you are reading this book, you have reached this stage of the "game" – all that came before *was* fun and exciting, and now you learn to live from mindful consciousness. And while life is still fun, you will find it deeper, richer, easier, and more peaceful. It feels SO good to feel connected again!

Death Can Awaken the Soul

by Gayla Lemley

My soul awakened after the death of my husband.

It started on a bright, warm, summer morning. As was our routine, my husband and I went for an early-morning run, ate breakfast, and read the newspaper. Afterwards, my husband went out back for a flight in his newly acquired Ultralight Trike (a motorized hang glider). I heard the engine and decided to step outside to watch him. He took off, the engine quit, and he crashed to the ground. I could hear trees breaking, and I ran to him as fast as I could…my mind racing wildly.

From that moment and throughout the ensuing days while he was in intensive care in a coma, all the spiritual powers held my hand. One night, I left his bedside very late and drove home in a torrential rain storm. I was so nervous, tired, and extremely sad, when a "person" dashed out in front of me. I later realized that it was him, following me to make sure I got home safely. I did, but ultimately my husband lost his life.

I do, however, continue to have visitations and obvious signs that he is watching over me. My soul has a deeper connection with all the energies that surround me daily. And I know without a doubt that the soul lives on when our human body leaves.

My soul awakened to so many possibilities, such as going back to school to become a Clinical Mental Health Holistic Therapist and remarrying. I now help others find their balance between the mind, body, and spirit – which can be done at any time during life, even when death presents itself.

Chapter 9
Thoughts, Feelings, & Our Vibrations

Connecting with your soul is so important, so profound, and so convenient – you can do it at any given moment, from wherever you are! This is certainly true when it comes to connecting with your soul through your thoughts. You always have the power to consciously focus more on what you *do* want than on what you *don't* want. And because your thoughts determine your vibration (the energy you transmit to the Universe), they determine what experiences you attract into your life.

But you don't have to wait for external manifestations to let you know about your thoughts and vibrations, because you're always receiving feedback through your feelings. All feelings are valid and helpful, as they let you know whether or not you're aligned with your soul. Simply put, so-called "negative" feelings let you know that you're not focused on what your soul's focused on (a valuable piece of feedback, which could save you years of struggle), and positive feelings indicate that you are moving in the direction of your soul.

We experienced the power of thought firsthand several years ago when a life coach encouraged us to shift a single word in our thinking (and speaking): to replace "I *have* to…" with "I *get* to…" when we talked about our work. We immediately felt the emotional/vibrational difference, and we soon noticed these inner changes reflected in our external lives – as our business began to flourish like never before!

Thoughts, feelings, and vibrations make quite a powerful team! The pieces in this chapter will help you harness this power in fun, easy, effective ways – such as shifting your perspective, making conscious choices, overcoming challenges, and changing your life story! We hope these pieces guide you toward an ever-closer connection with your soul.

Begin with What's Right

by Peggy Nolan

I remember all too well what it was like waking up in the morning and running through my "everything is wrong" list: the car that needed a new battery, the job that drained me, the husband who walked out. My list of wrongs was never-ending and perpetually stuck on repeat. It drowned out the voice of my heart's deepest longings. My list of wrongs got in the way of my joy, happiness, and freedom. It was my ball and chain.

Then one day I read this quote by Thich Nhat Hanh: "Begin with what's right. That is a good place to start."

This was the cosmic dope slap and attitude adjustment I needed to connect with my soul – not only to heal but to realign with my true self. I began my mornings with a new list, my "everything is right" list: the house I lived in and could afford on my own, my beautiful daughters, a job that paid me very well for my expertise and time, my friends who stood by me through thick and thin, my family, my yoga practice.

Even on days when I felt like staying in bed all day, I'd begin with what's right: a physical body in good working order, food in the fridge, a roof over my head, clothes in my closet, shoes on my feet, coffee.

If you're stuck in the negative loop of what's wrong in your life, begin experimenting with what's right. Start with your physical body: eyes that see; ears that hear; your ability to speak; two arms for hugs; life-sustaining organs; your brain that allows you to think, create, dream, and imagine. Start there. Begin with what's right.

Breathe, Balance, Begin Again

by Shelley Lundquist

On one of my routes for my daily walk, I pass a retaining wall that rises from the sidewalk, forming a bridge to the higher ground. Every time I pass it, I walk up that incline and along the ledge, just as I did as a little girl.

Where once there was a skip in my step, there is now a decided wobble. At some point over the years, I seem to have lost my balance. With each step I teeter precariously, all while telling myself what terrible balance I have. And then I fall. Funny how that works, isn't it?

After my morning meditation today, I headed out for my walk feeling balanced and rooted in a place of peace and acceptance. As I approached the welcoming arc of the wall and began my climb, again I felt myself start to teeter. This time, though, I stopped, took a deep breath, released my limiting belief, and whispered, "My natural state is balance." I noticed an immediate change. My shoulders dropped, and I felt myself grounded on the ledge. I had no idea how tense I was.

I whispered those magical words to myself with every step: "My natural state is balance. My natural state is balance…" until I reached the far side and descended the decline with the ease and grace of a geisha.

My mind was reeling as I brought myself to awareness. My own belief that I could not do it had manifested repeatedly because I kept giving it energy. Without even realising it, I was self-sabotaging my every attempt, which led to disconnecting from my body and my soul! What a powerful lesson!

What I love most is that the lesson is universal, and it doesn't just apply to maneuvering retaining walls. When we tell ourselves something is hard, we make it so. When we welcome opportunities and take one step at a time with ease and grace, we discover how effortlessly we can achieve anything we choose.

The Miracle of Choice

by James Kelly

The miracle of choice allows you to experience that all your unhappiness is a choice. You may think that your misery is caused by things that happen *to* you and not by your decision to disconnect from your soul. This is what I believed until about 20 years ago, when someone asked me a simple question that changed my life.

At the time, my partner had just broken up with me and I was utterly miserable. A few months later, I met her at a party, and it was obvious she was interested in someone else. She noticed my distress and asked, "Did you make your happiness depend on me?" I was silent. I could tell her question was genuine, and I knew in that instant my life had changed.

A miracle had happened: in that moment, I allowed myself to remember *choice*. I realised that relationships could not make me happy or miserable. I realised that making my happiness depend on others was the result of a choice to disconnect from my soul. And that left me free to remember the real cause of my happiness: connection with my own soul!

For years after that awakening, I avoided intimate relationships. I sensed that unless I deeply experienced connecting with my soul, I would end up deciding again that other people could make me happy (or unhappy). Part of me didn't want to wake up. Part of me wanted to find someone else and believe that they were the cause of my happiness. Part of me didn't want to be responsible for my misery and my happiness. But I had changed inside, and there was no going back.

Now when I am happy and in a relationship, I know that my happiness has nothing to do with the other person but only with my inner connection with my soul. If I am sad when they are not around, I ask for a miracle: the miracle of choice!

The miracle of choice reminds you that your sadness is a choice and only your decision to stay connected with your soul leads to true happiness.

Change Your Story, Change Your Life

by Skywalker Payne

Do you wake up with energy and a smile on your face? Or do you pull the covers up over your head and wish you could stay in bed because you dread facing another day?

Have you accepted that the story of your life consists merely of a secure job that lets you save for retirement (when you can *finally* live your dreams), along with nagging headaches, recurring insomnia, and a general sense of dissatisfaction?

If so, maybe you need to change your story.

Perhaps you bought the story of career, stability, and a guaranteed income – as I did. I sacrificed my love of writing and performance to become a nurse, only to painfully admit that this is a profession I will never understand or love. So I changed my story to this one: *I am a writer and a storyteller. My work contributes to creating a more compassionate world. These talents are gifts that demand to be shared.*

The decision to change my story – and my life – was an incredibly important one, but it was not a one-time-only action. I reinforce this decision daily by taking deep breaths and reclaiming my creativity and life purpose. Limiting beliefs rise up daily like threatening bears, but I face them fearlessly. I tell them my new story, and they lumber away.

If you're ready to change your story, too, you can start by reflecting on the fears associated with attachments that prevent you from living your dreams. Is that guaranteed income really necessary? Do you need the big house and two cars? Is a title worth unending stress?

Once you let go of attachments, fear dissolves, and you can begin to re-vision your story. You understand that *now* is all that is. This moment is the time to begin to live your dreams and your life purpose.

Although this transformation may be challenging, it doesn't have to be frightening. Equanimity, mindfulness, self-compassion, and gratitude empower you to change your story. To wake up every day and know you're living the life you were born to live makes changing your story a worthwhile effort.

Appreciating Divine Delay

by Barbara Schiffman

As technology speeds up our lives, our desires for instant results also escalate. But at the soul level, we truly have all the time in the world and there's no need to rush.

I've come to appreciate what I call "Divine Delay." This phenomenon has common elements apparent mostly in hindsight, though I sometimes become aware of them while they're occurring.

One is a sense of confusion when my determination to make things happen gets thwarted at every turn. Another is disappointment when people I trust begin letting me down. My frustration also builds to a high boil, which makes the situation more of a struggle.

But then something occurs to reveal that it is actually a good thing that what I wanted did not happen – at least not yet! This releases my tension, and I can allow forward movement to flow.

I first began noticing Divine Delay when I needed to value a real-estate asset in my mom's estate. As her executor, I struggled for two whole years to resolve what was in fact a rare situation – until I "accidentally" found a real-estate attorney who was familiar with it! In the interim, the asset gained value, so it was actually a good thing we hadn't filed her estate taxes earlier, as they would have needed to be redone.

It's truly a matter of soul perspective. When roadblocks feel like setbacks, they are often just detours. When I listen to my soul, or at least "go with the flow," a Divine Delay's benefits usually get revealed.

Divine timing often requires Divine Delay. The positive results of my particular delays have demonstrated that even when events are moving s-l-o-w-l-y for no apparent human reason, my soul's always working behind the scenes to generate results worth waiting for.

Harnessing the Power of Your Emotions

by Sonia Miller

Emotions are the language of the soul. However, few people know how to speak this language and even fewer understand its sheer power and essential role in creating the lives we want. Whether navigating challenges or pursuing dreams, our emotions hold a key to our untapped power.

The key to harnessing the power of our emotions lies in how we relate to them. Most people have a relationship with their emotions that is based on control. Either we are controlling our emotions or they are controlling us. However, control only serves to keep the door to our inner wisdom shut tight. Why? Because what we resist persists. The more we avoid, suppress, or distract ourselves from emotions we find uncomfortable, the more power they gain over our life and the further we get from the clear understanding that moves us in the right direction.

How then do we open the door to our greatest clarity? *We choose to feel.* Emotions are not problems to solve or questions to answer. They are energy that moves through us. Like electricity, this energy simply exists. Allowed to run amok, electricity can burn down a village. Channeled correctly, it can illuminate a city. The same is true for your emotions.

Emotions have the power to connect you with your soul – the bigger part of you that is connected to Source Energy. The smaller part of you – your human self – is like a costume that your soul wears in this lifetime. Emotions happen at the human level, not the soul level. When they flow freely, with acceptance, they loosen, release, and reveal your soul's power. When you control them, it is as if you are zipping up the "small you" costume – keeping your soul's power trapped and hidden away. The "small you" connects with the "big you" by unzipping your costume and letting your soul shine through.

Are you ready to harness the power of your emotions? Next time you find yourself trying to "zip up," hit the pause button and ask yourself, "Might this be a good time to choose to feel?" And once you have chosen to feel, stillness usually follows. This will be the time to listen to your soul. It will have something important to say.

Finding Freedom in a Forgiveness List

by Brenda Reiss

Have you ever written a forgiveness list?

As a Radical Forgiveness Coach, this is a tool that I have taught and used for years; but the amazing, liberating power of this exercise never struck me as fully as it did when I shared it with my friend who was battling cancer. While in remission for the second time, she was feeling a lot of heaviness – particularly when she thought of her parents and some ex-loves. She knew that she couldn't hold onto the blame, anger, and pain of unforgiveness and fully love herself. She wanted to release this burden and make space for laughing, painting, and enjoying life…while she still had time.

I encouraged her to write down the names of everyone who tugged at her belly or heart when she thought of them. As she made her list, some names came quickly; others took longer to emerge. She sat with each name and asked how to best release the energy. Sometimes it was just a matter of saying, "I release you and love you." When it came to her parents, she wrote letters not only *to* them but *from* them.

Through this process, she made a profound shift. She realized that her pain had not been about the other people but about her own unwillingness to forgive. She released her sense of victimhood and, for the first time in years, felt that life was happening *for* her rather than *to* her.

When she completed her list, she felt light. Free. Joyful. Healed.

Her cancer did come back, but this time she wasn't in any pain. Her journey home was a conscious, beautiful experience as she wasn't taking along any baggage. She was experiencing true freedom, and it all started with the willingness to forgive.

I feel so honored that my friend included me in her journey of forgiveness. And I feel blessed to be able to share this tool – to help all of us release old hurts, live to the fullest, and embrace the most powerful energy in the universe: love.

Opening to the Sacred Journey of Learning

by Tanya Levy

I often wonder where the desire for learning comes from. What sparks any of us to learn about yoga or energy healing or to engage in a formal learning experience, such as enrolling in a program to become a carpenter or a nurse?

I believe that all learning journeys are sacred. Picking up a book that speaks to our soul, applying to a program, or joining an exercise class are all answers to our soul's call for renewal. Our job is to be open to this call.

Learning starts with cultivating a beginner's mind. I often equate this to starting a new day planner. You would not enter an appointment for 2015 in your day planner for 2014, because that year has passed. Having a beginner's mind is like cleaning off a day's agenda so that new appointments can be written in it. To put it another way: if our minds can hold a chalkboard's worth of information each day, opening to learning means taking time to *clear off* that chalkboard to make space for something new. This allows you to let go of past information or beliefs that may block new material from entering (such as the belief that "learning is difficult"). Each step we take in learning is like a new beginning. As we learn, we become new.

Openness to learning also requires trust. Trusting the teacher that you have chosen to provide the information you need to learn. Trusting yourself to be able to learn. Trusting the learning process: the taking in, the understanding, the integrating, and the applying of new information or skills…until the once-new material becomes familiar and applying it becomes second nature.

Despite the similarities, the specifics of the learning journey are unique for each individual. The ultimate opening to the sacred journey of learning lies in making it your own and allowing it to become part of your own personal lens and also part of how you see the Divine. Trusting in the Divine to help you learn allows external support to be there for you when you need it. And doing so connects you in beautiful ways to your soul.

A Joyful Sensation

by Milada Sakic

One of the most vivid times that joy came through was during the war back home in Bosnia. It was midday, and bombs and grenades were falling outside our building while we were running between the underground shelter and our place. We were 100 yards from the front line, living with no electricity or tap water, scarce meals, and the daily insanity of war. Suddenly, a peaceful feeling came through so strongly and intensely: *ALL IS WELL.* Pure joy spread throughout my whole body – healing, calming, and uplifting me.

Before this experience, communicating with my soul's guidance had been a very intellectual process for me. I was mostly tuning into words and images, which felt like a stream of infinite, all-knowing consciousness that came through just like my own thoughts – until the day when this soulful joy simply landed into my body, as if it had always been there.

Although this experience occurred spontaneously for me (and under extreme conditions), I have since learned that anyone can consciously call in these soulful sensations. To experience this for yourself, the only tool that you require is your awareness.

Start by asking a question that you would like some energetic support around. Sit comfortably and tune in as if you were listening to your body's response. Then, translate the vibrational sensation in your body into a word that feels like a close match. If it *feels* like a vibrational match, it *is*!

When a word, image, or sensation comes through – for example, *peace* – simply breathe it in and affirm: *I am peace.* Then, peace will integrate into your consciousness and your cells, releasing a new awareness or "aha" understanding around the question that was on your mind.

Next, experience and translate a new sensation that comes through into one word or sentence. This time, for instance, it may be *joy.* Simply affirm: *I am joy.* Or you could say, "Yes, please" – as in, "Yes, I am willing to breathe in joy and become this energy."

Try it! It's one of the most rewarding soulful practices that really works to instantly raise your vibration!

Taking Off the Blinders

by Bonnie S. Hirst

After an especially dark period in my life, I felt like my soul was broken. In an attempt to heal, I secured imaginary blinders around my realm of vision. I believed that if I kept my soul buffered from outsiders' condemnation or acquaintances' compassion, I would be able to keep the pain of past events manageable.

My blinders were meant to be my protection from absorbing additional heartrending emotions. I kept them on day and night. Without realizing it, though, my blinders created a fulcrum of angst – every thought became about me and my fear of more bad things happening. I was oblivious that life proceeded without me as I spiraled deeper into despair.

One morning, my soul nudged me to go outside. As I stepped onto the back deck, the sun emerged above the mountain ridge, its gentle rays showering light onto the flowers in my backyard. The vibrant golden irises leaned into the sun's magnificence and took me with them. My closed heart began to blossom, and the blinders that were once secured so tightly around my vision slowly dissipated. I'd forgotten how beautiful Mother Nature could be. For the past few years, my blinders had been my cocoon, my refuge, and I had been unable to see the beauty around me.

A monarch butterfly, its delicate wings outlined in black, flitted from iris to iris, and my soul opened wider. My heart warmed, and I felt capable of joining life again. Detaching what was left of my imaginary blinders, I enjoyed the sunshine as it graced the flowers, the butterfly, and me. I felt renewed. I felt the awareness that my soul was yearning for.

When reminders of difficult times come back to me, whether it be the loss of a loved one or other tragic events along life's journey, I strive to remember how good it felt to remove my blinders.

I heard my soul ask for the sunshine, and I took my blinders off.

White Flag

by Fiona Louise

I've always struggled with my inner critic. For many years, I allowed it to drown out the loving, caring voice of my soul in favour of judgements, chastising, and thoughts that I wasn't good enough, worthy, or loveable. Soon enough, I believed all of it. I hid in the shadow of my true self – a lesser version of me, a frightened me who was too paralysed by the "what-ifs" to experience life. I felt like I was trudging uphill, waist deep in mud, whilst others were already at the top, enjoying the view. When I realised that I could be free, however, a momentous shift occurred: instead of battling constantly with my inner critic, I waved a white flag.

My white flag wasn't defeated surrender; it was a truce to negotiate terms. My white flag meant that I was surrendering my old conditioning, fears, restrictions, and limiting beliefs. In return, I offered compassion and understanding to my inner critic, for I knew that the good intention behind my critic's words was to protect me and keep me safe – it had just become a skewed, self-deprecating, nonsensical story over the years. I encouraged my critic to let me leave my shell. As I pushed past the fear with my critic's voice raging in my ears, I realised that life wasn't so scary after all – which shocked my ego into silence and allowed my soul's voice to gently nudge me back to the right path with renewed confidence and vigour. All I had to do was push through the fear. My critic realised that this new life was far more rewarding.

I won this battle through kindness, and I continue to nurture my critic with kind words and love. I still have fearful thoughts now and then, especially when I'm doing something really important. But as I remind my critic that I'm safe, its fears fade to a peaceful expectation.

Waving the white flag was a small act, but surrendering enabled me to move beyond fear; to connect with my soul; and to live a happy, loving, abundant life.

Are you ready to wave your white flag?

Emotions Are the Doorway to the Soul

by Tree Franklyn

In my late teens and 20s, I suffered from severe depression.

I used to lie in bed every night and pray that by some magical stroke of mercy, the bed would swallow me up while I slept and I'd finally be granted a pardon from this life sentence. And every morning, I woke up, sinking a little deeper into my bed, into my depression, as I realized I was still alive.

One particular morning, I became so angry I yelled, "I DON'T F***ING WANT TO FEEL THIS ANYMORE!!"

My body let out a blood-curdling scream of desperation, the intensity of which surprised me. I lay in bed for a moment, shocked at the power from which the scream emerged.

And then I heard, *Feel it more.*

I didn't exactly hear it with my ears. It was more like a whisper from the depths of my soul, a small urging from within.

My first reaction was defensive. "Are you f***ing kidding me?" (I was pretty angry back then.) But as my ego subsided and my mind quieted, I heard it again: *Feel it more.*

I closed my eyes, somehow trusting, and took a deep, long breath.

Before I could exhale, a surge of raw, unfiltered sorrow emerged from deep within me and radiated out through every cell of my body.

Scared and trembling, I continued to breathe. And feel. And cry.

There was no resistance. I had surrendered. Like a wave, it washed over and through me, and then was gone. There was nothing left but silence. And peace. The most profound peace I had ever felt. I felt a divine union with God, with my soul, with life.

Since that day, though it didn't happen all at once, my depression has dissolved into a radiant, inner joy; and when painful emotions arise, I recognize that they're here to help me connect more intimately. By embracing and accepting my emotions without any attempts to resist or judge, it opens a doorway into my soul, showing me who I really am.

In that simple act of surrender, I'm released from depression's painful grip.

Dissipate Your Blocks by Connecting to Them

by RoseAnn Janzen

Since our natural state is love and joy, then any other feeling, emotion, or thought is telling us that something is out of alignment with our natural state. When we do not address these misaligned feelings, we store them in our body and energy field as blocks, pain, aches, or illness.

Here are ways you can find and resolve old feelings, emotions, and thoughts that can cause blocks:

- Ask your body to show you where you have a specific emotion, thought, or feeling stored. Pay attention to every itch, gurgle, etc., that shows up, and pick one at a time to focus on. Then ask what that one is specifically (e.g., "Body, where do I have a block to receiving clients stored?").
- Ask Source to show you what block you have to a specific thing (e.g., "Source, what is my biggest block to receiving clients?").

(You can do this process with your eyes closed or open. If you keep your eyes open, it is best if you put yourself into an alpha state first by unfocusing your eyes.)

After you have asked your question, pay attention to what visuals, words, sounds, feelings, etc., show up. Keep asking if you need to know more until you know you have all the information you need.

The next step is to ask to be shown how this is affecting your life now. Then ask to be shown what your life would be like without that.

Finally, go back to what your life is like with that block or emotion and ask yourself if you want to keep it or if you are ready to let it go. When you are ready to release it from your life, simply take it with your hands and set it on the ground or give it to Source and say, "I release you with blessings of pure love and light. Thank you."

As you release these old energies, feel the joy of reconnecting and returning to your natural state of love.

Being Before Doing

by Christy Whitman

If I could share with you just one secret that would amplify your ability to manifest the outcomes you desire, it would be this: *One hour of inner work is worth seven hours of outer work.*

I first learned this principle from Jack Canfield, one of my earliest mentors, nearly 20 years ago. It is, without a doubt, the biggest reason that I am able to accomplish so much in so many different aspects of my life.

Now, just to clarify: by "inner work," I don't mean that I meditate for an hour each day. I mean that before I take any outer action, I first take some time to clarify the intention behind it. I deliberately decide how I want to *feel*, and I get into that state of *being* before I *do* anything.

Action that is infused with energy and intention produces results that are astonishing compared to what can be accomplished with action alone. It's like the difference between using a hand-powered device versus an electric one that's plugged in and fully charged by a live current.

If you look at anything that exists in the manifest world – from the objects in the room you're sitting in to your very own body – you'll see that behind every external form there is an invisible, internal current that animates it, calls it into being, and brings it to life. Some people refer to this energy as *spirit*, *nature*, or *life-force*; others call it *God*, *nature*, or *soul*.

Although different words are used, they are all describing the same phenomenon: Everything in physical form is created first in the realm of the non-physical, and every outcome we achieve begins with an intention. This means that the more you bring yourself into energetic alignment with the intention behind your actions, the more powerful your actions become.

For the past two decades, I've found this to be true in my own life: one hour of inner work – intending, visualizing, aligning, and allowing – is worth seven hours of outer work. Try it for yourself and see!

Don't Forget to Remember

by Sharon Rosen

There we were, my friend and I, talking on the phone many years ago, philosophizing as we often did: about her job and whether it was time to make the leap from corporate drone to self-employed healer, and about my latest in a string of relationships and a pattern I was beginning to see clearly and finally felt ready to heal and break free from.

Then, in the midst of our conversation, something suddenly shifted, and we settled into that truth space that carries its own quiet hum. Each of us was alive with a clarity that hadn't been there when we began. And I said to her, "See, we forget to remember that we know what we know!" In a moment of active listening and open inquiry, two confused people managed to shift into two soulfully embodied wise women.

Since then, "Don't forget to remember" has become a mantra I've lived by and shared with others.

Life has a tendency to cloud over the brilliance and wisdom we each were born with – a situation described by this wonderful Talmudic fable:

When babies are born, they have full knowledge of God and the deeper mysteries. But at the moment of birth an angel comes and puts a finger just above the lip, whispering, "Shhhhhh, forget everything, speak not of what you know." This creates the little hollow between the nose and upper lip, and is why we spend our lives searching for something that is right under our nose all along.

If we're always running around looking for something that's right under our nose anyway, what might be the best way to tune into that knowing?

STOP!

Simply stop. Stop looking outside yourself for wisdom, for truth. Take time to sit quietly – no formal practice needed. Watch the play of light across your wall. Place one hand on your upper chest and breathe into your heart as if it had a nose. (It has its own brain – why not a nose?) Rest in the questions themselves; take the time to see and feel what emerges.

And don't forget to remember what you already know.

Advance Confidently in the Direction of Your Dreams

by Peggy McColl

"If one advances confidently in the direction of his dreams,
and endeavors to live the life which he has imagined,
he will meet with a success unexpected in common hours."
- Henry David Thoreau

This is my all-time favorite quote. It contains a powerful formula that can bring you everything your soul desires. Let's explore the profound message behind these words:

If one advances... Find a way to move toward your goal every day. You can make small, progressive steps or giant leaps forward. Either way ensures that you are advancing.

...confidently... Confidence is a muscle that, when exercised, will become stronger. If you're not yet feeling as confident as you'd like to be, imagine what it would feel like if you *were* confident. By doing this, you will ignite the feeling of confidence within you until it expresses itself outwardly.

...in the direction of his dreams... As I've said, "If you don't like where you are going, change direction." Do the things, think the thoughts, speak the words, and feel the feelings that take you toward your dreams.

...and endeavors to live the life which he has imagined... Imagine what it will be like when you are living the life that you truly desire. Think about it all the time. Feel what it will feel like. Visualize yourself already in possession of your goals. Act as if you have already achieved them.

...he will meet with a success unexpected in common hours. When you are following Thoreau's "formula," you WILL meet with success. However, the success may be "unexpected" in the sense that you might not know *how* it will materialize. Your job is simply to decide what your dream is, advance toward it, and be confident that it will materialize – perhaps in ways that pleasantly surprise you!

Thoreau's quotation is so powerful that I recommend that you write it out and post it where you'll see it every day. Read it often. Carry it with you. And, most importantly, follow the formula so that you can realize your soul's deepest dreams.

Think Joy: From Words to Wellness

by Dana Ben-Yehuda

Remember the famous phrase from *The Little Engine that Could*? "I think I can! I think I can!" Say those words out loud – several times – and see how that shifts your energy.

The power of the word is well known; the expressions we use can cheer us up or bring us down. We're not always aware, though, of just how our words impact our thoughts, our moods, and even our bodies. If you say disempowering words – such as "You can't fight City Hall" – you'll feel a drop in your energy…and in your body. (Just from writing these words, I can already feel my shoulders sag.)

Thankfully, however, the opposite is also true: When we say (or even just *think*) positive words – such as "I think I can!" or any other words that inspire – we feel energized and empowered. If you want to feel better in your body, talk about what feels good.

The power of words is augmented when we add the element of imagination. By thinking about sights, tastes, or other sensory experiences, we can affect our emotions and even our physiology! Think of lemons long enough, and your mouth will water. If you want your movement to be smooth, think about gliding like a swan.

For an even more powerful experience, you can imagine a scene that combines numerous senses. For instance, close your eyes and imagine a lovely, secluded beach. The sand feels warm and smooth beneath your feet, and the air smells like flowers. Stand in the sunshine and invite the light into your body. Let it flow down your neck and back. Feel the sense of ease that comes. Did you let out a breath? Do your shoulders feel more relaxed?

Whether you realize it or not, the words you use – out loud or even silently in your thoughts – affect you every moment of every day. When you deliberately harness the power of your thoughts and words, you can consciously create a life of joy and wellness. It all begins with a single word.

Think "Joy."

Cornered by the Soul

by Star Staubach

"Heroes aren't born, they're cornered."
- Mickey Rooney

It was 3:30 in the morning, and I was awake again. It had become a routine, one I did not enjoy. I lay there wanting to get back to sleep, but the sleep wouldn't come. My frustration grew to anger as nearly an hour and a half slipped by. I felt myself entering the emotional "danger zone" when I heard a voice whispering inside my head: "You can either lie here and continue being angry, or you can get up and do something about it."

"I don't know how to change this situation," I told the inner voice. "What do I get up and do?" "Go for a run," the voice replied. "Me, run? At 5:00 a.m.? I am NOT a runner!"

It sounded crazy at first, but I eventually pushed beyond the initial rejection, trusted the whisper, and went for a run. Instantly, I felt my anger begin to dissipate.

A little over a year later, I ran a full marathon. If you would have told me on that sleepless morning that I would not only start running but actually complete a full marathon, I would have called you crazy. That morning I had felt completely stuck, backed into a corner. But my soul somehow broke through all my anger and resistance and got me to start my day on the right foot. I listened to my soul's whispers and took one simple action, and my life instantly changed.

Each of us have moments of feeling cornered. They usually occur right before we demonstrate to ourselves that we truly are the hero we've been waiting for. When we wake up to this realization, we liberate ourselves from the pain of waiting on someone else to be a hero for us. Our soul has an omnipresent awareness of this expanded version of ourselves. The more we resist it, the more we experience difficulty and pain – until we eventually feel the discomfort of being cornered…and do something about it!

Are you feeling cornered? Rather than resisting, why not celebrate this space, trusting that your soul is summoning the hero within. My hero emerged from a simple calling to go for ONE run. Your small step awaits you. Will you honor your soul and greet your inner hero?

Big Life Changes

by Robin Friedman

Are you moving, divorcing, or changing jobs? Have your children left the nest, or did a loved one pass away? These big life changes are a prime opportunity to connect with our soul. Most of us build our identity around our roles in life and the people we relate with. If we take all that away, who are we?

This is the question posed by gurus and meditators throughout the ages. In times of transition, life itself is our very own spiritual mentor, leading us inward to connect with our soul.

If you find yourself feeling stressed or anxious because of a life challenge, try these four steps:

1. *Harvest the good.* Acknowledge and cherish the good times you experienced in the phase that is passing, and feel them sinking into your soul. This experiential wisdom is now a part of you, and nothing can ever take it away.
2. *Deliberately bless and release the past and all those involved.* Honor their essence by wholeheartedly loving and releasing them to find their own soul's highest purpose.
3. *Ask and intend for your future to be better, richer, and deeper.* There is always an upside to everything. Search for the pearls of goodness in your new situation. What possible highest good could come out of this? Imagine something more wonderful than you ever expected happening.
4. *Release your prayer for the positive to the Universe.* Allow it to come about in the best way possible and be totally present in the current moment. When you find yourself lost in thought, try these things: feel your body, breathe deeply, look around, smile. When you are present *in* the moment, you will find the present *of* the moment, which is where we fully connect with our soul.

The truth is, even though we are a multifaceted, eternal soul, we will all go through many life challenges and changes. We can grumble and resist, or we can harvest the learning and make our soul a more beautiful jewel to shine and share its light in this world.

Let Go of How Life "Should" Be

by Shelley Lundquist

I listened as my client lamented the unfairness of life, remembering well the days I shared similar thoughts.

"I should be married with kids by now! I just want to be happy!" She went on to describe how clearly she set out her expectations to every potential suitor from the get-go. With no understanding of the defiant and expectant energy she was bringing to each date, she had no inkling at all of why she was still alone.

Over a few sessions, we reframed her belief that she needed someone else to fill the void she felt in her life. We got to the root of the problem, which was that she believed she was unlovable. During her breakthrough, she came to see how her fear was sabotaging potential relationships before they could even get started. In learning to love and accept herself, she let go of her need for control. In accepting responsibility for what she was willing to bring, both to her own life and to a relationship, she realised she didn't have to postpone her happiness; she could have it now.

Her life was transformed as her outer world began to reflect the beauty of her inner world, and she radiated love from her true self.

On her dates, she became more light-hearted, comfortable, and open. Just a few short months later, she arrived at her session full of news and excitement. She and her new beau were taking a trip together to Machu Picchu, Peru, above the Sacred Valley to the Intihuatana Stone – The Hitching Post of the Sun. "I've always felt called there but never thought I'd go! Isn't it amazing?" she beamed.

And I smiled back at her, knowing that when we let go of our ideas about the way life "should" be, we open to possibility, and life flows in beautiful and unexpected ways. The Universe always has so much more waiting for us than we could ever dream of.

Releasing Your Roles to Uncover Your Soul

by Nikki Ackerman

Our soul is such a sacred place. Oftentimes, however, we become disconnected from our soul as we get caught up in busy, chaotic lives, filled with many roles and responsibilities.

In my own life, I play many roles: I'm a daughter, granddaughter, sister, holistic practitioner/business owner, social worker, and friend. I know how easy it is to become caught up in these roles and forget who I am at the very core of my being. Like many people, I long to find a peaceful place deep within myself – a place beyond roles and responsibilities, a place where all is well.

One day, I felt especially called to reconnect with my soul, so I decided to spend some time alone. I sat down in one of my favorite rooms – with no TV, no cell phone, no computer…just me. The day was warm, and the open window allowed a gentle breeze to fill the room. The only sound was the melodious birdsong drifting in through the window. The scene could not have been more peaceful.

Even in this idyllic setting, however, I couldn't relax. My chest felt tight, and my head was swimming with thought after thought: *I need to check on Granny. I need to draft my next newsletter. I need to spend more time with my friends and family. I hope my client is doing better…*

Before I became completely overwhelmed, I took a deep breath and observed these thoughts one by one. I noticed the various roles they represented, and then I gently released them – allowing them to flow away without judgment. Layer after layer disappeared. I began to sense that, at the very core of my being, there was something more to my existence – something beyond and beneath these thoughts and these roles.

I continued to focus on my slow, deep breath, feeling it enter the center of my body more fully. I felt my heartbeat slowing and my thoughts settling. At last, I felt at peace in this sacred space and connected with my soul – that place that is always there, just below all of the noise and the roles.

Embracing the Gift of Freedom

by Tanya Levy

Think of a time when you felt free. Where were you? Who were you with? What were you doing? Being aware of the people, places, and situations that brought you freedom in the past can give you clues about how to feel free in the present. When we feel free, we are more closely connected with our soul, for the essence of our beings is more fully present. If we take the time to reflect on the experiences that help us feel free, we get clues to what makes us feel most alive.

Think of a time when you felt encumbered or trapped. Where were you? Who were you with? What were you doing? Being aware of the people, places, and situations that halted your freedom can give you clues about what creates disconnection from your soul. For when we aren't feeling free, our souls can feel unexpressed and lost. Reflecting on those times helps us see more clearly what we need to release to help us be more fully present.

Think of a time right now when you feel free. Where are you? Who are you with? What are you doing? What people, places, and situations help you feel free? How can you invite more of this feeling and experience into your life? Begin to notice when you feel free. Pay attention to what roots you in feeling free. Nurture those moments that allow you to be free in your own body, mind, heart, and soul.

Think of a time in the future when you see yourself being free. Where are you? Who are you with? What are you doing? What people, places, and situations speak freedom to you in the future? Allow your soul to speak. Listen to your needs, wants, desires, and dreams.

Sit quietly with a blank piece of paper. Write about (or draw a picture of) the people, places, and situations that speak to you of freedom in the past, present, and future. Let your soul speak to you of freedom, and set your soul free.

Better Living Through the Law of Attraction

by Lynnette Caldwell

For many years, the Law of Attraction was one of the best-kept secrets ever. Now, thanks in large part to *The Secret*, it's not much of a secret anymore! Still, I don't see many people consciously applying this powerful principle in their lives. Many people are aware of it, some are not, and some just think it's hogwash. But I can tell you from firsthand experience that IT REALLY WORKS!

It's extremely exciting to see people use the Law of Attraction to connect with their souls and to excel in all areas of life. Sadly though, most people don't believe that they can excel in even *one* area, let alone *all* areas. I have devoted most of my life to helping people realize that they *can* live the life they desire – offering "SOULutions" to their problems by introducing them to the Law of Attraction.

The first thing to know about the Law of Attraction is that it is the most powerful law in the universe. Just like the law of gravity, it applies to all people in all places, whether you know about it or not!

With the Law of Attraction, we attract our experiences through what we think, what we believe, and how we feel – all of which sends vibrations (or signals) to the universe, attracting matches and delivering them into our experience. For instance, if you feel appreciative of things in life, the Universe will send you more things to be grateful for. The same applies if you feel bad and send out lower-energy vibrations – you'll get more to feel bad about. You can also apply this to specific areas of life, such as money: abundant thoughts and feelings bring you more abundance, while thoughts and feelings of lack and scarcity will bring you more of the same.

Another great feature of the Law of Attraction is that it comes with a built-in "navigational system": our feelings and experiences! These always let us know if our thoughts have been predominantly in the direction we want to go or whether we need to back up and re-route our thoughts.

By working with the Law of Attraction, you can let your thoughts and feelings guide you to the fulfillment of your soul's desires. And when you use this process deliberately, you realize a deeply empowering truth: *You are in charge of your experiences!*

Make Each Moment a Masterpiece

by Jasmine Sreenika Crystalsinger

How perplexing is our perception of time! Tedious moments seem to stretch into eternity while cherished memories often slip by as quickly as grains of sand scattered by the wind.

Whether we're anxious about the future or trapped in remorse over the past, one thing's for sure: we can't stop the passage of time. We can, however, decide to make the most of the time we have – to live each moment to the fullest!

Here is an exercise to help you do exactly that:

Imagine that you have completed all you came here to do. You've left everything behind to transition to the next adventure on your soul's journey. Before you move on, though, you look back and see an exciting blur of images. This is your life. Every moment. Every chance you took and every opportunity you let pass you by. From this perspective as the observer of your own life, you see how every detail was part of a perfect plan.

Rewind to the present moment. Right here, right now. What do you choose within the space of your next breath? How do you say yes to life? If a regret from the past or a worry about the future rushes in to cloud your contemplation, return to your breath. As you inhale, feel your abdomen expand. As you exhale, feel your body release any and all resistance. Inhale again, and feel how you receive possibility in the most palpable way. How is this the only moment that counts? Feel the richness of this perfect pearl of possibility, this golden thread in the majesty of your life's tapestry. Open your heart. Allow your soul to sing. Make this moment a masterpiece.

Make *each* moment a masterpiece.

Anything Worth Doing Is Worth Doing Poorly

by Mary Lou Stark

Most of us have heard the phrase, "Anything worth doing is worth doing well." But have you ever heard the phrase, "Anything worth doing is worth doing *poorly*"? This was one of my mother's favorite expressions; and although I've heard it many times, it took a long time for me to make sense of it.

Whether it's a child learning to walk, a young adult learning to bake, or an adult learning accounting, it is impossible to go immediately from never having done something to being an expert. As we learn, we begin by doing it poorly. If we are fortunate, the people around us will celebrate our successes and encourage us to try again when we stumble.

As adults, we tend to forget that part of learning is being imperfect along the way. Rather than picking ourselves up and trying again, we get mired in the self-talk that repeatedly tells us, "I'm no good. I can't learn anything. I'll never get this right."

When our soul is connected to the Divine, we lift ourselves out of the quagmire, give ourselves a virtual hug, pat ourselves on the back, and move forward.

For me, the easiest way to reconnect is to pause, take three deep breaths, and ask myself the following question: *What is the Truth (with a capital T) of this situation?* This always brings me back to my core belief that *all is love.* Since I am part of the *all*, then *I* am love. And since I am love, I am capable of doing that which is mine to do. So then I ask myself: *Is this truly mine to do?*...and move forward accordingly.

Learning something new is only one of the times we may find ourselves doing something poorly. It is equally as important to continue doing something you enjoy doing, even when it is not one of your talents. Don't be afraid to do something poorly if it brings you joy. God says, "Make a joyful noise unto the Lord," not, "Sing only if you can do it really, really well!"

The Soulful Gift of Jealousy

by Robin Friedman

What does jealousy or envy feel like to you? A stabbing pain, a clenching gut, a feeling that "it's not fair"? This strong emotion is actually a message from your soul. It is saying, "This is important. I want this. Something's missing. Pay attention."

When you feel jealous, it's actually a wonderful sign. It means that what you are jealous about is actually ON your radar. You are probably not jealous of Bill Gates or a supermodel, right? But if someone in your neighborhood goes on a European vacation while you stay home all summer, you may feel jealous. Or if a friend who was about your size suddenly gets toned and fit, you might experience envy. These things *are* possible for you, or you wouldn't feel jealous.

Here are two simple steps that you can take to view jealousy from a soulful perspective:

1. Say, "Bless their fun vacation [or fit body or any other object of jealousy], and bless mine, too!" This takes you out of *constricting, wanting* energy and into *blessing, allowing* energy.
2. Find out the essence of what you want, and see if you can give that to yourself. For the vacation: is it the time off or the adventure of new places? How can you give that essence to yourself right now? Perhaps you can drive to a nearby city you haven't explored or go for a walk on the beach at night. Being envious of your friend's new healthy body is saying something to you. How can you be more fit or feel better about your body as it is? Ask what feeling your soul is asking for, and see if you can find a way to satisfy that request. Perhaps a new exercise class or buying a pretty dress will make you feel more happy and confident.

Our emotions are like the instruments on our car dashboard: they tell us when some important need is not being met. Be grateful when you feel jealousy or envy, and know that your soul is telling you that this *is* possible for you, too. And remember to say, "Bless their good, and bless mine, too!"

The Art of Problem Solving

by Shelley Lundquist

In the midst of dealing with problems, I've spent countless hours running scenes and scripts through my head and reeling from the aftermath of their fallout as though all those conversations and calamities had actually taken place. As it happens, I was actually magnifying the problem.

We all manifest what we focus on, whether we want it or not, because energy flows where attention goes. When we allow ourselves to be prisoners of our fears, we stay stuck. If we want different results, we need to tune our awareness.

In the stillness between breaths, where I connect with my truth, I came into the awareness of all the negative energy my thoughts and ensuing behaviours were bringing to my experience. With that new consciousness, I naturally shifted my perception. Instead of deciding to have a problem with something or someone, I decided to see an opportunity to bridge the gap and open to possibility.

Now when any negative thoughts or emotions arrive unexpectedly, I return to the stillness. From this space, I'm able to connect with my soul and decipher what I need to learn in order to dissolve the distraction of negativity and move forward successfully. I listen within, knowing that negative thoughts and emotions are *always* a soul call for positive action. It's my response that matters. Aligning my choices to honour who I am is all I ever need to do.

In knowing I am here to bring more love into the world, I consciously choose strategies that serve my intentions and trust that the outcome will serve me. As I take purposeful action, I open and allow the abundance of the universe to flow to and through me. And before I know it, I have crossed the chasm and moved into a solution.

When I radiate loving kindness and approach every opportunity with an open heart – rather than viewing the experience as a problem to be solved – I feel alive, awake, and at peace. In bringing the best of me to any situation, my actions are inherently synchronized for success in graceful harmony with the rhythm of the universe.

Living in Courage

by Debra Oakland

Over four short years, I lost my 21-year-old son; my baby girl in the eighth month of pregnancy; both brothers; and, a short time later, my father to prostate cancer.

One thing I learned through these losses is that we can either move through grief or stay stuck in it. I made the decision to honor the memory of my loved ones by carrying them in my heart as precious gifts. Out of this loss and grief, I found myself growing stronger, more resilient.

While grieving, I made it a daily practice to go inward on a sacred journey that no one else could take for me. Living from the inside out was more challenging some days than others, but I was determined – knowing that those who had transitioned still loved me as I still loved them, and they would want me to be happy.

As part of my healing process, I began writing, speaking, and living in courage in a way that supported my life and the lives of others. Connecting with my childhood dream to write was extremely healing. I no longer concerned myself with silly thoughts like "What if someone does not like what I write?" or "Who would want to read what I have to say?" – I had nothing to lose; I had already been through the fire.

During this time, I rekindled my love of stories and storytelling. I remembered just how much our stories matter and how they can change lives. We have all been through the fire in one way or another. Simply by telling our story, our hero's journey, we create a bridge that escorts others to a place of love, peace, healing, and inner joy.

Telling our stories takes courage. They are not always easy to share. But when we face our challenges, we find an inner strength that connects us with our passion and our purpose.

I have had to flex my courage muscles often throughout my grieving process, and courage has become a welcome traveling partner.

Staying out of the Quicksand

by Karen Hicks

Quicksand is a great metaphor for being "stuck in drama." Once in, it's tough to get out. The potential to sink into the drama heightens when we find that we're surrounded by it. Through social and print media, we are invited into other peoples' lives and encouraged to pass judgment. Reality TV offers up luxury plates overloaded with intimate details of relationships, trauma, and lost love. We're surrounded by gossip. And at times, we might even initiate our own drama!

At some point, though, the cost of living this way outweighs the benefit. Prolonged exposure to drama dims your inner light. Judgment and criticism become second nature. It becomes harder to see the silver lining. Compassion eludes you. You may even find yourself tired much of the time, with reduced interest in anything vibrant and life-giving. Living in drama definitely doesn't serve your higher purpose.

The good news is that there are ways out! The first way is to spend time with yourself and discover your gifts, talents, and values. They reflect the core of your identity and need nurturing in order to shine. Take intentional action every day: meditate, practice yoga, journal, paint, or go for a walk. Question your actions. If your thoughts and words take away from someone's dignity, then they are taking away from your own. Choose actions and words that are supportive.

In addition to spending time alone, look for community groups (online or in person) that align with your vision for yourself. Spend time with people who share your values and support your soul's growth.

The more you do these things, the brighter your inner light will shine and your world will change. Instead of feeling drained and scattered, your energy will increase. You will have more inner peace, and you will see the silver linings. And before too long, instead of drowning in quicksand-like drama, you'll find yourself firmly supported by the earth as you stand on your own two feet!

Using Challenges to Create Life-Pearls

by Barbara Schiffman

When my mother traveled to Japan, she always brought home beautiful pearl necklaces. She gave several to me when I was young. I put them away, unable to appreciate their beauty – or their metaphor – as they looked like "old-lady jewelry." But as I grew older (and hopefully wiser), I came to treasure my lustrous strings of pearls, which I now love to wear. They have become my glowing reminders of how life's challenges are catalysts for "life-pearls."

Challenges for humans often feel like the grains of sand that slip into an oyster's shell. This sand irritates and annoys the tender mollusk as it rubs against the iridescent inner shell on both sides. Eventually, bits of shell stick to the sand and ultimately create a precious gem. The rougher the sand and the longer the irritation, the bigger the pearl.

This process is not fun for the oyster, but without the sand the pearl cannot be formed. Fortunately, pearls are so strong and reflective – energetically and visually – that they justify the sand's actions. Although the process is painful for the oyster, the result gives it meaning and purpose.

In our lives, challenges – whether disasters or opportunities – are necessary for our human perspectives to shift and our lives to expand. Like the oyster's sand, they are gifts even when they feel like punishment. They help grow our souls.

Most humans wish for life to be easy, happy, and smooth all the time. But then there would be no *contrast* (an Abraham-Hicks Law of Attraction concept I particularly like). These contrasts are the essential yin-and-yang of life. They provide experiences, lessons, and memories that allow our souls to evolve.

When facing a new (or recurring) challenge, remember to bless it for being your "sand." It is another opportunity to grow a beautiful life-pearl! Each lesson has value, especially for our souls. Each life-pearl is a challenge that has been overcome, survived, or maybe even enjoyed. Eventually, you will become the beautiful string of life-pearls your soul has created through you.

Get Distracted

by Sallie Keys

What do you do when you can't find the answer you need? What so many people do is to keep searching for the answer in their own mind, thinking more and more, harder and harder. The problem with this approach, however, is that our mental chatter and inner noise can drown out the very answers we need! We often become so focused on trying to figure things out all by ourselves that we don't leave enough room for Spirit to come through with guidance that will truly serve us.

When you can't find the clarity you are seeking, the single best thing you can do for yourself and your sanity is to *stop* thinking and *allow* the answers to come to you. The problem is, however, that it's almost impossible to do that when you're in the middle of trying to solve a problem. That's when it's time to get distracted!

When you take your directed thought process out of the picture, you allow the guidance you need to flow through to you without interference. The best way to do that is to direct your main focus toward something else for a while – preferably, something repetitive that commands your full physical attention but doesn't require you to actively focus (such as washing dishes, taking a shower, or walking).

What you'll notice is that repetitive tasks such as these result in a more relaxed state of mind and ultimately allow the ideas and insights to flow freely. That's when your soul and Spirit can come through to you with the most ease.

How will you distract your mind and allow Spirit to flow through you today?

Listen Up – Your Failure Is Talking!

by Stephanie Cornett

Bam! You've been knocked to the ground. Stunned, confused, bloody knees, and head spinning.

Suddenly, you're still. You're paying attention. You might even begin to ask yourself some hard questions: *Why did this happen to me? What can I do to make sure it doesn't happen again?*

For me, the blows were coming so fast and furious that I began to call myself "Job" – you know, the one who had every trial imaginable thrown at him to test his faith. I teetered on the edge of giving up all faith in anything good. I was asking the questions but wasn't really listening for the answers.

I knew I was being called to greater things. My soul had been speaking to me since I was a small child – encouraging me to share my message. With each passing year, however, I refused to answer the call and step into my significance. The failures kept coming until I had a virtual tsunami of failure washing over me and was forced to get real with myself or drown.

My soul said, "I have not given up on you. I just have a much better place for you. When you did not listen to my gentle prompts, I had no choice but to take drastic measures to get your attention."

I didn't want my soul to have to get tougher, so I decided to get still, listen, and take action. Each day, I put one foot in front of the other and walked my spiritual path. I created visioning workshops and vision walks and invited others to join me, which they did! I now consult with individuals, organizations, and corporations on how to recognize and engage their unique gifts to change the world, which is amazing!

I learned that when failures – big or small – come your way, when something isn't working, get quiet. Meditate. Write. Call a trusted friend. And most importantly, tune into your soul. It may not be telling you to quit your job, move, or get a divorce. It may simply be asking you to change your strategy.

One thing is certain: your soul is saying, "You weren't born to live a life of insignificance; you were born to be a force in the world."

Consulting the Inner Observer

by Alice Chan

I am a firm believer that human beings are spiritual beings having a human experience. In other words, we are souls who have taken on physical bodies in order to have experiences not possible in the spirit realm. Even though our human selves do not remember why we signed up for this particular tour in the physical world, our souls do. Therefore, our souls always know the truth about why we are here and what is best for us from moment to moment. Our soul's wisdom – which is synonymous with intuition and inner wisdom – is always within us. We just need to remember to consult it.

Connecting to my intuitive wisdom partly involves cultivating the inner observer, who impartially watches the unfolding of events. These events are not inherently good or bad; our human judgments make them so. At every choice-point, my inner observer sees what my ego wants me to do out of fear and self-protection versus what my soul knows is the right action for my highest good. So, by remembering to consult my inner observer, I connect to my soul's wisdom.

As an example, when I was new at my job two years ago, one colleague felt particularly threatened by my presence and unceremoniously put me down publicly in a meeting. My attuned inner observer saw two alternative reactions to the situation: On the one hand, my human self felt justifiably hurt and had the sharpness of mind and tongue to put up a spectacular retort, thank you very much! On the other hand, my all-loving soul saw this instead: My colleague had to be harboring deep-seated insecurities and self-hate to feel threatened by what I was trying to do for the good of our collective organization. My soul felt compassion for this person. In a split-second's decision time, I chose my soul's reaction. In doing so, I did not condone my colleague's behavior but simply chose not to escalate the situation.

By consulting my inner observer, I've been able to connect with my soul's wisdom time and again. I love knowing that this wisdom is always available to me – and to us all – as much a part of us as our own hearts.

Moving Through Fear

by Katie Power

It's hot! I need air! I became weak and couldn't breathe. My heart clenched as sheer panic set in.

This happened to me a few months ago while driving in the middle of rush-hour traffic. I was having what turned out to be my first-ever panic attack. Interestingly, right as it began, I saw an image of being buried alive in my mind's eye and became instantly claustrophobic.

I have always felt squeamish in small spaces, but it wasn't until my teen years that this really started interfering with my daily life. I began avoiding elevators (even if it meant climbing 10 flights of stairs) and public bathrooms (worrying I'd somehow get locked in).

I saw this panic attack as my soul's way of telling me it was time to release this age-old, debilitating fear, which I believe stemmed from previous lifetimes. It reminded me that I am eternal, fear is just an illusion, and I had a choice to release it.

From then on, I decided I would approach fear differently. Instead of running from it or allowing it to take over my mind and body, I would surrender to it. I would acknowledge its presence and let it roll through me while recognizing that it was just stuck energy. I would call upon my soul and ask what I could learn from the experience. I would get the answers by listening to my heart and paying attention to my thoughts and feelings. I would remind myself that God and His angels were always there to help and protect me and that everything was going to be okay.

I now feel grateful for this experience because it served as a tremendous opportunity for my soul to grow and heal. I have also learned a lot about myself through this process, including that I am so much stronger than my fear ever was. (And, just in case you didn't already know, so are you!)

Thank You, Ego!

by Yvonne Peraza

As I began my spiritual journey, I kept hearing about this thing called an ego. I learned that it was the internal voice of fearful thinking and that I should treat it like a small child.

At this time, I was also thinking about how frequently I'd been getting sick and how I didn't have enough time for what I truly wanted to do. I blamed my situation on my job and my family – and also on my ego, which I thought was responsible for filling up any free time that I did have with fearful thoughts and emotions. Finally, I decided that I'd had enough and I was going to take action: I would retire early from my corporate career. My children would be old enough, and they wouldn't need me as much. My plan was set, or so I thought…until my ego asked an innocent but profound question: "Do we have enough?"

I thought my ego was trying to fool me into fearful thoughts. She asked me again and showed me a picture of my plan's possible outcome. It was not pretty. Oh no! I quickly realized that this plan of mine was not a good one. My family would be negatively impacted if I quit now. So, my ego suggested that I work longer. I held my breath with tears in my eyes. This wasn't what I wanted to hear.

Suddenly, I felt an internal hug. It was my ego. She was worried and only wanted the best for us. I hugged her back and felt such a deep love between us.

I realized that the ego does not necessarily play the role of the child or the "bad guy" – it can also serve as a protector, a provider of comfort, and a voice of reason. I began to love my ego – not because it was a "wounded child" who needed nurturing, but because I realized that my ego wants what's best for me. She has my highest interest in mind. She offers wisdom and loving guidance, which helps me feel safe and protected as my soul navigates my spiritual journey.

The simple yet powerful act of loving my ego has shifted everything in my life.

Thank you, ego! I love you! I am FREE!

The Soulful Power of Intentional Choice

by Molly M. Cantrell-Kraig

Choices have the power to change our lives. When we intentionally focus our energy on a choice, we infuse it with the formidable power of our emotion, intellect, and kinetic (outwardly expressed) energy, which magnifies its power.

Oftentimes, however, we feel powerless to choose. We become convinced that an outside force holds all the power: a boss, a spouse, a circumstance. When we delegate our choices to others, we relinquish our power. But when we take ownership of our choices, we harness their full power – and our own!

Furthermore, reclaiming our power of choice automatically increases our "power magnet" – because we are creating power consciously and with intention, the strength of our "signal" draws more power to us.

To reclaim your power of choice, start by making small changes in the language you use:

- Instead of "I can't afford it," say, "I choose to spend my money in another way."
- Instead of "I have to," say, "I get to."
- Instead of "He/she is making me," say, "I choose to…"

Reclaiming ownership of choice restores your personal power. It also raises several important questions: *What is the guiding principle on which your choices are made? What makes those choices powerful? And how do you know that they truly are your choices?*

The true power of your choices comes when they are aligned with your soul. Your soul is your inner compass, a lodestar to guide all your choices. To help you detect this "compass," spend a few minutes each day in meditation. When you connect with your soul, it will tell you whether or not a potential choice is in alignment with your highest good and your highest power. And each time you act in alignment with your soul's compass, your ability to make good powerful, soulful choices increases.

Free will is one of our greatest gifts. When you exercise your choices with soulful intention, you harness, amplify, and manifest your soul's power in all areas of your life.

Embracing Change

by Ronda Renee

We know that things are bound to change; it's inevitable. Life is full of shifts and transitions. So why is it that, more often than not, we still resist change? I'm not talking about the changes we set about making intentionally. I'm referring to those unplanned changes that pop up in our lives and are often seen as obstacles keeping us from what we want.

What I've learned about these "unwelcome" changes is that when they occur, there is something greater at work. When your life is not going according to your plans and suddenly makes a sharp left turn, it is always about something more than external circumstances, even if it doesn't look or feel like it at the time. These types of changes are the work of your soul. More often than not, you are being knocked *on* path, rather than *off*. You are being led somewhere.

When you are faced with challenges or obstacles in your life, use the ADAPT formula to embrace what is happening and take full advantage of what the changes are offering you.

- *Allow* whatever emotions you are feeling. It's okay to be scared, frustrated, disappointed, or even angry. Just allow those feelings to move through you.
- *Discover* your inner resources. You have within you what it takes to navigate this change. You will not be faced with something that you are not equipped to handle.
- *Accept* what is happening. It is in our resistance to a change that we create our own suffering. Accept that what *was* is gone. What *is to be* awaits you!
- *Participate* with what is happening and allow the change to lead the way to where you are meant to go. What is it trying to show you? Where is it leading you?
- *Transform* your perspective and your thinking about who you are, and become the person you were meant to be.

Embrace change as a gift from your soul. Trust that you are always on your path. And know that you will end up in exactly the right place.

The Inner Personalities and Your Soul

by Anne Aleckson

It was a warm, early-summer morning in 2004, and I was standing in the lounge room with my baby son crawling around my legs as my husband and I stood screaming at each other.

Things had been getting worse and worse between us, but today was different. Today I felt myself reach the point of no return…I was done with this relationship and the constant fighting, and I was ready to put an end to it and move on to find some joy and peace in life.

Little did I know that in making this decision, I was going to discover something about myself that would ultimately save my life: I discovered that within me were a number of inner personalities that were controlling my every action; and I realised that rather than being controlled by them, I could work *with* them to better my life.

I found within me three types of inner personalities:

- *The unhelpful personalities* – the fearful parts of me, such as my wounded inner child who likes to keep me safe within my comfort zone.
- *The neutral personalities* – the parts of me that operate on automatic pilot (like my inner personality of the car driver – once I learned to drive and gained confidence, it became a neutral and automatic part of me).
- *The helpful personalities* – those parts of me that know my life purpose and how I can live a joyful life. I consider the soul to be part of this group.

While I lost a husband, I gained invaluable insight into myself – which paved a path back to my soul!

If you, like me, want to live a happier life where you are contributing to the greater good through your purpose, then it might be time for you to find a process to heal your unhelpful inner personalities and unleash the power of your soul. Allow your helpful personalities to come to the fore, and allow them and your soul to guide you to the life you dream of living.

Moving from Human Emotions to Soulful Feelings

by Heather Boon

We are most connected to our soul and to everyone around us when we're ready to open ourselves and be completely vulnerable.

"Not so easy to do!" I hear you say. "Be vulnerable in a world where it feels like everyone is trying to get what they want, without thought for anyone else?"

I understand this concern, and I'd like to offer a different perspective that you may find useful in your own soul journey, as it has been a powerful catalyst for me in mine. Every day we hear and feel the words: *I'm happy, I'm sad, I'm depressed, I'm angry, I'm frustrated, I'm excited*, and so on. These words come from those around us and from our own internal dialogue, which runs an incessant commentary on how we're "feeling."

But are these really our true *feelings*? My experience is that they are simply human *emotions*, sourced from ego, which we are experiencing each day. They are here, and they are gone. Fleeting emotions, like waves, wash over us constantly. Some gently, some crashing over and around us – leaving mayhem. We can become numb from the intensity of the never-ending roller-coaster ride they offer, from the highest highs to the lowest lows.

As entrancing as these emotions may be, the energy vibration they carry comes from our lower chakras and will undoubtedly keep us disconnected from our soul...and from those around us.

True *feelings*, on the other hand, come from our soul – in the form of love, joy, and compassion – and carry a much higher vibration than human emotions. These feelings are not fleeting; they are grounded in the very essence of who we are, in our own divinity.

The bridge between human emotions and soulful feelings is our heart. When we go into our heart, feel our divine feelings, and recognise our emotions for what they truly are, we become vulnerable and find instant connection with our soul.

Try this for yourself: experience how different your world becomes when you detach from human emotions and embrace your divinity through your true feelings.

True Reality Creation

by Solara Sophia

Ever since I was a little girl, I have been head over heels in love with magic. I've always been completely captivated by the notion of manifesting something seemingly out of nothing. As a young adult, I began to avidly study and practice this art. Today, I apply it through a process of manifestation that I call "True Reality Creation."

Through True Reality Creation, I connect with the infinite, divine potential within myself and co-create my life experience. Here are four of my favorite ways to do this:

- *Thinking and Speaking Empowering Beliefs with Heartfelt Conviction:* I become aware of my conscious thought patterns, so that I can align my dominant thoughts with what I want to create. Within 17 seconds of focusing on a specific thought, we begin attracting it; and our spoken words energetically empower our beliefs (repeated thoughts) to materialize. I like to write out lists of empowering beliefs that I want to come true, which I think and speak throughout the day. These thoughts become my stream of consciousness and, in time, they always show up!
- *Embodying a Positive, High Vibration:* This is how I receive my desires. I do my best to consistently embody high vibrations, such as love, joy, peace, wellness, and prosperity. Acting "as if" my desires have already manifested helps me to stay receptive.
- *Trust:* I know, believe, and trust that the Universe will always grant my wishes. I commit to the outcome and surrender the "how."
- *Inspired Action:* I only take aligned, inspired actions that will move me closer to my dreams and visions.

I invite you to try the True Reality Creation process yourself! As you do so, remember that your feelings are your compass. They let you know if your dominant thoughts are aligned with what you'd like to co-create. The degree to which you feel positive is the degree to which your thoughts are aligned with what you truly want. Negative feelings indicate resistance and remind you to shift your focus – to realign with your desires and reconnect with your soul!

Feel All of It

by Elizabeth Kipp

"Accept what the moment brings," I told myself as the day began. Even in this intention, though, I could not accept what the moment brought. I fell utterly short of that. Today brought a full range of humanness and delivered as much anguish as it did joy.

Today is the birthday of my niece, Sarah K. Marvel. Sarah recently lost her battle with heroin addiction. Today is a joyous remembrance of Sarah and her amazing gifts, and of sobering reminiscence of the violence visited upon us by the dreaded disease of addiction. I feel bitter about addiction and deeply sad about how it took Sarah and so many others. This disease tears at humanity and brings so many down in collateral damage.

I tapped all of my tools for stress reduction: diet, exercise, prayer, fellowship, and more. I was grateful that I had such power at my side assuaging what I felt around Sarah's untimely passing. I cried for life cut short; for mother, sister, family, and friends bereft of their beloved; and for the powerlessness around not being able to alleviate the grief around this situation. I prayed for grace and ease for all.

This is what it means to be human – to feel all of it, from the towering heights of joy for this bright, generous soul who brought such song to all, to the depths of grief. I felt it and let it express itself. It may dissipate in time, or it may be with me forever.

"You cannot change the past," I try to tell myself. "You cannot know the life journey of another." While true statements, they catch in my throat right now. I may not be able to fully accept what the moment brings, especially around this subject. But I will be able to sleep tonight. I am closer to practicing acceptance over resentment thanks to the tools so many have shared with me, and thanks to the healing power of The Divine. I will remember Sarah with her beautiful singing voice as I slip into sleep tonight. May she rest in peace, watch over, and bless us all.

Whether you're feeling grief, elation, or any other emotion, remember that we connect with our soul by allowing ourselves to feel – letting all of our emotions flow through us.

How to Make Soulful Decisions

by Stacey Hall

I used to feel bogged down with confusion and anxiety each time I needed to make a decision. I would weigh the pros and cons, ask others what I should do, and then take even more time to consider my options. One day, though, I received inspiration from God that made this process much easier and helped me see that every decision is motivated by either love or fear.

I call this insight "The Solution Process," which consists of five questions that I ask my God-given spirit to help me identify the best possible decision in any situation:

- Coming from fear, why would I choose to not do (fill in the blank)?
- Coming from love, why would I choose to not do…?
- Coming from fear, why would I choose to do…?
- Coming from love, why would I choose to do…?
- Which answer felt the strongest in my body…not the best, not the worst, just the strongest?

Rather than listen with my mind, I feel the energy of the answers. Whether the strongest feeling is from love or fear, that is the one I choose. I allow my soul to help me make the best choice.

At first, I practiced on small choices, such as whether to attend a business networking function versus spending time with my husband, or whether to eat chocolate versus a piece of fruit. It worked so well I began using it for big decisions, such as attending a dear friend's funeral in another state or staying home to attend to my own wellness. Without The Solution Process, I would have gone to the funeral and compromised my own health. With the process, I listened to my soul and stayed home, guilt-free, and was able to provide comfort to her loved ones in other ways.

This process has helped me tremendously. Now, when I'm having a hard time making a decision, I go through the questions and within just a few minutes I'm able to identify the answer. It's such an easy process with powerful (and soulful) results!

Allow Yourself to Feel Lost

by Angela Boyle

When I think about being lost, I think it is because I do not know where I am going, as if there is a place I am meant to be that I just haven't discovered yet. But what if feeling lost is actually the destination (at least for now)?

Right now, I am attempting to settle into a new life with my family in a new country, Malaysia. Every day, my kids astonish me with how easily they embrace the new. They get up and excitedly put on their school uniforms. Once they are dressed, they run from one new situation to the next with big smiles and open hearts. I, on the other hand, seem to feel like I am standing naked on the top of a massive cliff, knowing that I have to jump, but feeling absolutely paralysed in fear and loneliness.

From this place, I start to run, too; but, unlike my children, I run in the other direction! I run from one thing to the next, hoping that the next thing I do will make me feel better – despite the fact that in my heart I know I have done everything but the one thing I actually need to do for now: *nothing.*

Today is the first day since we arrived that I have stopped and listened to my body. In this moment, I can hear the soft whispers of my heart saying thank you. Thank you for taking the time to hear that right now feeling lost is totally normal – feeling lost physically because you have no sense of direction in this new place, and feeling lost emotionally because you are trying to navigate your way through the range of feelings that come and go as quickly as they arrived: excitement, sadness, joy, hope, wonder, and despair.

And what do I feel right now, in this moment? Absolute peace. It seems that in allowing myself to feel lost for now, I actually found exactly what I have been looking for. I have been still long enough to listen to my body, and it has connected me with my soul.

The Gift of Suffering

by Shelley Lundquist

I couldn't believe what I was reading! For all the patience and kindness I had shown her, here I was bearing the brunt of an attack by a so-called friend for not being who she wanted me to be!

So began a cascade of physical reactions to the thoughts that were darting through my mind. The tightness in my chest, the tension in my shoulders, the racing of my heart, and the anger I felt spreading through my body like wildfire were blaring signals for me to pay attention. On more than one occasion in the past, I had let my emotions rule the roost, righteous in my wrath, cape billowing behind me on the wind, all while pointing a finger and ready to battle with anyone who I believed had wronged me. *Never* did that take me where I wanted to go.

Thankfully, we all have a built-in beacon – the mind-body connection – to guide us on our way.

I realized that this suffering that I was experiencing was ultimately a gift. My triggered emotional and physical responses were messages from my higher self, telling me that I was out of alignment with the truth of who I am and that I needed to do something differently to get back into balance.

I *know* I cause my own suffering when I give energy to judgmental and limiting beliefs about myself, others, and the way I believe the world "should" be, and yet, here I was at it again.

Ironically, my friend's lack of acceptance had led to my own ego-based reaction and judgment of *her*. In my frustration, I had closed my heart to her pain and created my own. With that revelation, my heart flooded with compassion. I released my judgment, moved from resistance to acceptance, and was guided to that place of peace within me – to my authentic core.

I'm grateful for the gift of awareness that suffering brings. And I'm also grateful that when we have the courage to open our hearts to compassion for ourselves and others, we move away from suffering and into the flow of living.

Recollection of Days – Memories Within the Seashells

by Kylie Mansfield

As the ocean is bound to the shore, so the echo of what's gone before is bound to the shell, forever sighing into the years…

To me, a memory is like a seashell, for each little shell captures and holds the echoes of the past within. I have a beautiful jar of these seashells sitting beside the sink in my bathroom. I call them my "Recollection of Days." Most of these shells were collected through the sunny days of my childhood, the flurry of my teen years, and the golden moments of my adult existence. Encased within the protective outer layer of each shell are the whispers of my life.

If you were here with me, we could choose a shell and listen to the memory that echoes within. Listen. Can you hear it…?

The little girl is waiting in the car. A breeze straight off the sea wafts through the open window, tousling damp hair and cooling tempers. The scream of gulls mingles with the sound of the waves and the creaking of the elderly pine trees that line the path along the beach. The waiting becomes too much for her, and she unbuckles her seatbelt and leans right out of the window, straining to see past the row of pines to the huddle of caravans nestled beneath.

Mrs. Ball was there. The little girl knew she was – *wished it to be so.* It could not be a proper summer holiday without the little van and the elderly lady within – the lady who painted stories onto the smooth, white stones that she collected from the beach. The little girl would go for a walk later, just to make sure.

If you were here with me now, looking at this shell, I know you would sense that little girl's excitement. *I feel it still…*

All of my shells are precious – even the not-so-pretty ones – for each and every one contains an echo of the girl I was and the woman I have become. Even as I write this, a new shell appears – adding itself to my recollection of days.

Another whisper of my life's events.

Chapter 10
Following Our Purpose & Passion

We all have a unique purpose – a reason for being here on Earth. Your purpose may be to bring beauty into the world through your paintings while ours is to bring love into the world through our writing. Each purpose is equally important. When we're living our purpose, everything seems to flow. We wake up excited to be alive and feel a mix of invigoration and peace – elation and calm. We go through our days grateful that we get to share our gifts.

Conversely, if our purpose and passion have taken a back seat, we'll most likely feel tired and dull – wishing for something more. When this happens, our soul will always call us back. And if we're open to it, we'll begin to see signs pointing in the direction that we need to go.

Because each purpose is unique, they don't come in a one-size-fits-all package. We can't look to anyone else to tell us what our purpose is, which can sometimes feel very frustrating – knowing that we have to figure it out on our own. But since we are the only one who can hear our soul's whispers, we are the only one who can feel our soul's calling.

Sometimes, we may find that our purpose goes against what others want for us or what is accepted in society, and we might feel the need to squash our desires for fear of being ostracized or ridiculed. Leaping into our dreams isn't for the weak of heart. It's for those of us who are bravely showing up for our life and reaping the rewards because of our ability to stay open to our soul's whispers.

Your soul will never steer you in the wrong direction, and it always has your best interest at heart. Trust it. Allow it to guide you. Listen to its whispers. And give yourself permission to follow your purpose and passion. In this chapter, you'll find pieces to help you do exactly that.

Live Your Unconquerable Life

by Peggy Nolan

"It matters not how strait the gate, How charged with punishments the scroll.
I am the master of my fate: I am the captain of my soul."
- William Ernest Henley

The news sucker-punched me. I had lost another friend to cancer. My friend never waffled on about life being unfair or unkind. Even when he knew he was dying, he took piano lessons, rode his Harley, and trained in his beloved martial arts. My friend was a brave and fearless warrior with an unmistakable soul message:

LIVE! Quit sitting on the sidelines of life waiting for an invitation. Make memories with those you treasure. Do what you love doing. Plant your garden, play with your kids, take piano lessons, or travel the globe. You are the captain of your soul. Go live your life!

Nearly 12 years ago, I had a little run-in with breast cancer. It was my "Holy crap! I could die from this!" wake-up call. The truth is that we're all going to die someday. Yet, all too often, we put off all the good stuff until "someday" – only to find that "someday" is a fancy lie we tell ourselves.

When I got my wake-up call, I couldn't wait for someday anymore. A week before I started chemo, I took my daughters to Playa del Carmen, Mexico. We went horseback riding in the ocean, snorkeled, tubed down the Xel-Há River, and climbed the great Mayan pyramid. I've been exploring the world and creating memories like this ever since, as often as possible.

As I navigated my journey through breast cancer, the poem "Invictus" by William Ernest Henley found its way to me. I taped it to my bathroom mirror as a reminder that no matter how impossible things seemed, my soul was and is unconquerable.

The poem continues to resonate as the "menace of the years" marches on. Every time I read it, I am reminded, like my friend, to live my soul's deepest longing and to unapologetically experience joy and live an unconquerable life.

Uncover Your Brilliance

by Joanna Lindenbaum

One of the most profound ways of connecting inwards that I know is to truly, fully uncover your brilliance.

In some ways it sounds so obvious, but way too often it gets overlooked. We go to school, we get credentialed, we find jobs, we start businesses…yet some of us never actually get to the core of who we are and what are true talents and sacred gifts are.

When you don't fully know your brilliance, you…

- don't fully value yourself.
- feel misaligned with your work.
- can't find the courage to fully stand up for yourself at work.
- feel disconnected from your deepest self.

Discovering my own brilliance has been a process, an inner journey that has evolved over time. It began when I was working as a curator in the art world in my 20s. While I truly loved the curatorial work I was doing, I would wake up in the middle of the night in sweats, knowing that I wasn't fully living my path. It took becoming physically ill because of my misalignment before I had the courage to explore what my true purpose and brilliance was.

If you would like to get to your core brilliance, here are some journaling questions that can help guide you:

- What activities are you naturally brilliant at? (Activities can include things like being a good listener, making people smile, keeping the peace, or knowing the exact right colors that go well together in a room.)
- What do people seek you out for? (Again, think about the types of examples I give above.)
- What activities feel effortless to you?

As you answer these questions, don't judge or censor yourself. Be as honest as you can be. And enjoy the brilliance that you uncover!

Honor Your Soul's Purpose

by Veronica Mather

Are you living the life your soul desires, or do your current circumstances merely reflect the expectations of people around you? It can be difficult at times to decipher which is which.

Reflecting back to when we were young can be an important tool in remembering who we really are. It can assist to remind us of the activities we were naturally drawn to before life's distractions and society's ideals impacted our way of thinking, influencing and potentially changing our true soul's calling.

When I was younger, I used to sit under an apple tree in our backyard and write. Writer's block wasn't a part of my world. Self criticism and lack of belief didn't even factor in. I could write a story from start to finish without stopping, and I loved every minute.

Gradually though – as I devoted more time to school, friends, sports, and other commitments – my writing was pushed aside. I always felt that something was missing, but I could never quite work out why my life felt incomplete.

Writing wasn't to become a part of my world again until I was in my 30s. When it did, I felt like I had regained a central part of myself that I never wanted to lose again! I felt like I had reconnected with a huge part of my soul's purpose.

Are you honouring *your* soul's purpose? Reflect back to when you were younger. What activities were you drawn to? Was it art, caring for animals, sitting with an elderly family member, or being active outdoors? Did you feel happiness and contentment? Is this passion still a part of your world? If not, ask yourself why?

As we grow, many of us lose that amazing capability to do what makes us happy without feeling self-conscious. Peer pressure, fitting in, being ridiculed, or having our behaviour questioned can mark our soul and damage our true self. Being different takes a strong person, and the fear of being good enough can cloud our hopes and pursuit of dreams. Your past is not your future. But using positive recall and weaving happy memories into your present is a great way to honour your soul's calling and to live your life without regret.

Unshackle the Golden Handcuffs

by Kim Steadman

By all appearances, my life was good. But the day wouldn't even be half over, and I would already be dreading the next day. It took massive amounts of gratitude games and "count-my-blessings" exercises to remain semi-optimistic. The usual "Pollyanna Kim" was in a perpetual funk, and I didn't like it. Why was I like this?

Okay. The truth was, I knew why. But to bring about the change I needed would take a giant leap of faith – something that I had put off for about three years. Why so long? Was it fear, apprehension, or uncertainty? Yes to all of the above and much more.

Over the past few years, I had allowed myself to make career decisions that were not aligned with my core values. I wasn't following my soul's true passions and purpose. So I decided to make a huge jump and unshackle the golden handcuffs of job stability.

I quit my lucrative, corporate career, which had been contributing to much of my stress and was taking a toll on my physical body and spirit. The minute I uttered the words "I'm resigning" to my boss of 17 years, I knew it was the right thing to do because I started feeling some of the toxicity inside me melt away and peace begin to fill in the crevices.

Was it a bold leap? You bet it was! Did everyone understand? Absolutely not! Do I have a supportive husband on this journey? Fortunately, yes! Have I replaced all that income yet? No, but that's part of the new journey, which is helping me to appreciate the smaller and simpler things in life.

Gone are the days of the familiarity of corporate life. But now, without the golden shackles, I have the peace of mind to explore new creative endeavors and follow my soul's whispers. I told my parents that I don't know what I want to be when I grow up. But I have the rest of my life to figure that out.

Do you have golden handcuffs that need to be unshackled?

Self Renewal

by Julie Jones

Do you ever feel absent from your own life? Do your needs, desires, passions, and purpose seem out of reach? Are you so involved in doing everything that you simply forget to *be*? Do you frequently neglect the present moment…and yourself?

If so, this might be a great time for you to practice self renewal.

Self renewal is about returning to yourself and being present in your world and regaining your power and passion for life. It is the reconnection with your soul's longing and purpose.

While there is not a prescription for self renewal, I believe that it begins with two types of awareness:

- *Inner Awareness* – Sit quietly and take a deep breath. Scan your body, from the bottom of your feet to the top of your head. Notice, without judgment, if there are areas of stress, pain, ache, cool, or heat.
- *Outer Awareness* – Take a moment to stop, look, and listen. Notice what you see, hear, and smell.

Taking a moment to notice can help you connect on a soul level. Noticing your body grounds you in your physical experience. Noticing your surroundings helps you become present in the moment. It can also raise powerful questions about your life: *Does your world bring you joy? Does it reflect your passion and purpose? Does it reflect who you are?*

When I went through this process, I realized that I was disconnected from my passion for soul service. I decided to take action by offering a silent blessing to everyone I encountered. Sometimes I prayed for them to experience peace or hope; other times I simply offered a smile. After a few days, I began to notice that more people would speak to me, hold the door or elevator, or smile back. The more I offered, the more I received – and the more I wanted to offer!

Your experience with self renewal may be very different from mine; but I hope that you also reconnect with your body, your world, and your soul – and find your passion for life reinvigorated and renewed.

Embrace Your Enigmatic Essence

by Jasmine Sreenika Crystalsinger

Every life you touch is marked by your enigmatic essence. I define this as a proprietary blend of greatness only you possess – a magnetism only you can unleash because no one could ever copy, steal, or replicate it, no matter how hard they tried. It is utterly unique to you.

To help you discover your enigmatic essence, answer the following questions:

- If your soul were a perfume, how would you describe it? What head, heart, and base notes combine to compose its unique fragrance of impressions, sensations, and desires?
- If your soul were a musical instrument, what would it sound like? What melodies, harmonies, and ornaments would it weave into the tapestry of your life?
- If you asked someone you love what makes you special, what would they say?
- If you asked them how you make them feel, what would they say?
- What combination of gifts and qualities goes into making you YOU?
- If you had to distill your enigmatic essence down to a few words, what words would you choose?

Spend some time imagining what new thoughts, feelings, intentions, and actions you would entertain if you allowed yourself to embrace your enigmatic essence – to show up from a place of deep knowing and self-acceptance. In what ways would you stretch and surprise yourself if you fully radiated your unapologetic truth?

When you fully embrace your enigmatic essence, you come home to yourself. Your passion becomes your purpose, your self-expression an epiphany for the world.

Follow Your *"Heck Yeah!"*

by Jenny McKaig

"Just give me five minutes," he said. "There's someone you *have* to meet."

"I don't have time," I said. "I've really got to go." But I heard my soul's voice telling me, *Stay. Meet the person he's talking about.* Something within me lit up when I heard that inner voice, so I decided to follow its advice. "Okay," I said. "But just five minutes."

He introduced me to the woman. We shook hands, exchanged business cards, and promised to follow up. And that was it. Five minutes later, I really did have to go.

A few days later, she sent me an email: "We need to talk to you."

Who "we" was, I didn't know; but before I had a chance to think it over, my soul said *Yes.* In fact, what it actually said was, *Heck yeah!*

It seemed that my soul had recently gotten in the habit of speaking to me more often. Two weeks earlier, I'd heard its clear inner voice tell me: *I'm ready for more speaking gigs. I'm ready to be seen on a larger scale by bigger audiences.* I'd more or less put this message out of my conscious mind, but it came rushing back when I spoke with the woman and her business partner.

We met over breakfast, and I learned that they were founders of a worldwide organization that promoted speakers. They wanted to arrange speaking engagements for me. Was I interested? *Heck yeah!* my soul said.

"I'd be delighted," I translated for my soul.

"How long do you need to prepare?"

"A month," I said.

Three hours later, I received a call. "Can you speak next Tuesday?"

"Yes," I said. *Heck yeah!*

I started speaking for that organization, saw crowds around the world, and co-authored an international bestselling book with the woman who I "really had to meet." And I learned that dreams come true when we listen to our soul – especially when it gives such an emphatic *yes* – or, as my soul puts it, *Heck yeah!*

Uncensored Expressions

by April Williams

I used to meticulously formulate my words, my feelings, and my every action. I neatly placed them together in order to belong. I had become so afraid of others' judgment that I nearly lost myself. I had become a hollowed-out version of the girl I once was. My soul and I almost completely detached from one another.

It wasn't until years later, after the birth of my first son and dealing with postpartum depression, that I awakened from the state of autopilot I had placed myself in. With this awakening, I realized that by muting my true self, I was being cut off from my soul.

So began my journey of reconnecting with my soul.

Through this journey, I have learned that my soul speaks in many ways, yet it speaks the loudest through uncensored expression: no calculated confinements, no adulterated arrangements, no fitting into specified standards. Just real, raw truths – flowing freely forward through written words, magical music, and spoken secrets.

As long as I allow for organically orchestrated rhythms of expression to flow out of me, I am connecting more closely with my soul – for all that comes from this innocent, judgment-free place is my soul speaking, shamelessly showing itself not only to me but to the whole world.

When I pause long enough to admire the beyond-breathtaking beauty that I opened up to, I find an endless amount of worldly wisdom; unconditional love; and a better understanding for my true self as a whole, which is lit by the eternal fire of my soul.

So if you want to try connecting with your soul today, allow yourself to open up completely, let go of any fears that surround you, and then admire as your uncensored self shines through – allowing your soul to speak and connect not only with you but with the whole wide world.

Shine Like a Diamond

by Sharon Kistler

The eyes are the windows to the soul, yet some people are afraid to have you look them in the eye. Perhaps they do not want you to see into their soul. They may feel the need to hide away the parts of themselves that they are not happy with or have a hard time accepting. They may not believe in their own inner beauty.

When you feel self-doubt or are afraid to be seen, it is a sign to look deeper to unearth the "Diamond Soul" in all of its brilliance! The many facets of self, like the many facets of a diamond, shimmer and sparkle as you attract and shine your own unique light.

A jeweler uses a loupe to look deeper into the diamond's essence. He looks through the lens and holds the diamond up to the light to discover its many unseen facets, even its inclusions or perceived flaws. Likewise, you can hold your Diamond Soul to the light of your awareness in order to see yourself in your full glory!

The process of revealing your Diamond Soul is all about believing in yourself and seeing your truest value. It's about taking the time for further self-discovery to see your greatness.

When you shine light on your soul, you'll see that the kingdom of the Divine truly is within you – the sacred place that stores all its glorious riches, your voice of the spirit, the core truth of who you really are. When you shine a light within, your soul tells you about the gifts that you already have…and about your unlimited potential!

Each diamond, just like each person, has a unique sparkle quality all its own. Are you ready to discover *your* sparkle, *your* gifts, and *your* brightest potential? Are you ready to reveal your own capacity for creativity, kindness, forgiveness, and love? Are you ready to believe in your brilliance?

Are you ready go out and shine your soul sparkle like the diamond you are?

Do More of What You Love to Do

by Thea Westra

When you spend hours in a row, seemingly lost in time and completely engrossed in an activity that you love, you can be certain that you're connected to soul.

Discovering what you truly love to do is sometimes straightforward, yet it isn't always. Embark on a journey of self-discovery, and try many new things. You may need to dedicate time and patience. It's all about tuning in to the signals from soul and noticing when passion is present or when an activity has an almost cathartic element to it.

Our soul informs us that life is about much more than a schedule full of duties and chores, things we do because we need to do them. Many of us even aspire to make a living by doing lots more of what we most love to do!

Free time offers us an opportunity to explore and embrace activities that we truly love, so be sure to schedule time to play and wander where your heart wants to take you. When we engage more often in the things that we really enjoy, which make us come alive, we fill the well. It enables us to give more of ourselves and to truly express the soul being. We radiate, and this energy is sensed by those with whom we come into contact.

Soul loves to connect with other soul beings. It's our job to make that possible by becoming the person we were meant to be. Expressing out into the world the purpose that we were designed to fulfill is the direction that soul will always lead us towards.

In our busy lives, contending with the distractions of modern living, we do not find much opportunity to connect with our own soul, let alone others.

It's vital to create room for free play and for trying out the activities that attract us. When you're drawn to a pursuit and you ignore intuition, you're really pushing away your soul's purpose.

Allow for free time to dabble, explore, and engage more often in the things that you know you love to do. This is the place where you can reconnect with your soul.

Stay in Your Soul Zone

by Heather A. Nardi

What is your *soul zone*? To me, being in your soul zone means living a positive, fulfilling, and purposeful life. It means listening to your soul – your inner voice. It means living your values, your passions, and your life purpose. When you're in your soul zone, you feel joy and peace.

My soul zone includes living a holistically healthy life and helping others to do the same. This passion and purpose came to light through experiences with my daughter. For seven years, she struggled with anxiety and depression. She saw therapists and took prescription medications, but to little avail. This all began to change when we explored holistic modalities such as flower essences, which helped her greatly. In helping her, I stepped into my soul zone!

Although your passions and purpose may be very different from mine, you can still use many of the same approaches for discovering and staying in your soul zone:

- Determine your core values and beliefs – how you think about yourself, your life, and the world around you. Follow your values, which will help when making decisions that affect family, career, friendships, and your soul zone.
- Surround yourself with those who empower you, and let go of anyone who drains your energy – with as much grace and kindness as possible. Take charge of your life and wellbeing!
- Be grateful for everything in your life, even the struggles. It can be tempting to let challenges keep us from feeling happy, but setbacks can often be our greatest teachers. My family's challenges have helped me to understand and support others.
- Remember that change starts from within. When you want to become more positive, change your thoughts to focus on joy and love. Use mantras or affirmations to help you develop a more positive perception of yourself.

Most of all, let your soul shine in a positive light – and share your soul zone with the world!

Your Inner Child Holds the Map

by Michelle McDonald Vlastnik

I would like to offer you a new perspective on the mind-body-soul connection: I invite you to view your soul and your Inner Child as one and the same.

Having a connection with our Inner Child is vital for our wholeness and overall wellness. This relationship has a direct correlation to our Oneness of Self and to the All.

It is my belief that our soul knows our Divine life-purpose plan and that our Inner Child holds that map. As we travel on our awakening quest, we begin soul searching, looking for meaning and purpose. Think back to what you loved as a child, because those passions are the seeds for your Divine life purpose.

As a child, I loved exploring outside and looking for hidden clues to solve mysteries. I would talk to Mother Nature and ask her to make the wind blow. At age five, I met my best friend and most significant spiritual teacher for this lifetime. I felt so free to be me when I was with him, whether I was being girly, tomboyish, scared, or tough, he showed me unconditional love before I even knew what it was called. That feeling of being a free spirit was the "X" on my map. We were inseparable until his death at age nine. Afterward, I unknowingly disconnected from my Inner Child and did not reconnect until age 38.

Our soul is our Inner Child, and our Inner Child is our Authentic Self. All of these parts come into alignment for the Oneness needed to create a clear communication within our Highest Self. Our journey is about the Inner Child that has been dormant or lost – a quest of awakening, remembrance, and reconnection to the innocence of our Light.

Our spiritual journey often requires different perspectives for learning. I hope that this unique way of thinking brings a fun, new, and innovative way for you to connect with your soul. May you find the "X" on your map and the treasure of the freedom to be your-Self.

Listen to the Voice Within

by Jenny McKaig

"Let's go for a walk," my friend said.

I agreed, not realizing that the "walk" would soon become a hike and then a climb…straight up a steep cliff covered with jagged rocks. Had I known this from the start, I probably wouldn't have agreed to join her – and I certainly would have worn something other than flip-flops!

I eventually did make it to the top of the mountain, though, and was rewarded by a breathtaking view. Sitting near the cliff's edge, I gazed out over the wide expanse of ocean, clear-blue water stretching out as far as the eye could see. The salty scent of the ocean wafted up on the gentle breeze, and the sun soothed me with its warmth.

As I sat, enjoying the moment of peace, I heard a whisper from within me: *Write, write.*

I did follow this call to write – a calling that has become my profession. More importantly, however, in this moment of grace, I connected with the voice of my soul.

Many times over the years, this wise inner voice has offered its benevolent guidance, speaking to me in clear, distinct words: *Finish what you start. Go back to Canada. Go to school for writing. Write a book. Write several books. Get married. Start a family. Learn to surf better.*

I've allowed this voice to guide me through many significant changes: out of a job I didn't love and a relationship that didn't fit, and into a life that better reflected my higher self. And I've let it serve as a lifelong connection with God, the Universe, and Life itself.

Several years ago, my friend bought me a magnet with the words: *You always know.* I've learned that this is true – the voice within us knows. And when we listen to its guidance, we connect with our path and our purpose, the wisdom of our soul, and more joy than we ever thought possible.

Honoring Family, Culture, and Individuality

by Manpreet Dhillon

We live in a society that emphasizes individuality. This focus has many benefits. It encourages people to identify who they are at their core, connect with their truth, and express their authentic selves – all of which is beautiful!

Individuality is an expression of a person's completeness, which includes their experiences, their beliefs, and their values. And, because we are also social beings, our individuality is also affected and informed by family and cultural influences and, in some cases, obligations.

While North American culture generally promotes individualism, many other cultures embrace a more collective approach to family. In these cultures, individuals are more likely to prioritize family needs over their own. This may mean sacrificing personal preferences or beliefs, or staying in situations based on the fear of letting the family down.

Balancing between family and cultural obligations can make it challenging to express true individuality. In trying to achieve this balance, it is important to be aware of what aspects of your cultural and family obligations resonate with you and which aspects do not.

A compassionate approach is of utmost importance, as it allows you to honor yourself as well as those in your family and culture. Remember that their belief systems served them as a whole and usually provided each individual with a sense of belonging and acceptance. As a leader in your own life, however, it is important to discover how else you can bring in a sense of belonging and acceptance for yourself and those around you. Be willing to let go of any past programming or beliefs that aren't in line with who you truly are. In doing so, your life will move into greater alignment with who you are, and you'll find greater connection with your authentic self – and your soul.

It's true that family and culture sometimes pose challenges to your individual expression, but they can also be a beautiful part of your true, authentic self. It is time to honor all aspects of our life – including family and culture – so that we can connect with all aspects of our true self.

Calling Out Your Talent

by Fiona Louise

What is your special talent? Standing on one leg? Balancing a spoon on your nose? Fixing electronics? Is there something you've always wanted to try but fear held you back? What makes your heart soar when you accomplish it? Have you heard gentle urgings to try something new or return to a project you discarded many years ago? This is your soul speaking to you, rekindling the fire in your belly to use your talent to connect.

Doing something fun, that you enjoy, elicits your feel-good hormones, making you feel alive and revitalised. This is what your soul wants for you. Your soul wants you to be blissful; so give yourself permission to set aside time to play, enjoy, and create! Unleash your inner child, re-lighting that amazing curiosity and sense of wonder. If you've always wanted to paint – start! If you've always wanted to speak Hindi – start! If you've always wanted to master the backwards flip on the trampoline – start! The key is to have fun!

As I began listening to my soul again, I found my hand reaching for a pen. Soon, scribbles on scrap paper became dedicated journals, and I now carry a notebook ready for whenever inspiration strikes. My soul was always there, waiting patiently for me to connect. Now that I have, words flow effortlessly! This talent is my connection with my soul, but you may have another way that is unique to you.

The possibilities are endless, and no matter what you choose, if it resonates then you are connecting with your soul. Be creative, happy, and relaxed, and *feel* your soul connection! It feels like bliss – the best kind of uplifting inspiration you can experience. You literally have a spring in your step, which is helpful if your talent is gymnastics!

So, what is your talent? Singing, woodcarving, baking, crocheting, swimming, teaching? Have you felt the urge to pick up the paintbrush again, tinker with old cars, or putter in the garden? It doesn't have to be grandiose, just something that makes your heart soar.

What talent will connect you to your soul today?

The Power of Reading

by Christena Alyssandratos

As a busy mother of two beautiful daughters, I often enjoy those quiet moments when I can pick up a book and immerse myself in the pages. I always look forward to the end of the day when I get to relax, pour myself a cup of hot tea, curl up under a cozy blanket, and read. I love feeling like time is standing still, even when the hours are quickly passing. It's in those moments that I feel connected with my true self.

I believe that reading a book can be a life-changing experience. I know it was for me.

I remember one afternoon years ago, when I put my daughter (who was four months old at the time) down for her afternoon nap. I had recently decided that it was time to start a new health regimen in order to lose those last few pounds after having a baby. I stood before my bookcase to see if I already had any books on healthy weight loss. I was immediately drawn to a book I had purchased a few years back and had never bothered to read. I pored through the pages, reading it every free moment I had – mostly when my daughter napped and just before I went to bed. I became drawn to the author's words and message. It was like she was speaking directly to me.

I soon realized that this book was about much more than just weight loss, and reading it led me toward a journey of self-empowerment. I discovered that the author was the founder of a coaching program. After my daughter was born, I knew I wanted to find work that was more meaningful and fulfilling. So I took a leap of faith and signed up for this program and become a Master Empowerment coach.

That book helped me discover my true passion by connecting me back to my soul. While your experiences may be quite different from mine, I know that you, too, can connect with your soul and your passions through the power of reading.

Activate Your Dream Life

by Priscilla Stephan

What if I told you that your soul already knows the exact lifestyle that will allow you to live your dreams? Would you believe me?

It's the truth. Your soul already knows your unique path to living an abundant and joyful life. Everything about you – including the components of your dream life, the lessons and contributions you are here to experience, and your purpose and how to monetize it – is already contained within your soul's blueprint (what I call your "Soul's DNA").

Our dreams are like clues from our soul, guiding us to live our best life. In fact, they are divinely implanted within us to support us in fulfilling our destiny and purpose. Our job is to go within, listen, and take action. Activating our dream life is the most profound act of love we can take for ourselves and the world. In doing so, we honour ourselves and the gifts we were born to share.

I know this because I've lived it. Every morning I pinch myself as I sip my coffee poolside at my San Diego home. This is because a year ago my life was radically different. I was sharing a one-bedroom apartment with my mother in Long Island, New York. I was going through a massive move, recovering from heartbreak, transitioning my business, and wondering: *When will my life really start?* Fast forward to today: I live in my dream city with a man who loves me, and I do work that's deeply fulfilling. I live an activated life, and you can, too.

On my journey to activating my dream life, I've uncovered a few simple but profound steps that will support you in activating your own:

- Get really clear on what *you* want (not anyone else's dreams).
- Have faith in yourself.
- Believe in your dreams (work through the reasons and beliefs that have stopped you).
- Be relentless, and have fun on the way to achieving your dreams.

Also, give yourself permission to have what you truly desire and stay flexible regarding how it shows up for you. And remember to listen to your soul and let it guide you. Dreams DO come true. So, what dreams are you ready to activate in your life?

Light Up

by Barb Heite

Light up and shine, beautiful soul.

You are wonderful just as you are. When talking about your passions and your heart's desires, you naturally light up…with a twinkle in your eye and music in your laughter. Your smile sparkles and radiates; and when you beam your natural beauty, the world is a little brighter. Your presence is a gift to the world.

You are uniquely brilliant, a child of God meant to let your light shine, illuminate the world, touch and inspire others, connect and share unconditional love. You are resilient, even when you don't feel that way. With each choice you make, you find new adventures that contribute to your happiness. You naturally light up as you move forward in your life journey, creating your own miracles, finding the answers through your personal experiences…stretching and growing.

Unwrap the gifts found in the treasure of being YOU: a heart full of creativity, kindness, curiosity, generosity, bravery, softness, and love. Your spirit thrives through everything you do. You glow outwardly, your inner bliss spilling out – your enthusiasm, your zest for life serving as an inspiration to us all as we watch. You are beautiful.

There is no wrong way to walk your path, just choices in the bends and bumps that you will experience. Your attitude will determine how you will feel as you walk your journey. When you believe in yourself, your world will open up to unexplored possibilities. As you listen to your inner voice, your heart, you will discover that your dreams can come true.

My wish for you is to have the courage to dream big, to dare, to take leaps of faith, to know your inherent worth, to know that you are loved beyond measure, and to always remember that when you are naturally being you, the world is graced with your inner beauty.

We all rejoice when you light up.

Live Your Passion

by Veronica Mather

Are you living a life that you always dreamed of? Or are you just going through the motions? Do you wake up each morning feeling passionate about the day to come? Or do you find it a struggle just to get out of bed? Taking time to honestly evaluate our present circumstances is something often left for "another day," but let's make that day *today*! Right now, take some time to reflect on these questions:

- Are you happy?
- What kind of life do you want to be living?
- What are you passionate about?
- What goals do you want to achieve?
- What do you want your life's legacy to be?

If the life you're currently living isn't full of joy, fulfillment, and passion, perhaps you'd like to take one (or more) of the following steps:

- *Meet new people.* Their different energy and ideas can be inspiring. Reach out to people who have successfully forged a path that you desire to follow.
- *Get training.* This will help you gain expertise and also boost your confidence.
- *Volunteer in your area of interest.* Not only is the work itself valuable, but you may gain useful skills and knowledge and make contacts within your chosen area. Volunteering can also help you to determine whether or not the work lives up to your expectations.

Some people instinctively know what they want to do from a very young age. But it's also okay to discover your soul's purpose later in life. Goals often change as we grow and evolve. Our destiny can be an ever-changing journey of hopes and dreams. There is nothing wrong with changing your mind.

It takes energy and dedication to follow the life your soul yearns for. But when you live your passion, achievement and contentment are destined to be part of your life. There is never a reason good enough to put your dreams on hold. Now is your time.

Making Your Divine Contribution

by Ronda Renee

"What am I here to do?" We've all asked ourselves this question, perhaps repeatedly. But what if this question is the very thing keeping you from connecting with your soul and fulfilling your purpose?

You see, the moment we project our purpose outside of ourselves is the moment we actually move away from it. Your purpose is not a "doing." It's not a project or a mission. It has nothing to do with what you do (for money or any other reason).

Your true purpose is actually a state of being – what you contribute through your presence. I am not simply talking about your body being somewhere, but about the specific energetic presence that you were meant to contribute to the world – what I call "Your Divine Contribution."

When you know what it is, you can make Your Divine Contribution in the very next room you walk into. You don't have to wait until you get your act together, until your family accepts you, or until you make it big and are reaching millions with your message.

What you do need to do is to get to the core of who you really are and who you were meant to BE – not just who you've learned to be, think you should be, or think you have to be in order to be seen as valuable to society.

Once you understand that your sole (and soul) purpose is to show up as your unique energetic signature, you realize you can effortlessly make Your Divine Contribution anywhere and everywhere you go.

Your energetic signature, what I call your Divine Coordinates®, is the specific set of energies that you were designed to contribute to the world. No one else has your exact energetic signature. So, if you don't identify those energies, align with them, and bring them to the world, then something essential is missing from the world: you.

The world is counting on you for something that only you can provide. The true you is the biggest contribution you can make to the world – Your Divine Contribution. Don't make us wait any longer!

Embrace Your Spiritual Talents

by Marcia Sandels

"Teach me how to trust my heart, my mind, my intuition, my inner knowing, the senses of my body, the blessings of my spirit. Teach me to trust these things so that I may enter my sacred space and love beyond my fear, and thus walk in balance with the passing of each glorious sunset."

- Lakota prayer

This prayer captures my intention on how to connect with your soul via your spiritual talents, or metaphysical senses. The soul is our inner essence, our connection to Divine Source. Each of us *IS* a soul, rather than *HAS* a soul…living in a human body. We are here to learn from earthly experiences and also to express our highest selves.

The Divine provides spiritual guidance through metaphysical communication with your soul. The definition of "metaphysical" is "that which is beyond your five physical senses," or your Extrasensory Perception (ESP) or unseen talents.

Our spiritual, God-given talents include intuition (our inner-knowing capacity without conscious reasoning); mental telepathy (mind-to-mind communication with another); soul writing (stepping away from ego-self and allowing the soul to express itself); and the "clairs": clairvoyance ("clear vision" with the mind's eye – seeing an event in advance), clairaudience ("clear hearing" – hearing angels, guides, or deceased loved ones), and claircognizance ("clear knowing" – what one needs to know is revealed when one needs to know it).

I find that I need to be calm and quiet to receive these divine soul communications and have experienced each of these spiritual talents and more. Because children are still closely connected to Spirit, they often display these talents by way of seeing, hearing, or knowing about deceased loved ones. Some people seem to be more adept at these talents, but we all have them to some degree. The key is to be open and receptive to your spiritual talents. You may be surprised and delighted at what you're capable of! We are blessed to have these talents from our Creator God. And So It Is.

Finding Passion and Purpose Through Our Struggles

by Jasmine Sreenika Crystalsinger

What do you desire? What whispers to your soul so fervently that you can't stop daydreaming about it? What petrifies you when you think of surrendering to the electricity of its invitation, of communing with your calling? Do you suspect how many people you could serve, how much joy you could have, and what legacy you could leave behind if you fueled your life with passion and poured the very best of who you are into your purpose?

When I work with women of vision, their most common question is: *How do I find my purpose?* I answer by asking more questions: *What do you love to give? What does that look and feel like? What are you most excited to share with others?*

Sometimes the answers to these questions lie hidden in the intense struggles we have surmounted ourselves so that we might inspire others to overcome them. For instance, if you've overcome fear or self-doubt, you may be able to help others do the same. Sometimes our external circumstances can point us toward our passion and purpose. If you've moved to a new country, experienced physical challenges, or passionately worked for a certain cause, your experiences and wisdom could benefit others in similar circumstances.

This definitely holds true for my own life. As a child, I remember taking books to birthday parties and crying when I had to knock on doors to sell Girl Scout cookies. My shyness made me feel painfully isolated and at times incapable of connecting with others and sharing the gifts I kept hidden inside. The turning point came when I left a promising career in linguistics to enter a national conservatory for acting in the Netherlands. In acting, I found my authentic voice and connected with my passion for expression and turned it into a heart-centered business where I get to help others step into the spotlight as well.

The struggles that you've overcome provide clues to help you identify your passion and purpose. The main question to ask is: *What makes you feel the most luscious, vibrant, and free right now?* Toy with several possible answers. PLAY and allow your curiosity to reveal delightful possibilities. Fall head over heels for your life purpose and let it transform you into a luminous testament of love.

Soulful Accountability

by Stacey Hall

Does the word "accountable" lower your energy? I ask because it used to lower mine. Emotionally, I would automatically resist the concept of "accountability" – although logically it seemed like a perfectly fine concept.

This aversion to accountability puzzled me since I completely embrace the concept of "integrity," and they seem to be a well-matched partnership.

I finally discovered the source of my unease with accountability when I recalled how I was introduced to the word (which is how most of us were introduced to it): As a child, I was often asked by my parents and teachers if they could count on me to do whatever it was they wanted me to do. Being accountable meant doing what *others* wanted me to do rather than doing what *I* wanted to do. Accountability meant being confined or limited, rather than being free.

Yet, to be a person of integrity means to be someone who can be counted upon. I chose to be a person of integrity, so I also chose to change my relationship with accountability.

I prayed and meditated, and I began to realize how important it is for me to fulfill my God-given purpose here on Earth – which meant that I was willing to be accountable to God. I made a list of everything that I intended to do to fulfill that purpose. This list has developed into a series of "I AM" statements about what I choose to count on myself to be, do, have, and accomplish – in other words, my "Soulful Accountabilities" – toward fulfilling my purpose.

I wake up every morning affirming and embracing my Soulful Accountabilities with this statement: "I AM making God smile, I AM healthy, I AM purposeful, I AM playful, I AM productive, I AM spiritually and financially prosperous, I AM loving, I AM loved, and I AM grateful." And then I get into action to complete activities that are in integrity with my Soulful Accountabilities.

I invite you to consider: what are your Soulful Accountabilities toward fulfilling your purpose?

Childhood Clues to Your Life Purpose

by Linda Wheeler Williams

If you want a glimpse of your life purpose, look back at your childhood. The soul gives us clues every step of the way, from the day we are born.

My earliest memories of what my life purpose could be was being a good listener. As a child, I would hide under furniture and very quietly listen to the adult conversations. Maybe my purpose was to be a court stenographer, because I could recite every word of the conversations – a fact that was not always appreciated by the adults!

Another glimpse of my life purpose came from the many funerals I attended as a child. Because my parents were caregivers for family members and neighbors, we regularly experienced death at our home. I don't remember being sad about this; I just knew it was part of life's process.

A third clue arrived when I started attending church regularly with an older neighbor (who I called "Grandpa"). My favorite subject at church was angels. I especially loved seeing their majestic pictures in the family Bible or the Bible storybooks my parents bought me. Angels and Heaven stayed on my mind. I would sit in my swing and look up at the heavens and say aloud to the angels, "I've just *got* to go to Heaven."

As an adult, I suffered through years of pain and disappointments, causing me to forgot about the life-purpose clues my soul had provided during my childhood – until 1999. That's when my journey of rediscovery began. Following a final emotionally traumatic experience, I sold everything, moved almost 1,800 miles away, and dedicated myself to seeking and *living* my life purpose.

With help from my childhood clues, I discovered this purpose as a personal-success coach who focuses on healing and forgiveness. In this role, I use my childhood skills of listening and compassion. I also teach others not to fear death – sharing what I learned as a child: that this is a natural part of life, that our loved ones are still with us, and that we can always call upon angels for assistance and guidance.

When you reflect on your childhood memories, what clues do they provide about *your* life purpose?

Leap Toward Your Dreams

by Lisa Anna Palmer

When we connect with our soul, we gain greater clarity about what we want to create in our lives. But we often find that our heart's desires live in that sacred yet scary space beyond our comfort zone – a place we may not want to go because it's, well…*uncomfortable!*

So often, we trick ourselves into thinking that our comfort zone is "safe," when ultimately it keeps us small, stunts our growth, and prevents us from living our dreams. All of our dreams are patiently waiting for us just beyond our comfort zone – excited for us to bravely leap toward them.

If you think about what may be holding you back from making the leap, one word usually comes to mind: fear.

It creeps up when you get excited about living life to the fullest; just when you are ready to move forward, your mind bombards you with "shoulds," "can'ts," and "don'ts" until your thoughts slowly eat away at your courage.

However, your heart's desires won't disappear simply because you ignored them. You might repeatedly follow their call…only to turn back each time you bump up against the limits of your comfort zone – leaving you with a nagging frustration and lack of fulfillment. Follow this pattern often enough, and you'll end up in an awful place: the land of regrets.

One way to avoid this all-too-common pitfall is to shift your thinking. Notice that fear presents an opportunity to demonstrate courage. For instance, I was so afraid of public speaking at the age of 25 that I couldn't give a speech at my own wedding! Since then, I have shifted my thinking and realized that courage cannot exist in the absence of fear. Now at 44, I look for opportunities to grow by speaking in front of increasingly larger audiences.

You, too, can begin by taking it one step at a time…and create the life you desire! Go ahead, venture beyond your comfort zone! Leap toward your heart's desires so that when you look back on your life you will be grateful that "I wish I could have," was replaced by "I am so glad I did!"

Shine Like the Star You Are

by Kylie Mansfield

The greatest injustice we do to ourselves is endeavor to be normal.

Allowing society to smother the light within us all, to snuff out what doesn't fit into the dark void of conformity, and to steal our spark is a sad loss. For in conforming, we become what conformists strive to be: Unnoticed. Part of the group. Completely the same as everyone else around us. And, dare I say it...*normal!*

There is nothing radiant about being normal. And that's the injustice of it. In striving to be normal, we deny ourselves the experience of shining like the stars we were made to be. Our own lights are dimmed, obscured amongst the sea of humanity. For where there is no light, there can only be darkness; and nothing beautiful can bloom in darkness.

So I say this to you: Make a choice right now, today, to step out of the darkness and into the light – after all, it is only a matter of choice, and you only get this one life to truly make a difference!

Invest the time into nurturing your own light – that tiny, sputtering spark deep within you. Ignite it. Fan it until it becomes a bushfire within your soul.

Do it by choosing to be different, by embracing the uniqueness that is you, and by surrounding yourself with loving people in order to keep your light from wavering.

Only then shall you be able to shine like a star!

Remember that you are never really alone. Have you noticed that not even a single star in the heavens shines all by itself? It always has other stars beside it, each unique, each individual, each beautiful; and together, they light up the night sky in the most spectacular way.

And while people *always* look up to admire the stars in the sky, not once have I heard anyone say that a star is "normal"!

Be the unique *you* that you were always destined to be. Forget about striving for normal. Strive to be luminous, dazzling, and radiant!

And above all: *SHINE*!

It's Not Too Late

by Shelley Lundquist

When I was nine, I already knew that I was going to be a writer and would travel the world helping people. I already fancied myself quite the wordsmith – scribbling poetry, conducting interviews, and journaling at every chance.

But the years slipped by, and it was time for me to "grow up" and be responsible. I avoided my writing for years thereafter because I could not bear the truth that emerged in its revelations – the truth that I wanted *more.*

After 20 years of being weighed down by the agony of unacknowledged passion, I'd finally had enough of the waiting. In the stillness, I could hear my soul's pleas for me to honour my heart's desire. Yet, even as I found the courage to begin to forge a new path, part of me feared that it was too late for me to follow my dreams and create a more joy-filled life. But the Universe, as it always does, provided me with exactly what I needed to realign my thoughts with purposeful direction.

The message I most needed to hear was divinely delivered to me through the wisdom of my six-year-old grandgirl, Emma. At the bottom of a drawing she made for me, she'd written, "It's not too late. It's never not time."

Tears of hope and joy streamed silently down my face upon reading those words. How could this be? I had never spoken to her of my fear. Yet here was my answer, laid bare for me to see. As the excitement that comes from opening to possibility washed over me in the miracle of that moment, I felt freer than I had in years.

Today, I am living my dreams, honouring who I am, allowing myself to be guided by the wisdom of my soul and the signs around me – always remembering that it's not too late and it's never not time. The time is always *now.*

Conclusion

You may have reached the end of the book, but you are just beginning a soulful journey of endless possibilities. You now have 365 tools that you can choose from at any given moment to support you in continuing to connect with your soul! We hope that you'll read this book over and over again – letting your soul guide the way to the perfect passage at the perfect moment. Let it become part of your spiritual practice and allow the miracles to flow!

One of our central messages in this book is that connecting with our soul can be fun and easy. We hope we've shown that it truly doesn't take much time at all to align with your higher self and with the Universe – sometimes just a simple shift in perspective, taking a deep breath in, petting your cat, or doing something creative is enough to raise your vibration. Your soul is just waiting for you to connect, and we promise that the more you connect with this wise part of you, the more your world will continue to open up in magical ways.

If you enjoyed this book, please be sure to share it with your friends and family! Helping someone connect with their soul is a beautiful gift! We would also be so grateful if you left a positive review for us on Amazon, which will help it reach even more people. And we would love for you to join us on our Facebook page, where you can share some of your favorite pieces, connect with the authors, and be part of our community: www.facebook.com/365waystoconnectwithyoursoul.

However you choose to connect with your soul moving forward, please honor yourself for living openly and soulfully – this is a brave path to take, and we're so grateful that we're on it together.

Hugs, love, and gratitude,
Jodi and Dan

Contributor Biographies

We're so excited to introduce you to each of the authors who contributed to this book. We came together, from all across the world, to show that connecting with our soul can be fun, easy, and life affirming!

Our souls know no boundaries. It doesn't matter how different our external circumstances are; in our hearts – where it truly matters – we are all the same. Collaborative books such as this really bring that point home. Bringing people together from all walks of life to share one central message is powerful and uplifting. It has the ability to change lives.

Some of the contributors are already accomplished authors with bestselling books, and others are sharing their words in print for the very first time – bravely leaping into their soul's calling with the hopes that you'll take their stories into your own heart.

We introduce each of the authors on the pages that follow, and we hope you enjoy meeting them and getting to know them! Please feel free to reach out to them individually and share how their piece helped you connect with your soul – they would love that!

About the Editors

Jodi Chapman and Dan Teck are a husband-and-wife team who loves living soulfully and joyfully. Since 2005, they've been living their dream of writing books and creating products that inspire others to connect with their soul and live fully and passionately.

Jodi has a BA in English/Technical Editing and Sociology, and Dan has a BA in Religious Studies and an MFA in Creative Writing. Together, they have over 30 years of experience with editing and publishing and have sold over 25,000 books. They have written 20 books, 10 ecourses, and over 1,000 blog posts/articles.

Jodi is the author of the award-winning blog, *Soul Speak*, and the creator of Soul Clarity Cards. Dan is the author of the personal-growth blog, *Halfway up the Mountain*. They are the co-creators of the *Soulful Journals Series*, the *365 Book Series*, and a number of soulful online communities.

They live in Oregon with their sweet cats. They enjoy hanging out at the beach and working, creating, and playing together.

They feel truly blessed to be able to spend each day together, doing what they love. And it's their heart's desire that their books and products bring joy to everyone they reach.

Learn more about Jodi here: www.jodichapman.com

Learn more about Dan here: www.halfwayupthemountain.com

Learn more about their *Soulful Journals* here: www.soulfuljournals.com

About the Contributors

Nikki Ackerman, RMT, is a holistic business owner and a Master in Usui/Tibetan Reiki, Karuna® Reiki, and Holy Fire® Reiki. Through her soulful practice, she desires to provide others with peace, balance, and wellness.

Ashton Aiden is a manifestation coach, brainwave-entrainment engineer, and an advocate of self-actualization. He created his website to educate the public about the powerful benefits of brainwave entrainment and to explore the far-reaching potential of the human mind. www.brainwavelove.com

Anne Aleckson is the "Soul Speaker" giving a voice to the power within. Creator of The One-Minute-Miracle emotional healing technique and the Higher Guidance weekly video message, she helps others find their purpose, create income, and awaken and activate the connection to their higher guidance. www.AnneAleckson.com

Aprile Alexander is an Australian artist, a creativity coach, and an intuitive energy healing practitioner. She helps people and animals clear energy blockages and move forward in life, to more easily express their God-given magnificence. She works with clients from any country in the world by phone. www.TimeForFlourishing.com

Karrol Rikka S. Altarejos is an intuitive empath coach, Reiki Master/teacher, and certified crystal/vibrational healer. She nurtures empaths to embrace, empower, and embody their gifts. www.karrolrikka.com

Christena Alyssandratos is a certified Master Empowerment Coach who is dedicated to empowering women to discover their authentic selves. She is on a mission to support and encourage women to create a radiant and joyful life by attaining their goals, releasing their fears, and stepping into their greatness.

Dana Ben-Yehuda, MAmSAT, a Certified Alexander Technique and Reconnective Healing practitioner in California, helps dancers and musicians release muscular tension for freer movement, better spinal alignment, and more expressive performance without pain. She helps computer users alleviate stress and pain. www.alexandertechniquestudio.org

Sarah Dennison Berkett is a certified spiritual teacher, Reiki Master, animal intuitive, reflexologist, author, crystal healer, and angelic life coach. www.beamerslight.com

Heather Bestel is a coach, mentor, and founder of The Happiness Garden online retreat. She loves supporting women in putting themselves first and offers a free *Magical Me-Time Starter Kit* here: www.heatherbestel.com.

Polina Blair holds a Masters in Health Care Administration. She is a wife and mother and works full time in the health-care field. She lives in the US, but is originally from eastern Europe. She is a passionate person who uses creativity every day to solve problems and bring more joy. She is also passionate about making jewelry and teaching workshops.

Cathie Bliss, MBA, cultivated a career in international business for two decades. When her daughter developed severe special needs in the 1990s, she reoriented to the healing arts, becoming a Certified LifeLine Practitioner and Intuitive Astrologer. Visit www.CathieBliss.com for her heart-centered offerings.

Heather Boon blends her intuition and soulfulness with her extensive business experience to provide the perfect mix of logical and intuitive guidance. She assists her clients in identifying the key piece that will be the catalyst to grow themselves and their business. www.heatherboon.com

Natasha Botkin is a master intuitive energy healer, writer, teacher, and modern-day Sacred Heart High Priestess. Using her multi-dimensional divine wisdom, she guides youth and adults by transforming heart and soul with passion, creative play, and healing energies through nature and all five elements. www.magicalblessingshealingcenter.com

Angela Boyle is originally from Australia and is currently living in Malaysia with her husband and young family. She is an author and social worker whose professional and personal life experience inspires a beautiful dance of words on a page. Her writing comes from the heart with the hope of touching something in yours. www.beingmebooks.com

Shannon Brokaw currently resides in Nevada with her two dogs. When she is not curled up with a book *du jour* or writing, she can be found on an airplane headed to an international destination or dreaming of it. She enjoys nice naps and a good dram of whisky.

Andrea Bryant is the creator of *Soulful Animal*, an inspirational website dedicated to helping animal lovers discover and embrace their life purpose. She offers a free *Life Purpose Workbook* to help heart-centered souls discover their calling. www.soulfulanimal.com/free-workbook

Lynnette Caldwell is a Law of Attraction life, business, and wealth practitioner. Prior to starting her business, she worked as the corporate communications and marketing director for a music-publishing company. One of her best assets is being "SOULution" oriented. She excels at helping others help themselves, and she loves creating win-win situations.

Christine Callahan-Oke is an empowerment coach, mom, inspirational writer, and positive thinker. Through coaching and writing, she offers practical tips and straightforward wisdom to help people achieve their potential, see the beauty in everyday moments, and live authentically. Download her free *5 Keys to Loving Life* guide here: www.YourInspiredLife.ca/free-guide.

Molly M. Cantrell-Kraig is a former single mother who established the Women With Drive Foundation to create a channel for elevating and empowering women and helping them chart a new course to prosperity. In building her nonprofit, she built herself.

Stacy Carr is a stay-at-home mom who has sought a more spiritual, soulful life since the birth of her first child in 2014. She enjoys reading and do-it-yourself projects, but most of all she enjoys her days at home with her son. She lives with her family in Indiana.

Cindia Carrere is an intuitive for entrepreneurs, specializing in energy alignment for total-life abundance. A certified life coach and award-winning author, she mentors clients to clear blocks in their energy and money grid to maximize their capacity for deserving and receiving wealth and happiness.

Anissa Centers is a multiple award-winning motivational speaker, trainer, and television news anchor with 20 years of communication expertise teaching women and men how to find their voice, speak their truth, and feel comfortable doing it. www.AnissaCenters.com

Alice Chan is a lifelong student of consciousness, passionately devoted to knowing her heart and returning to her true self before her personality took over and led her to believe that acceptance and love must be earned. She hopes to inspire others to know their hearts and true selves. www.dralicechan.com

Nita Chapman is a retired registered nurse who lives in the New Mexican mountains. She lives a life of peace, joy, and gratitude. She's a nurturer who lives for her children, her animals, and her dear friends – if anyone needs support, she is always there to help.

Cindie Chavez, "The Love & Magic Coach," is a certified life and relationship coach and an Energy Leadership Master Practitioner. She loves helping creative, busy women create more love and magic in their lives. www.cindiechavez.com

Laura P. Clark works with professionals using a unique blend of spiritual-awakening tools to help her clients hear their own inner wisdom more consistently, understand it with greater clarity, and act upon it more courageously to lead an inspired life filled with joy and abundance. www.soulwiseliving.com

Helen Clear is a healer, Reiki Master, and multidimensional transformational coach. She teaches Multidimensional Reiki at all levels and provides weekly meditation sessions. She assists in the transition from 3D to 5D – helping to access each person's unique multidimensional potential. She has a private practice in New Jersey. www.Healingin5D.com

Vanessa Codorniu is the founder of *Intuitive Leverage*™, an eight-week intuition boot camp that trains people to leverage their sensitivity in life and business! With more than 10,000 intuitive sessions and hundreds of students, Vanessa is an acclaimed psychic intuitive, clinical hypnotherapist, and international intuition trainer. www.vanessacodorniu.com

Rachel Cohen is an intuitive energy worker, self-compassion coach, multimedia artist, small business owner, and mother of two. Her three favorite words are sacred, sensual, and nurturing. She loves writing as a vehicle for exploring the depths of her inner worlds and chanting as a means for lounging luxuriously in them.

Marva Collins-Bush holds an MA in Psychology and a BA in Metaphysics. She is a Certified Metaphysical Practitioner, ordained metaphysical minister, Certified ARTbundance™ Coach, and author of three books: *Screams from the Heart of a Woman; My Daughter, My Mother, Myself;* and *Dances with Divinity*. www.earthmotherdivinesage.com

Keyra Conlinn is a coach, an educator, and an author who, through her company, Dare to Be Global, strives to motivate people to step out of their comfort zones, step beyond linguistic and cultural barriers, and step into new experiences and new lives by raising their personal and cultural awareness.

Stephanie Cornett is a transformational expert who helps individuals, brands, and organizations unlock and activate their unique gifts and become a force in the world through vision/mission discovery and strategy work. She is the creator of Be a Force Life and Business Consulting. www.stephaniecornett.com

Clarissa Coyoca, a former UCLA arts administrator, is currently earning her Master's in Spiritual Psychology. She believes love is the solution for life's challenges and applies that philosophy in facilitating support groups for divorcing women and in her one-on-one work supporting individuals on their own journeys into their hearts and souls.

Jasmine Sreenika Crystalsinger is the CEO of Artangelis Inc. and founder of Video Goddess Academy. As an actor and director, she helps high-achieving female entrepreneurs ignite their intuition, share their sacred message, and transform self-doubt into six-figure celebrity success. www.videogoddessacademy.com

Jan Deelstra is a coach and award-winning author who has been leading the charge for empowering women since 1984. Merging spirituality with psychology, she utilizes her background in social services, experiences with "miraculous forces," her intuitive gifts, and her passion for writing to inspire women to emerge into their fullest potential.

Reverend Scott M. Dehn has 18 years of experience in metaphysics. He has been teaching Reiki, coaching spiritual values, and is currently using his ministry to share New Thought. He has formal training in Science of Mind, professional photography, and a BS in Holistic Nutrition.

Jimena DeLima is an Usui Reiki Master/teacher, and a certified angel/oracle card reader. She is an avid lover of the healing arts and divides her time between Australia and the United States, where she uses her expertise and gifts to empower and support souls through their healing journey. www.palihealingarts.com

Manpreet Dhillon has an MA in Organizational Management and is a success coach, certified personal and business coach, and co-founder of Be Your Own Best Friend (a South Asian Women's network). She empowers women to reclaim their purpose/passion and move to the next level of their personal and professional lives.

Linda J. Dieffenbach, BSW, is a holistic healer and coach with over 10 years of experience. She works with individuals, couples, and groups, helping her clients to reduce stress and anxiety, overcome barriers and challenges, and heal their relationships. She also provides healing services for animals. www.wellnessinharmony.com

Jody Rentner Doty is a writer, minister, healer, seer, and a bit of a mystic. Her words are inspired through meditation on the divine belief that every moment guides our journey. She lives in the Pacific Northwest. www.jodydoty.com

Gretchen Duhaime mentors high-achieving, creative, professional women to achieve their next level of success.

Jerri Eddington, EdD, is the creator of Energy Connections and the co-creator of Lighten Up and Thrive, which is a sacred vision of sharing our expertise and wisdom as transformational life coaches. She facilitates powerful, transformative programs that help others experience joyful living for mind, body, and soul.

Tandy R. Elisala, CPSC, ACH, CHt, is a #1 international bestselling author and coach. She helps stressed women conquer overwhelm so they can live with passion, grace, and ease. She is passionate about helping women recognize their power within to be, do, and have anything they want. www.tandyelisala.com

Gabriele Engstrom's love for holistic health, science, and spirituality has made her a unique healer and energy worker. She supports people who forever search for equilibrium on a physical, emotional, and spiritual level. www.gabrieleengstrom.com.au

Lori Evans is an educational health expert and holds a BA in Education in the fields of English and Health. For nearly 10 years, she has worked as a Premier Private Pilates Coach teaching people not just about Pilates but inspiring them to tune in to their bodies. www.lorievans.biz

Nancy Ferrari is passionate about her professional duality as a media personality and as a Soul Destiny© guide and mentor. Nancy is the producer and host of *The Nancy Ferrari Show* and co-host of *Connecting People, Changing Lives*, a web/TV talk show, both within the Spark It Network.

Kimberly Brazier Flatland is the creator of Soulfirmations – Affirmations for Your Soul and Love Your SoulSelf. As a writer and speaker, she is passionate about creating a soulful movement by teaching others how to embrace their true spirit.www.loveyoursoulself.com

Arielle Ford is a gifted writer and the author of 10 books including *Wabi Sabi Love* and the international bestseller, *The Soulmate Secret.* She has been called "The Cupid of Consciousness" and "The Fairy Godmother of Love." She lives in California with her husband/soulmate, Brian Hilliard, and their feline friends. www.soulmatesecret.com

Tree Franklyn is an author and creator of the popular, whimsical TreeDoodle art, starring unapologetic and incessantly happy "Stick Girl." She helps soul-centered, empathic women understand their sensitivity and manage their emotions so they can reconnect with their authentic selves and channel their sensitive energies for positive outcomes.

Robin Friedman is a life coach and certified EFT practitioner and hypnotherapist. She leads groups and classes, sharing self-empowering tools. She loves helping people change their energy, which transforms their outer life naturally. She created the popular tapping home-study program, TAP Your Way to Transformation. www.EnergyToolsForDailyLiving.com

Amy Gage is a writer and poet who is passionate about authentic creative expression and inspiring others to feel more love, openness, empowerment, magic, and beauty in their lives. She has healed from deep depression and insecurity, and she shares her journey to joy and creative expression at www.moondancemuse.com.

Karen Gibbs lives in Queensland, Australia, and enjoys motivating and inspiring others through her writings, blog posts, and Facebook coaching. Her first book was published in 2002 when she also won the Excellence in Business Award. Her inspiration comes from lessons learned while spending time with her horses. www.KarenGibbs.com.au

Sandy Jabo Gougis is a Zen Buddhist Priest, Reiki Master, and life coach. She lives with her husband and a pack of rescued animals. Bringing the creed "How may I help you?" to all of her endeavors, she is offering a free sample coaching session here: www.cancercarecoaching.com.

Michelle Anne Gould is a soulpreneur, mother, founder of Abundant Spirit Education, and creator of SoulMagic™. She supports people who are committed to enhancing their lives through personal transformation, unlocking and activating abundance from within. She awakens people to their unique, infinite magic. www.abundantspiritedu.com

Leah Grant has been transforming lives as an ICF Master Certified Coach since 1997. She is certified in NLP and emotional intelligence. She is the creator of Ecstatic Meditation and part of the team developing Delphi Village – a transformational entertainment complex outside Las Vegas. She is a multi-published personal-growth author.

Deena Gray-Henry is a certified SimplyHealed™ practitioner, a gift healer, and a life coach who intuitively and quickly helps release blocked energy and increase high energy, peace, love, freedom, and abundance. People, animals, homes and businesses have experienced lasting results and success. www.DeenaGH.com

Stacey Hall, LSH, CNTC, CAC, CRTS, is a spiritual healer, success coach, speaker, author of the bestselling *Chi-To-Be! Achieving Your Ultimate B-All,* and co-author of *Attracting Perfect Customers…The Power of Strategic Synchronicity.* Access her *Attraction Tips* to attract the aCHIevement of goals with ease for free at www.chi-to-be.com.

Mariët Hammann is the creator of *Living Life in Full Colour.* She's an art-based functional therapist, coach, MARI Practitioner, Food & Spirit Practitioner, JourneyCircle Facilitator, Right Brain Business Plan Facilitator, biblical counselor, SoulStory connector, joy jumper, motivational mover, colorful soul, creative genie, dream duster, and eternal optimist. www.soulcolourstudio.com

Elizabeth Harper is an internationally acclaimed artist, color seer, and author. Her work has been featured in popular magazines including *Woman's World*, *Redbook*, and *Health.* She is a magazine columnist, regular contributor to Australian radio, award-winning author of *Wishing: How to Fulfill Your Heart's Desires*, and co-author of *365 Days of Angel Prayers.*

Annalene Hart is a creative soul and life coach, poet, and visionary artist who creates soul paintings. She inspires her clients to pursue and realize their dreams. She conducts individualized Magical Child sessions to help activate the participant's innate creativity and imagination. www.mydivineenchantedlife.wordpress.com

Ellouise Heather is a wellbeing coach and creative writer. She is passionately committed to helping women who are suffering and recovering from illness find joyfully inspired new meaning in life. For helpful tips and insights, be sure to visit her blog: www.ellouiseheather.com.

Barb Heite has an MA in Human Dynamics, is a certified vulnerability coach, and is the author of *Beautiful Mess...A Journey to the Universe Within*. She writes, speaks, and coaches with a unique approach to healing through nurturing therapy, which explores alternative natural approaches to healing the mind, body, and spirit.

Kristen A. Hemming is a Wiccan Clergy running Green Tree Temple in British Columbia. She is a clinical hypnotherapist, Reiki practitioner, and intuitive specializing in helping others lose weight and overcome their fears and phobias. www.kahemming.com

Nukhet Hendricks is a coach, truth seeker, spiritual rebel, intuitive, land-locked ocean lover, and beach-bum wannabe. She considers herself a bridge to the Divine for her clients and connects them to the Divine and their inner knowing. She offers a free ebook here: www.nukhets.com/thelittlebigbookofmagic.html.

Karen Hicks lives in Ontario, Canada, with her partner, daughters, and dog. She is passionate about people discovering their brilliance and assists this journey through her coaching practice. She practices hypnosis, EFT, and NLP, and might even have a soft spot for Crossfit!

Ayesha Hilton is a bestselling author, speaker, and business strategist. She is passionate about living an inspired life and inspiring others to do the same. She is the founder of the Inspired Life Club where she helps others live an inspirational life full of creativity and joy.

Bonnie S. Hirst enjoys stories with happy endings and spending time with family and friends. When life tries to shorten her stride, she prays, consults with her guardian angels, reads self-help books, and writes. She can often be found in her kayak on a peaceful mountain lake. www.Icantquotescripture.com

Dortha Hise is the "Chief Overwhelm Eliminator" at Pretty Smart Virtual Services, a full-service virtual assistant company whose purpose is to rescue their entrepreneur clients out of overwhelm. She created a free *Reignite Your Joy Guided Journaling Promptings* ebook to support others in their grief: www.prettysmartvaservices.com/promptings.

Cindy Harpe Hively is a transformational intuitive and a healing catalyst for women. She's the "Goddess Creatrix" for *In Her Fullness*, an Awakened Living mentor, columnist, and published author. She empowers spiritual women and teaches them how to create an abundant life that they love by strategizing and optimizing each key area of their life.

Sharyn Holmes is an Australian multi-passionate intuitive artist, jeweler, writer, healer, women's mentor, and creatrix of *Gutsy Girl*. With creative fire and gutsy energy to boot, she leads empowering and transformative personal-development and creativity workshops and ecourses to help others manifest the life of their dreams.

Cindy Holtfreter, CPCC, SEP, is a soulful living and leadership coach and the founder of *Body & Soul Leadership*. With 20 years' experience as a leadership coach and 10 years in corporate executive leadership, she is living her purpose and passion by incorporating transformation, leadership, and healing into her practice. www.BodyAndSoulLeadership.com

Daria Howell, LMT, is a health and wellness expert who specializes in helping people discover their own ageless beauty and wellbeing. A craniosacral therapist and lover of dancing, cooking wonderful food, and musing on spiritual topics, she lives with her husband in Oregon. www.DariaHowell.com

Alicia Isaacs Howes, founder of *Your Soul Story* and international *Soul Connection*™ expert, specializes in guiding others to align more fully with their brilliance using her *Purpose, Passion & Prosperity*™ system. She helps people love their life and allow it to love them right back. www.yoursoulstory.com

Allanah Hunt is an author and teacher working with women to build self-awareness, self-confidence, and a sense of identity, and to create lives of freedom. Her book *Beyond the Pain: Living with Power & Freedom after Separation & Divorce* is a comprehensive guide to reclaiming personal power after loss.

Susan Huntz-Ramos is a certified life coach, holistic wellness coach, and Reiki practitioner. With guidance from Spirit and the angels, her passion is teaching individuals how to tap into their own inner wisdom, inspiring a healthy balance to their mind, body, and life. www.susanhuntzramos.com

Lisa Hutchison understands the challenges of maintaining a connection within and to the Divine in an overwhelming world. She empowers empathic helpers and artists to find balance in life through stress management. She is a free-spirited, passionate, licensed psychotherapist, teacher, and published writer in *Chicken Soup for the Soul*.

Lacey Dawn Jackson is an author, internationally-known psychic, and speaker. She has been called the "Abundance Babe" because of the impact she has in helping others obtain their dreams and manifest their heart's desires. Find her latest book, *7 Steps to Finding Your Authentic Self* at www.GroovyGreenGoddess.com.

Murray James, RN, is a Life in Balance coach and an energy intuitive, assisting people to find harmony and peace in their lives. Mindfulness is at the heart of his work. He offers harmony coaching sessions and energy clearing sessions by phone to people anywhere. www.murrayjamescoaching.com

RoseAnn Janzen is an author, truth seeker, authenticity advisor, and Akashic guide who helps intuitive entrepreneurs and creatives embody their divine self so that they are operating from their highest place of power, peace, and impact in their life and work. For a free *Spirit Assessment*, please visit: www.revealyourlife.com/spirit-assessment.html.

Jack V. Johnson is a natural-born mystic and lifelong spiritual seeker. Over the years, his personal path has led him to meditation, Reiki, shamanism, qigong, and other practices. He enjoys sharing his experiences and insights and helping like-minded seekers on their own paths. www.soulfulpath.com

Tia Johnson is an intuitive healer, speaker, author, University of Pennsylvania graduate student, and a *Huffington Post* blog contributor. She created her spiritually based business in 2010 after a two-year healing period she underwent following the deaths of her grandparents. She was a speaker at MindBodySpirit Expo™ and the DivaGirl® Conference.

Julie Jones is a nurse, researcher, aromatherapist, energy practitioner, health and wellness coach, inspirational speaker, and author. Her supportive coaching with small steps inspires and empowers people to move from sick care to health care – restoring balance for wellness. www.restoretobalance.com

Nancy Merrill Justice is an author and intuitive business mentor for entrepreneurs. She draws on her 25 years of successful entrepreneurship to help her clients master "mindset of success" techniques applicable to any business, so they can achieve their dreams and succeed at their highest potential in their business and personal lives.

Gina Karas is a full-time sales assistant in the construction industry. She's an avid scrapbooker, blogger, art journaler, and aspiring author who loves photography, reading, and traveling. She loves living on the California coast and spending time near the ocean. www.californiascrappin.com

Sue Kearney is "Chief Inspiration Officer" at Magnolias West, a coaching and branding spiritual business. Part technology and neuroscience geek, part partially tamed hippie, she is passionate about and dedicated to helping women with heart and soul rock their businesses and share their awesome with the world!

Jenna Kelland, PhD, is a Certified Holistic Nutritionist™ and owner of Spark Wellness. She offers nutrition education to moms, helping them to have balanced, energized lives. A self-employed mom of three, she involves her children in growing and preparing food so they can appreciate the physical and emotional nourishment it provides.

James Kelly created the *Miracle Choice® Board Game*. Since its rapid spread to different countries and requests for more material, he developed the Certified Facilitator Game Training and other online material about the power of inner choice. He lives with his family and two cats in Scotland. www.miraclechoicegame.com

Sallie Keys is an Akashic energy healer who uses a combination of energetic and spiritual healing modalities to assist her clients in manifesting the level of abundance they desire in their lives. She does this by clearing away what is blocking them from experiencing who they truly are, which enables them to express that to the world.

Rachel Kieffer is a certified holistic nutrition and health coach. For over 30 years, she has worked with thousands of women on transforming their relationship with food and their bodies and creating radiant health through consultations, online programs, and writing. Visit www.Healthnutgirl.com to sign up for her inspiring newsletter.

Christine King's soul journey began in 1979 with the death of her husband, after which she received a powerful spiritual message that her life purpose was to assist others on the spiritual path. She has 35 years' experience as a metaphysical teacher and soul guidance practitioner helping people live their purpose.

Elizabeth Kipp, founder of Elizabeth Kipp Media, LLC, is a health facilitator and empowerment coach who helps people grasp the power of their own healing. She helps people resolve conflict and generate communication skills so they can tap into their own healing ability and build effective health-care teams. www.elizabeth-kipp.com

Sharon Kistler is an author, speaker, and life coach with international accreditation. She inspires people to awaken to their greatness so they can live a life of purpose and success. She created the Your New Life Journey program and founded The Amazing Woman Organization and The Success Network. www.sharonkistler.com

Chrystal Kubis is a life-navigation specialist, passion igniter, and master empowerment coach. Utilizing her wide toolbox of modalities gathered over 18 years of training and experience, she serves as a powerful facilitator of freedom and has led trainings on personal transformation and empowerment across the country. www.chrystalkubis.com

Cindy Jones Lantier is a certified professional coach, tapping practitioner, spiritual mentor, and an ordained minister. Knowing there are as many paths up the spiritual mountain as there are people wanting to scale it, she works with women who are trying to carve out that path for themselves. www.cindyjoneslantier.com

Jennifer "Elemental" Larkin leads a global initiative to empower and inspire people into greater freedom and conscious choice. Join her worldwide movement and receive access to a massive vault of content celebrating the power of coaching, training, and mentoring. Join her growing tribe of powerful beings here: www.mentoringvault.com.

Destrie Sweet Larrabee lives in Ohio with her wonderful family and beautiful cats. She enjoys life, Lake Erie, and learning along the way.

Janice Lawrenz is a life enhancer and an empowerment catalyst for mamas. Her inspiring, passionate mission is to help mothers awaken their feminine identity, unlocking blockages so they can live their true purpose and authentically go beyond "just being a mom." www.AwakenYourTruePurpose.com

Gayla Lemley is a licensed therapist with Turning Points Therapy & Holistic Wellness. She is experienced in traditional and holistic methods to bring balance, which empowers and helps people live their soul life to its fullest and realize their dreams and potential. www.tptholisticwellnesspartners.net

Nicole Levac is a writer, transformation guide, wife, and mother. She helps women heal their relationship with themselves so that they can be present as themselves in the different facets of their lives, which empowers them to give more freely of themselves as they experience their life. www.nicolelevac.com

Tanya Levy is a counselor in a community college and an inspirational photographer. She has worked in the human-services field for 25 years. She is a strong and passionate advocate for the healing power of each individual's own learning journey. www.facebook.com/heartladyinspiration

Joanna Lindenbaum has supported thousands of women in creating lives and businesses that are fully aligned with their soul. She is the creator of the Your Sacred Business program where she helps entrepreneurs build their income while learning to love themselves deeply. www.soulfulcoach.com

Courtney Long, MSW, LC, CHt, ATP®, is an angel communicator, life-purpose intuitive, psychic medium, author, and speaker. She inspires adults, teens, and kids to joyfully activate the angels' assistance, open their intuition, and discover their purpose and gifts. www.CourtneyLongAngels.com

Fiona Louise is an author, intuitive, and natural therapist who provides motivational and entertaining firsthand insight into emotional and spiritual healing. She offers inspirational healing retreats and workshops. She is a co-author in the bestselling *Creative Thoughts Journal* and a forthcoming book on intuition. www.fiona-louise.com

Shelley Lundquist is an international bestselling author, motivational speaker, and self-mastery and success coach who uses her intuitive gifts and transformational breakthrough processes to guide men and women in creating their best life – a peaceful, harmonious life of joy and abundance that acknowledges body, mind, and spirit. www.letmemoveyou.me

Arwen Lynch-Poe, Professional Joy Seeker, is known for her ability to guide others to their own joy using humor, compassion, and tarot as tools. With over 10 novels, she loves to help writers finish their own books. She lives in New Mexico. www.tarotbyarwen.com

Tae Lynne is a former type-A driven career woman turned writer and blogger. Forced to slow down by chronic illness, she discovered her true purpose as the "Kindness Junkie." Join her on her mission to stop hatred, fighting, and bullying and help change the world at www.60secondstokindness.com.

Puja Madan is a women's life coach, speaker, and author. She contributes regularly to the *Huffington Post*, *MindBodyGreen*, and *Elephant Journal*. She offers meditations, live events, and coaching programs to hundreds of spiritual entrepreneurial women on a mission. www.pujamadan.com

Kylie Mansfield lives in South Australia and comes from a family of avid storytellers and book lovers. For as long as she can remember, she has amused, soothed, and entranced herself with stories. She is currently studying an Advanced Diploma of Professional Writing at the Adelaide College of the Arts.

Sheelagh Maria has been working closely with Spirit as a clairvoyant channel for nine years, ever since Archangel Michael saved her son from death. She offers advice to business owners and intuition to lightworkers. Receive clearings on business, abilities, and abundance here: www.sheelaghmaria.com.

Lori Kilgour Martin is an angelic counselor and musical theatre artist from Canada. She is a co-author of the book *365 Days of Angel Prayers* and is grateful to be included in this caring circle of lightworkers while working in partnership through service with the Divine Realm. www.diamondheartangel.com

Veronica Mather is a writer and keen photographer. She is passionate about animal welfare and shares her life with her husband, Dale, five rescued sheep, and two high-spirited dogs, Max and Blaze.

Peggy McColl (aka "The Bestseller Maker") is a *New York Times* bestselling author and an internationally recognized expert in helping authors, entrepreneurs, and specialists understand the Law of Attraction, create valuable products, build their brand worldwide, make money online, and create international bestsellers. www.peggymccoll.com

Carolyn McGee empowers women to walk with spirit to enhance and embrace divine guidance in soul and body. She is passionate about helping others release blocks, trust their intuition, and turn on the river of abundance so their life flows with ease and grace. www.carolynmcgee.com

Kat Ellis McIntyre is a shamanic astrologer, writer, and teacher based in Sydney, Australia. She is the founder of The Soul's Journey, a healing space dedicated to supporting individuals through deep transformation. She guides people on their sacred journey of coming home to themselves. www.facebook.com/thesoulsjourneys

Jenny McKaig is CEO, writer, and coach at www.JennyMcKaig.com; international bestselling author and senior editor for *Empowering Women to Succeed*; certified awakening coach; and award-winning writer who empowers people with transformational stories to elevate success. In addition to language, she loves surfing and ultimate Frisbee.

Pam McKinney is a Certified Crystal Healer trained by the Hibiscus Moon Crystal Academy. She is a certified Soul Journeys® Akashic Records consultant, a certified Usui Reiki practitioner, and a certified Soul Journeys® Heal Your Money Story coach. www.connecttoyourlight.com

Josh Medici is an aspiring writer and soul searcher who's on a quest to find grace through gratitude. Sadness and pain are no longer his enemies. He now sees them as much a part of his journey as the happiest days. When he is not managing his marketing business, he is writing about the things that inspire him.

Sonia Miller, BA, MSW, is the bestselling author of *The Attraction Distraction: Why the Law of Attraction Isn't Working for You and How to Get Results – Finally!*, which reaches international audiences with translations available in five countries. She draws upon 25 years as a speaker and coach to illuminate people's blind spots and expose their untapped power.

Colleen E. Millett is an enthusiastic entrepreneur who loves helping others use challenges as opportunities for growth. Through her coaching at Brite Life Transformations, she inspires women to bring their highest self forward by stepping out of the shadows and into their light!

Patricia Missakian is the founder of the Akashic Records Institute, a school for spiritual development and growth. Patricia guides her students to break free of any limiting beliefs to achieve full potential. She believes that together we can elevate the vibrations of the Earth and play our part in its transformation.

Rev. Kathryn Morrow is an author, educator, nutritional and spiritual counselor, EFT and intuitive coach, and relationship expert. She has an MS in Holistic Nutrition and a PhD in Theology. She facilitates healing and manifesting from a heart-centered connection, empowering others to live the life of their dreams full of passion and purpose.

Susan Mullen is a gifted intuitive and leading expert on intuitive living. She is a certified intuitive coach and founder of the Pilot Light Intuitive Sessions, where she lovingly guides clients to their next right step. She is a frequent radio guest, blogger, and animal advocate. www.SusanTMullen.com

Dedra Murchison is a writer, artist, and money-mentor coach who wants to teach the people of the world to sing in perfect harmony with their souls. In her free time, she writes, sings, dances, and creates from her heart. www.rm2cg.com

Heather A. Nardi is a healer, a flower and gemstone essence practitioner, and a holistic coach. After discovering holistic modalities to help her child, her soul's work is to help families who are struggling with mental-health disorders work through the pain using these remedies as well.

Hue Anh Nguyen is an intuitive coach in the field of energy medicine. With 20 years of energetic experience, her unique gifts and intuition enhance and empower others to improve their quality of life as it did in her own healing of Fibromyalgia and her marriage. www.Polarity4Harmony.com

Peggy Nolan is an international bestselling author, blogger, podcaster, sometimes poet, yoga teacher, and third-degree black belt who is always stubbornly optimistic. She loves to help others vanquish fear, slay doubt, let go, and move forward. She lives in New Hampshire with her husband, Richard.

Cathleen O'Connor, PhD, is a metaphysical teacher, bestselling author, speaker, and intuitive coach who loves helping people harness the power of the mind and heart to co-create miracles in all areas of life. She blogs about career and wealth for Numerologist.com and offers women's retreats through Spiritual Living. www.cathleenoconnor.com

Debra Oakland is the founder of *Living in Courage,* a spiritual oasis for overcoming life's biggest challenges. As a courage advocate, her story has been featured in major media outlets including online, TV, radio, magazines, and bestselling books. She is eagerly anticipating the release of her own book in 2016.

Nadean Ollech is a walker, writer, and a spiritual life coach at Healed Daisy Intuitive Guidance. She has a degree in Religion. She coaches clients through their life journey, focusing on oracle cards, psychometry, and energy readings. Her goal is to help woman connect to themselves and live their best lives.

Diana Onuma is a family mediator, coach, and Reiki practitioner who is passionate about empowering people to be their best selves by shining brightly, celebrating their authentic power, and living fearlessly. She's offering a free 30-minute Boldness Breakthrough session here: www.circleofgrowth.co.uk.

Bree Orata is curious by nature and is inspired by miracles, art, and simplicity. She is out to create an orgasmic life. A lover of all things beautiful, her mantra is to appreciate the pleasures that are present in the everyday. www.thebreespot.com

Carol Owens lives her life in a heart-centered connection with other mindful souls. She spends her days playing with her grandkids and her dogs, hanging with her husband, writing books and blogs, and connecting and assisting others to follow their soul's passion. www.carolowens.com

Karen Packwood is a clairvoyant, healer, and #1 bestselling author who loves to work with people who have suffered extreme trauma in life. Her mission is to prove that it is possible to come back to a place of joy no matter how broken someone may have been. karenpackwood@gmail.com

Karen Marie Palmer is a success/mindful coach, Kundalini yoga instructor, conscious dog trainer, and non-profit business leader who teaches simple strategies so anyone can live their dream life. She is working to bring environmental education, animal advocacy, and kindness to public schools. www.itsalldivine.org

Lisa Anna Palmer launched her business as a career and leadership coach and Certified Passion Test® Facilitator in 2011 and has helped hundreds of people gain greater clarity about what is most important and leap out of their comfort zone.

Skywalker Payne is a published writer who has shared the world of stories in cities and towns across the United States. Now living in Alaska, she blogs and produces books and videos. Her works envision a world of compassion, courage, and peace. http://skywalkerstorytellerworks.com

Tanya Penny, Abundance Catalyst and Freedom Coach, teaches and supports healers, coaches, and women-on-purpose to break through fear and self-doubt, and heal illness and trauma so they can step into self-confidence and create a healthy body and a balanced lifestyle filled with passion and purpose. www.tanyapenny.com

Yvonne Peraza is an angelic gypsy whose free spirit and unconditional love touches all who come in contact with her. She spends her days learning and expressing herself through creativity. She shares her life with her husband, children, and pets. www.yvonneperaza.com

Debbie Perret is a physiotherapist and wellness advocate with an emphasis on healing chronic pain and depression. Her research examines multiple diverse paths to personal and planetary health, which she believes are inextricably entwined. Find out which rabbit holes she is currently exploring at www.DebbiePerret.com.

Kathy Perry is known for "Taking the Eek! Out of Geek" and is a social-media and energy-empowerment coach. She is a BrainTrust member on Small Business Advocate Radio. She is a professional speaker and co-author in *Stepping Stones to Success* with Deepak Chopra and Jack Canfield. www.kathyperry.com

Ashley Pierson is a writer and founder of the *Better Eating Project.* She delights in creating new recipes to inspire others to find joy in cooking. Ashley has a BS in Nutrition from Michigan State University. www.bettereatingproject.com

Katie Power is a spiritual messenger and intuitive healer who enjoys channeling spirit and helping others to connect with the wisdom of their soul. She has a BS in Nutrition and a passion for living a healthy, balanced life. She's happily married with two beautiful boys, Grant and Warren. www.KatiePower.com

Annie Price is a spiritual healer who uses heartfelt, intuitive guidance to empower others in their divine purpose and in living the joyful expression of their soul. Her Fearless, Fun & Free™ program assists in permanent weight release. She has a BA in Psychology and loves being Mom to three teenagers. www.SoulSoaring.com

Donna S. Priesmeyer is a media professional who promotes artists, authors, musicians, healers, and spiritual teachers in creative pursuits. She enjoys connecting to Spirit through nature; gardening; traveling; reading; writing; art; playing with her furry children; and spending time with her husband, family, and friends. www.PriesmeyerMusicMedia.com

Laura Probert, MPT, is an expert physical therapist, healer, and teacher. Her blogs, online challenges, and classes redefine healing and help others be brave. She gets illegal amounts of happiness from cheese, dark chocolate, and writing stuff that inspires people to take action toward their dreams. www.LauraProbert.com

Mimi Quick is known as the "Prosperity Muse." She is a psychic business mentor and owner of the Spiritual Business Institute – a spiritual coaching and training company that empowers spirited entrepreneurs to create prosperous, aligned businesses and lives doing what they love. www.MimiQuick.com

Radavie is an emotional-wellbeing healer and shaman. She is recognized for her specialty in resolving inner-child wounds that secretly block the flow of success. Since 1981, she has followed her soul's calling by assisting her global cliental, specializing in healers, therapists, entrepreneurs, and those in service to others.

Michelle Radomski is a mandala artist, graphic/book designer, and author. For 35 years, she's created customized, colorful, and inspiring designs for purpose-driven individuals and organizations. She helps her clients become more visible, remember and connect to the power of their voices, and make a more meaningful impact in the world.

Akasha Rainbow is yet another beautiful incarnation of the Great Divine. Through her writing, she seeks to call all of us into a visceral knowing of ourselves as an indestructible soul expressed perfectly in the here and now so that a new world future of peace, harmony, and super-human potential may be born. www.awakentheflame.com

Helen Rebello is a transformational therapist, teacher, and peaceful pathfinder – guiding female service professionals back to their hearts to uncover their unique, tranquil pathway and travel from over-stretched surviving to thoroughly-thankful thriving. She is currently creating an online oasis of calm at www.thetranquilpath.co.uk.

Gia Reed is a registered healer, certified energetic life coach, Reiki Master, mentor, author, blogger, and speaker dedicated to healing and awakening. She assists clients across the globe in connecting to their soul through distant healing. She is the author of *The 7 Day Life Transformation*. www.TheNewEssenceofHealing.com

Brenda Reiss loves coaching women who want to move from living a life in recovery to the passionate possibility life is meant to be, using her wisdom and certifications as a Radical Forgiveness® coach, Soul Journeys® Akashic Record consultant, and Heal Your Money Story coach. www.Besoulstrong.com

Ramona Remesat is a spiritual life coach, Angel Therapy Practitioner®, speaker, and co-author of the Amazon bestseller *365 Days of Angel Prayers*. She helps open-minded coaches, consultants, and entrepreneurs who struggle with limiting mind-stories crush their fears and doubts and align with their purpose. www.ramonaremesat.com

Ronda Renee is the creator of the Divine Coordinates® process, Your Divine Navigation System®, and The Business in Your Soul®. She is committed to helping others live and work from their soul and gain clarity, purpose, and direction for their life and business. www.DivineNavigation.com

Rev. Aliza Bloom Robinson is a master spiritual facilitator, speaker, author, ordained Unity Minister, and founder of www.Divine-Awakening.org. She has walked a Spirit-led life through both the valleys and peaks of experience. She facilitates the discovery of peace, purpose, passion, and fulfillment in living a dream-filled life.

Jane Duncan Rogers is an award-winning coach, author, and speaker. She works with spiritually inclined women who are challenged by loss of any kind and are ready to awaken to the gift in their situation so they can embrace life fully and make the contribution they were born to make. www.wildwisdom.co.uk

Helen Jane Rose is the author of *Wake Up: Spiritual Enlightenment Uncloaked* and *To Fear, With Love*. She is a soul-conscious coach, meditative/automatic writing mentor, and Master Reiki Healer. For more information, advice, and to get free chapters from her book, please visit her blog and website: www.soulconsciousbeing.com.

Sharon Rosen is a writer, healer, teacher, and guide for women hungry to find their balance within life's chaos. She's especially passionate about helping those who've experienced a life-altering diagnosis or loss to reclaim their footing and live with presence, hope, and grace. www.heartofselfcare.com

Sharon Rothstein is a long-standing student of spirit and a teacher of many. She is a Feng Shui practitioner in the school of Black Sect Tantric Buddhism and studied under Professor Thomas Lin Yun. She is grateful for this opportunity to be showcased in her first published collaboration.

Barbara Royal is a Master Prayer Practitioner, Interfaith Certified Spiritual Director, Certified Angel Therapy Practitioner®, soul lesson card reader, and the founder of Bio Spiritual Transformation – a method that invokes the Power of I AM to create health and wellbeing in one's life. Email her at miraclesofwellness@gmail.com for appointments.

Katja Rusanen is a spiritual life coach, Soul Plan Reader, inspirational speaker, and author. Her transformational and practical spiritual life coaching helps people develop their intuition and use the superpower within to navigate their lives with ease and make fulfilling decisions. www.katjarusanen.com

Maria Angela Russo's passion is to inspire others to awaken to their own divine essence. She is an existential psychotherapist and LCSW; a trained SoulCollage® facilitator; and has recently published her spiritual memoir, *The Growing Soul*, and contributed chapters to two other books. www.TheGrowingSoul.com

Cynthia L. Ryals is a writer, coach, speaker, and spiritual messenger gifted in guiding others in rediscovering their highest self and life's purpose. She believes that reconnecting to our soul is key to consciously creating a life that feels good; honors our truth; and, ultimately, heals the world. www.myevolvedlife.com

Jenni Ryan is a mother of two boys and a leadership mentor in network marketing. She has spent the last 10 years working on personal growth. www.JenniRyan.com

Milada Sakic is a transformational teacher, intuitive healer, and astrologer. She helps highly conscious entrepreneurs fully align with their purpose and clear their money blocks. Receive her complimentary three-part Soul Evolution Kit here: www.energyhealingimmersion.com/soul-evolution-kit.html.

Qatana Samanen, PhD, has helped people connect with their soul through their chakra guides for over 30 years. She remains in awe of the brilliance, wisdom, and power these guides bring to helping people create lives of greater peace, joy, and love.

Marcia Sandels is a former public-school teacher. Her interests include spiritual and inspirational writing, and she is the author of the book *Living Beyond the Veil: How My Mystical Incidences May Help You and/or Your Rainbow or Crystal Children.* She is also a world traveler and fine-arts enthusiast. Find her on Facebook at "Marcia Sandels, Writer."

Nishaan Sandhu brings people and plants together to inspire body wisdom, vitality, and natural health. Through her unique integration of clinical herbalism, holistic aromatherapy, and dynamic-eating psychology coaching, she assists individuals who seek lasting relief from chronic pain, anxiety, weight challenges, digestive distress, fatigue, and mood imbalances.

Melissa Sarazin is the caretaker of A Sacred Vision Life, a unique system that focuses on partnering with the sacred women archetype to help us remember, reconnect, and realign with our personal power to activate the leader from within. www.sacredvisionlife.com

Barbara Schiffman is a Life&Soul Balance Coach, Akashic Records advanced teacher, and clinical hypnotherapist. She blends scientific concepts and intuitive principles into life improvement tools at www.YourLifeandSoul.com. Her books, *The Akashic Muse* and *Living in Balance for Boomers*, and DailyOM e-courses help people create balance, peace, and joy.

Kristin Schmidt is a wife, mother, author, speaker, women's mentor, global community thought leader, and tech-savvy entrepreneur with middle-American core beliefs. She inspires and motivates women around the world not only to live their lives authentically but to live pretty lives while being their true selves. www.createaprettylife.com

Isla Selupucin is a mindful mother and intuitive empath. She is the creator of www.littlebeeandbutterfly.com, a website that journals her spiritual stories and connections. She lives in Turkey with the loves of her life: her daughter, Ceyda, and husband, Koray.

Laurie Seymour, MA, a provocative speaker, author, and master facilitator, knows that life's deepest answers shine when we connect with our inner resources. Her research proved that unlocking potential brings enduring transformation, so she left her career as a psychotherapist and founded *The Baca Journey,* offering guidance for discovering our magnificent truth.

Cathy (Cat) Smith works as an IT Project Manager and has studied various energy-healing modalities, including Reiki, kinesiology, and energy scans. Her focus is on assisting others with living happier and healthier lives by identifying and clearing blocks in energy to help reduce pain, stress, toxicity, and emotional imbalances.

Lynn M. Smith is a tapping expert who focuses on money mindset. Her passion is helping women entrepreneurs overcome their financial self-sabotage, enabling them to earn more and create a bigger impact. www.lynnmsmith.com

Maura Smith is a fulfillment coach who helps people find clarity and live deeply. Through her unique programs that combine intuitive energy healing, training, and coaching, clients learn to invest their time in what really matters to them and express themselves through a lifestyle that makes them feel truly alive. www.maurasmith.com

Solara Sophia helps heart-centered women step fully and confidently into their Divine power so they can manifest their dream reality. www.solarasophia.com

Marianne Soucy is author and coach at *Healing Pet Loss* and *Give Your Dream Wings*. Her sacred spirit journeys are a foundation for her work. She connects pet owners with their pets in the afterlife and helps spiritual entrepreneurs, healers, and authors manifest their dreams while staying connected to self and spirit.

Astra Spider, Abundance Shaman, empowers spiritual folks and soul-centered entrepreneurs to step into abundance, open to money flow, and create the beautiful lives of their dreams. She manifested her dream home, and blissfully resides there with her special guy and their six amazing animal babies. www.oneexpansion.com

Jeanette St. Germain is a spiritual alchemist with a passion for empowering others to embrace their own inner radiance. She offers intuitive guidance, energetic healing, and public events that include inspired angelic messages, clarity of life purpose, and deep rejuvenation through all layers of the mind, body, and spirit. www.sophiastouch.com

Mary Lou Stark, Book Enchantress, has explored multiple paths, including metaphysics, in her spiritual journey. She partners with writers and first-time authors, lovingly supporting them in revealing those ideas that are dear to their hearts and focusing a clear light on the core points of their message.

Star Staubach is a speaker, *Huffington Post* blogger, light reflector, "BS" excavator, life coach, world traveler, and busy mom of three. She understands the power of connecting with the soul to support the richness of this mind-body-spirit connection.

Kim Steadman is the chief curator of www.TheReFeatheredNest.com where moms can find encouragement to repurpose and redesign their life after the kids fly the coop. She is the author of the soon-to-be-released book *My Little Book of Empty Nest Quotes & Wisdom.*

Priscilla Stephan is an intuitive business strategist and dream-life activator who supports women in creating more freedom, profit, and ease in their lives and businesses. Her holistic approach to success allows her clients to live their dream lifestyle while sharing their brilliance and embodying their purpose with confidence.

Jaden Sterling is an award-winning, international bestselling author of *The Alchemy of True Success: Activate Your Mind, Revitalize Your Body, and Reignite Your Spirit.* He is an intuitive business coach who guides conscious entrepreneurs to build a business they love that will benefit their family, their community, and the world.

Autumne Stirling is a mother, writer, and advocate for mental-health awareness. A survivor of childhood trauma, she lives with complex mental-health issues and is grateful to have received extraordinary treatment. She currently works at a yoga studio and plans to continue writing and focusing on assisting those with PTSD.

Steve Tallamy lives in Poole, England, and is a lover of the simple things in life. Along with a deep connection with nature, he believes in sharing his joy with many, which he does on his blog: www.stevetallamy.com.

Vicki Talvi-Cole is a light weaver, energy tracker, intuitive healer, teacher, and channel. She inspires and navigates others to live their life as an adventure – empowered through their self expression, activated by their spirit and soul journey. She offers "Sol-utions" by phone, in person, or partnering with Horse. www.VickiTalvi-Cole.com

Stella Tassone is a loving soul from Australia who loves to love. She is a mother, certified angel-card and Reiki practitioner, and massage practitioner. She currently works with children who have special needs and enjoys assisting people in remembering who they are. www.stellatassone.com

Beth Shekinah Terrence is a shaman, holistic health practitioner, recovery coach, speaker, and writer. Her mission is to support others in living a heart-centered, balanced, and joyful life through discovering the healer within. She works with individuals, groups, and organizations locally and globally. www.bethterrence.com

Lori Thiessen lives in Alberta, Canada, where she works as an architectural tech during the day, moonlights as a writer, and is mom to five almost-grown-up kids. She is a certified NLP Practitioner, Toastmaster, and runner. www.couragefinder.com

Christine Tomasello is the founder of Joyful Coaching, where she empowers people to make the ordinary extraordinary. Her coaching is based on the principle that insight and action work together to create transformation. She helps her clients discover the joy in their life, no matter where they are on their journey. www.joyful-coaching.com

Debbie Lamb Turner is passionate about walking alongside others on their journey in life, helping them recognize their divine nature, and exploring ways to step boldly into ridiculously amazing lives! Her insightful book, *The Path that Beckons* (available in early 2016), offers useful and playful practices. www.thepaththatbeckons.com

Carol Tuttle is a master energy healer and the bestselling author of five books. Her online learning platforms are all designed to help individuals love and live their truth. She is the creator of Energy Profiling, Dressing Your Truth, The Child Whisperer, Chakra7, Healing School, and SoulPrint Healing for Affluence. www.thecarolblog.com

Sherry VanAntwerp is an intuitive coach and speaker. With over 20 years in corporate business, raising children, and triumphing over traumatic losses, she now helps women discover their self-worth and create fulfilling lives. Her perspective on life, loss, and purpose drives her mission to help women create their own life transformations.

Lumi Vasile guides people who feel that something is missing from their life into a journey of awakening, where they remember and connect with their Divine Essence; ascend to higher levels of consciousness; find meaning, purpose, and joy; and co-create with Spirit the life of their dreams. www.JourrneysIntoTheLight.com

Susan Viljoen is a wise magician. Using life coaching, horses, and labyrinths, she helps clients uncover and trust their own answers by inspiring curiosity. Her nimble open-mindedness and creative expertise ground and encourage her clients on their journey to transformation. She lives in Johannesburg, South Africa.

Michelle McDonald Vlastnik is a Michigan girl living in an Arizona world. Her divine purpose is to assist with the conscious shift and to help with the healing of Mother Earth. Her movement is finding the freedom to be "yourSelf," because there is something magic about being authentic. www.Facebook.com/HighEnergySixSensoryPersonalTraining

Linda Voogd is a holistic therapist, addictions counselor, and adjunct professor. She offers ongoing workshops and life coaching. She helps others create healthy beliefs, attitudes, and thought patterns that propel them toward personal transformation. She has over 30 years of experience and runs a private practice in northern New Jersey.

Tracy Una Wagner, CHT, is an intuitive transpersonal life coach who works with the spirit realm by using creatively fun approaches to guide people to reach their goals, dreams, wishes, and desires. She empowers individuals to finally know true abundance by living their uniquely authentic life journey. www.versatileinspirations.com

Catherine Walters is dedicated to assisting energy-sensitive spiritual people to transform their obstacles, stress, and inner-child wounds into energy, passion, and joy. She is a lifestyle coach, hypnotherapist, Reiki Master/instructor and yoga teacher. www.guidedchange.com

Rozlyn Warren, CHt, ESLC, is a Certified Akashic Records practitioner, mystic, and publisher of *Lean Toward Happy* magazine. She directly engages her clients' inner guidance and works in their Akashic Records to guide them in realigning with their soul, loving themselves so fully that they naturally see the world through the eyes of love.

Thea Westra is the author of *Time for My Life: 365 Stepping Stones* and the owner and creator of Forward Steps. Her mission is to help others step forward in life and to add wings to their unique life journeys. Receive a free copy of her *179 Forward Steps* ebook here: www.forwardsteps.com.au.

Kathy White is a mother, art therapist, creator of *Child Soul Cards*, and founder of Joyful Parents. She is dedicated to supporting soul-filled, loving parent-child connections. She's also a Certified Facilitator of *The Work of Byron Katie* and trains and coaches many individuals, businesses, and organizations all over the world.

Christy Whitman is the *New York Times* bestselling author of *The Art of Having It All.* As the CEO and founder of the Quantum Success Coaching Academy, a 12-month Law of Attraction coaching certification program, Christy has helped people worldwide to achieve their goals and lead more empowered lives. www.ChristyWhitman.com

Kate Whorlow lives in the United Kingdom and helps women who are wishing to transform their lives to achieve joy, peace, and prosperity. She has been a natural-healing practitioner since 1998 and now combines a variety of therapies in her practice. Her healing program is called Fall in Love with Life.

Monica Wilcox is the spiritual columnist for *FemCentral.com*. She's a featured blogger for numerous sites and magazines. When her fingers aren't tapping laptop keys, she enjoys exploring dark corners and dank basements. www.twitter.com/Monica_Wilcox

April Williams is a dreamer, believer, mother, lover, nature admirer, reality inquirer, and hope-infused inspirer. With passions for helping people rediscover their power within and creating positive change, she is a true visionary who can usually be found weaving whimsical words with visions of vibrant futures for all.

Linda Wheeler Williams is a personal-success coach, spiritual teacher, and angel communicator who specializes in forgiveness. She lives in Phoenix, Arizona. www.lindawheelerwilliams.com

Cat Williford, MCC, has helped thousands of women move from debilitating perfectionism and fear into experiencing deep self-love and success on their terms for the past 22 years. Founder of *The Modern Goddess* and *The Authenticity Advantage*, she is a coaching-profession pioneer, speaker, writer, and frequent expert on TV, radio, and print. www.catwilliford.com

Holly Worton is a coach and PSYCH-K® facilitator. She works with women to quickly and easily change their beliefs at the subconscious level so they can create the business and lifestyle of their dreams.

Acknowledgements

This book is truly a labor of love, and there are so many beautiful souls who we would like to acknowledge. First and foremost, a huge thank you to each of the contributors. Without you, this book would not exist. You believed in our vision right from the start and trusted us to bring it to life. You shared your hearts on the pages and also in our Facebook community. We have become friends and love the supportive tribe that has come from this collaboration. We're so grateful for all of your love and help throughout this process – from answering surveys about how something should be done to helping us figure things out along the way. Thank you. This book is for all of us!

From Dan: First, last, and always, thank you to Jodi. You are my heart, my soul, my life, my world, my everything. Thank you for all you do and for all you are. Thank you for sharing your soul, your life, and your love with me every day, forever.

Thank you, also, to all the people who have inspired me throughout my lifetime – including everyone who has contributed to this book, everyone I've connected with through online groups, and all the people who I haven't directly connected with but who inspire me through their words and lives. The way so many of you have modeled soulful authenticity – by truly showing up and vulnerably sharing your deepest selves – inspires me to dig deeper, share more of myself, shine brighter, and live my best life.

Thank you to the many people who have helped me develop my writing – in classes, workshops, and writing groups over the past 25 years. Your guidance, support, and encouragement have given me the confidence to use writing as a way to connect with my own soul and to help others do the same.

Thank you to Esther Hicks for bringing the Teachings of Abraham into my life (and into the world). Your messages of freedom, love, and ever-expanding joy have awakened me and transformed me forever, calling me "gently down the stream" toward my inner being, my source, my soul.

And thank you again, Jodi. (As I said, you are first and last and always for me!) I have so much appreciation for you – not just for the role you play in my life, but for the love you constantly emanate and share with the whole world. You are a constant source of inspiration, joy, and love. I feel so blessed to be sharing every step of this journey with you. I love you.

From Jodi: I would like to thank Dan for being such a rock star in every way imaginable. Thank you for all the hours and hours of editing that you put in to bring this book to life. Thank you for being my daily "grounder" when things became overwhelming. Thank you for being such a great partner in work and life and for loving me like you do. My life truly began the moment you walked into it, and my heart has been expanding and fluttering ever since. You are my absolute everything, and I love you eternally.

Special thanks to my mom for listening and supporting me always, especially over the last few years. It's so nice to have a mom who is also my best friend. I'm so grateful that she's part of this book – it's an honor to share this with her.

Loving thanks to my dear friends who love me unconditionally and who have supported me during each step of this journey. I don't want to name names for fear of leaving someone out, but you know who you are. And I'm so grateful that you're in my life.

I would like to thank my angels, spirit guides, and loved ones on the other side who put this idea in my head and lifted me up when I feared I had taken on too much. Their loving guidance is such a gift, and I'm so grateful.

Lastly, we would like to thank you, the reader. We're so grateful that this book called to you and that you listened to your soul and picked it up. We wrote it for you, and we hope that it's helped you connect with your soul!

An Invitation

This is the first book in our *365 Book Series*, and we would love to invite you to learn more about the books and join us as a contributing author, a reader, or both!

In addition to this book, we currently have two additional collaborative books on the way!

365 Moments of Grace

This book will contain personal stories of grace, miracles, and transformations from beautiful souls all around the world to show how magical our world is and how connected we truly are.

365 Ways to Lift Your Spirit

This book will contain loving ways that we can pull ourselves up when we're feeling down and also keep the good feelings flowing and expand on them when we're already feeling great!

You can learn more about our current and upcoming books from this soulful series here: www.365bookseries.com.

26362814R10249

Made in the USA
Middletown, DE
26 November 2015